PRAISE FOR
TIME TO LEAD

"Meticulously researched. Steenkamp shows what today's managers can learn from past great historical leaders. Each case study is organized around a particular dilemma, and is interesting in its own right. The book is easy to read, yet provides incisive leadership principles that have withstood the test of time. The self-assessment questions and leadership tests make the book highly actionable. A must-read for any (aspiring) corporate and nonprofit leader."

—**Hermann Simon,** Founder and honorary chairman, Simon-Kucher & Partners Strategy and Marketing Consultants, management guru, 2019 Thinkers50 Hall of Fame inductee, and author of *Hidden Champions*

"Steenkamp has written a remarkable book on leadership that I strongly recommend to all those who might think 'leadership' is something mythical and hence 'too big to study.' Drawing on his well-renowned knowledge of marketing, he engages in a truly interdisciplinary approach that unveils, on the basis of sixteen cases of impressive leaders, the relevant dimensions of the phenomenon of leaders and leadership. This already makes reading this book worthwhile. On top of that, the book proposes a strong and convincing set of self-assessment tools that can help (aspirant) leaders to reflect on their own style of leadership. And it even helps them to make a decision when their time is over . . . "

—**Wim van de Donk,** King's Commissioner (governor) of the State of North Brabant, The Netherlands, Extraordinary Professor of Public Administration, Tilburg University, and former president, European Group for Public Administration

"A masterwork of leadership across history and its application for today's leaders. J. B. Steenkamp takes us through history's most decisive leaders and events, identifies the essence of their leadership approach, and expertly ties it to well-established, contemporary leadership methods. Most important, Steenkamp provides us with a framework and method to assess our own leadership and reach our leader development goals. This is a must-read for anyone who wants to learn and apply the lessons of history's leaders to their own leader growth."

—**Colonel Todd Woodruff,** Former Director of Leadership and Management Studies, the United States Military Academy at West Point

"Ancient models of leadership are an old story, beginning with ancients like Plutarch, but Steenkamp is the first to rival Plutarch by comparing ancient and modern models through the use of psychological categories drawn from Isaiah Berlin and others. Steenkamp's handling of Alexander the Great is characteristic: The conqueror who wished to become a god proves to be a shrewd evangelist for his own cult. The author's modern parallel to Alexander is apt: Charles de Gaulle, who sold the greatness of France to the French, but as a way of selling himself."

—**Fred Naiden,** Professor of history at the University of North Carolina and author of *Soldier, Priest, and God: A Life of Alexander the Great*

"Steenkamp explores the essence of leadership, all of which I have seen displayed in my thirty years in the pharma industry, for good and for bad. My career highs and lows were closely associated with the experiences of a leader that either inspired me or drove me to the depths of despair. Steenkamp reminds us of how a great leader can impact the culture and engagement of any enterprise."

—**John Bamforth,** Founder of Ciara Biosciences, Director, Eshelman Institute for Innovation, and former Vice President, Eli Lilly and Co.

"Backed by great histories and supported by Steenkamp's own expertise, this is essential reading if you want to improve your personal leadership skills. Managers in private and public organizations alike will be grateful to Steenkamp for this new great book."

—**Xavier Orendáin,** President, Chamber of Commerce, Guadalajara (Mexico)

"Enlightening and inspiring! There's a lot we can learn from leaders of different times and apply in our current companies. Steenkamp found the way to show the reader how to apply all those historic experiences to our times."

—Alejandro Romero, Director General, Geolife Swiss

"I am enlightened after reading *Time to Lead*. It discusses types of leadership in a concise yet insightful manner. I highly recommend the book as a practical guidance to managers as well as all those who aspire to be in a leadership position. I liked the global scope of the book, pulling in leaders from all parts of the world. *Time to Lead* is definitely a book worth reading repeatedly."

—Guo Xiuling, Founder, Sand River Cashmere

"It is academically gratifying to read a book that uses illustrative examples so well to express a notion that is always in vogue. Leadership has been a topic of great interest for many decades. Of the many styles that deeply resonate with me is servant leadership. Steenkamp dealt with it so eloquently and portrayed it in such a vibrant way. His choice of nurse Nightingale is spot-on, not only for her servant leadership style that could be tangibly seen and felt; but with a great degree of humility she helped save lives and took that as her calling in life. As for Martin Luther King, his style could fall under charismatic leadership par excellence, yet Steenkamp masterfully chose him to better portray servant leadership, as King was willing to give up everything to ensure the survivability of his belief to serve the people and gave his life doing just that! Steenkamp's book is powerfully illustrated with vivid examples that have stood the test of time and a must-read for people who are interested in the art of leadership."

—Moustapha Sarhank, Servant leader and seeker of enlightenment, Executive Chairman, IBAG, S.A.E., and Senior Fellow, Olsson Center for Applied Ethics at the University of Virginia

"J-B Steenkamp has again managed to combine his exhaustive capacity for research (in this case historical) with an almost uncanny ability to distill his knowledge into simple, usable, and practical conceptual frameworks for action in this fascinating treatise on leadership. In this navigation through and synthesis of the very real leadership actions, approaches, and game-changing outcomes of sixteen world leaders spanning more than 2,400 years of history, he has been able to extract seven foundational leadership styles and two fundamental truths around leadership impact—grit (the tenacity to persevere despite obstacles) and clear and consistent vision. Part history book, part academic leadership study, and part personal development guide—it's a worthwhile journey for anyone who aspires to have true and lasting impact."

—**Rob Malcolm,** Director, Hershey Company, Senior Adviser, Boston Consulting Group, and former President, Global Marketing, Sales, and Innovation, Diageo

JAN-BENEDICT STEENKAMP

Foreword by Major General Cameron G. Holt

TIME to LEAD

Lessons *for* Today's Leaders *from*
Bold Decisions *That* Changed History

**FAST
COMPANY**
Press

Fast Company Press
New York, New York
www.fastcompanypress.com

This work is being published under the Fast Company Press imprint by an exclusive arrangement with Fast Company. Fast Company and the Fast Company logo are registered trademarks of Mansueto Ventures, LLC. The Fast Company Press logo is a wholly owned trademark of Mansueto Ventures, LLC.

Distributed by Greenleaf Book Group

For ordering information or special discounts for bulk purchases, please contact Greenleaf Book Group at PO Box 91869, Austin, TX 78709, 512.891.6100.

Design and composition by Greenleaf Book Group
Cover design by Greenleaf Book Group
Photographs of Deng Xiaoping and Margaret Thatcher appear courtesy of the National Archives. Photograph of Nelson Mandela © South Africa - The Good News (https://www.sagoodnews.co.za/) (no changes made). All other images (© Georgios Kollidas, ra3m, Loulouka1, Volosovich Igor, DianaFinch, giannimarchetti, Hennadii H.) used under license from Shutterstock.com.

Publisher's Cataloging-in-Publication data is available.

Print ISBN: 978-1-7343248-2-2

eBook ISBN: 978-1-7343248-3-9

Part of the Tree Neutral® program, which offsets the number of trees consumed in the production and printing of this book by taking proactive steps, such as planting trees in direct proportion to the number of trees used: www.treeneutral.com

TreeNeutral

Printed in the United States of America on acid-free paper

20 21 22 23 24 25 26   10 9 8 7 6 5 4 3 2 1

First Edition

To those who shaped my leadership ideas—my late parents, my brothers Thomas and Paulus, my wife Valarie, and my late doctoral supervisor Thieu Meulenberg

ALSO BY
JAN-BENEDICT STEENKAMP

Private Label Strategy: How to Meet the Store Brand Challenge, with Nirmalya Kumar

Brand Breakout: How Emerging Market Brands Will Go Global, with Nirmalya Kumar

Global Brand Strategy: World-wise Marketing in the Age of Branding

Retail Disruptors: The Spectacular Rise and Impact of the Hard Discounters, with Laurens Sloot

CONTENTS

Foreword xvii

Preface xxi

Acknowledgments xxvi

1. Leaders and Leadership Types 1

PART ONE: ADAPTIVE LEADERSHIP— MODIFY ACCORDING TO THE CIRCUMSTANCES   19

2. Clovis Attends a Mass 20

3. Bismarck Unshackles a Nation 31

4. Deng Seeks Truth from Facts 46

Reflections on Adaptive Leadership 63

PART TWO: PERSUASIVE LEADERSHIP— CHANGE THE MINDS OF YOUR FOLLOWERS   69

5. Themistocles Erects a Wooden Wall 70

6. Campbell-Bannerman Shows Magnanimity 85

7. Roosevelt Lends a Hose 100

Reflections on Persuasive Leadership 118

PART THREE: DIRECTIVE LEADERSHIP— DEFINE THE MARCHING ORDERS   125

8. Cortés Scuttles His Ships 126
9. Thatcher Closes a Pit 139
Reflections on Directive Leadership 154

PART FOUR: DISRUPTIVE LEADERSHIP— BREAK WITH THE PAST   159

10. St. Peter Discards One Thousand Years of Religious Doctrine . . 160
11. Fisher Launches a Ship 171
Reflections on Disruptive Leadership 187

PART FIVE: AUTHENTIC LEADERSHIP— SET THE EXAMPLE   193

12. Washington Stops, Twice 194
13. Mandela Goes to a Match 209
Reflections on Authentic Leadership 226

PART SIX: SERVANT LEADERSHIP— PUT FOLLOWERS FIRST   233

14. Nightingale Carries a Lamp 234
15. King Goes MIA 249
Reflections on Servant Leadership 264

PART SEVEN: CHARISMATIC LEADERSHIP— BUY INTO THE LEADER, THEN FOLLOW THEIR VISION   273

16. Alexander the Great Says No 274
17. De Gaulle Understands the *Pieds-Noirs* 292
Reflections on Charismatic Leadership 311

18. Where Do *You* Go from Here? 319

APPENDICES: LEADERSHIP ASSESSMENT TOOLS   328

Appendix A: Grit Scale 329

Appendix B: Hedgefox Scale 332

Appendix C: Steenkamp Assessment Instrument

          for Leadership Styles (SAILS) 334

Notes 346

Index 371

About the Author 387

LIST OF FIGURES

1.1: Hedgehog-like vs. Fox-like Qualities

1.2: Leadership Styles

2.1: Germanic Kingdoms in 480 A.D.

2.2: The Rise of the Franks

3.1: Europe after the Congress of Vienna

3.2: Reunification of Germany

3.3: Dropping the Pilot

4.1: Deng Xiaoping, 1979

5.1: Persian Empire in 500 B.C.

5.2: The Persian Wars, 499–479 B.C.

5.3: Battle at Salamis

6.1: Map of Southern Africa in 1899

6.2: Henry Campbell-Bannerman, 1902

7.1: Franklin Roosevelt at One of His Fireside Chats

7.2: Social judgment theory applied to Roosevelt's persuasive leadership

8.1: Aztec Empire

8.2: Route of Cortés

8.3: The Valley of Mexico

9.1: Margaret Thatcher, 1983

10.1: Peter's Vision

11.1: Jacky Fisher, 1915

11.2: Diagram of HMS *Dreadnought*

11.3: HMS *Dreadnought* at Sea

12.1:   George Washington as Commander in Chief
        of the Continental Army
12.2:   Apotheosis of Washington
13.1:   Nelson Mandela, 1993
14.1:   Florence Nightingale, 1858
15.1:   Martin Luther King Jr., 1963
SL.1:   Expectation-Disconfirmation Theory Applied
        to Servant Leadership
16.1:   Empire of Alexander the Great
16.2:   Battle at Issus
16.3:   Successor (Diadochi) Kingdoms in 301 B.C.
17.1:   Frenemies—Churchill and de Gaulle, 1944
 A.1:   Using SAILS for 360-Degree Feedback

LIST OF TABLES

4.1: Results of Reform and Opening Up, 1978–1988

7.1: Party Divisions in U.S. Congress, 1928–1940

7.2: Purchases versus Lend-Lease by Great Britain in World War II (in billions of dollars)

SL.1: Service Leadership in Theory versus in Practice

FOREWORD

LEADERSHIP MATTERS

Leadership is arguably the highest leverage ingredient driving the outcomes of virtually every human endeavor—and has been throughout the ages and across the globe. Effective leaders have harnessed the potential of populations to accomplish the greatest of human achievements and unleashed the depths of human depravity. Speaking for myself and apart from the important outcomes of effective leadership, I also believe that leadership matters because the people I lead matter.

There are literally thousands of books written on the subject. Most practitioners of leadership, including myself, have read dozens of them and attended multiple leadership courses during their careers. Yet I have found through my own experiences as a leader—from the boardroom to the battlefield—that the vast majority of leadership books should be placed gently in the trash can where they belong. Leadership is fundamentally about people, and people are messy creatures. Deterministic leadership "recipes" promising desired outcomes if only you effectively carry out prescribed steps or credibly exhibit desirable behaviors are, quite simply, hogwash.

LEADERSHIP IS INTENSELY PERSONAL

Leadership is dependent on the leaders themselves, those who would be led, and the context. Every year I host a weeklong seminar for mid-career officers selected for the Air Force's biggest leadership test—Squadron Command. Throughout the week, they experience storytelling from a number of leaders and hear the expectations the Air Force has of them as they are entrusted with America's sons and daughters, various leadership tools, and the national security context we all face.

When it is my turn to speak to them directly, many are at first surprised—and then somewhat relieved by the advice I give. I do not focus on what worked for me so they can follow suit. I do not even attempt to provide a definition of a "good" Squadron Commander. Of all the time they will spend in preparation for command, I urge them to spend the most time learning who *they* really are as a leader—not who they think the Air Force wants them to be. The Air Force does not look for "Squadron Commanders" from among the people we have; we look for the right people and make them Squadron Commanders.

There is no one successful leadership style or set of behaviors, and you cannot be someone you are not. You can, however, become more effective as a leader given who you are. The real value of studying other leaders is not in attempting to become more like them. The value in studying other leaders is in deepening your understanding; your understanding of leadership, yes— but also your understanding of yourself.

LEADERSHIP IS A JOURNEY, NOT A DESTINATION

Experienced leaders will want to read *Time to Lead* more than once and seek to understand why they made the decisions they did in various leadership settings. I have noticed in my own leadership journey that there are many similarities, or at least common threads, in how I approached decisions and situations. These similarities are mostly explained by my own dominant leadership style. The vivid examples within each leadership style and the self-assessment instruments provided by Professor Steenkamp will help cement that understanding. Perhaps even more useful, however, is understanding why you chose vastly different approaches in different leadership situations. Professor Steenkamp's careful selection of case studies across cultures, situations, and time will help you understand why you applied elements and artifacts of other, non-dominant, leadership styles to different settings. Even the most experienced and successful leaders can, and should, improve.

Through my own journey of self-reflection, I have learned from my successes and failures as a leader. I have also learned as much or more observing other leaders—both good and bad. Within my context as a senior military leader, I have had the honor to lead men and women who have made personal decisions to serve their nation and to serve a purpose higher than themselves. Through the successes, I have always believed the values and quality of the people I lead gives me an unfair advantage—an "ace in the hole." For all my shortcomings as a leader, I have found the people entrusted to my care incredibly forgiving. Yet with the sense of service they share, they consistently demand two things from me or any leader—*competence* and *caring*—and you can't fake either one! I have also learned in the organizations I have led, whether in an office setting or a combat zone, that there is a critical social contract between the leader and the led. Loyalty is *owed,* trust is *earned,* and the leader trusts *first*!

YOU ARE IN FOR A TREAT

I had the honor of meeting Professor Steenkamp and his wife during one of my visits to the Kenan-Flagler School at the University of North Carolina (UNC). We immediately hit it off, diving right into discussions of leadership and how proud we both were of the Air Force officer students I had entrusted to their instruction and mentoring. To this day, however, I know more about Professor Steenkamp and his wife through the positive impact they had on my officers, Lieutenant Colonel Karen Landale and Major Dan Finkenstadt, who successfully completed their Ph.Ds studying under the Steenkamps' leadership. Both Karen and Dan are brilliant officers and leaders in their own right, yet I can see Professor Steenkamp's fingerprints on them—both in terms of the agility and discipline of their thinking and in the sense of indebtedness and endearment both officers feel for the Steenkamps. I have encountered few scholars like Professor Steenkamp. Not only does he understand leadership as a theoretical construct of styles and traits and behaviors, he has a rare intuition about leadership within the context of history as an interpersonal pursuit that can be forged and honed and deepened experientially if properly examined.

In *Time to Lead*, Professor Steenkamp actually practices effective leadership himself to guide us; not simply on *what* to think about leadership, but *how* to think about leadership. He leads us to consider singular decisions that changed the course of history— decisions made by 16 leaders applying their own dominant tendency of the seven leadership styles pre-sented within a full diversity of contexts—time, culture, followers, situation, and leader identity. In this way, Professor Steenkamp leads us to optimize our own "sense-making" ability. His disciplined storytelling within a well-conceived theoretical framework produces a vivid *mental map* to deepen our understanding of who we really are as leaders. This book will give you the tools to deepen your wisdom, clarify your thinking, and improve your outcomes as your own story of leadership unfolds. Enjoy!

—Major General Cameron G. Holt
Deputy Assistant Secretary of the Air Force,
Washington, D.C.

PREFACE

I MAKE EXTENSIVE use of principles of leadership in my teaching, executive work, and the business cases I have written. This is only logical, as marketing and leadership are closely aligned. The core of marketing is getting customers (your "followers") to do what you want—also the essence of leadership. In marketing, this goal can be achieved in at least seven different ways: (1) product adaptation to local needs (discussed in my book *Global Brand Strategy*); (2) persuasion (discussed in my book *Private Label Strategy*); (3) putting pressure on the customer (a well-known salesperson technique); (4) offering a product that disrupts the competition (discussed in my book *Retail Disruptors*); (5) creating an authentic brand story (discussed in my book *Brand Breakout*); (6) going out of your way to serve your customers (discussed in my wife's book *Services Marketing*); (7) imbuing your brand with a higher purpose that customers buy into (discussed in *Global Brand Strategy*).

Leaders adopt these seven approaches too. Here, they are called "leadership styles." You will encounter all of them in this book. While my work as a marketing professor has been enriched by my study of leadership, in this book I will use my marketing knowledge to deepen our understanding of leadership. Don't get me wrong. This is not a book about marketing leadership. It is about leadership in general, be it in corporate, military, public, or nonprofit organizations. Rather, where relevant, I will use marketing principles to further elaborate on a particular leadership style.

In this book, I explore these seven leadership styles and bring them to life using great historical leaders. History has fascinated me for as long as I have been able to read. I have always been interested in historical events and even more in the underlying causes behind these events, seeking to understand why and how things happened as they did. This has been of profound benefit for my academic career. Studying history in this manner has greatly enhanced my conceptualization skills, that is, the ability to relate often seemingly disparate ideas and events to each other. That is not an innate capability. I credit my intensive study of history for this.

In my teaching, I use lessons from history to guide present action, across different audiences—undergraduate, MBA, executive MBA, executive development, and PhD teaching—as well as in my consulting and in my work with the military. I have explained to U.S. special ops how they can change opinions abroad through a stepwise process, pioneered by President Franklin D. Roosevelt, and elucidated to the U.S. Army how the Thucydides Trap (outlined by the Greek historian Thucydides in the fifth century B.C.) can be used to understand strategic challenges in relation to present-day China. I use the epochal Battle of Gaugamela in 331 B.C. to instruct PhD students around the world how to navigate the review process of their articles, an ordeal that makes a root canal treatment feel like a pleasant massage.

Since reading biographies of Alexander the Great and Roosevelt at the tender age of ten, I have believed in the role of great people in shaping the course of history (the "great man" theory). History is not only shaped by the outcomes of anonymous social and economic forces, penetratingly analyzed in such seminal works as Paul Kennedy's *The Rise and Fall of the Great Powers*, Jared Diamond's *Guns, Germs, and Steel*, David Landes's *The Wealth and Poverty of Nations*, and William McNeil's *The Rise of the West: A History of the Human Community*. Great leaders have played a critical role in history since the dawn of civilization.

Recall the immense impact of Buddha, Confucius, Jesus Christ, and Muhammad. The course of world history would also have been very different if Alexander the Great had not refused an offer no sane man would refuse.

Or if General George Washington had followed the example of Oliver Cromwell and the urgings of his fellow officers. Imagine if Deng Xiaoping had stuck to the teachings of the "Great Helmsman," Mao Zedong. This raises intriguing questions. Why were these leaders so successful? How did they get others on board? What was their primary leadership style and what was behind that, and how can we learn from them today? Which leadership insights can we acquire through the lens of history? These questions motivated me to write this book.

Everybody can improve their leadership qualities by reading about other leaders, how they resolved their dilemmas, and why they were successful. Take Alexander the Great and Dr. Martin Luther King. Both drew inspiration, and learned, from historical examples—Achilles and Xenophon in the case of Alexander, Mahatma Gandhi for King. If these men, who routinely are ranked among the greatest leaders of all time, turn to the lives and leadership example of previous leaders to improve their leadership skills, then so can we, lesser mortals, to an even greater extent. Niccolò Machiavelli understood that well. In *Il Principe* (*The Prince*), one of the most important political treatises ever written, he wrote that among all his possessions, none was prized as much as "a knowledge of the actions of great men." In the second century A.D., in his seminal book *Parallel Lives*, Plutarch drew leadership lessons from a series of concise biographies of famous Greeks and Romans, arranged in tandem. President Harry S. Truman kept a copy of *Parallel Lives* at hand in the White House. He said that in Plutarch's book, he could find everything worth knowing about the leaders of his time—how they behaved, what made them tick.

This book is about the actions of great men and women, and what we can learn from them. It is not a theoretical treatise on leadership; rather, it illustrates leadership through the actual lives of great leaders—and derives lessons that are relevant for us here and now. Having taught for nearly forty years, I recognize that most people learn more, and better remember what they have learned, from case studies than from theoretical expositions. You will encounter real people making real decisions, and experience the struggles they faced and the hurdles they had to overcome.

Still, you may wonder what you can learn from historical leaders. Is not everything different today? Actually, it is not. As the French say, *l'Histoire se répète* (History repeats itself). As of this writing, I could effortlessly identify leaders of different shades and qualities in politics, business, public service, and nonprofits, ranging from consensus-minded to authoritarian, from deeply ethical to opportunistic, from humble to narcissistic, all mirroring the historical leaders in this book. It is critical to realize that with the test of time, people's evaluation and understanding of a person's leadership qualities can change dramatically, making leaders that have endured particularly relevant. Consider three examples of recent hallowed leaders who have fallen from their pedestal.

1. Any leadership book written in 2000 would have included a hagiography of General Electric's CEO Jack Welch, who in 1999 was named "Manager of the Century" by *Fortune* magazine. Yet the global financial crisis of 2007–2008 laid bare the toxic foundations of the edifice Welch built.

2. Mark Zuckerberg was hailed as one of the world's greatest business leaders only shortly before the scandal over Facebook's privacy practices broke. His shaky and evasive performance in U.S. congressional and European parliament hearings led many to doubt his ability to run such a powerful company.

3. Carlos Ghosn was regarded as a visionary titan, a man who had the foresight to build the Renault-Nissan-Mitsubishi Alliance into one of the biggest players in the automotive industry. While I was writing this book, he fell from grace and many of the achievements held up during the Ghosn years have been revealed to be smoke and mirrors.

The advantage in turning to historical persons for leadership lessons is that their virtues and vices, their accomplishments and failures, are by now firmly established. My view is inspired by Peter Drucker, whom many regard as the most influential management thinker and consultant of the twentieth century. In a 2016 article in the *Harvard Business Review*, entitled "Why Peter Drucker's Writing Still Feels So Relevant," Hermann Simon, founder of the global strategy consultancy Simon-Kucher & Partners and a management guru in his own right, asked Drucker whether he considered himself more a historical writer or a management thinker. "More a historical writer," Drucker answered. He explained that the human being has changed relatively little during the known course of history. We therefore gain more valuable leadership insights from historical analogies and examples rather than by embracing the latest management fads.

Drucker's view is echoed in an insightful article called "History Lessons" that appeared in August 2018 in *The Economist*. The article argued that running a country is a greater test than running a corporation, and "those who have passed through the fire surely have something to teach modern-day [corporate] managers." The article briefly discussed leadership lessons that can be gleaned from great historical figures, and concluded, "Bosses should read more history books." This is sound advice but history books are not generally written with leadership lessons in mind, and biographies tend to be long—for example, a recent biography of Deng Xiaoping is nine hundred pages.

This book fills the void by providing compact descriptions of multiple past great leaders and the leadership lessons today's (corporate) managers can learn from their actions.

ACKNOWLEDGMENTS

THIS BOOK IS a product of five decades of my study of great leaders—reading countless biographies, studying them in a wider context in general history books, observing others in action, and applying these leadership lessons in practice—in the multitude of leadership positions I have held in many organizations in various countries and continents. I am grateful for my colleagues in all these and other organizations.

My greatest mentor on everything concerning leadership was my late father. I am supremely fortunate to have had a role model who was a successful leader in every domain he was active in, from politics (president of the Netherlands Senate, founder of the Christian Democratic Party) to business (CEO of our family's food company De Hoorn, independent director of a dozen companies, including KLM Royal Dutch Airlines and ING), from academia (dean at Eindhoven University of Technology) to nonprofits (chairman of the Pastoral Council of the Catholic Church in the Netherlands, vice chairman of Catharina Hospital). My father took his leadership cues from historical leaders, and before I was even a teenager he spent his (admittedly limited) spare time explaining to me what we can learn from historical figures. He would have loved to read this book.

My late mother tutored me on the importance of ethics and to never compromise on my core beliefs. My eldest brother, Thomas, was a mayor for more than twenty-five years, and he demonstrated the importance of developing and nurturing relationships with followers. My middle brother, Paulus, was a senior manager at Royal Dutch Shell and a board member of the Shell-BASF joint venture, and is vice president of the Navigators Europe, a nonprofit organization. He taught me some of the challenges posed by leading very different organizations. My wife, Valarie Zeithaml Steenkamp, was chairman of the American Marketing Association and senior associate dean at the Kenan-Flagler Business School. She taught me how to "read" people and understand what makes them "tick." Her undergraduate degree in psychology nicely complements my undergraduate degree in economics. My *Doktorvater* (PhD supervisor) Thieu Meulenberg instructed me on the rigors of academic thinking. I have benefited tremendously by learning from all my mentors, testing my ideas, and observing their behaviors.

I am deeply grateful to all the executives, leadership experts, and history scholars with whom I have discussed my ideas and whose valuable feedback made the book much stronger. I want to acknowledge with special gratitude my brother Paulus, who read the entire manuscript, line by line, and gave me unvarnished Dutch-style comments. He also served as an invaluable sounding board for my ideas, and provided many invaluable recommendations to make them better. Tojin Eapen (University of Missouri) also gave incisive suggestions spanning the entire book. I thank Dave Hofmann, senior associate dean at UNC and renowned leadership expert, for his encouragement and his willingness to generously share his deep knowledge on the theory and measurement of leadership with me.

I thank Kate Bollinger (independent medieval historian), Steven M. Burgess (University of the Witwatersrand, South Africa), Maj. Dan Finkenstadt (Naval Postgraduate School, Monterey), Fiona Fitzpatrick (Fiona Fitz Consulting), Lt. Col. Karen Landale (United States Air Force), Miguel Angel Lopez Lomeli (ITESM, Mexico), Mark McNeilly (Lenovo), Markus Saba (Eli Lilly), and Col. Todd Woodruff (West Point) for providing feedback on parts of the manuscript. I thank Erin Mitchell for proofreading the manuscript and Frank Wagenknecht for preparing all the maps. Finally, I thank Sabrina Baker, my personal trainer at the Meadowmont Wellness Center, who always reminds me of the old Roman wisdom *mens sana in corpore sano* ("a healthy mind in a healthy body").

Finally, I want to acknowledge all those who hold leadership positions in companies, nonprofit organizations, and the public sector. If they find this book useful, it is worth all of my efforts.

LEADERS AND LEADERSHIP TYPES

LEADERSHIP HAS BEEN a feature of humanity since its early beginnings. Hundreds of thousands of years ago, our ancestors hunted big animals for survival. When hunters faced prey that could overpower them, coordination was needed, and coordination required leadership. Leadership became ever more important as the complexity of human societies increased: from small bands of hunter-gatherers (twenty to fifty people) to villages (several hundreds of people) to cities (several thousands of people) to kingdoms encompassing many cities (several hundreds of thousands of people) to empires (millions of people).[1] And, as human complexity increased, the number of leaders, and the complexity of the demands placed upon them, increased.

Today's complex society would come to a standstill without leadership. It is not an exaggeration to state that leadership is one of the key issues of our times. Countless people occupy leadership positions, whether in government, companies, churches, nongovernmental organizations, schools, nonprofit organizations, or elsewhere. Leadership courses and programs are among the most popular offerings in the executive development programs of many business schools. For example, at UNC's Kenan-Flagler Business School, programs for which the majority of content is about leadership account for two-thirds of the total revenue of Executive Development. When I did a Google search on "leadership," I got over five billion hits! Clearly, leadership is on the minds of many people.

WHAT IS LEADERSHIP?

Leadership is the ability of an individual to influence others to achieve a common goal.[2] This definition contains five components. First, leadership is *relational*. It exists only in relation to followers. Without followers, there is no leader. Second, leadership involves *influence*. Without influence, leadership does not exist. But where does influence come from? The most obvious source is positional authority. The CEO of a corporation has more influence than an assembly-line worker. Yet, you can also influence followers over whom you have no authority by methods such as rational persuasion, inspirational appeal, consultation, ingratiation, personal appeal, forming a coalition, or relentless pressure.[3]

Third, leadership is a *process*. Leadership usually does not happen in just one particular instance, but often involves a complex system of moves/actions to accomplish a goal over a period of time. Fourth, leadership includes attention to *common goals*. By common, I mean that leader and followers have a mutual purpose. Leaders direct their energies toward others to achieve something together. This requires awareness of the current state, some vision of a desired future, and an ability to move from where you are to where you want to be.

Finally, leadership is about coping with *change*. The common goals are often different from what the organization has done hitherto. Part of the reason why leadership is so important is that the (business) world has become more competitive and volatile. Major changes occur ever more often and are more and more necessary to survive and compete effectively in this new environment. As leadership thinker John Kotter puts it, "More change always demands more leadership."[4]

LEADERSHIP TRAITS

Leadership scholars have long debated what makes great leaders. Do great leaders need to have particular traits? Academic research has identified a long list, which includes the following core qualities:

- **Intelligence:** a person's ability to learn information, to apply it to life tasks, and solve complex problems.
- **Self-confidence:** the ability to be certain about one's own competencies and skills. It includes a sense of self-esteem and self-assurance and the belief that one can make a difference.
- **Integrity:** the quality of honesty and trustworthiness. Leaders that have integrity are believable and worthy of our trust.
- **Sociability:** the inclination to seek out and develop relational networks. Leaders who show sociability are friendly, courteous, tactful, and diplomatic.
- **Emotional intelligence:** the ability to identify, control, and express one's own emotions, as well as the ability to handle relationships with others judiciously and empathetically.
- **Humility:** the quality of not thinking you are better than other people. It does not imply low self-esteem but rather a keen sense of one's own cognitive or emotional limitations.
- **Grit:** the courage and determination that make it possible to continue doing something difficult or unpleasant.[5]

Are all these traits necessary? Interestingly, as you shall see in this book, the leaders differed greatly on these traits—some were highly sociable, others not; some showed exemplary integrity, others not at all; and so on.

However, all these leaders had one thing in common: They all displayed grit. Setbacks did not cause the leaders in this book to give up; rather, they redoubled their efforts. They persevered in the face of opposition and disappointments. Or, as per the title of R&B singer Billy Ocean's biggest hit, "When the Going Gets Tough, the Tough Get Going."[6]

Grit is the common denominator that ties together the lives of all the leaders in this book. They all crossed the river, so to speak. Grit is required to be a great leader. Appendix A of this book contains the Grit Scale, a self-assessment tool you can use to determine how gritty you are. You can take the test now or wait until you have reached chapter 18, where I will discuss the scale and will tie your score back to specific parts in the book.

THE HEDGEHOG AND THE FOX

In the book *The Hedgehog and the Fox*, published in 1953, the Russian-British philosopher Isaiah Berlin quoted the seventh-century B.C. Greek poet Archilochus: "The fox knows many smaller things, but the hedgehog knows one big thing."[7] According to Berlin, the distinction between hedgehogs and foxes marks "one of the deepest differences, which divide . . . human beings," whether they are poets, scientists, managers, or politicians.[8] This distinction is highly useful for the study of leadership.

HEDGEHOGS

Hedgehogs are people who relate everything to a single central vision, which serves as their universal organizing principle. This vision shapes how they think and feel, how they understand the world. Hedgehogs are risk takers who agree with the Persian king Xerxes (who we shall encounter in chapter 5) that "big things are won by big dangers."[9] Hedgehogs focus on end goals, gains, and outcomes, have a long-term view, and have a mindset of reshaping (organizational or environmental) constraints. They tend to brush aside criticism and command the attention of their audience with their captivating vision. People are moved by big ideas, by a vision of a different (better) future. Hedgehogs think in certainties: "If I do X, I will get Y." Hedgehogs offer simple (not necessarily simplistic) solutions to complex problems. There is a reason why most gurus are hedgehogs: By reducing complexities to a few general rules, they offer a clear path forward to other, more uncertain minds.

In stark terms, *hedgehogs know much better where they are going (ends) than how to get there (means).* They are strategic visionaries rather than astute operators. This leads to the key potential weakness of hedgehogs: the failure to establish a proper relation between ends and means. In other words, their end goals can easily exceed the means at their disposal. According to historian John Lewis Gaddis, their trap is: "If you fail to prepare for all that might happen, you'll ensure that some of it will."[10]

King George III is an example of a particularly stubborn hedgehog. His overriding vision was royal sovereignty, which led to behaviors that pushed his American subjects away, while he did not have the means to suppress the revolt. Adolf Hitler was also a hedgehog. His evil overarching goal of world domination under the "superior" Aryan race and the concomitant destruction of Jewry were there for everyone to see. However, he failed to align means with ends—Germany was simply not strong enough to take on the Soviet Union, the British Empire, and the United States simultaneously.[11] President Ronald Reagan was a successful hedgehog. Not a man of details, he had three overarching goals: smaller government, lower taxes, and strengthen the nation's military. He achieved two out of three, which is an impressive result. Notwithstanding these successes, Reagan struggled with aligning goals and means. Lowering taxes and spending more on the military led to a significant increase in the budget deficit. This had to be rectified by his successor, George H. W. Bush, who lost the subsequent election in 1992 because of his broken promise not to raise taxes.

FOXES

Foxes pursue many ends, often unrelated and sometimes even contradictory, related to no clearly defined overarching goal. They might not even have a clear end goal at all. *Foxes know much better how to get to somewhere (means) than where they are going (ends).* They are operational rather than strategic leaders. They distrust grand schemes and simple explanations. They are prudent, cautious, detail-oriented, seeing everywhere obstacles and complexities. They have a relatively short-term view and focus on process rather than outcome. They have a good understanding of the means, but less of the ends. They tend to adapt to (organizational or environmental) constraints. Foxes think in eventualities: "If I do X, I might get Y, or possibly Z." While foxes are keenly aware of the complex array of constraints they potentially face, this awareness can easily lead to paralysis. In Gaddis's words, "If you try to anticipate everything, you'll accomplish nothing."[12] Foxes struggle with articulating a clear priority among the many ends they want to achieve, which may leave their followers in confusion as to what the marching orders are.

President Bill Clinton is an example of a fox. He was one of the best political operators of the twentieth century, being able to switch course after he lost the midterm elections of 1994 and work with the Republican Congress. However, unlike Reagan, he was not driven by an overarching vision that captivated the nation. Another example is German chancellor Angela Merkel, who has been widely admired for her coolheaded leadership in the EU. Rather than entertain grand ideas of a "historic mission" or "strategic vision," she aimed to solve today's problems. Yet she has also been criticized as being too cautious and as squandering an opportunity to prepare Germany's economy for the future.[13]

A third example is British prime minister David Cameron. He was an effective, but also opportunistic, politician who led the Conservative Party in 2010 back to power after having been in the opposition for thirteen years. However, he made the mistake of using a referendum on Brexit as a means to fight off the rise of the U.K. Independence Party (UKIP) and to quell dissension in his own party. He lost, resigned, and the United Kingdom entered years of political turmoil.

Initially, Berlin sharply contrasted hedgehogs versus foxes—you had to be one or the other. His distinction was used by political scientist Philip Tetlock, who found that foxes were consistently better predictors of future political events than hedgehogs.[14] However, shortly before his death, Berlin acknowledged that some people are foxes as well as hedgehogs and some people are neither.[15] Thus, we have four Aesopian possibilities, depicted in Figure 1.1.

Figure 1.1 Hedgehog-like vs. Fox-like Qualities

	Fox	**Eagle**
Yes	• Pursues many, often unrelated, more immediate ends • Sees the trees rather than the forest • Focus on means, costs, small things • Cautious • Adapts to constraints • Pitfall: Lack of direction, strategic paralysis - if you try to anticipate everything, you'll risk accomplishing nothing *Examples: Bill Clinton, Angela Merkel, David Cameron*	• Aligns long-term vision with available means • Sees how the forest is built up by trees • Stretches goals over time or purposefully increases means • Calculated risk taker • Understands which constraints can be bent to your will, which ones cannot • Pitfall: Constant balancing act between ends and means *Examples: Augustus, Abraham Lincoln, Josef Stalin*
	Ostrich	**Hedgehog**
No	• Ends are not clearly defined • Sees neither forest nor trees • Failure to reconcile multiple, conflicting, unclear ends with limited means • Clueless • Unable to accurately assess constraints • Pitfall: High certainty of leadership failure *Examples: Louis XVI, Theresa May, George W. Bush*	• Guided by a single, central long-term vision • Sees the forest rather than the trees • Focus on ends, gains, big things • Risk taker • Reshapes constraints • Long-term vision trumps short-term complexities • Pitfall: Failure to establish a proper relation between ends and means - if you fail to prepare for all that might happen, you'll ensure that some of it will *Examples: George III, Adolf Hitler, Ronald Reagan*

Fox-like qualities (means)

No   Yes

Hedgehog-like qualities (ends)

Note: Examples in the same cell do not imply moral equivalence.

EAGLES

I call leaders who combine the qualities of the hedgehog and fox, eagles. Eagles can see far in the distance—that is, have a farsighted vision— which they combine with great tactical agility. They excel in aligning potentially unlimited ambitions with necessarily limited capabilities. *Eagles know where they are going (ends) and how to get there (means).* They can deal with immediate priorities yet never lose sight of long-term goals. They may seek to increase their means before embarking on their journey. Alternatively, they stretch their goals over time, attempting to reach certain goals in the short term, put off others until later, and regard still others as unattainable.[16]

One example of an eagle is the Roman emperor Augustus. His overriding vision was to create a new political structure for the Roman Empire that would provide stability after a century of civil war. As we know, he succeeded beyond expectation in that goal. One noteworthy feature of his eagle-like leadership was that he scaled down his ambitions to align them with the (huge) means of Rome. The best example is that, after three Roman legions were destroyed in the German Teutoburg Forest in 9 A.D., he sensibly decided to make the Rhine the northern boundary of the empire.

Abraham Lincoln is another example of an eagle. His overriding central goals in his presidency were preservation of the Union and emancipation of American slaves. To achieve these twin goals, his maneuvers were as foxy as one could imagine—resorting to deals, bribes, flattery, arm-twisting, and outright lies.[17]

A third example is Soviet dictator Joseph Stalin. His overriding goal was to strengthen communism at home, and, in the process, the Soviet Union, under his sole leadership. To achieve these goals, he used a variety of means, including outmaneuvering rivals and forced industrialization, as well as a pact with Hitler, and, later, with Britain and the United States. By 1945, he had achieved all he wanted, and the Soviet Union was the second-most powerful country on Earth.

OSTRICHES

A more sorrowful group are leaders who are neither a hedgehog nor a fox—they are essentially hapless leaders. I call them ostriches, which, in the words of the Roman statesman Pliny the Elder (23–79 A.D.), "imagine, when they have thrust their head and neck into a bush, that the whole of their body is concealed." *Ostriches neither have a clear idea where they are going (ends) nor how to get there (means).* They lack a compelling, overarching central vision. If they pursue ends at all, they are unrelated and even contradictory, and they fail to accurately assess the means at their disposal or to link means with ends. You will find ostriches in most organizations, but they may be disproportionately present in large, bureaucratic organizations with high job security, and an emphasis on "going with the flow." Chapter 11 describes such a case—the Royal Navy before the arrival of Admiral Jacky Fisher.

The French King Louis XVI was clueless about what to do in the face of rising public unrest, which resulted in the French Revolution. His incompetence cost him his head. Another example of an ostrich is British prime minister Theresa May, who succeeded David Cameron. She called an election in 2017 to push through Brexit, which she lost, largely due to her own incompetence. She agreed to a Brexit agreement that was unacceptable to many of her own Conservative members of Parliament, and was forced to resign after three miserable years in office. She is regarded as one of the worst prime ministers since World War II.[18]

In the United States, President George W. Bush also falls in this category. His defining decision was the invasion of Iraq, which was done without clear end goals, based on faulty information, something acknowledged later by Secretary of State Colin Powell.[19] The Iraq war cost trillions of dollars and thousands of casualties, allowed the emergence of Iran as the dominant power in the region, and diverted attention from the much greater military threat of an emerging China. Not surprisingly, he is rated as one of the worst presidents since World War II.[20]

WHICH AESOPIAN METAPHOR ARE YOU?

I will assess each leader discussed in this book using this Aesopian clas-
sification. As you will see, it leads to some interesting insights. You may
also wonder: What am I? Am I a hedgehog, a fox, an eagle, or an ostrich?
The Hedgefox Scale, in Appendix B, allows you to answer this question. In
chapter 18, I will tie your score back to specific parts of the book.

LEADERSHIP STYLES

Leadership, whether the leader is a hedgehog, a fox, an eagle, or an ostrich,
can come in many different forms, based on the person's personality traits
and competencies, and the organizational and cultural context. Theorists
have structured different manifestations of leadership by distinguishing
leadership styles. Leadership style consists of the attitudinal and behavioral
pattern of a person who attempts to influence others.[21]

In my work, I have identified seven leadership styles: adaptive, persuasive, directive, disruptive, authentic, servant, and charismatic. While there
may be others, these are certainly among the most important ones. These
seven leadership styles can be distinguished from each other on several
dimensions (Figure 1.2). The influence of the leader versus the follower is
the primary dimension on which adaptive, persuasive, directive, and disruptive leadership can be contrasted. Follower influence is greatest for adaptive
leadership and smallest for disruptive leadership. Authentic and servant
leadership are differentiated from the others by the exceptional moral
standards to which the leader is held. These leadership styles demand an
unusual degree of integrity and even self-sacrifice. Charismatic leadership
is distinguished from the others in that the leader is imbued with (near)
messianic quality.

Figure 1.2 Leadership Styles

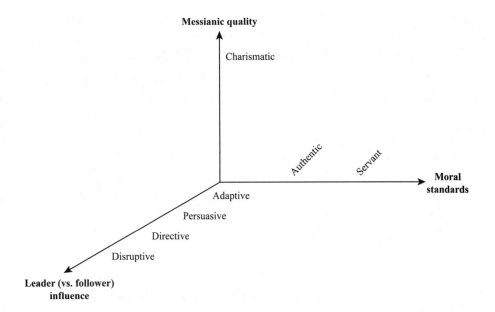

ADAPTIVE LEADERSHIP—MODIFY ACCORDING TO THE CIRCUMSTANCES

Adaptive leadership calls for a high degree of flexibility of the leader to modify their goals and values as required by either the organizational context or the environment. Most leaders are not so rigid that they are unwilling to adapt the process, and even the common goals, if required by circumstances. But this willingness to adapt, even to jettison one's own views, in view of changing circumstances is central to adaptive leadership. A key challenge for adaptive leaders is to remain credible even after they have changed their position. If they do this too often or too abruptly, they may be considered a weathervane, or perhaps even a sell-out, to their followers. Taken to the extreme, adaptive leadership becomes Machiavellian—leadership where the end justifies any means.

PERSUASIVE LEADERSHIP – CHANGE THE MINDS OF YOUR FOLLOWERS

All leadership involves some degree of persuasion—even Hitler and Stalin could not lead by terror alone—but persuasive leaders have made it an art. Persuasive leaders excel in moving their followers toward a position they did not hold before. Their outstanding feature is that they are able to change the hearts and minds of their followers. To achieve this, persuasive leaders must not only make rational arguments, but also frame their ideas in ways that appeal to their followers' emotions. They also (appear to) involve followers in the decision-making process so that the followers "own" the decision. The extreme case of persuasive leadership is manipulative leadership, where the leader persuades their followers by telling lies and making promises they have no intention to keep.

The key difference between adaptive and persuasive leadership is the locus of change in order to achieve the desired goal. In the case of persuasive leadership, the primary focus of the leader is to change the minds of their followers in order to attain the desired goal, while in the case of adaptive leadership, the leader changes their own position.

DIRECTIVE LEADERSHIP – DEFINE THE MARCHING ORDERS

Directive leadership characterizes a leadership style where the leader initiates ideas, projects, and tasks, and gives followers clear instructions about their responsibilities, including what is expected of them, how to perform the task, and the timeline in which it should be completed. Directive leaders tend to focus on their own experiences and opinions above others. They set the direction of the vision and the mission. This means their followers are not required to offer suggestions or provide feedback to the leader. Their work performance is judged by how well they are performing their assigned tasks.[22] If pushed too far, directive leadership becomes autocratic leadership, which is clearly unproductive, as followers have information and insights that are not used. Followers feel stifled and unfulfilled. They may talk behind the leader's back instead of confronting the leader, for fear of repercussions, and the best employees will leave.

DISRUPTIVE LEADERSHIP –
BREAK WITH THE PAST

Most people hate change, and the same applies to organizations. There is a built-in inclination in organizations, especially bureaucratic organizations, to stick with the established and proven way of things. After all, followers know what they currently have, while it is uncertain what change may give them. Furthermore, as Machiavelli already observed in *The Prince*, in any organization, there will be many people who benefit from the existing state of affairs and have a strong motivation to resist change by any means. Disruptive leaders have the vision and the courage to engineer change in their organization, notwithstanding the barriers. They break the rules to forge a different and (presumably) better future. But there is always the danger that they move too far ahead of their followers, or move too fast. In this case, disruptive leadership often leads to organizational chaos, and a premature end to the leader's career.

AUTHENTIC LEADERSHIP –
SET THE EXAMPLE

As the name implies, this leadership style is about the authenticity of the leader and their leadership. Is their leadership genuine and "real"? Do they not only talk the talk but also walk the walk? Authentic leaders understand their purpose, have strong values about what they see as the right thing to do, act upon their values, and are passionate about their mission. A survey conducted among U.S. workers asked them to select the one characteristic that was the most important for a person to lead them. Leading by example came out number one, with 26 percent. Strong ethics or morals—another integral aspect of authentic leadership—was the second most selected trait

(19 percent).[23] While authentic leadership is intuitively appealing, if pushed too far, authentic leadership's strong sense of right and wrong can morph into rigid, moralistic leadership. The world is a messy place, which requires leaders to sometimes compromise on their values to reach their goal. In such situations, if the leader rigidly sticks to their values, they may not be able to achieve their goals.

SERVANT LEADERSHIP – PUT FOLLOWERS FIRST

Robert Greenleaf, one of the leading scholars on servant leadership, provides the following description of the servant leader:

> The servant leader is servant first . . . It begins with the natural feeling that one wants to serve, to serve first . . . The best test is this: Do those served grow as persons? Do they, while being served, become healthier, wiser, freer, more autonomous, and more likely themselves to become servants? And, what is the effect on the least privileged in society? Will they benefit, or at least not further be harmed?[24]

Compared to other leadership styles where the ultimate goal is the well-being of the organization, the central focus of the servant leader is serving others. They put followers first, empower them, and are committed to helping them grow professionally and personally. Servant leaders lead in ways that serve the greater good. Hence, social responsibility looms large in servant leadership.[25] Servant leadership is one of the hot topics in management these days, but, if pushed too far, it becomes utopian leadership. The world is a tough place and many followers are self-serving. In fact, the academic discipline of economics is largely built on the notion of people pursuing their own interests. Further, if servant leaders serve their followers at the expense of the organizational goals, they ultimately harm the followers as the organization fails. Servant leadership might be ineffective when it ignores these realities.

CHARISMATIC LEADERSHIP — BUY INTO THE LEADER, THEN FOLLOW THEIR VISION

Charismatic leaders excel in their ability to formulate and articulate an inspirational vision, and by employing behaviors and actions that foster an impression that they and their mission are extraordinary. Individuals choose to follow such leaders in organizations not only because of formal authority but out of perceptions of extraordinariness.[26] Charismatic leaders act as a strong role model for their followers, who identify with these leaders and want to emulate them. They make their followers part of something larger than themselves. These leaders are convinced beyond doubt about the "justness of their cause." However, some would-be charismatic leaders approach the area of vision backwards. They believe that, if the cause is good, people will automatically buy into it and follow the leader. But that is not how charismatic leadership works. People buy into the leader first, then into the leader's vision.[27]

Charismatic leadership is an extraordinarily powerful way to lead. However, pushed to the extreme, it can easily lead to hubris. You are so adored by your followers that you may develop a feeling of invulnerability, which can lead to your downfall. They may also follow you, rather than having internalized your vision. That means that if you leave the organization, the progress toward attaining the goals set out by you is interrupted. Without you, why should they bother?

YOUR LEADERSHIP STYLE

Which leadership style (or styles) do you exhibit, or aspire to? You will find a measurement instrument—the Steenkamp Assessment Instrument for Leadership Styles, or SAILS—to help you answer that question, in

Appendix C. In chapter 18, I will redirect you to specific parts of the book, dependent on your scores.

ABOUT THE LEADERS INCLUDED IN THIS BOOK

Every leader discussed in this book took significant risks and had qualities that transcend time. Some were kings or military commanders, others were politicians or nonprofit leaders. Some were highly educated, others received little formal education. Some were morally upstanding, others decidedly not. Some had to overcome barriers of sexism or racism. The leaders chosen span 2,500 years of history and come from (present-day) China, France, Germany, Great Britain, Greece, Israel, South Africa, Spain, and the United States. But one characteristic was shared by them all: Their leadership changed the course of history. The world as we know it would not be the same without their leadership. As leaders, they had to take great risks, often with the odds stacked against them. We, living in the twenty-first century, can learn from their true stories and the struggles they faced. We can also be encouraged by them. If they were able to persevere and succeed, is there any pertinent reason we cannot do so as well?

You might wonder why I chose these sixteen men and women. It is not an exhaustive list, of course, and if your favorite leader is not included here, this does not mean they are undeserving. Indeed, there are many other people I would like to have included, but that would result in a book of a thousand pages or more, and you might not want to read it. Yet, I did not select these case studies at random. Two criteria helped me in the selection process.

First, I drew on the four functions of historical examples, outlined by Carl von Clausewitz in his famous book *On War*.[28] More specifically, I searched for leadership case studies: (1) that may be used as an *explanation* of a particular leadership style; (2) that serve to show the *application* of a leadership style in practice; (3) that prove the *possibility* of a leadership style across different circumstances; and (4) that allow me to derive *general insights* from the multiple case studies grouped under a particular leadership style. Don't get me wrong—I am not claiming that a particular leader used that leadership style exclusively. Social reality is too complex for that, and most leaders therefore display some amalgamation of styles. And, as Figure 1.2 shows, leadership styles exist on a continuum, and demarcations between them are not as clear-cut as what you would encounter when, say, studying physics. Having said this, I do believe that the leadership style under which a person appears is the most outstanding, prototypical one for that person. For example, while George Washington obviously exhibited directive leadership—how can you not as a general?—in my view, his truly outstanding leadership style is that he is one of the most authentic leaders the world has ever seen.

Second, I focus on a single seminal dilemma facing the leader, and the decision made by the leader in question to solve that dilemma. As you will see, each of these decisions changed the course of world history. In each case, there was an alternative response available to the dilemma facing the leader, which, at the time, might often have seemed a safer bet. That makes the decision especially noteworthy as exemplifying true leadership. With the benefit of hindsight, the right course of action may now seem like the logical thing to do. Yet, hindsight is misleading. In hindsight, I should have invested all my money in Amazon in 1997. Unfortunately, I did not . . . This approach allows me to keep the chapters relatively concise, and the examples crisper.

FORMAT OF THE BOOK

This book is written in an accessible manner and organized in seven parts, one for each leadership style. Each part contains two or three case studies on individual leaders, each in a separate chapter. These chapters all follow the same format. The first section briefly describes the wider context that gave rise to the dilemma facing the leader. Next comes a short biography of the leader up to the time the decision had to be made. Then, the focus shifts to the seminal decision made by that person to resolve that dilemma. I conclude by drawing lessons about that case study. Each part concludes with reflections on the leadership style by comparing the leaders in that part, and provides some questions to think over in order to decide whether that leadership style suits you.

Part One contains three examples of adaptive leadership, examining the seminal dilemmas facing the Frankish king Clovis (c. 466–511), German chancellor Otto von Bismarck (1815–1898), and Chinese supreme leader Deng Xiaoping (1904–1997). Examples of persuasive leadership are the subject of Part Two, and include the Athenian politician and admiral Themistocles (524–459 B.C.), British prime minister Sir Henry Campbell-Bannerman (1836–1908), and U.S. president Franklin D. Roosevelt (1882–1945).

Two examples of directive leadership style are introduced in Part Three: the fearsome Spanish conquistador Hernán Cortés (1485–1547) and Britain's Iron Lady, Margaret Thatcher (1925–2013). Disruptive leadership, by the Apostle Peter (c. 1–64/68) and British admiral Jacky Fisher (1841–1920), is the subject of Part Four. Part Five deals with authentic leadership and presents case studies involving dilemmas facing U.S. general and president George Washington (1732–1799) and Nelson Mandela (1918–2013), South Africa's first black president.

Part Six is devoted to servant leadership and features British nurse Florence Nightingale (1820–1910) and civil rights activist Dr. Martin Luther King Jr. (1929–1968). Finally, Part Seven focuses on charismatic leadership and features Alexander the Great (356–323 B.C.) and French general and president Charles de Gaulle (1890–1970).

The final chapter, chapter 18, circles back to *you*. Where do you go from here? How can you apply the themes and lessons of the book in your life and organization? Then, in the appendices, I provide three unique self-assessment tools—the Grit Scale, the Hedgefox Scale, and SAILS—that can help you assess your leadership potential and style, and provide specific recommendations on what to do, dependent on your scores on these leadership assessments.

PART ONE

ADAPTIVE LEADERSHIP — MODIFY ACCORDING TO THE CIRCUMSTANCES

2

CLOVIS ATTENDS
A MASS

"I shall make Gaul the empire of the Franks."
—CLOVIS

Leadership Dilemma: How could Clovis bring the Franks, a weak tribe at the periphery of the former Roman Empire, to greatness?

CONTEXT

In the fifth century A.D., the western part of the once invincible Roman Empire (broadly, Western Europe and North Africa) was overrun by Germanic tribes, including the Vandals, Visigoths, Ostrogoths, Burgundians, and Franks. The empire gradually disintegrated until its "formal" collapse in 476, when the Germanic war lord Odoacer deposed the last Western Roman emperor and sent the imperial regalia to Constantinople. By 480, the western part of the empire was divided

Figure 2.1 Germanic Kingdoms in 480 A.D.

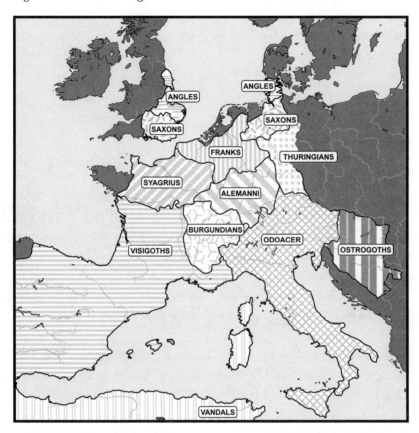

into a number of Germanic kingdoms (Figure 2.1). The most powerful Germanic kingdom was that of the Visigoths, who occupied Spain and much of central and southern France. Two rival powers were the Vandal kingdom in North Africa and the kingdom of Odoacer in Italy. In the early 490s, Odoacer's kingdom was conquered by the Ostrogoths, led by their great king Theodoric.

Among the least impressive Germanic kingdoms was that of the Franks. The Franks were a loose confederation of Germanic tribes, which were divided into two groups. The Salian Franks dwelt in (roughly) what is today Belgium, while the Ripuarian Franks inhabited the area along the river Rhine. The area occupied by the Franks was neither large nor rich. The Frankish tribes were ruled by many "kings"—more accurately, royal chieftains. Nothing would suggest that the future would belong to the Franks—until Clovis burst upon the scene. His goal was to make the Franks the preeminent power in Gaul (roughly present-day France). But how could he achieve that?

CLOVIS

Clovis was born in the year 466. His father was one of the "kings" of the Salian Franks, whom he succeeded in 481. He was a pagan but he married a Catholic princess, Clotilda. The extent of his territory was a pretty restricted corner of Belgium.[1] Gregory of Tours, a late-sixth-century Gallo-Roman historian and bishop of Tours, wrote a famous book, *History of the Franks*. From these pages, a complex picture of Clovis emerges. His crude, cunning, and savage qualities are painfully evident. At the same time, however, he appears as a courageous and decisive war leader, and a shrewd strategist.[2]

The exact chronology of events is not always completely clear, but, fortunately, this is not crucial for the purposes of this book. In 486, Clovis conquered the area around Paris by defeating a remnant of the Western Roman Empire under a local warlord called Syagrius. He next pressed eastward against the Alamanni and the Ripuarian Franks and extended his territory deep into Germany. He picked quarrels with other kings of the Salian and Ripuarian Franks. In a series of Mafia-like hits, using deception and treachery, he eliminated all his potential rivals, thus ensuring that only his dynasty would rule the Franks. But these were all relatively weak adversaries. Standing between him and his goal to gain the ascendancy in Gaul stood the vastly more powerful Visigothic kingdom, which possessed the richest part of Gaul, Aquitaine. Yet, to the astonishment of all, in the period from 507 to 511, he was able to drive the Visigoths out of most of Gaul (Figure 2.2). By the time of his death in 511, Clovis had transformed a minor Frankish state into a major power, second only to that of the kingdom of the Ostrogoths. How did he accomplish this? One crucial decision made all the difference.

Figure 2.2 The Rise of the Franks

Lands gained by Clovis 482–511

From Syagrius 486	From Ripuarian Franks by 509	Lands gained by Clovis's sons 511–36
From Alemanni 505–7	From Visigoths 507–11	—— Frankish boundary 482
		●●●● Frankish boundary 511

Source: Based on Heather (2013), p. 210

CLOVIS CONVERTS TO CATHOLICISM

In 496, Clovis made a decision whose effects can still be felt today. He converted to orthodox Christianity (i.e., Catholicism) and was baptized, together with many leading Frankish nobles, by Remigius, the bishop of Rheims. His conversion was later shrouded in legend. Gregory of Tours wrote that the conversion was a consequence of a promise made in the midst of a battle with the Alamanni in 496 when things looked bleak for the Franks. I quote from Gregory:

> Jesus Christ, whom Clotilda asserts to be the Son of the living God, who art said to give aid to those in distress, and to bestow victory on those who hope in Thee, I beseech the glory of thy aid, and with the vow that if thou grant me victory over these enemies . . . I will believe in Thee and be baptized in Thy Name.[3]

According to Gregory, the Franks then miraculously got the upper hand and defeated the Alemanni decisively. As a child, I already knew this story. Clovis's conversion earned France the title of "the eldest daughter of the Church." His conversion did not come out of the blue. Rather, it was the result of a shrewd analysis of the political-strategic situation. Indeed, the decision was preceded by intense debate at the Frankish court—should they remain pagan, become Arian, or become Catholic?[4] Why would that matter so much?

As we have seen (Figure 2.1), by 480 A.D., the Western Roman Empire was carved up into a number of Germanic kingdoms. There existed an unbridgeable religious chasm between the German overlords and the Roman subjects, who constituted the large majority of each kingdom. With the exception of the Franks, who were pagans, the Germanic tribes were Arians while the Roman population was Catholic. In a nutshell, Arianism denies the divinity of Christ, which was—and is—a cornerstone of the orthodox Christian faith. The Roman population regarded Arianism as heresy. While this may seem like a minor theological dispute, it was actually a huge issue. In its importance, compare it to the division between Shiites and Sunnis in Islam, a division that continues to fuel intense conflict in the Middle East thirteen hundred years after the dispute arose.

To complicate matters further, after the Roman civil administration melted away in the late fifth century, it was not replaced by a Germanic civil administration. Administration required literacy, fluency in Latin, and many years of education. The Germanic tribesmen were more interested in military prowess, which was more profitable and crucial for the survival of their kingdoms on Roman soil. So, who *did* prevent the total collapse of civil administration? The Catholic Church, which was the only administrative structure left in Western Europe. The leaders of the Church were a network of bishops in every major city of the empire, arranged in a hierarchy, diocese by diocese, with "metropolitan" bishops (later called archbishops) at their head, and looking to the bishop of Rome—the pope. (This is essentially still the structure of the Catholic Church today.) This did not mean, however, that there were incessant sharp tensions between the German overlords and the Church hierarchy. Relations could be quite cordial at times, but the divide was always there. No churchman would ever compromise over the divinity of Christ. Moreover, sometimes Catholics were actively persecuted.

In sum, by the late fifth century, bishops were no longer purely religious authorities—they had become major political players. Without their help, conquering, let alone holding and effectively governing, a territory was challenging.[5] Clovis understood this and saw an opportunity to take advantage of it. Remaining a pagan offered short-term benefits, in that he could expect no opposition from fellow pagan Franks. Clovis also understood, however, that remaining a pagan did not yield long-term benefits. Christianity was young and dynamic. It represented the future, while the Frankish gods represented the past. And Clovis was not the kind of person to look back. As Gregory emphasized, initial meetings between Clovis and Remigius, the bishop of Rheims, were conducted in secret. Clovis told Remigius, "but there remains one thing: the people who follow me cannot endure to abandon their gods; but I shall go and speak to them according to your words."[6] The alternative to conversion to Catholicism was conversion to Arianism. Had Clovis desired to live with his fellow Germanic kings on terms of equality and friendship, converting to Arianism was the prudent course of action. But "nothing was more foreign to his thoughts than friendship and alliance with any of the neighboring tribes. His desire was to reduce them all to a state of subjection to himself."[7] Clovis needed to play a different game to gain the upper hand. Since the Ostrogothic and Visigothic kingdoms were stronger than his kingdom, he needed to find support elsewhere. His seminal insight was that Gaul was worth a mass.

Clovis knew that if he accepted the Catholic religion, he would be the only Catholic king in all of the former Western Roman Empire. By becoming Catholic, Clovis bridged the chasm between German and Roman. Gregory's enthusiasm, and his eagerness to link Clovis's conversion to divine intervention, shows that Clovis made the shrewd choice. In Gregory's account, the Mafia-like leader of the Frankish war band was suddenly transformed by his conversion into a new Constantine. God's support for Clovis was evidenced by various alleged miracles, a sure sign that he had found favor in the eyes of the Church. As the Catholic champion, he would find it much easier to gain the allegiance of the Gallo-Romans and the Catholic Church. With his power reinforced by the support of the Church, Clovis proceeded in his conquests.[8]

Clovis's clever use of the advantages of posing as champion of the Catholic cause played out most clearly in the conquest of the large swath of Visigothic territory in southern France, which was rich and heavily populated. Taking on the Visigothic kingdom was the gamble of his life. He enlisted the support of the episcopate and the large Gallo-Roman population in southern France by choosing his casus belli carefully. When he declared war in 507, he justified it not as a naked land grab, but rather to stop the persecutions of Catholics by Visigothic king Alaric II: "I take it very hard that these Arians hold part of Gaul. Let us go with God's help and conquer them and bring the land under our control."[9] It is telling that he astutely refers to his enemies as Arians, not Visigoths.

In moving his army south toward Visigothic territory, Clovis trumpeted his Catholic credentials. As he passed through the territory of Tours, which was claimed to be under the special protection of St. Martin, he was careful to preserve the strictest discipline among his soldiers to further ingratiate himself with the Church and sanctify his undertaking. When a Frankish soldier transgressed his command, and Clovis heard about it, the response was immediate: "[q]uicker than speed, the offender was slain by the sword, and the king said: 'and where shall our hope of victory be if we offend the blessed Martin?'"[10] In Tours, he publicly displayed his reverence for the patron saint. All this made for good publicity, which would soon serve him well. In the spring of 507, he decisively defeated the Visigoths and over-ran southern France. After Clovis's victory, the Eastern Roman emperor Anastasius awarded Clovis a consulship. Although a purely honorary title, it meant that Clovis's conquests received the consent of the emperor, still regarded as the highest authority in the former Western Roman Empire.[11]

Clovis's sons would further extend Frankish territory to the east and south. The grip of the Franks on their vast lands was never in doubt, given that they alone among Germanic tribes had crossed the divide with the majority Roman population. While all other Germanic kingdoms had dis-appeared by c. 700, the Frankish empire was destined to be long-lasting.[12] Its western part would become France (the name says it all), which would remain an independent and powerful world player up to the present day.[13] Its eastern half would morph into the Holy Roman Empire of the German Nation, and, eventually, Germany. Seventeen kings of France would be named after Clovis, as well as four Holy Roman emperors.[14] Fifteen hundred years later, Charles de Gaulle, who is the subject of chapter 17, commented: "For me the history of France begins with Clovis . . . The deciding element for me is that Clovis was the first king to be baptized a Christian."[15] Not a bad legacy for somebody who started as a rogue warlord.

LESSONS

It is ironic that Clovis's name and heritage would live in history, while his contemporary, the Ostrogothic king Theodoric the Great, who in every respect was more laudable than the Frankish schemer, is all but forgotten. According to historian Norman Cantor, Theodoric, in his personal qualities, was the greatest Germanic king before Charlemagne.[16] Theodoric actively tried to revive Roman institutions, brought peace and prosperity to Italy, and attempted to synthesize Ostrogothic and Roman culture. Yet, in the end, Theodoric failed. After his death, the Ostrogothic kingdom disappeared from history, and the leadership in Western Europe passed to the Franks. A key reason, if not *the* key reason, was that Theodoric was unwilling to exhibit flexibility on the one aspect that was the root cause of the unbridgeable chasm between the Ostrogothic people and the Romans—Arianism. He was unwilling to give up Arianism.

Clovis, on the other hand, while being a ruffian, exhibited adaptive leadership where it really mattered. He was the only Germanic king who adopted the faith of his majority Roman subjects, and was therefore served by them, and especially by their clergy, with a loyalty which no Goth, Vandal, or Burgundian king could ever win. According to historian Charles Oman, "Not least among the causes of Chlodovech's [Clovis's] easy triumphs and of the permanence of his kingdom may be reckoned his adherence to Catholicism."[17] Referring back to Isaiah Berlin's distinction between hedgehogs and foxes introduced in chapter 1, Theodoric was a hedgehog, while Clovis was an eagle. Clovis had a single overarching vision: "I shall make Gaul the empire of the Franks." However, he modified the means to achieve this in a fox-like manner. During his career, he always aligned means and ends.

Oman concluded that "He [Clovis] was granted a measure of success that was refused to kings of far better disposition."[18] He is not the only leader who is judged by his outcomes rather than by the moral quality of his character. I think it is fair to say that in his personal behavior, President George W. Bush was a man of higher moral quality than his predecessor, Bill Clinton, who even faced impeachment on grounds of perjury to a grand jury. But unlike Bush, Clinton exhibited adaptive leadership—after he lost control of Congress, he made a turn to the right, saying, "the era of big government is over." Regardless of whether he was sincere in his change of mind or not, Clinton is seen by presidential experts as a much better president than Bush—with one of the biggest differences being on the aspect of "ability to compromise," where Clinton ranked #4 of all U.S. presidents and Bush #42.[19]

Smart adaptive leadership implies that you carefully analyze your situation and identify the key issue(s) standing between you and the goal you want to reach. Clovis's life reveals a four-step procedure for adaptive leadership.

First, you identify the key barrier(s) that limit your effectiveness as leader to achieve organizational success. In Clovis's case, that was the religious chasm between him/his Franks and the majority population.

Second, you assess what your competitors are doing. Do they face the same barrier? If so, being a first mover gives you an edge. If they have already crossed that bridge, you may still have to do it, but the benefits will be less. In Clovis's case, the other Germanic kingdoms had not embraced Catholicism, which offered Clovis a unique opportunity. Because he was the first, it was risky (Clovis was worried about the reaction of his followers), but, as the Romans said, *fortis Fortuna adiuvat* (fortune favors the brave).

Third, once you have changed your position, make sure that your followers, and the wider world, become aware of it. After having convinced his Franks, Clovis exhibited his newly found religious fervor publicly—for example, in Tours, by displaying his reverence for St. Martin and executing a Frankish offender.

Fourth, benefit from the aura created by what you did. Clovis's services to the cause of the Catholic Church negated his moral shortcomings in the eyes of contemporary ecclesiastical historians. Writes Gregory of Tours: "God prostrated his enemies before him and increased his kingdom, because he walked before him with an upright heart, and did what was pleasing in His eyes."[20] Quite a statement, given Clovis's life!

Companies have used investments in corporate social responsibility as an insurance policy when things go wrong.[21] One such example is BP. In the late 1990s, before almost any other oil majors, it acknowledged its role in global warming and joined the battle against climate change with tangible and meaningful action. Its green efforts were communicated to the world with massive advertising, which resulted in a "green" aura, quite remarkable for an oil company. This helped the company mitigate the fallout of the 2010 *Deepwater Horizon* oil spill, the largest marine oil spill in the history of the petroleum industry. Research showed that BP's green aura significantly reduced the adverse effects such as brand switching and downward pressure on prices.[22]

CHAPTER TAKEAWAYS

- Clovis was an eagle who pursued his overarching goal of making the Franks masters of Gaul through a variety of means. His chief opponent, Theodoric, was a hedgehog on the issue that really counted (religion).

- Clovis converted to Catholicism because he understood that in the long run, getting buy-in from his Gallo-Roman subjects and the Church was the route to success.

- It is unclear whether Clovis's conversion was sincere, but the effect of his adaptive decision was a deciding moment in the history of France, and of Western Europe.

- Clovis's life highlights several adaptive leadership principles:

    ° One's leadership may be judged as much, if not more, by its outcomes as by one's moral quality.

    ° Having few, if any, strong convictions makes adaptive leadership easier.

    ° A four-step procedure to adaptive leadership:

        ▫ Identify the key barrier(s) that would limit the effectiveness of you as leader to achieve organizational success.

        ▫ Assess what your competitors are doing.

        ▫ Change your position, and make sure your followers and the wider world are aware of this.

        ▫ Leverage the aura created by your new position when you face tough times.

BISMARCK UNSHACKLES A NATION

"A man of extraordinary flexibility."
—HISTORIAN ROBERT GERWARTH

Leadership Dilemma: How could Bismarck unify Germany against fierce opposition?

CONTEXT

The French Revolution and the ensuing Napoleonic wars spread the message of liberty, fraternity, and equality across Europe. After the defeat of Napoleon at Waterloo in 1815, the allies Great Britain, Russia, Austria, and Prussia were determined to push the twin genies of nationalism and liberalism back into the bottle. Autocratic regimes were brought back where they had been swept away by the French armies. The Austrian chancellor and foreign minister Klemens von Metternich was the architect of this system, which was put together during the Congress of Vienna (1814–1815).[1] Its glue was a shared sense of legitimacy and the unity of conservative interests that transcended state borders. The Vienna system was based on the following principles:

- In the interest of stability, Europe's legitimate crowned heads of state had to be preserved.
- National and liberal movements had to be suppressed.
- France had to be kept in check.
- Relations among states had to be determined by consensus among like-minded rulers.[2]

The system worked well for some three decades, but in 1848, revolutions against this suppressive order broke out all around Europe, starting (where else?) in France. However, within a few years, all revolutions were suppressed and promises of liberal constitutions and democracy, made during the revolutionary heydays of 1848, were conveniently forgotten. In 1852, Louis-Napoleon, nephew of the great Napoleon, abolished the short-lived Second French Republic and became Emperor Napoleon III. For reasons of national and personal prestige, he could never accept the Vienna system. He saw himself as a champion of nationalism, being convinced that his uncle had failed because he opposed the national will of Germany and Italy. He was continuously mulling over vague schemes for redrawing the map of Europe. According to the historian A.J.P. Taylor, "If there was a stable point in his unstable mind, it was resentment against Austria, the country of Metternich and of stability."[3]

Thus, in the 1850s, the European political map looked much like the one created by the Congress of Vienna. There were five Great Powers— Great Britain, Russia, France, Austria, and Prussia (Figure 3.1). They all understood that the large area in the center of Europe was central to continental stability. This area was fragmented into many states, the two

Figure 3.1 Europe after the Congress of Vienna

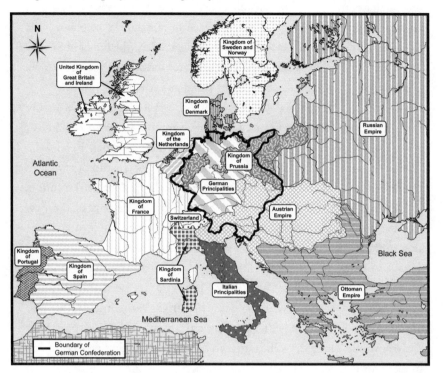

largest by far being the Kingdom of Prussia and the Austrian Empire. Austria commanded the greater respect and legitimacy by virtue of its size, its history dating back to the Middle Ages, and its illustrious Habsburg Dynasty. While the Germans were politically dominant in the Austrian Empire, they constituted only a minority of its population. Prussia was an upstart, having become a kingdom only in 1701, but was militarily formidable, ethnically more homogenous, and much better governed than Austria. The relationship between Austria and Prussia was central to European stability.

Figure 3.1 shows that the German heartland was flanked by two large and powerful states, France and Russia. Since the seventeenth century, France had strived to keep Germany divided because it was keenly aware that a unified Germany would be a formidable power right on its doorstep. To thwart French designs on central Europe, the Congress of Vienna had created a new entity called the *Deutscher Bund* (German Confederation), providing a common defense against outside aggression. It was too strong to be attacked by France, but too decentralized to threaten its neighbors. The German Confederation had a permanent Federal Diet, which met in the city of Frankfurt. The Diet's members were the ambassadors of the thirty-nine German states, with the Austrian envoy being its permanent president.[4]

By the 1850s, national feeling among Germans in all walks of life was on the rise. More and more Germans wanted a German Reich. But what, exactly, was "Germany"? What should a new German Reich look like? If the status quo had to change (something Austria did not want in the first place), Austria favored the *grossdeutsche* (large-German) solution, in which the Austrian Empire in its entirety would be part of the new German nation. This would automatically give Austria the leading position in this new entity. Prussia, on the other hand, was inclined toward a *kleindeutsche* (small-German) entity, excluding Austria, with the Prussian king, Friedrich Wilhelm IV (r. 1840–1861), as its head. But being a strict adherent to the Vienna system, Friedrich Wilhelm only wanted *kleindeutsche* unification with Austrian agreement. This was something Austria would never do voluntarily, and the Prussian king was not ready to fight for it.[5]

In sum, while most Germans longed for German unification, in practice, conflicting views within Germany and conflicting interests between Prussia, Austria, and France led to a stalemate. It required a political Houdini to resolve this. That person would be Otto von Bismarck.

OTTO VON BISMARCK

Otto von Bismarck was born on April 1, 1815, in Schönhausen, in the Prussian province of Saxony. The Bismarcks were reasonably well-off, but by no means wealthy. They were Junkers, members of the landed nobility. Junkers constituted the backbone of the Prussian apparatus—its army officers, many of its civil servants, and some of its statesmen.[6] Bismarck studied law, but during his time as a student he stood out mainly for the many duels he fought to avenge (perceived) slights. He also frequently clashed with the university authorities.[7] He went on to become a civil servant, where he neglected his duties. He took an unauthorized leave of absence for six months to pursue a romance across Europe. After his position had become untenable, he was automatically liable for compulsory military service, which he tried to evade on account of (imaginary) ailments. The hard-nosed Prussian military did not fall for this. A silver lining was that because of the *von* before his name, he immediately became a lieutenant. He hated the rigid discipline and barely served the minimum mandatory time without being court-martialed. While he had no difficulty ordering others around, he could not stand being on the receiving end.[8] In 1839, he returned to run the family estates.

In 1847, Bismarck, at age thirty-two, was chosen as a representative to the newly created Prussian Diet. The large majority of the Diet belonged to various liberal groups. Bismarck quickly gained a reputation as a royalist and reactionary politician with a gift for provocative rhetoric. In speech after speech, he castigated any attempt to limit the absolute power of the king or the inherited privileges of the landed nobility.[9] He also branched out into journalism and became one of the chief contributors to the *Kreuzzeitung*, the mouthpiece of the ultraconservative faction, led by General Leopold von Gerlach, the Prussian king's military adjutant.[10]

Bismarck was made the Prussian envoy to the Federal Diet in Frankfurt in 1851. He arrived at this post as a friend of Austria; in fact, this is why his mentor, General Gerlach, had recommended him in the first place. In 1859 he was appointed ambassador to Russia, and then ambassador to France in May 1862. What he really craved, though, was to be in the center of power. However, while Friedrich Wilhelm IV and his successor Wilhelm I (r. 1861–1888) appreciated Bismarck's extreme conservatism, neither of them liked or fully trusted him. They regarded him as a troublemaker and "a red reactionary thirsting for blood."[11] But developments were occurring that would work in his favor.

Wilhelm I came into conflict with the increasingly liberal Prussian *Landtag*, or the Chamber of Deputies (lower house) of the Prussian Diet. A crisis arose from 1860 to 1862, when the *Landtag* repeatedly refused to authorize funding for a far-reaching reorganization of the army. New elections in 1861 and 1862 to break the stalemate yielded the opposite result— an unequivocal shift to the left. The king's ministers could not convince legislators to pass the budget, yet they were unwilling to defy parliament. The king was unwilling to make concessions.[12] Things came to a head when, in September 1862, the *Landtag* again overwhelmingly rejected the proposed budget. General Albrecht von Roon, the minister of war, advised the king to recall Bismarck to Prussia. Roon had known Bismarck since the latter was a teenager and thought he was the tough reactionary that could break the stalemate. Grudgingly, the king gave in. Wilhelm I asked Bismarck how he would get around a hostile *Landtag* when all his other ministers had failed. Bismarck answered: "My responsibility is only to my sovereign. If I cannot serve Your Majesty with parliament, I will do without the legislature."[13] He proved good to his word.

On September 23, 1862, Wilhelm appointed Bismarck prime minister and foreign minister, positions he would retain for the next twenty-seven years. In this period, he emerged as the colossus of European politics. He would destroy the conservative, legitimate consensus of the Congress of Vienna, be the first European leader to introduce universal male suffrage (long before liberal Britain), and introduce the most comprehensive system of social welfare the world had ever seen. All these decisions were directly in contradiction to his deeply held conservative beliefs.

Bismarck was able to accomplish this because of unsurpassed adaptive leadership, which has received its own name until this day, *Realpolitik*— politics based on considerations of given circumstances and factors, rather than explicit ideological notions or moral and ethical premises.[14]

BISMARCK UNIFIES GERMANY

As a staunch conservative, Bismarck should have had special appreciation and admiration for Austria, which, at the time, was hated by liberals all over Europe as a brutal police state, the symbol of reactionary oppression.[15] However, while he was the Prussian envoy to the Federal Diet in Frankfurt (from 1851 to 1859), he became increasingly convinced that Austria used the Federal Diet as an instrument to lock Prussia into the position of junior partner. This created a dilemma for Bismarck.

On the one hand, if Prussia was ever going to realize its destiny and unify Germany under Prussian leadership (*kleindeutsche* option), the German Confederation in its present form had to be destroyed and Austria had to be excluded from German affairs.[16] As Austria would never abdicate its dominant position voluntarily, any means, including war, fomenting ethnic unrest in the polyglot Austrian Empire, or an alliance with (supposedly "revolutionary") Napoleon III, should be considered.[17] In other words, the Vienna system had to be destroyed. On the other hand, as an archconservative, he was strongly committed to conservative institutions and the legitimacy of crowned heads. He hated liberalism, and he supported the principles upon which the Vienna system was built.

These two views were irreconcilable. Bismarck decided that his personal convictions should not dictate what he should do as the Prussian leader. In reaching this conclusion, he differed sharply from his erstwhile mentor Gerlach, to whom he owed so much.[18] Like the Ostrogothic king Theodoric (see chapter 2), Gerlach could not bring himself to accept the idea that strategic advantage could justify abandoning one's personal principles. In Gerlach's words, "My political principle is, and remains, the struggle against the Revolution."[19] Gerlach stuck to his beliefs—and is all but forgotten in history—while Bismarck's subsequent adaptive leadership created a united Germany for the first time since the Middle Ages.

Bismarck succeeded in unifying Germany under Prussian leadership via three wars fought between 1864 and 1871 (Figure 3.2). While Bismarck would have preferred to accomplish unification without war—where the outcome is inherently uncertain—he did not expect Austria and France to acquiesce to Prussia's expansion of influence without a fight. He was correct in this assessment.

The specifics of the subsequent political maneuvers have filled countless pages and are less important for the purposes of this book. Briefly, Bismarck lured Austria into joint action against Denmark in 1864 on behalf of the pan-German cause. The issue at hand was the future of the North German duchies of Schleswig and Holstein, which were dynastically linked to the Danish crown. After a brief war fought in the name of nationalism—so that Napoleon III would be less inclined to intervene—Schleswig and Holstein were detached from Denmark. This was the first nail in the coffin of the Vienna system. Holstein was to be administered by Austria and Schleswig by Prussia.

Next, Bismarck started to stir up trouble in the two duchies and engaged in political moves to foment conflicts with Austria over Schleswig-Holstein in the German Confederation.[20] Bismarck also dropped a political bombshell: He proposed the creation of an all-German Federal Assembly based on universal male suffrage to reform the German Confederation. This was nail number two in the Vienna coffin. Everybody immediately realized that this proposal did not come from an inner democratic conviction of Bismarck. After all, he treated the Prussian legislature with contempt and had always insisted on the privileged status of the nobility at home.

Figure 3.2 Reunification of Germany

Nevertheless, his old conservative friends were horrified. They could not understand why Bismarck was going against everything that conservatism and legitimism stood for. Yet, it was a supremely astute political maneuver. No Austrian government could possibly accept universal suffrage. It would empower the ten or so non-German subject nationalities in their struggles for representation and autonomy.[21] Predictably, Austria's reaction was violent. War was becoming inevitable.

Bismarck isolated Austria by dropping hints to Napoleon III that French neutrality might be rewarded with some lands west of the Rhine. Any understanding with France, especially if led by a scion of the Bonaparte family, directly contradicted what the Vienna system stood for—nail number three. Further, Bismarck stirred up trouble in the Austrian Empire. He initiated discussions with Hungarian leaders, who chafed under Austrian domination, about uprisings that would coincide with a Prussian assault. Here, we have the archconservative advocate of legitimate authority inciting people in another country to rebel against their own legitimate government: nail number four.[22] Finally, he made common cause with Italy, which coveted the Austrian-held area around Venice. Italy would attack Austria at the same time as Prussia would attack, pinning down Austria's large Italian army.[23] This would result in another transfer of territory taken from a legitimate ruler: nail number five.

The resulting Prussian-Austrian war in 1866 was over in a few weeks. Austria was evicted from German affairs. The German Confederation was abolished; Prussia annexed the northern German states that had sided with Austria, and established the North German Confederation under its indisputable leadership: nail number six. So as not to antagonize Napoleon III at this stage, the South German states remained outside this new entity.[24]

In the meantime, France was growing ever more alarmed. Napoleon III thought Prussia would never be able to defeat Austria, and certainly not so quickly and convincingly. Bismarck knew that to complete the unification of Germany, he still had to defeat Prussia's strongest opponent by far, France. He set about isolating France through deft political maneuvering.[25] In this, he was mightily helped by the incompetence and prevarication of Napoleon III, who was haunted his entire life by living under the shadow of his famous uncle, but who possessed none of his uncle's military genius, ruthlessness, and political decisiveness.

The two powers went to war in 1870, and France was soundly defeated. It was forced to give up Alsace and Lorraine to the new German Reich (with fateful consequences for the future). On January 18, 1871, the Prussian king Wilhelm I was proclaimed German emperor in the Hall of Mirrors at the Versailles Palace in France: the seventh and final nail in the coffin of the Vienna system.

With the unification of Germany, Bismarck had fulfilled his life goal and Germany was now, in his words, a "satisfied power." As chancellor of the German Reich, Bismarck played the role of peacemaker in Europe, until the new, rash emperor, Wilhelm II, who wanted to take charge of German policy himself, forced him to resign in 1890.[26] This was immortalized in the cartoon "Dropping the Pilot," published in the British satirical magazine *Punch* on March 29, 1890 (Figure 3.3).

However, Bismarck had created a problem that has haunted the world ever since. Once the vast, rich, and populous Germanic area was unified, it rapidly became the most powerful state in Continental Europe. A saying attributed to General Charles de Gaulle aptly summarizes the dilemma: "Europe without Germany is Europe without a heart. Europe with Germany is German Europe." Germany could only be contained by a coalition of other powers, which meant that Germany always felt encircled. France, resentful of having lost its preeminence in Europe and fearful of the ever-growing power of Germany, was invariably in the anti-Germany camp. Bismarck was able to manage the strategic complexities that resulted from German unification, but his successors, who lacked his brilliance, were not. Even so, Bismarck built Germany so well that his creation survived defeat in two world wars, two foreign occupations, and fifty years as a divided country.[27]

LESSONS

Henry Kissinger called Bismarck, together with Napoleon I, the most consequential European leader of the nineteenth century. Kissinger's

Figure 3.3 Dropping the Pilot

Source: Punch, 29 March 1890, public domain

admiration for Bismarck's *Realpolitik* (and his disdain for Napoleon III's grandstanding) is evident to anybody who reads his masterpiece *Diplomacy*.

Napoleon III was a hapless ostrich—he had no clear vision that guided all his scheming; for him, scheming was an end in itself. He also lacked an accurate understanding of France's military and economic means. Bismarck, on the other hand, was an eagle. The overarching vision that guided all his actions was to unify Germany under Prussian leadership. To achieve this, he modified his plans and his alliances in an exemplary fox-like manner. He understood that Prussia's means were insufficient to take on all opponents to German unity simultaneously. So, he played them against each other and continuously strengthened Prussia in the process until it was ready to take on mighty France. (Contrast this with the strategically insane policy of Hitler, who took on Britain, the United States, and the Soviet Union simultaneously.) Consequently, Bismarck is seen as a great, albeit controversial, leader, and his adversary, Napoleon III, is seen as a bumbler. Bismarck knew events could suddenly throw his calculations into chaos. He was always ready to ditch his own ideas and commitments when they seemed shaky. He was interested in winning, not in consistency.[28] What can we learn from Bismarck? I draw out four lessons.

First, the litmus test for successful adaptive leadership is whether you can discern from the tangle of adaptive tactical decisions the true long-term interests of your organization, and devise an appropriate strategy for achieving them. Too often, leaders lose sight of the ultimate goal, being occupied by tactics. They are not alone. Napoleon III was all about opportunistic, short-term, tactical schemes. Bismarck's tactics changed all the time, but they were always employed within the context of reaching toward his long-term goal.

Second, and related, adaptive leaders exhibit a high degree of flexibility in their tactics, but not in their strategy. What works best at any given moment is often highly time- and context-dependent. Bismarck often changed tactics, but not strategy. For example, to steer Austria to declare war on Prussia—and appear the aggressor—it had to be tempted beyond its capacity to bear. Thus, Bismarck introduced the proposal of universal male suffrage for the German Confederation. For him, this was a tactic to be used to reach the longer-term goal of evicting Austria from German affairs. If another tactic would serve his long-term goal better, he would have used that. But beware of the danger that tactical flexibility becomes the end in itself. My brother Paulus has frequently encountered colleagues at his company (Royal Dutch Shell) who appear primarily guided by the mantra, "What interests my boss, fascinates me." The executive's own views and thoughts are made subordinate to the higher echelons' thinking and wishes. While likely advancing said executive's career, it is doubtful that this leads to the best business results possible.

Third, analyze in which areas, if any, your personal background gives your adaptive leadership special credibility. Bismarck wanted to make working-class Germans loyal to the new German Reich, and to persuade them to resist the siren call of socialism (which, unsurprisingly, he hated). He pushed through the world's first comprehensive social security system. Compulsory accident, sickness, and old age insurance gave the German worker protections that were unheard of in the Western world. Given Bismarck's background, nobody could credibly accuse him of socialist leanings when he introduced this system. As Bismarck's example shows, few organizations have adequate "defenses" when somebody of their "own" proposes revolutionary change. Another example of this principle is U.S. president Richard Nixon's opening to China in the early 1970s. Nixon had made his name as a strident anticommunist crusader. When a leader with such sterling credentials decides to change his position on China, how could conservatives effectively oppose this? Imagine the uproar if that same policy would have been started by George McGovern or another liberal politician. My father came from a strict Catholic family in the Netherlands. So, when he became convinced in the 1960s that the Catholic People's Party should forgo its identity by merging with two Protestant political parties, his fellow Catholic politicians could not credibly accuse him of selling out the Catholic cause. It made him much more effective than if he had been "soft" on Catholicism.

Fourth, Bismarck was in a strong position to implement his strategy to unify Germany because Prussia had few foreign-policy interests beyond that goal. In contrast, France was occupied with Italy, the Near East, Britain, and an absurd adventure in Mexico. Austria had to deal with problems in Italy and the Balkans, as well as internally. In other words, Prussia could follow a "focus strategy" while its two key adversaries followed a "diversification strategy." We know from the marketing and strategy literatures that a focus strategy typically leads to better results than a diversification strategy because, in the latter case, a firm's resources are often spread too thin. Britain's largest grocery retailer, Tesco (2019 revenues: $84 billion), nearly went under because it expanded domestically into other sectors, including electronics, clothing, homewares, and garden centers, and internationally into other countries. As a result, it lost sight of its core market, grocery shoppers in the United Kingdom, where the hard discounters Aldi and Lidl made huge inroads.[29] After racking up a massive loss of $10 billion in 2015, it quit many geographical and sector markets. It was a close call, but Tesco was able to right the ship. Its business became much leaner and more efficient, and the company returned its focus to the shoppers and delivering value to them.[30]

CHAPTER TAKEAWAYS

- Bismarck was an eagle who pursued his overarching goal of unifying Germany under Prussian leadership with a variety of means. His chief opponent, Napoleon III, started out with vastly greater resources but squandered everything because he was an ostrich.

- In achieving his overarching goal, Bismarck went against his own deepest, conservative convictions and against those of the men who had supported him in his rise to power, like General Gerlach.

- Bismarck succeeded by having a laser-sharp focus on what he wanted to accomplish.

- Bismarck took on one adversary at a time, isolating or co-opting other adversaries who did not see the big picture.

- Bismarck's adaptive leadership has received its own name until this day, *Realpolitik*.

- The system Bismarck created and the country he forged proved impossible to manage by his less-brilliant successors. Two world wars were the direct (albeit unintentional) consequence of Bismarck's work.

- Bismarck's life highlights several adaptive leadership principles:

  ° Consider *Realpolitik* as a leadership option—leadership based on considerations of given circumstances and factors, rather than explicit ideological notions or moral and ethical premises.

  ° Discern from the tangle of tactical decisions the true long-term interests of your organization, and devise an appropriate strategy for achieving them.

° Exhibit a high degree of flexibility in tactics, but not in strategy—and do not confuse the two.

° Analyze and leverage areas where your personal background gives your adaptive leadership special credibility.

° Pursue a focus strategy over a diversification strategy.

4

DENG SEEKS TRUTH FROM FACTS

"It doesn't matter if a cat is black or white,
so long as it catches mice."
—DENG XIAOPING

Leadership Dilemma: How could Deng jump-start China's moribund Marxist economy?

CONTEXT

On September 9, 1976, Mao Zedong, the Great Helmsman and supreme leader of the People's Republic of China, died. The country and the world were apprehensive about what would come next. Long gone were the days when the Qianlong Emperor contemptuously told the British ambassador in 1795 that the Celestial Empire had no need for foreign wares, as all China needed was produced by his own people. In the nineteenth century,

China was humiliated by Great Britain in two so-called opium wars (1839–1842 and 1856–1860) and forced to open its economy to Western products (including opium!). In the late nineteenth century, the central authority of the Qing dynasty broke down. The Western powers and Japan divided China into different spheres of influence, and Chinese warlords effectively ruled much of the country. The corrupt and ineffective Qing dynasty collapsed in 1912, ending China's imperial period that had started around 2000 B.C.

From the late 1920s on, the Guomindang (or, Kuomintang) party, headed by Generalissimo Chiang Kai-shek, was the dominant force in China. Initially, it worked together with the fledgling Chinese Communist Party (CCP; founded in 1921) but the two parties soon had a falling out. In the 1930s and 1940s, the Guomindang and CCP engaged in a brutal civil war, which was suspended for a few years to jointly resist the full-scale Japanese invasion. The CCP emerged victorious, and, on October 1, 1949, Mao proclaimed the founding of the People's Republic of China. Chiang Kai-shek and his supporters fled to Taiwan, where their successors still remain.

Private enterprises were abolished, industry was nationalized, and land was redistributed to poor peasants. According to conservative estimates, more than two million landlords, well-to-do peasants, "bourgeois elements," and former supporters of the Guomindang were killed. Another two million were imprisoned or sent to labor camps.[1] In 1958, Mao launched the Great Leap Forward, which lasted until 1962. Its aim was to rapidly transform the country from an agrarian economy into a socialist society through accelerated industrialization and agricultural collectivization. Private plots were abolished and communal kitchens were introduced. These people's communes became the new form of economic and political organization throughout rural China. Like some twenty-five years earlier in the Soviet Union, it was a disaster. Production plummeted and the ensuing Great Chinese Famine cost the lives of up to 45 million people.[2]

After a few years of relative calm, Mao launched the Great Proletarian Cultural Revolution in 1966, which lasted until his death in 1976. Mao alleged that "bourgeois" elements had infiltrated the CCP, the government, the army, and society, aiming to restore capitalism. Mao insisted that these "revisionists" be removed through violent class struggle. Millions of people were persecuted and suffered a wide range of abuses, including public humiliation, arbitrary imprisonment, torture, hard labor, sustained harassment, seizure of property, and sometimes execution. A large segment of the population was forcibly displaced from cities to rural areas. One of my Chinese friends told me that, as a teenager, he was compelled to work three years in the countryside as an agricultural laborer and live in a cave. The worst phase of the Cultural Revolution was over by 1971, but it lingered on until Mao's death. The social and economic effects were again disastrous.

By the time of Mao's death, China was a basket case. Since 1840, China never had a period of peace and stability that lasted more than ten years. The country had been in constant turmoil and had suffered from repeated foreign aggressions, civil wars, peasant uprisings, and self-inflicted ideological frenzy.[3] All basic consumer goods, including food and clothing, were rationed. China's collectivized agriculture was barely able to feed its massive population, and 250 million peasants were suffering from hunger. The closing of the school system during the Cultural Revolution had led to calamitous conditions. One-third of the workforce had only a primary school education and less than 1 percent was college educated.[4] The economy was run via central planning, and Chinese GDP per capita was lower than that of Congo. Its failures were apparent, but trying something else would require a leader willing to adapt beliefs that were considered sacred in the pantheon of Marxist thought. That person was Deng Xiaoping. However, he had tried it twice before and suffered the consequences. Would he succeed now?

DENG XIAOPING

Deng was born on August 22, 1904, into a family of wealthy landowners in the southwestern province of Sichuan. After attending elementary and middle school in China, Deng went to France to study and work (1920–1926). While in France, he embraced communism and met Zhou Enlai, his later protector and first prime minister of the People's Republic. Deng traveled to Moscow in 1926, where he studied Marxist theory, party construction, and military affairs. At the time, the New Economic Policy (NEP) was in full bloom in the Soviet Union. It was aimed at developing a partial market economy in agriculture and in consumer goods, under the aegis of the Communist Party. The NEP was launched by Vladimir Lenin to jump-start Russia's moribund economy. Its successes were visible everywhere—a lesson that Deng would remember decades later.

Deng returned to China in 1927 and, in the ensuing decades, he rose steadily in the ranks of the CCP. He was one of the veterans of the Long March of 1934–1935 to evade the Guomindang army. From 1935 through the end of the civil war in 1949, Deng occupied a series of military and political leadership positions in the Red Army and its successor, the People's Liberation Army. He forged long-standing relationships with senior army officers, which would be of crucial importance in his later life.

In October 1950, the Central Committee of the CCP issued a new directive against "counterrevolutionary crimes." As the party boss responsible for the southwestern region of China, Deng responded enthusiastically to the call for action. The orgy of executions that followed took on such proportions that Mao felt compelled to caution Deng "not to kill too many people."[5] Yet, such zealous behavior did not go unrewarded. Mao admired Deng's exceptional capacity for work, his organizational talent, energy, and loyalty, and Deng's rapid ascent continued. In 1954 he was appointed deputy prime minister under Zhou Enlai, and in 1956 he was chosen as a member of the all-powerful Standing Committee of the Politburo of the CCP, becoming the sixth-ranked person in the party hierarchy.[6]

That same year, the CCP launched a national movement under the slogan "Let a Hundred Flowers Bloom," where citizens were encouraged to openly express their opinions of the communist regime. It was designed to uncover and root out "counterrevolutionaries." Mao conceived the idea and Deng was its main executor. The campaign was a great success, at least from Mao's point of view. Millions of educated people were unmasked as "rightist bourgeois elements" (because they had criticized the Party) and 500,000 were sent to labor camps.[7]

After initial hesitation, which he ascribed to his lack of adequate understanding of "Mao Zedong Thought," Deng became an energetic proponent of the disastrous Great Leap Forward. He regarded the people's communes as "a powerful instrument for accelerating socialist construction in the countryside as well as the optimal form of social organization in the future transition from collective property to state property."[8] But in the early 1960s, Deng took a field trip that opened his eyes. He witnessed firsthand that the commune system was not working. The increasingly apparent dismal failure of the Great Leap Forward led to a temporary decline of Mao's influence in the CCP and a (very) modest liberalization of the economy between 1961 and 1966. In 1960, some communes in Anhui Province had begun to experiment with the so-called family contract system, in which peasants were allowed to work their own parcel of land. They were obliged to turn over to the government a specified amount of the harvest and could keep everything they produced above the contract. It was so successful that, in 1962, Deng approved its expansion to other parts of China. Deng's newfound pragmatism was cogently expressed in a speech given in July 1962:

When it comes to ways of optimizing the relations of production, I rather think that we should take this attitude: to adopt whatever pattern will restore and develop agricultural output . . . "Whether white or black. A cat is a good cat so long as it catches the rat."[9]

This did not at all mean that Deng had become a free marketer. In another speech, he emphasized that China's fundamental task was to "consolidate the collective economy of the country, that is, consolidate the socialist system."[10] Still, Mao took great offense and accused Deng of being a "capitalist roader," and early in the Cultural Revolution (July 1967), Deng was placed under house arrest. Deng tried to get on Mao's good side again by writing obsequious letters praising the Great Helmsman for his "brilliant leadership," and thanking him for having sent Deng to Jianxi Province to reform himself through labor and study. Deng wrote that he regretted supporting the family contract system, and wrote, "from the bottom of my heart I wish the Chairman eternal longevity."[11]

Fortunately for Deng, Mao needed him, too. In January 1973, Prime Minister Zhou Enlai's health sharply deteriorated and only Deng had the organizational capabilities to relieve Zhou's burden.[12] Mao brought Deng back, despite strong opposition from the radicals in the Politburo (the so-called Gang of Four—headed by Mao's wife, Jiang Qing). In quick succession, Deng amassed key positions in the government, the CCP, and the armed forces, and by 1975, he occupied the third position in the party hierarchy.

In another twist in this already byzantine plot, in April 1976, Mao dismissed Deng and put him under house arrest, again. Deng was the victim of a vicious power struggle between the radicals and the moderates in the top of the CCP. This time, though, his fall from power did not last long. Mao died a few months later and his successor, Hua Guofeng, lacked a strong power base. Hua was able to arrest the Gang of Four, but only with the help of the army's top leadership, who were strongly pro-Deng. Deng's return became inevitable. In July 1977, he was restored to his top positions and, by 1979, he had emerged as China's de facto supreme leader. The epochal event was the December 1978 Third Plenary Session (plenum) of the Eleventh Central Committee of the CCP. Upon Deng's insistence and maneuvering, that plenary session proclaimed the slogan that would characterize Deng's subsequent policies: "Reform and Opening Up."

Figure 4.1 Deng Xiaoping, 1979

Source: NASA

DENG DECIDES TO REFORM AND OPEN UP CHINA

China's economic program until the late 1970s was based on the example of the Soviet Union. It relied on central planning, and emphasized heavy industry and collectivized agriculture. Deng had come around to reject these orthodoxies. The people, he said, needed to be given a stake in what they produced. Light industry (consumer goods) had to have priority over heavy industry, Chinese farmers should be liberated from their communes, and government needed to be decentralized.[13] China was simply too vast and complex for central planning. For Mao, ideology overrode practical experience. For Deng, practical experience overrode ideology—in other words, there is more than one way to skin a cat, so let's just use the one that is most effective. Deng's philosophy was summarized in the slogan "Seeking truth from facts." In an ironic twist, worthy of Deng's adaptive leadership, this slogan was first proposed by Mao himself in 1943. Deng boldly asserted that it contained "the quintessence of Mao Zedong Thought," notwithstanding the fact that the Great Helmsman's actions in the last two decades of his life were diametrically opposite to his own slogan. This is an example of how Deng astutely cloaked himself with the authority of the deceased leader while doing the very things that would make Mao turn in his grave.[14]

Deng perceived perhaps better than anybody else that the Chinese communist system had to adapt in order to survive. According to him, the superiority of socialism to the Chinese people must be revealed, not in ideology, but "first and foremost, in the rate of economic growth and in economic efficiency."[15] This required radical modernization of the Chinese economy. Deng identified four key areas—the so-called Four Modernizations: agriculture, industry, science and technology, and defense. For our purposes here, the first three are especially interesting, although the fourth modernization is casting increasingly large shadows on the world as we speak.

MODERNIZATION OF AGRICULTURE

In 1979, over 80 percent of the Chinese workforce was employed in agriculture. Productivity was abysmal and could hardly keep up with population growth. Agricultural reform was achieved by decollectivization and reintroduction of the family contract system. This was done gradually, from below at the district level, with the tacit approval of Deng, who was mindful of what had happened the previous time, before the Cultural Revolution. Local success stories powered ever wider adoption. For example, in Xiaogang in Anhui Province, hitherto one of the country's poorest districts, the family-contract system produced a sixfold increase in grain production, and the peasants' average income grew eighteenfold. As the Party cadres became more accustomed to agricultural reform, Deng was able to express himself more openly in favor of the family contract system, and its adoption accelerated. While in December 1980, only 5 percent of the production brigades were on a full family contract system, by June 1982 that had increased to 67 percent.[16]

To counter Marxist hardliners in the CCP, Deng was looking for a Marxist justification for this departure from received (Soviet) wisdom. This was found in Lenin's New Economic Plan and the works of Nikolai Bukharin, NEP's theoretician. Bukharin had defended prosperous peasants (his slogan to peasants was "Enrich yourselves!") and maintained that the growth of industry directly depended on a productive agriculture. Bukharin further supported a synergistic combination of planned and market regulations, and he recognized the important role of the price mechanism under socialism. This was the Marxist justification that Deng needed.[17]

MODERNIZATION OF INDUSTRY

The modernization of industry proceeded along several paths. Small-scale businesses were permitted. To counter opposition from conservatives, Deng's supporters resorted to brilliant casuistry. Marx's tome *Das Kapital* ("Capital") contained a story of a capitalist who exploited eight workers. So, if Marx spoke precisely of eight, it meant that the hiring of seven workers would not make one a capitalist. What true communist could argue with its founding father? So, on Deng's initiative, individual enterprises with no more than seven employees were permitted. This led to an explosion of small service enterprises—restaurants, shoe repair shops, barber shops, et cetera—absorbing millions of underemployed workers.[18]

China also modernized its industrial apparatus and infrastructure. For that, it needed to import heavy equipment and technology, and learn modern management techniques. Where would that money come from? On Deng's initiative, the government established in 1980 several Special Economic Zones (SEZ) in southern China, close to Hong Kong, Taiwan, and Macao.

The best-known SEZ was at Shenzhen, at the time an insignificant town on the border with Hong Kong. These zones were established to attract foreign direct investment. Producers in these zones could import materials and components free of many regulations and tariffs, and paid lower taxes on profits. The Chinese government also provided substantial subsidies for infrastructure. In 1984, China established similar arrangements in fourteen other coastal cities.

Initially, the SEZs were established as market enclaves, producing only for export. The export monies thus generated were used to import machinery and technology to upgrade China's industrial infrastructure. Chinese workers were also exposed to modern management techniques for the first time. Exports were further stimulated by a substantial devaluation of the official exchange rate.

However, enclaves smacked of the hated international settlements that existed in Chinese cities like Shanghai before World War II. Could they be defended on Marxist grounds? Researchers of the Chinese Academy of Social Sciences came to the rescue. They uncovered that, during Lenin's NEP, there existed a system of concessions with more than two hundred enterprises in which foreigners were permitted to invest heavily. How could an orthodox Chinese Marxist quarrel with the hallowed Lenin?[19]

MODERNIZATION OF SCIENCE AND TECHNOLOGY

During the "Let a Hundred Flowers Bloom" campaign, Deng had been Mao's right-hand man in implementing the attack on intellectuals. In the late 1970s, he had come around and understood that these attacks and subsequent events during the Cultural Revolution had devastated Chinese science and technology, without which China's modernization could not materialize. University entrance examinations were reintroduced. Academic merit rather than "proper class background" and "proper political thinking" (Mao's criteria) were the basis of admittance into universities. To speed up China's modernization in the sciences, Chinese scholars were encouraged to study abroad with financial support from the State. When my brother Paulus worked on his PhD at the Delft University of Technology in the early 1980s, he had one of the first Chinese scientists sent to the Netherlands co-working with him. His family was kept in China to ensure his return. To promote basic science, Deng set as rule that at least five-sixths of a scientist's workweek was to be spent on basic research (the remainder on physical labor and political education). Work propaganda teams were removed from scientific institutes, and the basic research of institutes would be under a leader trained in science.

RESULTS

The effects of the Four Modernizations on China were breathtaking (Table 4.1). In the first decade after Deng kicked off the Reform and Opening Up program, agricultural production increased 72 percent; agricultural efficiency, 41 percent; industrial production, 183 percent; and steel production, 87 percent. Exports increased nearly sevenfold. This generated the necessary revenues to import machinery and technology needed to make the economic modernization a self-sustaining process. Chinese people felt the benefits in their pockets—GDP increased 160 percent and GDP per capita, 126 percent. This built strong support for the modernization drive among the population, which continued to fuel economic growth in the 1990s and beyond. While China's economy in 1978 was smaller than Canada's—a country with one-fortieth of its population—in 2020, only the U.S. economy was larger. Hundreds of millions of people have been lifted out of poverty, and China has become the world's largest manufacturer, ahead of the United States, Japan, and Germany.

Deng officially retired from the political scene in 1992, but he continued to exert great influence on China's affairs until his death in 1997 at the age of ninety-two. China's rapid rise under Deng and his successors has also created geopolitical problems. The West believed that with increased economic prosperity would come political liberalization and a gradual move toward democracy, although that was never on Deng's mind. He reformed China to maintain the position of the party, not to weaken it. And since Xi Jinping came to power in 2012, the CCP has reasserted its leading role in China. Xi also pursues a more muscular foreign policy, challenging America's position in the world. One issue hotly debated today is whether the United States and China can escape the Thucydides Trap. This dilemma was first identified by the fifth-century B.C. Athenian

Table. 4.1 Results of Reform and Opening Up, 1978–1988

Year	Agriculture ($)	Cereal yield/acre (tons)	Industry ($)	Steel (tons)	Exports ($)	GDP ($)	GDP per capita ($)
1978	100	100	100	100	100	100	100
1979	106	109	108	108	135	108	106
1980	105	105	123	117	166	116	113
1981	112	110	125	112	215	122	117
1982	125	124	132	118	332	133	126
1983	135	133	146	126	324	147	138
1984	153	142	167	136	365	170	156
1985	155	137	198	147	379	192	175
1986	161	139	218	164	385	210	188
1987	168	142	247	177	500	234	206
1988	172	141	283	187	660	260	226

Note: Entries are indexed versus 1978. The value of agriculture, industry, and GDP are calculated based on constant dollars, while the value of exports is in current dollars. Industry figures refer to value added.

Source: Author's calculations based on World Development Indicators and World Steel Organization.

historian Thucydides, who famously wrote, "It was the rise of Athens and the fear that this instilled in Sparta that made war inevitable." When a rising power threatens to displace a ruling one, the most likely outcome is war. I lectured on this to the cadets at West Point, and they correctly identified that the last time a rising power was on course to collide with the established power was in the early twentieth century, involving Germany versus Britain (see chapter 11). We all know how that ended.

Notwithstanding the gathering clouds on the horizon, Deng's accomplishments themselves are not in doubt. Never before in world history has so much wealth been created in such a short time and have so many people been lifted out of abject destitution. And it all started with Deng changing his long-held Marxist beliefs.

LESSONS

The following joke appeared in *The New York Times* in 1997: Presidents Bill Clinton and Jiang Zemin (China) are each driving down a road and their two cars approach an intersection. Clinton turns right without signaling. But Jiang hesitates and asks his passenger, Deng Xiaoping, which way to go. "Signal left and turn right," Deng replies.[20] Adaptive leadership *pur sang*.

At first glance, Deng appears to be a fox—somebody who changes according to the situation. This is to misread his leadership. His overriding vision was to safeguard the primacy of the CCP. He pursued this goal with hedgehog-like persistence. Initially, he used traditional communist means like collectivization. But, while Mao never wavered from this even when the means clearly fell short of the aspirations—and hence was the prototypical hedgehog—Deng was willing to change. He became an eagle. This made him one of the most consequential leaders of the twentieth century.

Today's managers can learn a lot from his adaptive leadership style. Consider these facts. Deng led a huge organization, bigger in terms of "revenues" (GDP), "employees" (one billion), and "functional divisions" (ministries, party organizations, provinces) than any company today. He was appointed the boss of the organization when it was in chaos and nearly bankrupt, and left it economically strong, healthy, and poised for further growth. What CEO can rival that? Here are key lessons from Deng's art of adaptive leadership.

BIG PICTURE

Deng focused on the big picture. He distinguished between major and minor issues and devoted his efforts to where they would make the biggest difference for China: devising strategies, evaluating policies that were deemed crucial for the success of his goals, and getting buy-in from fellow officials and the public. He set the agenda, and his lieutenants, Hu Yaobang (general secretary of the CCP) and Zhao Ziyang (prime minister), carried them out as they thought best. Too often, leaders micromanage, either because they cannot distinguish between major and minor issues, or because they are afraid to lose control. You can see that in universities, companies, NGOs, and churches.

LONG-TERM FOCUS

Deng focused on the long term, and was adaptive in the setting of specific short-term policies in the light of long-term goals. In 1984 he struck the "one country, two systems" compromise with British prime minister Margaret Thatcher (who is the subject of chapter 9), in which Hong Kong would enjoy a high degree of autonomy for fifty years. He realized that this short-term concession was necessary to achieve his long-term goal of peaceful reunification, and to keep Hong Kong as a vital economic and financial hub for China. He also envisaged the same arrangement for Taiwan, but developments since Xi came to power make this a distant possibility at best.

Deng was keenly aware of the inefficiency of China's countless state-owned enterprises (SOEs). His long-term goal was to reduce the number of SOEs and make them more efficient by reducing their bloated personnel count. However, doing this too fast would create massive unemployment at a time when jobs were still scarce, which would undermine support for his Reform and Opening Up program. Therefore, Deng decided to adapt his position and postponed eliminating large numbers of SOEs until more jobs were available.

Deng's leadership of setting short-term policies in the light of long-term goals compares favorably with the behavior of many managers. In my work with companies, I am struck by how little managers think about the long-term goals for their brands. To meet quarterly sales targets, they often resort to deep discounts, despite the fact that this practice negatively affects long-term brand health.[21] In economic downturns, firms tend to cut back on advertising and R&D expenses, which has long-term adverse effects on market share and profits.[22] Similarly, capital intensive long-horizon businesses such as the oil and gas industry often cut back on maintenance and recapitalization expenditure during economic headwinds, and as a consequence suffer costly unscheduled plant outages several years down the road. Corporate leaders would do well to adopt a long-term focus more often and accept inevitable short-term criticism levied against them by financial analysts. If they follow the example of Deng and more clearly articulate their long-term goals and explain how certain short-term policies might be detrimental—or helpful—to achieve these long-term goals, it might render the financial markets more forgiving.

GETTING BUY-IN FROM HIS FOLLOWERS BEFORE PROMOTING GROUNDBREAKING POLICIES

Despite being China's paramount leader, Deng spent considerable time getting buy-in for his reform plans from his fellow party members. He carefully prepared for the annual meetings of the Central Committee, for they helped to forge a common perspective among the top members of the CCP.[23] He gave even more time to the preparation of party congresses, held every five years, in order to forge a consensus among the even larger numbers of delegates (several thousand) who would be crucial in implementing his plans in the next five years. While most companies have annual conferences for their most senior one hundred to two hundred executives, far fewer have large gatherings involving the echelon below—complete with open discussions and breakout sessions. Yet, as Deng, and anybody who has been around in bureaucracies for some time, knows, many decisions made in the C-suite are frustrated by lack of buy-in by managers in the sub-top.

In achieving his objectives, Deng moved gradually. Although he was already seventy-two when he became China's leader, and time was not on his side, he realized that moving too fast could undo the entire Reform and Opening Up program. In Chinese terms, his implementation trajectory was to "cross the river by feeling the stones," adapting his path, in part, on the basis of what worked.[24] Patience is not a virtue too many leaders have. If they know what they want, many want to have it accomplished today, not tomorrow. Dramatic reorganizations early in a CEO's tenure come to mind, usually under catchy slogans like "Clearing Rubble." How many managers—after having gone through a few reorganizations—feel that they really did much more than create unrest? Deng showed the wisdom of going one step at a time, while always keeping the long-term goal in clear sight.

To balance internal discussions with unified action, Deng embraced the twin notions of "inner-party democracy," and "democratic centralism." The top leadership needed to listen to constructive opinions in order to reduce the danger of serious mistakes (inner-party democracy). But, once a decision was made, party members had to implement it (democratic centralism).

DECENTRALIZED DECISION MAKING

Deng also advocated decentralized decision making, giving more flexibility to local officials, who would be more familiar with local conditions. He encouraged local initiative and experimentation. Deng's aforementioned family contract system is such an example. In today's multinational organizations, it is a constant struggle to balance central versus decentral decision making. Many good ideas are developed in local markets but never make it because the firm does not reward such initiatives.[25] Deng understood more keenly than some corporate leaders in multinationals that one-size-fits-all does not work when your market is diverse in needs and conditions.

THE DANGER WHEN YOUR PREDECESSOR IS STILL AROUND

A final cautionary note that goes beyond adaptive leadership. Deng's experiences show the dangers of trying to lead while your predecessor is still around, especially when your predecessor still wields considerable power. Twice, Mao, dissatisfied with the direction Deng wanted to take, intervened and sacked him. Business leaders also often find it difficult to hand over the reins.

Think about Ferdinand Piech (Volkswagen CEO and major shareholder) firing his successor Bernd Pischetsrieder, or Henry Ford II firing Lee Iacocca. Be wary of taking over as leader in such situations, especially if the former leader is a major shareholder. The risks are high.

CHAPTER TAKEAWAYS

- Deng started out as a hedgehog but became an eagle after he saw that communism did not work economically. Mao, in contrast, remained a hedgehog.

- Deng fell from power twice. The key factor was that he tried to set out a new direction while the ultimate arbiter, Mao, was still around.

- Deng initiated his market-oriented reforms by presenting them as a way to better achieve socialism ("signaling left and turning right").

- Many of his reforms were justified by obscure or contrived references to writings and precedents by communist heroes. This undercut opposition by hardliners.

- Deng's reforms gradually became more radical. This made opposition to his reforms more difficult because each incremental step was not regarded as unacceptably anti-Marxist.

- Deng's reforms were never meant to weaken the role of the CCP, but rather to strengthen it by delivering economic prosperity to the long-suffering Chinese population.

- Western hopes that economic reforms would be followed by political reforms have not materialized. How to deal with a powerful China is the greatest strategic challenge facing the West since the fall of the Soviet Union.

- Deng's life highlights several adaptive leadership principles:

    ° Focus on the big picture.

    ° Maintain a long-term focus.

    ° Get buy-in from your followers, even when you have great power.

    ° Prioritize your subgoals and stretch them out over time, without losing sight of your overarching vision.

    ° Allow for decentralized decision making within a common framework.

REFLECTIONS ON ADAPTIVE LEADERSHIP

IN ADAPTIVE LEADERSHIP, the locus of change is in the leader, not the follower. The leader adapts their own position in order to achieve the goal. Every leader has to be able and willing to adapt their views, perhaps only on minor issues, when the situation demands this. But adaptive leadership is way more than exhibiting some flexibility on minor issues. It concerns an ability to exhibit flexibility to change your position on important adaptive challenges you face in your work.

Taken together, the case studies on Clovis, Bismarck, and Deng highlight several key principles of successful adaptive leadership: (1) identify the adaptive challenge; (2) recognize that it is the leader who needs to change; (3) display mental flexibility; (4) maintain credibility.

1. IDENTIFY THE ADAPTIVE CHALLENGE

Central to adaptive leadership is the ability to identify adaptive challenges, according to Ronald Heifetz's theory.[1] The leader needs to identify the problem(s) that is hindering their success. Adaptive challenges are murky, systemic problems with no easy answer. It requires a leader with deep understanding of the situation to identify them. Few people in 500 A.D. had a clear understanding that religion would be a make-or-break factor for the future of Germanic kingdoms. Few contemporaries had Bismarck's deep understanding of how the Vienna system actually held Prussia down—and how to solve this. In hindsight, the wisdom of Deng's reform policies appears obvious, but anybody who had gone through decades of communist indoctrination would have found this solution inconceivable.

2. RECOGNIZE THAT THE LOCUS FOR CHANGE IS IN THE LEADER

Adaptive challenges are challenges that cannot be solved by other means, such as the leader's authority or expertise, through the normal ways of doing things in the organization, or by persuading followers to change their position. The lives and decisions made by the three adaptive leaders in this book illustrate this. Clovis could not force—or persuade—his Catholic population to become Arian; the Visigoths tried that and had failed miserably. In Bismarck's case, he initially tried working through the existing conservative organizational structures like the German Diet and the institutional framework of the Vienna system, but concluded that this would not allow him to reach his end goal, because Austria dominated these institutions. In Deng's situation, the system was broken. Urging the people to work harder in communes for a better common future for all had been tried and failed.

3. DISPLAY MENTAL FLEXIBILITY

The leader must possess mental flexibility in order to solve adaptive challenges and reach the leader's goal. Adaptive challenges force leaders to question their most deeply held beliefs when the values that made these leaders successful in the past have become less relevant, if not an outright hindrance to organizational success. Heifetz puts it as follows: "[A]daptive change is distressing for the people going through it. They need to take on new roles, new relationships, new values, new behaviors, and new approaches to work."[2]

Clovis, Bismarck, and Deng exhibited remarkable mental flexibility. All three had to give up some deeply held beliefs for "organizational" success. It is not clear whether Clovis's pagan beliefs were deeply held, but paganism was the faith of his ancestors so it probably had some meaning to him. There is no doubt that Bismarck was deeply conservative and Deng a dyed-in-the-wool communist. Yet all three correctly saw that their innermost beliefs stood in the way of success. In Bismarck's case, it is clear that he never changed his inner beliefs. Deng changed his beliefs about Marxist economics, although not about the political system and the primacy of the Communist Party. Whether Clovis became a sincere Catholic has been a topic of debate ever since his death. At one dinner, I had a long discussion about this with Dr. Kate Bollinger, an early-medieval historian, and we concluded that most likely his conversion was one of expediency.

Ideally, a leader's conversion is real (like Deng's), but adaptive leadership is possible regardless of your true beliefs, as long as you are able to separate personal opinion from public actions. Many leaders cannot pull this off. In fact, both Clovis's and Deng's main opponents were hedgehogs, who never compromised their convictions. Clovis's main adversary, the Ostrogothic king Theodoric, refused to give up Arianism, although that would have been clearly advantageous. Similarly, the Gang of Four put Marxist purity above economic prosperity. Turning to Bismarck's main opponent, Napoleon III—nobody would accuse him of being principled. Nevertheless, if he had one principle, it was nationalism. He failed to see that it actually undermined France's position until it was too late. While being principled is often seen as laudable, Theodoric, Napoleon III, and the Gang of Four have been relegated to the dust of history.

My father was clearly an adaptive leader. While he had strong personal values, he was willing to modify his actions (although not necessarily his beliefs) to reach a goal. When he was a leading senator for the Catholic People's Party (a predecessor of today's Christian Democratic Party) in the Netherlands, he had to vote on a new law that would permit abortion for pregnancies up to twelve weeks. Both he and my mother held strong personal objections against abortion. However, he knew that many people in society felt differently and that this law was the most restrictive arrangement the Catholic People's Party could get. So, he persuaded his fellow Catholic senators to support the law, which was then accepted. My mother, who was anything but adaptive, was furious. She argued that my father should have voted according to his conscience. Up to this day, one can validly argue both points of view. But in politics, like in business, the challenge is usually not to "be right," but to convince others, which usually requires a compromise on some of your views. Hence, there is no denying that adaptive leadership has proven time and again that it is a particularly effective leadership style.

4. MAINTAIN CREDIBILITY

A challenge for adaptive leaders is to convince their followers that their change of heart is sincere. If followers believe that the leader changed their position purely out of expediency, the leader's credibility may be fatally weakened. For example, in the 2004 U.S. presidential campaign, the credibility of Democratic candidate John Kerry was famously hurt by him turning against the Iraq war—after having earlier supported it—because it became politically inconvenient. His explanation is still hard to fathom: "I actually did vote for the $87 billion, before I voted against it."[3]

We know from marketing literature that the credibility of a source is essential in effecting change. The two dimensions of source credibility are trustworthiness and expertise. Trustworthiness means that the source can be relied upon, that the person is basically honest and is not trying to manipulate the audience. Expertise refers to the knowledgeability of the source: Does the person know what they are talking about?

Few would have regarded Bismarck as particularly trustworthy. This leaves expertise, which he used to full effect. During Bismarck's lifetime, his followers, including the newly minted German emperor Wilhelm I, understood that he alone possessed the skills to hold the political system together. Nothing in the literature suggests that Clovis was trustworthy, but because he was a pagan, his conversion was not incredible per se (German warlords had converted before, albeit to Arianism). Deng's credibility remained high. He had a history of trying mild reforms (so trustworthiness was not an issue), and his long experience gave him expertise, too. But adaptive leaders who cannot draw upon deep sources of trustworthiness and/or expertise will see their effectiveness undermined.

Adaptive leaders have to prepare their ground carefully. If you change your position, you need to ensure that you maintain credibility, especially if your change of mind puts you at odds with your followers. In that case, you need to develop a strategy to get their buy-in. Before announcing his conversion, Clovis had intensive discussions with his followers. We do not know the exact content of these discussions but, according to ancient sources, they were heated. Deng carefully prepared the ground by moving gradually and holding many meetings with his followers. He also trumpeted early successes to generate momentum.

To assess whether adaptive leadership is a style that suits you, consider the following questions.

1. Do you have a keen ability to identify adaptive challenges in your organization? What evidence do you have for this? Can you give examples?

2. Do you find it easy to see another person's point of view or do you struggle with that? What examples from your life can you give?

3. Would you generally describe yourself as a person of strong principles or more as a pragmatic person?

4. Which of your principles or convictions are untouchable? Can you foresee that these might come under attack at a point in the future? Under what circumstances?

5. Which adaptive leaders do you recognize in your own professional and/or personal environment? How do you relate to their style of leadership?

6. What feedback have you ever received that portrayed you as an adaptive leader?

7. In what situation(s) have you been where being an "adaptive leader" would have been most effective? What did you actually do, and what were the results?

PART TWO

PERSUASIVE LEADERSHIP — CHANGE THE MINDS OF YOUR FOLLOWERS

5

THEMISTOCLES ERECTS A WOODEN WALL

"'I never learned how to tune a harp, or play upon a lute; but I know how to raise a small and inconsiderable city to glory and greatness."
—THEMISTOCLES

Leadership Dilemma: How could Themistocles persuade his fellow Greeks to overcome their fear and make a final stand in an unlikely place?

CONTEXT

In 500 B.C., Greece consisted of a large number of fiercely independent city-states, the most important being Sparta and Athens. Most city-states were oligarchies, but Athens was embarking on one of the most radical political experiment in history. After Athens ousted its last would-be tyrant in 507 B.C., democracy, meaning "rule by people," was instituted.

To the east of Greece lay the enormous Persian Empire, which stretched from the Danube to the Indus River and from Sudan to the Aral Sea (Figure 5.1).[1] Founded by Cyrus (r. 559–530 B.C.), it was the first "world empire" in history. Ionia, the west coast of present-day Turkey, was part of this empire. It comprised a number of wealthy city-states, founded and inhabited by Greek colonists who continued to maintain close relationships with the mother country. The democratic revolution in Athens had been followed enthusiastically in Ionia: In 499 B.C., the Ionian cities revolted against their Persian-backed tyrants and replaced them with democracies. The cities appealed to the Greek city-states for help to ward off the Persians, and Athens sent help in response, but too little to make a difference. In 493 B.C., the Ionian Revolt was savagely crushed, but the ruling Persian king Darius (r. 522–486 B.C.) had not forgotten the Greeks' help.

In 490 B.C., Darius sent a large force across the Aegean Sea to conquer Athens. The army landed on the plain of Marathon, about twenty-five miles from Athens. Against all odds, Athens' new citizen army of around 10,000

Figure 5.1 Persian Empire in 500 B.C.

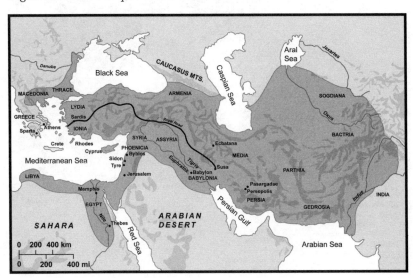

hoplites (heavily armed infantry) defeated the numerically superior Persian forces. The Athenians sent a runner to their city to announce the great news. This historical event is the basis for the marathon race, which has been a fixture of all modern Olympic Summer Games.

For Darius, there was now no going back; this humiliation had to be avenged. Yet, the Persian response was delayed, due to a revolt in Egypt and Darius's death. His son Xerxes (r. 486–465 B.C.) took up the cause and amassed a huge army of around 250,000 men, supported by 1,200 warships and 3,000 transport vessels, drawn from all parts of the empire.[2] It was the largest force ever assembled at that time. The close contact between the army and the fleet was the linchpin of Xerxes's strategy. The Greeks were not oblivious to Persian war preparations, and in 481 B.C., some thirty Greek city-states gathered in Corinth. After much discussion, they agreed to form a coalition against the Persians, with Corinth as the center of operations. A Spartan would be supreme commander of the allied forces.

Figure 5.2 The Persian Wars, 499–479 B.C.

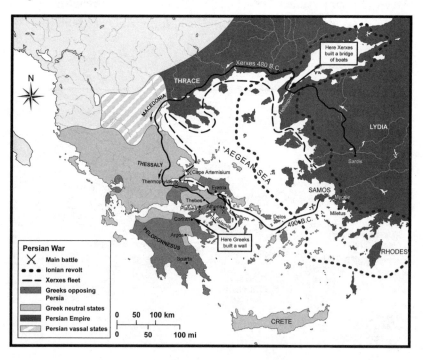

After crossing the Hellespont (Dardanelles) and marching through friendly territory, the Persian forces defeated a small Greek force at Thermopylae, in central Greece (Figure 5.2). This event was made into a Hollywood blockbuster, called *300*, released in 2007 and featuring Gerard Butler as the Spartan king Leonidas, who commanded the Greeks. The way to the Greek heartland now lay wide open. Athens was evacuated, and subsequently burned by the Persians. The Greek army withdrew to the defensive-line wall across the Isthmus of Corinth that separates the Peloponnesus from the rest of Greece.

The Greeks were demoralized, fearful, and divided over what to do next. Most important was where they should make their final stand. It would require a man of supreme persuasive abilities to get the member states to agree on—and execute—a common strategy. Fortunately for the course of world history, there was such a man on the Greek war council: the Athenian politician and admiral Themistocles.

THEMISTOCLES

Themistocles was born c. 524 B.C., the son of Neocles, who was, according to Plutarch, not of distinguished lineage.[3] As a teenager, he experienced the transition to a democratic government, which would open up opportunities for ambitious men like Themistocles, who previously would have had no access to power. The new democratic institutions required skills that previously had been unimportant. Earlier than other politicians, he understood that formerly disenfranchised and commonly ignored poor citizens offered a new power base. Naturally affable and gregarious as he was, he wooed the poor; and they, not used to being courted, duly loved him back.[4]

Themistocles was to prove himself a master of the new democratic system; "he could infight, he could network, he could spin . . . and crucially, he knew how to make himself visible."[5] Themistocles consciously relocated to a down-market part of Athens. This move marked him as a man of the people and allowed him to interact more easily with ordinary citizens.[6] He set himself up as an attorney, the first politician ever in the democracy to prepare for public life by practicing the law. He made some very useful friends among influential clients by getting them acquitted. This also allowed him to hone his persuasive skills.

On the back of his popularity with the common man, Themistocles was elected one of Athens' nine archons, or magistrates, in 493 B.C. Three years later, he fought at Marathon in the ranks of the hoplites. In the decade after the battle at Marathon, with his power base firmly established among the poor, Themistocles emerged as one of Athens' most influential politicians. During that period, he advocated the building of a fleet of triremes. Triremes were slim, ram-headed war galleys equipped with three rows of oars. Themistocles realized more clearly than any other Greek politician that Persia would return with a vengeance, and that the only way to survive the inevitable onslaught was to build a navy that could hope to face up to the Persian navy. The conservative faction of farmers and landed gentry in the Athenian Assembly opposed Themistocles's naval scheme. According to them, Marathon had shown what hoplites could accomplish.

Things came to a head when, in 483 B.C., a massive new seam of silver was found in mines near Athens. What to do with this windfall? The conservative faction proposed to distribute the mining royalties among the entire adult citizen body. This was bound to appeal to the lower-income groups, Themistocles's stronghold. However, Themistocles was able to persuade the Assembly to spend the money on a new fleet of one hundred triremes. This was an impressive feat of persuasive leadership—convincing the people who needed it most to forgo much-needed extra money. In addition, Athens was historically not a naval power, so building a fleet was madness to the conservative faction. If anything, the army should have been strengthened.

As word of the massive Persian buildup reached Athens, Themistocles was elected commander in chief (war archon) with extraordinary powers.[7] He directed the construction of even more triremes and the conversion of Athenian hoplites to rowers. In the hope of receiving a morale-boosting forecast, in the summer of 480 B.C., Athens sent representatives to consult the Oracle of Delphi. The answer was the most famous response in its entire storied history:

Though all else shall be taken within the bound of Cecrops
[Athens] . . .
Yet Zeus the all-seeing grants to Athens' prayer;
That the wooden wall only shall not fall but help you and your
children.[8]

But what was the wooden wall the Oracle was talking about? Some
argued that the wooden wall was the palisade, which in ancient days had
fenced Athens' citadel, the Acropolis. Themistocles had an answer of his
own. The wooden wall, he argued, was nothing less than the fleet they had
spent these last few years hurriedly constructing. This would mean evacu-
ation of their beloved city. He appealed to the Assembly by presenting a
radically new idea—that Athens was not walls and buildings but a community of people. When he finished speaking, the citizens rose as one and
cheered him. The vote was overwhelmingly in his favor. The Athenian population was evacuated to Salamis, an island off Athens. The die was cast. The
Athenians trusted their lives, families, and future to Themistocles's wooden
wall of triremes.

THE BATTLE OF SALAMIS

The Greek fleet of around 300 triremes had gathered in the narrow waters
between Athens and the island of Salamis (Figure 5.3). As the Persian navy
approached and the Greeks saw Athens burning, dissension among the
allied naval commanders—always simmering—erupted. The general feeling in the war council was to withdraw to the Isthmus of Corinth and fight
in defense of the Peloponnese on the grounds that, if they were beaten at
Salamis, they could not escape, while if they were beaten near the isthmus,
they could escape to their homes.[9] This reasoning was based on the belief
that naval defeat was more likely than victory. The mood was thus one of
profound defeatism. Themistocles was the only commander who worked
from the unquestioning assumption of a Greek victory.[10]

Figure 5.3 Battle at Salamis

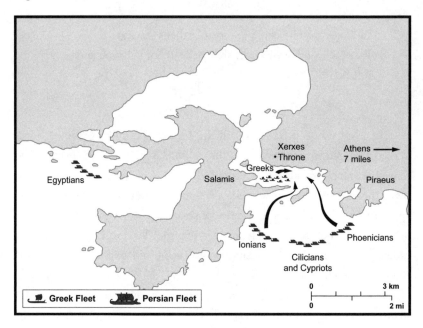

At Themistocles's prodding, Eurybiades, the Spartan commander in chief, called another war council meeting. Here, Themistocles argued that they would have to fight the Persians anyway. If they withdrew to the Isthmus of Corinth, they would fight in the open sea against a numerically superior enemy. Conversely, at Salamis, they would fight in a narrow sea where their numerical inferiority was much less of an issue. Themistocles was strongly opposed by Adeimantus, the commander of the Corinthian flotilla, who landed a low punch by declaring that Themistocles should shut up because he was a man without a city (recall that Athens had been occupied by the Persians). Now, the time for soft talk was over. Themistocles played his trump card. If Eurybiades decided to withdraw the fleet, Themistocles would take the Athenian evacuees on board and sail for Italy. It was a bluff—the fleet was not large enough to transport all Athenians, and any split of the fleet would sink all hopes of victory. Yet, it worked. Eurybiades changed his mind and he decided to give battle at Salamis.

But there was so much dissatisfaction with Eurybiades's decision that yet another war council was called, on September 19, 480 B.C.[11] Themistocles saw that the opponents of the Salamis strategy would carry the votes against him. He played his last card. He secretly instructed a messenger to go to Xerxes to inform him that the Greek disunity was complete, all will to resist the Persians had dissipated, they were preparing a hasty flight, and the Athenians were ready to switch sides. As the Persians were intimately aware of the defeatism and incessant infighting among the Greek commanders, this was credible information. Xerxes fell into the trap. He wanted to finish the war. Only an overwhelming naval victory while the weather held would achieve this. He ordered the fleet to take up their stations and sent an Egyptian contingent of 200 ships to block the western escape route. While the Greeks were still in heated debate, news came in that there was no escape anymore. There was now no alternative solution but to fight—live free or die.

The next day, September 20, the huge Persian fleet of 600 to 800 ships attacked. From the beginning, everything went wrong for the Persians. The sea was rough, favoring the heavier Greek ships. The number of Persian ships was too large for the narrow channel where the Greek fleet was lying in wait. The columns of ships were thrown into confusion just as the Greeks rowed upon them, and a melee ensued in which the heaviest (Greek) rather than the fastest (Persian) ships held the advantage. After a bitter fight of some seven to eight hours, the Persian fleet had lost about half of its ships, and the remainder withdrew.[12]

Xerxes had no option but to withdraw most of his army. Without naval support, there was virtually no chance his army could turn the Greek position at the isthmus. Moreover, his lengthy supply lines were now very vulnerable. To hasten Persian withdrawal, Themistocles spread misinformation that the Greek fleet would sail to the Hellespont to destroy the pontoon bridges. Terrified at the prospect of being cut off from his empire, Xerxes proceeded to retreat from Greece with all speed, leaving a force of around 90,000 strong in Greece. This army would have little chance to succeed unless Greek disunity could be exploited. For once, the Greeks were able (albeit, barely) to maintain a united front, and the Persian army was routed in a hard-fought battle at Plataea in August 479 B.C. In that same month (some claim, on the same day), a Greek expeditionary force destroyed the remaining Persian fleet at Mycale in Ionia.

The Persian Wars were over. A handful of city-states had defeated the mightiest empire in the world.

Salamis was the high point in Themistocles's career, which afterward headed south. He became increasingly arrogant—according to Plutarch, "he was, indeed, by nature, a great lover of honor."[13] His fellow citizens grew jealous of his prestige and power. In response, Themistocles felt compelled to remind them time and again of the great services he had performed.[14] In a democracy, such behavior is ultimately self-defeating. People want to move on. Following accusations of bribery, sacrilege, and a suspicious association with a Spartan traitor, he was exiled around 471 B.C. Ironically, he ultimately ended up in the Persian Empire and was made governor of a Greek city in Ionia, where he died in 459 B.C. Athens' lack of gratitude is not an isolated instance. Democracies are not given to showing gratitude to their leaders; they want to move on. Take Winston Churchill. Having led Britain in its darkest moments, he was voted out of office in the general election a mere two months after the surrender of Nazi Germany.

Salamis was arguably the most important naval battle ever fought. Greece emerged as the cradle of Western civilization. Athenian democracy would be a beacon of inspiration through the ages, not in the least to America's Founding Fathers. In the centuries after Salamis, Greece would lay the foundations of democracy, science, philosophy, literature, and the arts. Greek civilization would evolve into Hellenistic civilization after the conquests of Alexander the Great (see chapter 16). Rome would absorb and diffuse Greek civilization throughout its vast empire, and that influence has profoundly affected the world up to the present day. None of this would have happened without Themistocles. Hardly ever in world history has persuasive leadership led to more portentous consequences.

LESSONS

According to historian John Lewis Gaddis, Xerxes was a prototypical hedgehog—he was hell-bent on destroying Greece and pointedly refused to consider such trifles as autumn storms and Greece's inability to support a massive army.[15] According to Herodotus, he admonished his cautious advisor Artabanus with the following words: "If you were to take in account of everything . . . you would never do anything. It is better to have a brave heart and endure one half of the terrors we dread than to [calculate] all of the terrors and suffer nothing at all."

Themistocles was an eagle. His single central vision was to thwart Persia's designs on Greece. He understood that Persia would come back in full force to avenge Marathon. This gave direction to all he did. However, unlike Xerxes, he was flexible in his means. He shifted resources from the army to the navy. This was a radical insight. After Marathon, the trust in Athenian hoplites was sky-high. Yet Themistocles understood that the size of the Persian army at Marathon was trivial to what Persia would muster the next time around. However, Greek geography (mountainous terrain, poor soil) made it impossible for a large army to stay in Greece for a prolonged period without being supplied by the sea. He further understood that Athens' naval means were insufficient to meet his goal, and, hence, he agreed to a coalition where Athens was not formally in the driver's seat. He further resorted to lies, flattery, pressure, and subterfuge to keep the fleet together.

Time and again, Themistocles exhibited an amazing ability to analyze the situation correctly, unlike his fellow countrymen. However, to be right is very different from getting others to accept you are right. Since Athens was a democracy, and the Greek city-states were fiercely independent, Themistocles could only work through persuasion. Time and again, Themistocles's biggest challenge was not to come up with a solution, but to persuade his countrymen (who, according to Plutarch, were "stupid and hidebound second-raters")[16] to follow his lead. Fortunately, Themistocles "made a career out of persuasion."[17] Four persuasive instances stand out:

1. He persuaded the Athenians to build a fleet rather than pocket the money.

2. He persuaded Greek city-states to collaborate.

3. He convinced the Athenians to evacuate their beloved city.

4. He coaxed the allied fleet to fight at Salamis.

How did he do this? The life of Themistocles reveals five learnings.

RELATIONSHIP BUILDING

Themistocles excelled at relationship building. From early in his career, he "pressed the flesh." He toured taverns, markets, and docks, canvassing where no politician had ever thought to canvass before, making sure never to forget a single voter's name. This was crucial in persuading the Athenians to forgo the handout and to evacuate the city. This reminds me of my brother Thomas, who made his career within the Christian Democratic Party in the Netherlands. He went to regional and national congresses and talked with everyone. He knew the names of the delegates' spouses and children, and inquired after their welfare. As mayor, he made sure he got to know all key players and their families personally. This helped him when facing political conflicts, as they inevitably occurred. He was able to persuade people because he had forged deep relations with them.

DO NOT MAKE IT ABOUT YOURSELF

Despite being intensely proud and ambitious—according to Plutarch, "in his ambition he surpassed all men"[18]—Themistocles did not make it all about himself. He was willing to take a step back for the greater good. The Athenian fleet contingent was by far the largest in the Greek fleet, so it would be logical that Themistocles would command the allied fleet. However, at the Panhellenic Congress in Corinth, other city-states refused to serve under an Athenian. To solve this quandary, Themistocles made the masterly suggestion that leadership of the allied fleet be given to a Spartan. Spartans had no fleet to speak of. Nobody would feel threatened by this choice, and the landlubber Eurybiades was duly appointed as commander in chief of the allied fleet.[19]

Followers will often try to assess whether you are trying to get them to do something to further your own self-interest or for the greater good. If you give up something, they will be less likely to suspect ulterior motives. By stepping aside, Themistocles could not be easily accused of only furthering the Athenian cause. But Themistocles's action shows something else. Historian Peter Green describes Eurybiades as "a dull, well-meaning nonentity."[20] If you need to take a step back, it can be advantageous to support somebody who lacks an independent power base (and mind), and therefore is more prone to do your bidding.

INVOKE A TANGIBLE, IMMEDIATE, AND MANAGEABLE THREAT

Themistocles had "great insight into human nature."[21] He intuitively understood two principles of persuasion that marketing scholars identified only much later:

1. People give more weight to short-term outcomes than to long-term outcomes. After all, the longer the time horizon, the more uncertain it is that the expected outcomes will actually materialize.[22]

2. If outcomes are extremely negative, the associated feeling of intensive fear is psychologically so overwhelming that your followers are more prone to go into denial.[23]

Themistocles used these principles to persuade the Athenian Assembly to forgo a free handout of silver to themselves and spend it on a fleet of triremes. He did this by focusing on the more tangible, immediate, and manageable threat posed by Athens' commercial rival Aegina, against which Athens had repeatedly lost battles at sea. Plutarch explained Themistocles's persuasive tactics "not by trying to terrify the citizens with dreadful pictures of Darius or the Persians—these were too far away and inspired no very serious fear of their coming [denial], but by making opportune use of the bitter jealousy which they cherished toward Aegina."[24] In short, he used the lesser but closer, rather than the bigger but more distant threat to convince his followers.

In the 1930s, Winston Churchill repeatedly warned of German aggressive designs, but he was ignored. The idea of another world war after the horrors of World War I was simply too frightening a thought for the British population, and its political class, to entertain. Consequently, Britain long refused to respond to the rapid rearmament of Nazi Germany until it was nearly too late. Perhaps if Churchill had been able to identify Britain's "Aegina," the course of recent history would have played out differently.

USE FLATTERY

Themistocles also used flattery, especially with the (nominal) commander of the fleet, Eurybiades. Eurybiades lacked Themistocles's penetrating strategic insights and was easily swayed by the opinion of others. Themistocles held his tongue and used honey, not vinegar, to persuade him. When Themistocles made his case to fight in a narrow sea, he started his speech with: "With thee it rests, O Eurybiades! To save Greece."[25] It reminds me of my father, who had to listen to endless self-aggrandizing talks by Dr. Roelof Kruisinga, the leader of one of the three political parties that would be merged into the new Christian Democratic Party. I asked my father—I was a teenager at the time—why on earth he would listen to these ramblings? My father explained that Kruisinga did not really have a political agenda over and above self-promotion. By indulging him, my father made him an ally rather than an opponent.

As mayor, my brother Thomas often had to persuade the city councilors to support his proposals. In one difficult situation, he needed the support of one opposing councilor. He went to great lengths to acknowledge the opponent's arguments, expressing understanding of his position, yet stating that he was convinced that the councilor would place the interest of the city ahead of anything else. To everyone's astonishment, the councilor came around and voted in support.

DON'T FORGET THE STICK

Themistocles overlaid the carrot with the stick; when the "soft" side of persuasive leadership—flattery, taking a step back, networking—was not enough, he was willing to play tough. He threatened to pull the Athenian fleet out of the Greek coalition and sail for Italy and, when even that might not work, he made sure his colleagues were cornered. Themistocles explained his thinking: "as our men would not fight here of their own free will, it was necessary to make them, whether they wanted to do so or not."[26] Sometimes, when gentle persuasion does not work and risks are high, it may be necessary to give followers no choice.

I am the co-founder and executive director of AiMark, a nonprofit institute comprising a network of academics from all over the world, large companies, and two global market research agencies. My relationship with the market research agencies (who are co-founders with me) is one of persuasion. They provide data, and the academic network provides actionable insights based on these data. There was one senior executive in the leading market research agency who was consistently contrarian and negative, despite my best efforts of flattery and trying to engage him on his passion (soccer). Clearly, persuasion did not work. Therefore, at one crucial meeting, I changed my tune and threatened to pull the academic network out of a big joint collaboration if his market research agency would not be more cooperative. That would hurt their business. It would also harm academics who need these data, but, like Themistocles, I saw no other way forward. Fortunately for all parties involved, it worked, and the collaboration is going strong.

CHAPTER TAKEAWAYS

- Themistocles was an eagle while Xerxes was a hedgehog.
- Themistocles is the first major politician in the democratic age in world history.
- Themistocles was a genius ahead of his time, whose greatest challenge was to deal with his ostrich followers, who refused to see the danger posed by Persia because it terrified them.
- Western civilization was born in the Battle of Salamis.
- Themistocles learned the hard way that democracies have a short memory and do not want to be reminded of past great deeds.
- Themistocles's life highlights several persuasive leadership principles:
  - Build relationships with your followers.
  - Do not make it about yourself. Take a step back if this is necessary to achieve your goals. In that case, support somebody whom you can steer.

- ° Identify and use a smaller, more immediate threat if the real threat is too overwhelming—provided the immediate threat gets you on the trajectory to tackle the real threat.

- ° Use flattery to butter up your followers.

- ° Bring out the stick when you have no other choice, but then, wield it effectively.

CAMPBELL-BANNERMAN SHOWS MAGNANIMITY

"What a wise man, what statesmanship in insight and
faith, and what sure grip on the future."
—JAN SMUTS ABOUT HENRY CAMPBELL-BANNERMAN

Leadership Dilemma: How should Campbell-Bannerman deal with the
bitter legacy of the Boer War?

CONTEXT

In 1899, at the time Queen Victoria's long rule was drawing to an end, the
British Empire reigned supreme. Its latest area of expansion was southern Africa—it had captured the Cape Province from the Dutch in 1795

to secure the all-important route to British India. In the last two decades
of the nineteenth century, the empire had taken possession of Natal,
Bechuanaland (present-day Botswana), and Rhodesia (present-day Zambia
and Zimbabwe). There was, however, one hole in the British chain of possessions in southern Africa: the independent republics of Orange Free State
and the Transvaal. These republics straddled the land route between the Cape
Province and Rhodesia (Figure 6.1). Orange Free State and the Transvaal
were founded by Boers (Dutch for "farmer"), also known as Afrikaners, who
left the Cape Province in the 1830s in search of a life free of British rule.
The Boers were descendants of Dutch (and French Huguenot) immigrants
who had left Europe for the Cape Province in the seventeenth and eighteenth centuries.

Figure 6.1 Map of Southern Africa in 1899

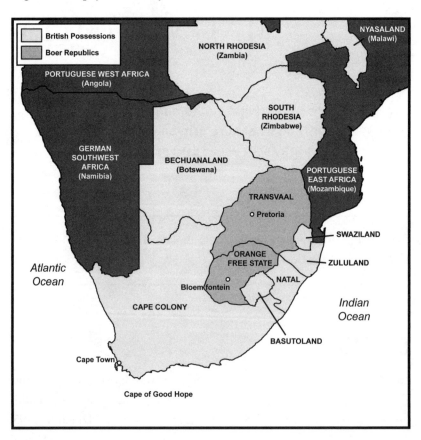

To Britain's frustration, the Boer republics stubbornly resisted British encroachments. Things came to a head after huge gold deposits were discovered near Johannesburg (Transvaal), and tens of thousands of (mostly British) foreigners streamed into the Transvaal. To maintain its independence and identity, the Transvaal government threw up discriminatory barriers to deny the new immigrants equal political rights. Negotiations to address this situation went nowhere. Alfred Milner, Britain's high commissioner for southern Africa, told Britain's colonial secretary Joseph Chamberlain that "I should be inclined to work up a crisis."[1] Inept handling of the rapidly escalating situation by Paul Kruger, the president of the Transvaal, exacerbated the situation and, in October 1899, the Boer War started.[2]

Initially, the well-armed Boers inflicted defeat upon defeat on the British. On November 15, 1899, they even captured and imprisoned the young Winston Churchill, who worked as a war correspondent for a British newspaper. But after Great Britain rushed in immense reinforcements, the tide began to turn. By September 1900, both Boer republics were conquered and annexed to the British Empire. The Boers, refusing to give up, resorted to guerilla warfare, in which they were surprisingly successful. The British responded by burning Boer farms, cutting down orchards, slaughtering livestock, and systematically herding Boer families into concentration camps. It was the first time in the modern age that war was waged on a civilian population, setting a dark precedent for future wars. The conditions in the concentration camps were terrible, not by design but because of incompetence. One out of five of the 117,000 internees, or some 23,000 people, mostly children, died from typhoid and other diseases in the camps. The plight of their families and British military pressure wore down the dwindling Boer forces, and in May 1902, the Peace of Vereeniging (named after the city, just south of present-day Johannesburg) was signed.[3]

The Peace of Vereeniging stipulated that people who declared their acceptance as subjects of King Edward VII could return home. For the rest, the peace terms were remarkably lenient. Yet, the Boers were far from reconciled with the new situation. The terrible loss of life—almost every family had lost loved ones in the infamous concentration camps—and the loss of self-government, bit deep. Article 7 of the peace treaty promised the Boers representative institutions leading up to self-government "as soon as circumstances permit," but this was all unspecified. In the meantime, the hated Milner governed the Transvaal and the renamed Orange River Colony.

In 1905, the Unionist (Conservative-Liberal Unionist) government proposed for the Transvaal what became known as the Lyttelton Constitution.[4] The Lyttelton Constitution provided a limited form of representative government, under which all executive responsibility was to remain in the hands of members of the legislature who were appointed by the British government, and His Majesty's governor was to be given a veto on any legislation. This was little more than a sop for the Boers. Nothing had even been proposed for the Orange River Colony. However, before the Lyttelton Constitution was approved by Parliament, the Unionist government fell and was replaced by the Liberal government under Sir Henry Campbell-Bannerman. This new government had to decide whether to go forward with the Lyttelton Constitution, amend it, or do something entirely different.[5]

HENRY CAMPBELL-BANNERMAN

Henry Campbell was born in 1836, the son of a prosperous, self-made Scottish merchant. He attended the University of Glasgow and the University of Cambridge. After spending ten years working for his father, he was elected to the House of Commons in 1868 as a member of the Liberal Party.[6] Three years later, a rich uncle, Henry Bannerman, left him a large inheritance on the condition that Campbell added "Bannerman" to his name. He never liked Campbell-Bannerman and actually preferred to answer to CB.

Campbell-Bannerman rose slowly in the ranks of the Liberal Party. In the House of Commons, he gradually built a reputation for solid competence and common sense, rather than for intellectual or oratorical brilliance.[7] In 1871 he joined the first Gladstone government (1868–1874) as financial secretary to the War Office, which had the rank of junior minister. CB knew next to nothing of military affairs, but he performed his duties conscientiously and competently. In the second Gladstone administration (1880–1885), he held various junior positions. His breakthrough came when he was appointed secretary of state for war, a position he held in the third (1886) and fourth (1892–1894) Gladstone governments, and in the Rosebery government (1894–1895).

After Rosebery's government fell in 1895, Campbell-Bannerman returned to the opposition benches, and in February 1899 he was elected as the new leader of the Liberal Party. CB accepted the job only because, there being nobody else, he saw it as his duty. In his words, "there is no room for shirking."[8] He received his baptism by fire soon after he became leader of the party. In October 1899, the Boer War started and it bitterly divided the Liberal Party. A faction of roughly one-third of the Liberal MPs, called Liberal Imperialists, headed by the brilliant H. H. Asquith, Edward Grey, and Richard Haldane, supported the (Unionist) government on South Africa. Another third, the Radicals, headed by David Lloyd George, were strongly opposed to the war, if not pro-Boer. In the middle, there was Campbell-Bannerman, and the remaining third of the party, who were "anti Joe, but never pro- [Transvaal President] Kruger"[9]—that is, they were against the machinations of Colonial Secretary Joseph Chamberlain, but that did not mean they supported the Boers.[10]

CB's main goal was to keep the party together, something that became ever more difficult as the war dragged on. The best historical parallel is how the Democratic Party in the United States nearly tore itself apart during the Vietnam War. As the Democratic Party experienced in 1968 and 1972, a divided party hardly ever wins. The same was the fate of the Liberal Party in the general elections of October 1900. Riding on the waves of euphoria of the (ostensibly) won Boer war (guerilla warfare was just beginning), the Liberal Party suffered a defeat at the polls.

The next year, CB learned about the horrors in the concentration camps in a meeting with a remarkable woman, Emily Hobhouse, who had toured the camps. CB was deeply moved by her account and decided to speak up. In a speech on June 14, 1901, he attacked the government's policy in conducting the war:

> What is the policy? That now that we had got the men we
> had been fighting against down, we should punish them as

severely as possible, devastate their country, burn their homes, break up their very instruments of agriculture . . . When is a war not a war? When it is carried on by methods of barbarism in South Africa.[11]

The phrase "methods of barbarism" caused a furor. CB was attacked by Unionists as well as by the Liberal Imperialists in his own party. He was accused of being a traitor and unfit to lead the country. One clergyman (!) wrote, "You are a cad, coward, & a murderer & I hope you will meet a traitor's or a murderer's doom." With typical British understatement, CB thought this "pretty stiff."[12] Yet, against all opposition and vile comments, he courageously stuck to his principles.

But in politics things can change quickly. The Boer War was over in 1902, and with it, the main cause of the deep divisions within the Liberal Party. In the ensuing years, the Conservative Party tore itself apart over the issue of free trade—which is a recurring pattern in this venerable

Figure 6.2 Henry Campbell-Bannerman, 1902

party—from the Corn Laws in the 1840s to Brexit in our times.[13] In December 1905, the government headed by Arthur Balfour collapsed, and CB was asked to form a new government.

In the subsequent general election of January 1906, his party won one of the greatest victories ever recorded in Britain's parliamentary history. Before the 1906 election, Campbell-Bannerman promised that there would be no legislation on Irish Home Rule (another deeply divisive issue, which has haunted the United Kingdom now for over two centuries).[14] That avoided a rift with the Liberal Imperialists. The composition of his cabinet reflected his desire to represent all currents of opinion in the party. He included Lloyd George, as well as the Liberal Imperialists Asquith, Grey, and Haldane.

CB soon established a command over the Commons that he had never enjoyed before. The occasion was a speech given by former prime minister Balfour that was contrived—full of irony, paradoxes, mock anguish—using rhetorical devices with which he had dominated the Commons during the preceding decade. CB retorted:

> [Balfour] comes back to this new House of Commons with the same airy graces, the same subtle dialectics and the same light and frivolous way of dealing with great questions . . . Enough of this tomfoolery. It might have answered very well in the last Parliament but it is altogether out of place in this.[15]

Campbell-Bannerman's reputation was changed within the space of a four-minute speech.

The man who had been no more than tolerated by half of his own party had become the embodiment of a new and more dynamic age.[16] He was now ready to take on the biggest challenge of his premiership: what to do with the resentful Boers.

RECONCILIATION WITH THE BOERS

Campbell-Bannerman was inclined toward self-government for the Boers, but he had nagging doubts about Boer loyalties. Moreover, the Liberal Imperialists in his cabinet were hesitant. So, he set up a cabinet committee, which included Asquith, the leading Liberal Imperialist. This committee came up with a draft constitution that was little more than the Lyttelton proposals. A number of influential voices urged continuity with the policies of the Balfour government, arguing that any bolder course would be "a leap in the dark" and "a dire calamity." They regarded the Boer leadership as irreconcilable, despite "smooth talk" by some of them.[17] To argue their case, the Boers sent one of their most brilliant leaders, the young General Jan Smuts, to the United Kingdom. He met various cabinet ministers but made no headway with his appeal for self-government. Britain had conquered the Boer Republics only three years before, and now Smuts was asking for his country back![18] The breakthrough came in a one-on-one meeting with Campbell-Bannerman on February 7, 1906. Despite the large age difference (CB was 69, Smuts 35), the two connected. Smuts was able to assuage the prime minister's doubts about Boer loyalties and thus reinforced CB's own deepest convictions that self-government was the right approach.[19]

The following day, the cabinet met. CB rejected both departmental advice and the proposals of the cabinet committee. In a brief but eloquent speech, Campbell-Bannerman appealed to his colleagues to treat the Boers with confidence and generosity, and to make a clean break with Unionist policy.[20] "I have made up my mind," CB said, "that we must scrap the Lyttelton Constitution and start afresh and make partners of the Boers." He spoke with such passion—all the more effective for being so out of character—that he was able to persuade his reluctant colleagues to unanimously accept his proposal.[21]

The idea of self-government for the Boer colonies was denounced by the Unionists in both houses of Parliament in the most extreme terms. In the House of Lords, Milner referred to Boer nationalism as the "insidious and absolutely consistent enemy of this country," and predicted that South Africa would be lost for Britain. Rudyard Kipling wrote a poem denouncing the sellout. Yet CB did not buckle under the weight of criticism. He asked the young under-secretary of state for the colonies,

Winston Churchill, to introduce the South African legislation in the House of Commons (the secretary for the colonies sat in the House of Lords). It was Churchill's first major speech in the house, and it was a smashing success. With the cabinet unified, the outcome of the vote was never in serious doubt, and the grant of self-government to the Transvaal and to the Orange River Colony was passed with a huge majority in the House of Commons, although only one Unionist voted for it.

Reconciliation with the Boers was CB's greatest accomplishment. Three years later, in 1910, the Cape Colony, the Transvaal, the Orange Free Colony, and the Natal Colony were brought together in the Union of South Africa, which was given the status of a self-governing dominion of the British Empire, next to Canada, Australia, and New Zealand. Campbell-Bannerman would not live to see this final victory of his policy. Ailing for a long time, he died on April 22, 1908.

The atmosphere in the Boer colonies changed dramatically. Nowhere was that more evident than in the mindset of the two leading Boers, General Louis Botha—who became prime minister of the Transvaal in 1907 and the first prime minister of South Africa in 1910—and General Smuts. When Botha attended the Colonial Conference in London later in 1907, he said in public, "Today, although a South African, I stand here as a British subject, a son and a brother of our great British Empire . . . I am a soldier and I did my duty then as a soldier; but I am ready to do that same duty today on behalf of the British Empire."[22] These words came from the man whose wife had wandered for months on the endless *veld* (grasslands) of the Transvaal, after having been driven from her home. The British also made a lifelong friend in Smuts, who opined, "They gave back our country in everything but name. After four years. Has such a miracle of trust and magnanimity ever happened before? Only people like the English could do it. They may make mistakes, but they are a big people."[23] Strong words from a man whose wife had been put in a concentration camp, where their firstborn child had died.[24]

Botha and Smuts proved true to their words. In the First World War, South Africa (under the leadership of Botha) staunchly supported Britain with men and materiel, defeated the Germans in their African colonies of (present-day) Namibia and Tanzania, and put down a rebellion by

pro-German Boers who wanted to reestablish the Transvaal as an independent republic.[25] According to Smuts,

> . . . if England had not given the Boers responsible gov-
> ernment in 1906, Boer would not have stopped Boer from
> fighting England and supporting Germany in 1914. And
> not only would there have been a new war in South Africa,
> but the Germans would have had their submarine bases in
> German East and German West and the history of the war
> and the world might have been different.[26]

Smuts would be a pillar of Britain and its Empire for four decades
(Botha had died early, in 1919). In World War II, as premier of South
Africa, he ensured the security of the Cape of Good Hope, ranked third on
Britain's list of strategic priorities, after the home islands and Singapore.[27]
He also served in Churchill's Imperial War Cabinet. The British historian
George M. Trevelyan provided the following verdict:

> In history he [CB] will live chiefly for one thing, the recon-
> ciliation of the white races in South Africa after the Boer
> War . . . it is . . . more than doubtful whether Great Britain
> could have survived the two world wars if South Africa had
> not been previously reconciled.[28]

At the Versailles Peace Conference after World War I, Smuts argued
in vain that Germany be given a similarly magnanimous treatment.
Unfortunately, then Prime Minister Lloyd George refused to listen, and
imposed a Carthaginian peace on Germany. History might have been very
different if Britain had followed the advice of the Boer who overcame both
personal and national bitterness. As in the case of Carthage versus Rome,
the replay would be even worse than the original war.[29]

Unfortunately, there was a dark side to giving the Boer colonies self-government: No arrangements were made regarding franchise to the black population. The Treaty of Vereeniging stipulated that the question of granting franchise to blacks was not to be discussed until *after* self-government. In his speech in the House of Commons, Churchill said that the Boers would regard extending the franchise to any non-white men as a breach of that treaty. But he was prescient, as he would be so often in his career, when he added, "We may regret that decision."[30] It took a man even greater than Campbell-Bannerman to right this wrong—Nelson Mandela (see chapter 13).

LESSONS

CB's leadership is first and foremost a message of encouragement to all of us who do not have the brilliance of Alexander the Great or Franklin D. Roosevelt. Neither did CB, who was in many respects an unlikely leader. In the words of biographer Roy Hattersley, he was neither "quick" nor "smart."[31] He had neither charisma, nor outstanding administrative competence, nor a lust for exercising political power.[32] Most of CB's career is more accurately characterized as pursuing many ends of minor importance (fox) than being related to a single central vision (hedgehog). But when it came to the most consequential decision in his life as a leader, his goal was clear while he was flexible in the means to achieve it.

So, what were CB's strengths? He was patient, imperturbable, honest, reliable, and courageous. He had common sense where others may have had lofty ideals, and he was a person of high integrity. He belongs with solid, perceptive leaders like Eisenhower, Truman, or Merkel.[33] CB held it to be inexpedient, as well as unethical, for a leader to jettison principles in order to win power.[34] According to biographer J. A. Spender,

> No man was ever more of a democrat and less of a demagogue than Campbell-Bannerman, and if there is anything that may be learnt from his example, it is that a man may

still . . . win popular applause and affection by bravely resist-
ing the tumults and excitements of the hour.[35]

CB's measured, principled stance on the relevant issues of his time stands
in stark contrast to the demagoguery and allegations of alternative facts we
have recently seen in countries around the world. Clearly, this unassuming,
solid leader has some lessons for us.

CB listened with an open mind to what others have to say. One example
is that, by all accounts, CB paid close attention to Smuts's exposition of how
the Boers would behave when given self-government. According to Smuts,
who described the prime minister as "a cautious Scot," CB said nothing,
but yet, Smuts felt that he had come through, that CB had listened.[36] CB
consulted intensively with his cabinet. According to his colleagues, CB's
cabinet was the most harmonious they had known. Said one of his colleagues, "As head of a Cabinet, he [CB] was cool, acute, straight, candid,
attentive to affairs, considerate."[37]

CB understood the wisdom of keeping your friends close and your enemies closer. He purposefully included the three leading Liberal Imperialists
in his Cabinet and made them feel welcome. This is what Foreign Secretary
Edward Grey wrote about him:

> From the moment his Cabinet was formed he made no
> distinction in personal relations, in intimacy and sympathy
> between those who had helped him and those who had made
> difficulties for him [i.e., Asquith, Haldane, and Grey] . . .
> Haldane was now at the War Office. Campbell-Bannerman's
> previous experience and knowledge enabled him to give spe-
> cial help . . . unsparingly and wholeheartedly to Haldane. In
> return, he expected loyalty from everyone."[38]

Grey's opinion is revealing because, while CB respected Asquith, he
held Haldane and Grey in contempt.[39] But CB realized they would be

much more dangerous outside the cabinet than inside. Outside, they could rally the faction of Liberal Imperialists and ally with the Unionists to attempt to kill CB's plan for South Africa. As part of his strategy to keep his enemies closer, he involved them in difficult decisions so that they "owned" them too. He appointed Asquith to the cabinet committee to consider solutions for South Africa. This went so far that, later, Asquith claimed that the Transvaal Constitution was worked out by him and the other committee members. Although this was a wildly exaggerated claim, it reduced opposition from within.[40]

CB made sure he remained the ultimate director of the process. In his "cabinet of all talents," he was the hub. All spokes centered on him. He was the indispensable man. Some of his colleagues were greater orators or more intelligent, but he was more seasoned, better balanced, warier, and cannier.[41] CB's signature accomplishment as a historical leader was due to his decisive intervention in a cabinet that was wavering. Lloyd George recorded what the prime minister told his cabinet: "I have made up my mind that we must scrap the Lyttelton constitution and start afresh and make partners of the Boers."[42]

CB gave others credit, perhaps more than was their due. He asked Churchill to open the debate on the proposals for self-government because CB's wife was seriously ill. CB was giving up, in his wife's interest, what should have been his finest hour. Many people would understandably begrudge their replacement; not so Campbell-Bannerman. He later wrote to Churchill a note of congratulation in which he said, "It is not only the greatest achievement of this Government (which is a comparatively small matter) but it is the finest & noblest work of the British power in modern times . . . a large part of the credit must be always attributed to you." Two things stand out here. First, CB's humility in that he called the honor the decision gave to his administration a comparatively small matter. Second, that he gave the young under-secretary such credit for a settlement that was CB's doing, not Churchill's. Only truly great people can do this. Not surprisingly, he made in Churchill a friend for life—which, sadly in CB's case, would not be long.

CB is an example of what management thinker Jim Collins calls a "Level 5 leader." According to Collins, the Level 5 leader sits on top of a hierarchy of leadership capabilities. Level 5 leaders blend deep personal humility with intense resolve. According to Collins's research, executives who possess this paradoxical combination of traits are catalysts for the rare occurrence of transforming a good organization into a great one.[43]

Finally, truly involving your followers in decision making may be easier if you lack burning ambition. CB is that most oxymoronic of politicians, one devoid of ambition.[44] If your self-worth and success are tied up in your leadership position, it is probably more difficult to invite followers—and especially those that disagree with you—to truly share in decision making. There were few university, political, or business-related committees on which my father sat that he did not chair. He was generally very successful in bringing opinions together in a workable compromise; that is, he was an effective persuasive leader. My father always maintained that a key reason why he was so successful was that he had no ambitions for lucrative positions for himself. That mindset made it easier for him to have others truly participate in the process and the outcomes, and to give them more credit than was perhaps their due.

CHAPTER TAKEAWAYS

- Campbell-Bannerman started as an ostrich, became a fox, and ended as an eagle in the area that cemented his place in history.

- Campbell-Bannerman persevered against opposition within his own party.

- Campbell-Bannerman co-opted and effectively neutralized his chief opponents in his own Liberal Party by including them in his cabinet and in key committees.

- Campbell-Bannerman was solid, honest, and reliable, rather than brilliant or a demagogue, riding the waves of popular passion. A modern-day parallel is Germany's Angela Merkel.

- Campbell-Bannerman is an example of a Level 5 leader—he combined deep personal humility with fierce resolve.

- Campbell-Bannerman's life highlights several persuasive leadership principles:
  - Keep an open mind to what others have to say.
  - Keep your friends close but your enemies closer.
  - Be open-minded and considerate, but at the same time, remain the ultimate director of the process.
  - Be generous in giving others credit, even more than they deserve.
  - Having others truly share in your decision making is easier when your self-worth and success are not tied up in your leadership position.

ROOSEVELT LENDS A HOSE

"Never forget what FDR has done for the
liberation of the Netherlands."
—DEDICATION WRITTEN BY MY FATHER, PROFESSOR PIET
STEENKAMP, WHO WAS THEN PRESIDENT OF THE DUTCH SENATE,
IN A BIOGRAPHY OF ROOSEVELT HE GAVE ME ON OCTOBER 5, 1985

Leadership Dilemma: How could Roosevelt persuade the American people
to support Great Britain in its life-and-death struggle with Nazi Germany?

CONTEXT

In the 1930s, the clouds of war were gathering over the world, again. After
Adolf Hitler became chancellor in 1933, Germany embarked on a massive
rearmament program—stealthily at first, but later ever more openly—in bla-
tant violation of the 1919 Treaty of Versailles. Yet France and Great Britain,

haunted by the slaughter of the First World War, elected to do nothing. It would not be long before Hitler started to make his moves. In rapid succession, Germany invaded the Rhineland (1936) and annexed Austria (March 1938), Sudetenland (October 1938, after the infamous Conference of Munich), and the remainder of the Czech part of Czechoslovakia (March 1939). Next, Hitler set his eyes on Poland. By that time, Britain and France finally showed some resolve and announced that a German invasion of Poland would lead to war. Undeterred, and after concluding a pact with the Soviet Union (the Molotov-Ribbentrop Pact) in August 1939, Hitler invaded Poland the following month, and Great Britain and France declared war on Germany. World War II had begun.

Across the Atlantic, the United States watched and decided to stay neutral. Why? There was certainly little love for Nazism. A poll in October 1939 showed that only 1 percent of Americans sympathized with Germany, versus 84 percent with Britain and France.[1] However, people were sick and tired of the prospect of being drawn again into European squabbles. The overwhelming majority of the American public was isolationist. Foreshadowing events in the late 1960s, antiwar demonstrations in 1935 in Washington and on university campuses across the country underscored opposition to any foreign engagement. A poll in 1937 revealed that 70 percent of Americans thought it had been a mistake to get involved in World War I, and a majority of Americans remained angry at the European nations for defaulting on their war debts.[2] There was a widespread belief that shameless war profiteers, international financiers, and armaments companies had duped the United States into that war. Another poll in December 1939 showed that around 80 percent of Americans wanted the country to stay out of war, even if Britain and France appeared to be losing.[3]

Besides, America had other priorities. After the Roaring Twenties, the Wall Street Crash in late October 1929 ushered in the Great Depression, the greatest economic calamity ever experienced by the country. Countless banks collapsed, and by 1933, one in four Americans were out of a job. Real GDP in 1933 was 26 percent below 1929.[4] For the first time in its history, it appeared possible that the fabric of U.S. society would disintegrate. Between 1933 and 1937, the U.S. economy witnessed a strong recovery, but in the second half of 1937 it experienced another deep slump—a depression within a depression.

The sudden and unexpected collapse of the mighty French army in a mere six weeks in May and June of 1940 redirected the minds of Americans to the international situation. Against all odds, Britain held out against Germany in the Battle of Britain that raged over its skies in the summer and fall of 1940. While sympathy with Britain grew steadily in the United States as more bombs were dropped on London, antiwar sentiment remained strong. In October 1940, 83 percent of Americans saw no need for the U.S. to enter the war.[5] Isolationists were vocal, both in Congress and in the country at large.

To counter Germany's industrial might, augmented by the economies of occupied countries, Britain imported massive quantities of war supplies from the United States. But by the end of 1940, Great Britain, which had singlehandedly financed the coalition war against Napoleonic France, and had propped up its allies in World War I, had hardly any dollars left to pay for its purchases in America. In short, Britain was broke. How to persuade the American population—and Congress—to help Britain without asking anything in return would require consummate skills. Enter Franklin Delano Roosevelt, America's thirty-second president, one of history's greatest persuasive leaders.

FRANKLIN DELANO ROOSEVELT

If ever there was a president born in privilege, it was Franklin Delano Roosevelt. Born in 1882, Roosevelt was a patrician in the true sense of the word—his family was wealthy *and* socially prominent, not merely "new money" like Joseph Kennedy. The pedigree of the Roosevelts and the Delanos (from his mother) was impeccable, and could be traced back to the mid-1600s. His mother was a domineering presence in his life. He was her only child and her husband had died early, in 1900. To deal with his mother, Roosevelt learned early on to hide his true motives and intentions. It became a model for how he later dealt with political associates and opponents. "Never let the left hand know what the right is doing" was a tactic he would use effectively in dealings with politicians who were unsympathetic to a plan of action he advocated. By keeping them in the dark, Roosevelt was repeatedly able to advance controversial policies because ignorance of his aims gave his adversaries limited time and opportunity to defeat him.[6]

Roosevelt was educated at Groton preparatory private school, Harvard University, and Columbia University. He was an average student, not because of lack of intelligence, but because academic work was not his highest priority.[7] After being admitted to the bar in 1907, he spent three years practicing law in New York. The most important consequence of that period was that, for the first time in his life, he had to deal with people who were underprivileged.[8] But his real calling was politics, not the law. In 1910 he was elected to the New York State senate, and he was appointed assistant secretary of the navy in the Wilson administration from 1913 to 1919. In 1920 he received the vice presidential nomination under Democratic presidential nominee James Cox. His youthful energy and his famous name (he was related to Theodore Roosevelt, who was president from 1901 to 1909) were seen as important assets. The election campaign gave him excellent schooling in national politics. He learned how to read the public mood and how to conduct future political races. He also built up a national network of political contacts, and he successfully projected an image to the party and the public as a viable future presidential candidate. However, pledging "a return to normalcy," the Republican candidate Warren Harding won the election by a landslide.[9]

Notwithstanding this heavy defeat, the future looked bright. Until disaster struck. In 1921 he contracted polio, which left him permanently paralyzed from the waist down.[10] It took him three years to recover, but he would never be able to walk even short distances without iron braces. Roosevelt made his public comeback at the Democratic Convention of 1924, and in 1928 he was elected to the governorship of America's most populous state, New York. This instantly made him a prominent Democratic candidate for the 1932 presidential election.

As governor, he honed his communication skills. Unlike his predecessors, he held frequent press conferences, and he was among the first leading politicians to recognize the importance of the novel communication medium of radio. In the spring of 1929, he gave his first fireside chat. He broadcast on Sunday nights, when the radio audience was largest. The advantages of radio were threefold. First, he reached many more followers (i.e., the public) with radio than any newspaper could. Second, with radio broadcasts, he was in total control of the message. Third, people could actually hear him speak. He gave listeners the feeling that they were holding a conversation with him.[11] Throughout the rest of his career, Roosevelt would use radio to lobby the public to put pressure on their legislative representatives to vote for his agenda. During his time as governor of New York (1929–1933), he pushed a progressive agenda to relieve the suffering of those hardest hit by the economic collapse that occurred shortly after he became governor.

In 1932 he became the Democratic presidential nominee, to run against incumbent Herbert Hoover. People were starving for inspired leadership after Hoover's hapless performance. Like Barack Obama would do some seventy-five years later, Roosevelt campaigned less on detailed policy proposals than on a message of change. People desperately wanted change, action—anything but the status quo, which clearly was not working. Obama used "Change we can believe in"; Roosevelt pledged himself to a "New Deal." It worked. Roosevelt carried forty-two out of the forty-eight states (472 versus 59 electoral votes), and the Democrats won large majorities in

Table 7.1 Party Divisions in U.S. Congress, 1928-1940

Election year	House of Representatives		Senate	
	Democrats	Republicans	Democrats	Republicans
1928	163	267	39	56
1930	217	217	47	48
1932	313	117	59	36
1934	322	103	69	25
1936	333	89	75	17
1938	262	169	69	23
1940	267	162	66	28

Source: Wikipedia

Figure 7.1 Franklin Roosevelt at One of His Fireside Chats

Source: National Archives and Records Administration

both houses of Congress (Table 7.1).[12] In the first hundred days of Roosevelt's administration, fifteen major bills were rushed through Congress. Not everything worked, but at least something was being done. He held his first fireside chat as president on March 12, reaching almost half of the U.S. population.[13] For almost every American, it was the first time they heard the voice of a president of their own country.

Many more fireside chats and press conferences would follow. Roosevelt's New Deal legislation was so radical and antiestablishment that he was branded "a traitor to his class."[14] Between 1934 and 1936, the economy grew by around 10 percent per year, and Roosevelt was reelected in a landslide in 1936, with further increased majorities in Congress.

As is the case with many presidents, Roosevelt's second term was less successful.[15] The Supreme Court had struck down several New Deal bills as unconstitutional. In response, Roosevelt proposed to increase the number of justices on the Supreme Court. His "court-packing" scheme was vehemently opposed by conservative Democrats and was eventually withdrawn. An emerging coalition between Republicans and conservative Democrats virtually ended Roosevelt's ability to enact more New Deal legislation after the 1938 midterm elections went badly, especially for pro–New Deal Democrats.

It appeared that Roosevelt's administration would end like so many two-term presidencies, if it were not for the fact that increasingly, domestic concerns were being overshadowed by the war in Europe. Britain was soldiering on, yet few believed that it could win on its own against Hitler's Third Reich. Roosevelt became convinced that it was in America's best interest to help Britain, but most Americans were wary, to say the least, of any kind of involvement with the war.

HELPING GREAT BRITAIN

As the 1930s progressed, it became increasingly clear to Roosevelt that the European democracies needed strong U.S. backing against a resurgent Germany. However, resistance to any involvement in Europe ran deep. Roosevelt's hands were further tied by the Neutrality Acts of 1935, 1936, and 1937, which imposed an arms embargo on countries that were at war. In press conferences and fireside chats, he did air his increasing worries about what was going on in Europe, but his early attempts (1935–1938) for international economic cooperation, arms reduction, and quarantining aggressors were unsuccessful, due to disagreements among international partners and fierce resistance in Congress.

After Hitler annexed the Czech part of Czechoslovakia in March 1939, Roosevelt proposed to revoke the embargo clause in the Neutrality Law and put trade with belligerents on a cash-and-carry basis: Belligerent nations could buy arms in the United States as long as the recipients paid in cash and arranged for transportation on non-American ships. This favored the Allies, as the Royal Navy controlled the seas. However, Roosevelt's proposal was voted down—Congress refused to believe that war was imminent, and, even if it was, like the population at large, they did not see a Nazi victory as a genuine threat to the homeland. After World War II started in September 1939, however, sentiment shifted in favor of a cash-and-carry policy.[16] Roosevelt moved deliberately, emphasizing that repeal of the embargo and instituting cash-and-carry would aid the cause of peace.[17] It is doubtful whether Roosevelt truly believed this, but he went to great lengths to hide any suggestion that he was more concerned with helping to defeat Nazi Germany than with keeping the U.S. out of war.[18] But it did the job—in November 1939 a new Neutrality Law was passed by Congress, whose main provision was the cash-and-carry clause.

In the first half of 1940, German U-boat attacks had significantly reduced the Royal Navy's destroyer force, crucial for protecting the merchant fleet. The new prime minister, Winston Churchill, implored Roosevelt to hand over fifty to sixty old destroyers. How could Roosevelt ever defend this? He had a masterly solution. In return for the destroyers, the U.S. would lease seven British naval bases in the Western Hemisphere. Roosevelt sold this to the public as an astute move to secure naval bases to protect the homeland. The strategic—and political—logic was undeniable. Ever since the promulgation of the Monroe Doctrine of 1823, no American in their right mind could argue against the desirability of naval bases close to the homeland being in American hands. Yet, it tied the U.S. ever closer to Britain, and to the war.

The next, and pivotal, step was triggered by a letter written by Churchill to Roosevelt on December 9, 1940, right after Roosevelt had been reelected to an unprecedented third term (the timing is no coincidence), which broke with the precedent set by America's first president, George Washington (see chapter 12). Churchill avowed Britain's commitment to fight until the end, but he informed Roosevelt that Britain was broke. By all accounts, the letter made a deep impression on Roosevelt.[19] However, cash-and-carry was already a radical departure from earlier embargoes, and Americans had not forgotten that Britain had never fully repaid its World War I debts. How could Roosevelt persuade Congress to forgo payment by Britain? Mulling over the problem for two days, Roosevelt himself came up with the idea for the famous lend-lease program.[20]

In what was perhaps Roosevelt's greatest public performance, on December 17, 1940, he appealed directly to the U.S. public, this time via a press conference. He started out by arguing that the best immediate defense of the United States was the success of Great Britain defending itself. Then, he proceeded to argue that, in such circumstances, talking about money for armament deliveries was "somewhat banal." It is worthwhile to quote what he said in full:

> Now, what I am trying to do is to eliminate the dollar sign. That is something brand new in the thoughts of practically everybody in this room, I think—get rid of the silly, foolish old dollar sign. Well, let me give you an illustration: Suppose my neighbor's home catches fire, and I have a length of garden hose four or five hundred feet away. If he can take my garden hose and connect it up with his hydrant, I may help him to put out his fire. Now, what do I do? I don't say to him before that operation, "Neighbor, my garden hose cost me $15; you have to pay me $15 for it." What is the transaction that goes on? I don't want $15—I want my garden hose back after the fire is over. All right. If it goes through the fire all right, intact, without any damage to it, he gives it back to me and thanks me very much for the use of it. But suppose it gets smashed up—holes in it—during the fire; we don't have to have too much formality about it, but I say to him, "I was glad to lend you that hose; I see I can't use it any more, it's all smashed up." He says, "How many feet of it were there?" I tell him, "There were 150 feet of it." He says, "All right, I will replace it." Now, if I get a nice garden hose back, I am in pretty good shape.[21]

Shrewdly, Roosevelt suggested Lend-Lease was just "one of several other possible methods," to give the public the illusion that they were not forced in a particular direction, but unsaid was that it was not at all obvious what other methods would work. Isolationists were not fooled by his garden hose metaphor, though. They understood that Lend-Lease would take the United States one major step closer to involvement in the war.

Stopping Lend-Lease was their last real chance to keep America out of the war in Europe.[22] The opposition was led by the influential America First Committee. According to them, the Axis powers (Germany, Italy, and Japan) were welcome to (try to) control the rest of the world; America would be strong enough to defend itself and the Western Hemisphere.[23] Some things never change. The illusion that the U.S. can divorce itself from the rest of the world is a recurrent feature of American politics.

Roosevelt knew he might expect a tough fight with the isolationists, so he took to the airwaves for a fireside chat on December 29, 1940. He started by saying that this was not a fireside chat on war but on national security. He outlined the danger posed by Nazi Germany and the key role Great Britain played:

> Does anyone seriously believe that we need to fear attack anywhere in the Americas while a free Britain remains our most powerful naval neighbor in the Atlantic? Does anyone seriously believe, on the other hand, that we could rest easy if the Axis powers were our neighbors there? If Great Britain goes down, the Axis powers will control the continents of Europe, Asia, Africa, Australasia, and the high seas—and they will be in a position to bring enormous military and naval resources against this hemisphere.

Next, he calmly and logically discussed—and debunked—a number of arguments against Lend-Lease. He argued that Lend-Lease was no charity but rather enlightened self-interest: "The best immediate defense of the United States is the success of Great Britain in defending itself, and . . . it is equally important from a selfish point of view of American defense that we should do everything to help."[24] If one accepted the fact that Nazi Germany was aggressive, powerful, and bent on world domination (contentions that at the end of 1940 were ever harder to dispute), the alternative to Lend-Lease would be to shed American blood. Seen in this light, Lend-Lease seemed a good deal!

Listen to the voice of Roosevelt, one of the greatest communicators of all time, explaining the rationale for Lend-Lease to the American people. At 33:53 ff., Roosevelt announces that the U.S. will be "the great arsenal of democracy." Knowing my parents at the time lived in Nazi-occupied Amsterdam, hoping against hope that one day they would be liberated by the Allies, I cannot listen to this fireside chat without getting goose bumps.

https://millercenter.org/the-presidency/presidential-speeches/december-29-1940-fireside-chat-16-arsenal-democracy

Discussion in Congress was fierce. Treasure Secretary Henry Morgenthau testified before Congress that, if it would not pass the law, Great Britain would have no option but to give up the good fight, which was a gross exaggeration.[25] Opponents claimed that Lend-Lease—formally titled An Act to Promote the Defense of the United States (which from a marketing point of view is much better)—would give Roosevelt (near) dictatorial powers. They alleged Roosevelt could (would) use these powers with reckless abandon, since it would be up to him to decide which countries would receive which defense materials. The president and others in his administration countered that claim by simply avoiding discussion of the dictatorship charge.

During a press conference on January 17, 1941, a reporter asked Roosevelt why he objected to any sort of limitation to his power on transferring war materials to other countries under the provisions of the bill. Rather than answering this question, Roosevelt flippantly replied, "I suppose they better put in standing on my head, too, and a lot of other things." It did the job. The general reaction in the press was that accusations about presidential dictatorship were an insult to his integrity.[26]

In the 1980 presidential debate between President Jimmy Carter and Governor Ronald Reagan, the latter—who, incidentally, was an admirer of Roosevelt—would borrow this tactic with great success. Carter went on the offensive against Reagan's record on Medicare. Rather than debunking Carter's detailed criticism, Reagan—who was never sure-footed on policy details anyway—simply answered: "There you go again." It was a masterpiece, one of history's famous putdowns that I can remember, watching the debate while I was traveling in the U.S. It defused Carter's attack, just like Roosevelt's retort cut off his detractors.

In early 1941, Roosevelt was able to gradually turn large portions of the public around. A poll on January 22, 1941, showed that 54 percent of the population supported Lend-Lease, a percentage that increased to 77 percent by early April, a month after the act was passed.[27] In March 1941, the Lend-Lease Act was passed by 260 vs. 165 in the House of Representatives and 60 vs. 31 in the Senate. Churchill described Lend-Lease in the House of Commons as "the most unsordid act in the history of any nation."

As Table 7.2 shows, in 1941 Lend-Lease already accounted for 35 percent of total deliveries to Great Britain (existing orders under

Table 7.2 Purchases versus Lend-Lease by Great Britain in World War II (in billions of dollars)

Year		Sept. 1939-Dec. 1940	1941	1942	1943	1944	1945	Total World War II
Total purchases		2.1	1.5	0.7	0.2	0.3	0.7	5.5
	Arms and munitions	0.6	1.2	0.6	0.1	0.1	0.0	2.6
	Foods	0.2	0.0	0.0	0.1	0.1	0.2	0.6
	Raw materials	0.4	0.1	0.0	0.0	0.0	0.0	0.5
	Other	0.9	0.2	0.1	0.0	0.1	0.5	1.8
Total Lend-Lease			0.8	3.4	7.4	8.7	3.6	23.9
	Arms and munitions	-	0.2	1.8	4.4	5.6	1.8	13.6
	Foods	-	0.3	0.5	0.6	0.8	0.3	2.5
	Raw materials	-	0.1	0.4	0.6	0.6	0.3	2.0
	Other	-	0.2	0.7	1.8	1.7	1.2	5.6
Lend-Lease (%)		0%	35%	83%	97%	97%	84%	81%

Source: Based on Carl (1957), p. 47. Carl's figures are based on the British Treasury Department.

cash-and-carry still had to be paid), and from 1942 on, practically all war materials were supplied under Lend-Lease. America would also supply billions of dollars to the Soviet Union, France, and other Allies. Lend-Lease was of enormous importance for the Allied war effort. The Battle of el-Alamein, Egypt (October–November 1942), was one of the first instances where Lend-Lease made a critical difference. Overwhelming British tank forces, many of them riding in American Sherman tanks, crushed the German Panzers of General Erwin Rommel's vaunted Afrika Korps. It was the turning point on the Western Front.

After Lend-Lease, Roosevelt took additional steps to align America closer to Britain. In May 1941, America started to patrol large areas of the North Atlantic, and in August 1941, Churchill and Roosevelt issued a joint declaration (the famous Atlantic Charter) proclaiming as one of the war aims, "the final destruction of Nazi tyranny." After incidents on the high seas, U.S. Navy vessels were ordered to shoot on sight, and in November 1941, the House voted to arm merchantmen.[28] America actively entered World War II after the Japanese Imperial Navy attacked Pearl Harbor. Upon hearing this news, Churchill "slept the sleep of the saved and thankful." He now knew Britain would survive.

Roosevelt died on April 12, 1945, shortly before the end of World War II. By the time of his death, victory was assured, not in the least thanks to his steadfast leadership.

LESSONS

Few people have more ably combined the hedgehog's sense of direction with the fox's sensitivity to its surroundings as Roosevelt, a true eagle. Long before the U.S. public was ready, Roosevelt had set his sights on thwarting the designs of Nazi Germany. Initially, he hoped to achieve it through soft means (e.g., asking Hitler to promise not to attack thirty specific countries), but over time, his means became more aggressive as it became increasingly clear that earlier methods did not work. Compare this with the purely hedgehog qualities of Hitler, who was unable to align his unlimited aspirations with limited German capabilities, and the ostrich-like qualities of Japanese war leader General Hideki Tojo, who neither had an accurate assessment of Japan's means (e.g., Japanese martial spirit that could overcome material inadequacies versus the U.S.) nor had a clearly defined end goal in mind when attacking the United States (a vague hope that the U.S. would simply give up).

Roosevelt is generally regarded as one of America's greatest presidents.[29] His supreme self-confidence, unsurpassed political intuition, resilience, and public persuasion skills are key qualities that help explain why he stands apart from almost all of America's other leaders. His self-confidence helped him walk (no pun intended) through the valley of the shadow of political death caused by polio, and through the trials of the Great Depression and World War II, the two greatest challenges faced by the country since the Civil War. His self-confidence was overlaid with, and supported by, his political intuition. He often sensed what was on other people's minds before they themselves realized it. Perhaps nowhere was this clearer than in his inaugural address on March 4, 1933, in which he put the finger exactly on the sore spot when he opened with: ". . . the only thing we have to fear is fear itself—nameless, unreasoning, unjustified terror which paralyzes needed efforts to convert retreat into advance."[30] Roosevelt's level of intuition about what was going on among the American public would, in my opinion, only be reached again by Reagan.

According to all accounts, the seismic event in his life was when he contracted polio. It is a perfect example of a transformative event that leadership theorist Warren Bennis calls a "crucible"—a severe test or trial. Crucibles are intense, often traumatic, and always unplanned. According to Bennis, extraordinary leaders find meaning in—and learn from—crucibles: "Like phoenixes rising from the ashes, they emerge from the adversity stronger, more confident in themselves and their purpose, and more committed to their work."[31] Without polio, Roosevelt would not have become the leader he would be. It taught the privileged patrician who had had few failures in life compassion with his less fortunate countrymen. This compassion would guide many of his policies during the Great Depression. It also taught him resilience in the face of adversity. As he once said, if you have spent two years in bed trying to wiggle your big toe, everything else seems easy.[32]

According to presidential historians, of all U.S. presidents, Roosevelt scores highest on persuasion skills.[33] How did he guide a reluctant and isolationist nation toward supporting Great Britain? He did it step by step. Roosevelt's own thinking evolved over the 1930s, but, after the fall of France, he knew it was nigh unavoidable that the U.S. would be drawn into this conflict. His persuasive strategy can be understood by turning to social judgment theory, a theory that is widely employed in marketing. This theory posits that people have two zones, or latitudes, around their initial attitude, which acts as anchor: latitude of acceptance and latitude of rejection. According to social judgment theory, if Roosevelt's message was too far removed from the public's opinion, they would reject his message because it would fall into their latitude of rejection. If, however, Roosevelt proposed a small change in America's stance, the public might accept it since it would fall into their latitude of acceptance. As a consequence, the public's opinion shifted a little into the direction of greater U.S. involvement ("assimilation"), with a new latitude of acceptance that also shifted a bit toward greater involvement. Roosevelt could then present a slightly more activist stand than before, and the process would repeat itself.

Although social judgment theory was proposed long after Roosevelt's death, as a supremely gifted persuasive leader he intuitively understood its principles. In his own words, "I knew we were going to war . . . But I could not come out and say a war was coming, because the people would have panicked and turned from me. I had to educate the people to the inevitable, step-by-step."[34] These steps included warnings of the impending dangers, repeal of the embargo, cash-and-carry, destroyers for bases, Lend-Lease, navy patrols in the Atlantic, shoot on sight, arming of U.S. merchantmen, and releasing the prohibition of U.S. ships to carry lend-lease supplies. Figure 7.2 illustrates the application of social judgment theory for two successive steps: repeal of the arms embargo and cash-and-carry. Notice how the latitude of acceptance shifts in the direction desired by Roosevelt. Notice also that initially, cash-and-carry would have fallen in the latitude of rejection, and, hence, would have been rejected by the population.

In sum, the task of persuasive leadership is to propose an opinion that is inside the latitude of acceptance of your followers, but in the direction you want your followers to move. After this opinion has been assimilated,

Figure 7.2 Social Judgment Theory Applied to Roosevelt's Persuasive Leadership

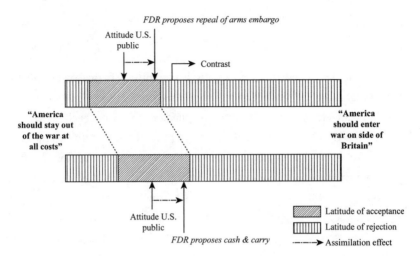

repeat the process, until the followers are where you want them to be. For this step-by-step change, it is important that the leader knows where their followers stand. How did Roosevelt know where the public stood? While he had superior political intuition, Roosevelt was also the first president to systematically rely on opinion polls.[35]

In the section "Reflections on Adaptive Leadership," we have seen that followers are more prone to accept divergent opinions from credible sources than from less credible sources. As a resident of the White House, Roosevelt almost by definition had significant credibility (although, just as we can witness in today's political atmosphere, there were large portions of society who hated him). How did he leverage that in the fireside chat in which he proposed Lend-Lease to the general public? By reminding his listeners of his first fireside chat in which he dealt with the domestic crisis that was ravaging the country. Harking back to those dark early days, he said:

> "I tried to convey to the great mass of American people what the banking crisis meant to them in their daily lives. Tonight, I want to do the same thing, with the same people, in this new crisis which faces America. We met the issue of 1933 with courage

and realism. We face this new crisis—this new threat to the security of our nation—with the same courage and realism."[36]

All listeners knew that, under his leadership, America overcame the Great Depression. Why not trust him in this new crisis?

Another element in the art of persuasion that Roosevelt used with great effectiveness is that people are more prone to accept divergent opinions from a friend than from a stranger. Roosevelt made his fireside chats personal, making every effort to create intimacy with his audience. For example, he used phrases like "Let us sit down together again, you and I, to consider our own pressing problems that confront us,"[37] and "I well remember that while I sat in my study in the White House, preparing to talk with the people of the United States, I had before my eyes the picture of all those Americans with whom I was talking . . .Tonight, I want to do the same thing, with the same people, in this new crisis which faces America."[38] This increased the effectiveness of his persuasive communications substantially.

Roosevelt explained difficult concepts with metaphors and examples. Think about his celebrated use of the garden hose to explain the reasonableness of Lend-Lease. In his first fireside chat, on March 12, 1933, he explained what banks do in a simple, accessible way, without appearing condescending. My father was a student of Roosevelt's tactics. When his effort to form one large Christian Democratic Party was ridiculed in the press, his response was, "The dogs bark, but the caravan goes on." The metaphor sentence stuck, and his critics in the press were put on the defensive.[39]

One last observation about communication media. Roosevelt was among the first politicians to use the new communication medium of the radio. There appears a recurring theme here. John F. Kennedy was the first to grasp the power of television, Barack Obama was the first to leverage the emerging new power of the Internet, and Donald Trump that of social media.

CHAPTER TAKEAWAYS

- Roosevelt was an eagle while his two main adversaries, Hitler and Tojo, were a hedgehog and an ostrich, respectively.

- To deal with his domineering mother, Roosevelt learned early on to hide his true motives and intentions.

- The combination of supreme self-confidence, unsurpassed political intuition, resilience, and public persuasion skills set Roosevelt apart from almost all of America's other leaders.

- Roosevelt's illness (polio) is an example of a transformative event called a "crucible." It gave Roosevelt persistence, resilience, patience, and compassion for others.

- Roosevelt was one of the greatest communicators of all time. He made his audience seemingly part of the conversation.

- Roosevelt employed a brilliantly executed, patient, step-by-step strategy to persuade a thoroughly isolationist country to help Britain.

- Roosevelt benefited from understanding the power of the new mass medium of his time, the radio. This is a recurrent theme. Leaders who are the first to embrace a new medium tend to do well.

- Roosevelt's life highlights several persuasive leadership principles:

  ○ Employ social judgment theory to change the opinion of your followers, step by step.

  ○ Leverage source credibility by reminding your audience of past events and successes.

  ○ Create intimacy with your audience—treat them as your friend.

  ○ Use metaphors and examples to explain difficult concepts.

REFLECTIONS ON PERSUASIVE LEADERSHIP

THE LOCUS OF change in adaptive leadership is the leader, while persuasive leaders excel in their ability to change the hearts and minds of their followers. The lives of Themistocles, Campbell-Bannerman, and Roosevelt illustrate important principles of persuasive leadership. Persuasive leaders (1) need to manage the gap between themselves and their followers; (2) maintain credibility; (3) excel in communication skills; (4) use distal followers to persuade proximate followers; (5) hide their ulterior intentions when required; and (6) appeal to their followers' self-interest.

1. MANAGE THE GAP IN VISION WITH YOUR FOLLOWERS

Persuasive leaders have to grapple with the gap between their goals and what their followers want. Themistocles, Campbell-Bannerman, and Roosevelt knew long before their followers what had to be done. Their greatest challenge was to manage the gap. One of my friends often says (privately) that he is surrounded by incompetence. He means that others do not see what is so obvious to him. While perhaps true, such an attitude does not help to persuade others to follow him. Rather, try to place yourself in the position of your followers and understand their reluctance and fear. Then, develop a gradual, step-by-step process to move them toward your desired direction, using the principles of social judgment theory. This requires a lot of patience but if you move too fast, you will lose them.

Another friend of mine is a senior manager at a large multinational company. Its CEO committed to substantial cost savings in his discussions with stock analysts. The division to which my friend belongs was expected to cut costs by several hundred million dollars in a short period of two years. As he told me, "Teams of McKinsey consultants were let loose on manufacturing plants across the world, catching their staff and managers by surprise." The leadership of the division did not understand the need for such a hurry, as the company was very profitable. Cost reductions are never popular, but failure to prepare the ground leads to resistance, and is a recipe for failure.

2. MAINTAIN CREDIBILITY

In Part One, the challenge was for the leader to change while maintaining credibility. Here, the issue is whether the leader possesses sufficient expertise and trustworthiness to persuade their followers. Roosevelt had an easier task in this respect than Themistocles or Campbell-Bannerman. Themistocles was not an acknowledged expert in naval warfare, and although he was right in arguing that fighting in the narrow seas was smarter than fighting in the open seas, his self-interest was obvious to all, which undermined his trustworthiness. In the case of Campbell-Bannerman, he had only recently become prime minister. His principled stand on South Africa made him trustworthy, but his expertise was less firmly established. On the other hand, Roosevelt had been president for many years when World War II broke out, and he had shown the nation that he was a safe pair of hands, having steered the nation out of the Great Depression.

3. EXCEL IN COMMUNICATION SKILLS

Persuasive leaders need to excel in communication skills, arguably more than most other types of leaders. After all, they want to persuade—as opposed to order or coerce—people to change their ways. Themistocles and Roosevelt were among the best communicators of their time. As I listened to Roosevelt's fireside chats, I marveled at their clarity, intimacy, and persuasive impact. Themistocles's oratorical skills are obvious from Herodotus's writings. Campbell-Bannerman, on the other hand, was a rather wooden orator, which paradoxically worked to his advantage when he advocated a change in policy that nobody was expecting. He spoke with such uncharacteristic emotion that it was clear to all how deeply the prime minister felt about the issue.

So, you can be a persuasive leader without possessing great communication skills, but that is rare. If you are a Campbell-Bannerman, what can you do? The good news is that you can improve your oratorical qualities. King George VI (r. 1936–1952) worked hard to overcome his stuttering condition, just in time to broadcast Britain's declaration of war with Nazi Germany in 1939. His tortuous journey was the subject of the critically acclaimed 2010 movie *The King's Speech*, featuring Colin Firth.

I was lucky that my father—who was a superb speaker—tutored me in oratory. He taught me to never read a speech verbatim from a prepared text; take special effort to vary the tone within and across sentences; exude energy; display passion about the topic (regardless of how boring it may be); and make eye contact with different people in the audience. While these appear obvious—especially when you read them here and now—how many people do it?

4. USE DISTAL FOLLOWERS TO PERSUADE PROXIMATE FOLLOWERS

It is sometimes useful to distinguish between two groups of followers: proximate and distal. Proximate followers are followers that are on your "team," for example, the parliamentary faction of your party (politics) or the people working for you at your church or in your business unit, while distal followers are farther away—think about voters, the congregation, and all company employees, respectively. Persuading proximate followers is typically crucial to reach your goals, but what to do if you encounter significant resistance among this group? You can deal with this situation by invoking distal followers (or even adversaries) to persuade proximate followers.

Time and again, Roosevelt put pressure on Congress, especially on members of his own Democratic Party (his proximate followers) by reaching out to the population (his distal followers). The one time this strategy failed spectacularly—his "court-packing" scheme—was exactly the instance where he failed to convince the American public to back his idea. Themistocles used the Persians to persuade his allies to adopt his point of view. Before that, he used the Athenian population to put pressure on his political rivals. Campbell-Bannerman's position in his party was greatly strengthened by his overwhelming electoral victory. Something similar happened in December 2019 when British prime minister Boris Johnson appealed to the country to allow him to push through Brexit over the opposition of part of his own Conservative Party. He won a decisive victory and Britain left the EU one month later.

When my father faced continued resistance from the leaders of the three parties to coalesce into one Christian Democratic Party, he switched from "The Hague" (the seat of parliament and hence his fellow politicians) to "the country." For two years he gave speeches at one local party organization after the other, which built a groundswell of support for the merger that literally overwhelmed the resistance in The Hague.

This strategy of reaching out to distal followers to induce change in proximate followers is a common marketing tactic, which is called a "pull strategy." In a pull strategy, a firm creates demand for a product by advertising it to consumers, who then demand that resellers stock it. This causes the product to be "pulled" through the sales channel. One celebrated example is the "Intel Inside" campaign. In the early 1990s, as the market for personal computers exploded, few people knew anything about semiconductor chips. Thus, PC manufacturers could just play one semiconductor manufacturer against the other. Intel's great insight was to promote the Intel chip to consumers. Over time, and after Intel invested hundreds of millions of dollars in advertising, people started to look for PCs that contained Intel chips, which forced PC manufacturers to use Intel, even if they might have preferred another brand. The effect was dramatic. In 2019, Intel's revenues exceeded $72 billion, versus $7 billion for AMD—a brand you probably have never heard of, which proves the point.

A pull strategy can also be used by smart entrepreneurs without deep pockets. Mr. Kips, a friend of my paternal grandfather, launched Kips liver sausage in Amsterdam in the 1920s. Bars were an important distribution channel at the time. How to get bar owners to carry Kips? Mr. Kips paid a number of freelance "sales reps" to go to bars, order a beer, and ask for Kips liver sausage. If the bar owner said he did not carry Kips, the "customer" responded that Kips was the only liver sausage he wanted and no other liver sausage would do. After multiple such experiences, bar owners felt compelled to carry Kips, which subsequently became the market leader in Amsterdam, and went on to become one of the most loved meat-product brands in the Netherlands. In today's world, bar visits might be replaced by buzz on social media, but the principle remains the same.[1]

5. HIDE YOUR ULTERIOR INTENTIONS

Successful persuasive leaders often hide their ulterior intentions—if their followers would know what their real endpoint was, they might not want to follow them anymore. Roosevelt was a master in this respect. Like that other great persuasive U.S. president, Ronald Reagan, it was difficult to get to know what he really thought. Roosevelt preferred to keep his options open and his thoughts shrouded. As his behavior on the eve of the Battle of Salamis showed, Themistocles was also a master in hiding what he really wanted too.

More controversially, persuasive leaders may sometimes revert to half-truths and deception. For example, to get Xerxes to leave Greece, Themistocles spread the false rumor that the Greek fleet would sail to the Hellespont to destroy the pontoon bridges. In the 1940 presidential election, Roosevelt vowed, "Our boys shall stay out of European wars," while he knew he would almost certainly break that promise.[2] In his fireside chat on December 9, 1941, he claimed that "Your Government knows that for weeks Germany has been telling Japan that if Japan did not attack the United States, Japan would not share in dividing the spoils with Germany when peace came."[3] In fact, the attack on Pearl Harbor caught Hitler completely by surprise. Roosevelt made that claim because he was concerned that the public would demand that the U.S. concentrate on defeating Japan while Roosevelt knew that Germany was the greater danger. Hitler, true to form, made Roosevelt's life easier by declaring war on the United States on December 11, 1941, so that for once, FDR did not have to use his legendary persuasive skills to convince Congress to declare war on the Third Reich too.

6. APPEAL TO SELF-INTEREST

Regardless of how good your cause is, there often is no substitute for appealing to your followers' self-interests. Themistocles did this when he advocated spending money on triremes by pointing to Athens' commercial rival Aegina. Time and again, Roosevelt emphasized that Britain was America's last line of defense. Campbell-Bannerman was up against public opinion that was still keenly aware of Britain's human and financial sacrifice in the Boer War. Illustrative is what King Edward VII wrote to the Prince of Wales: "After all the blood & treasure we have expended it would [be] terrible indeed if the country were handed over to the Boer."[4] We do not know the exact arguments used by Campbell-Bannerman in his decisive speech to his cabinet (no minutes were recorded). But we can be reasonably sure that the prime minister did not only appeal to higher ideas but also to the hard-nosed reality laid out the day before this cabinet meeting by the Boer general Jan Smuts, when Smuts told him, "Do you want friends or enemies? You can have the Boers for friends, and they have proved what quality their friendship may mean. You can choose to make them enemies, and possibly have another Ireland on your hands."[5]

Since you want to persuade your followers to change their beliefs, which are often vested in their own self-interest, do not solely count on lofty ideals to persuade your followers. Some will be convinced, but more often, your followers will ask the age-old Roman question: *Cui bono?* (Who benefits?)

To assess whether persuasive leadership is a style that suits you, consider the following questions.

1. Do you routinely analyze the gap between your goals and what your followers want? If so, have you been able to persuade your followers toward your point of view? What examples from your life can you give?

2. Can you draw on your expertise in your line of work to facilitate change in your followers? If not, can you build more expertise?

3. Do your followers regard you as a trustworthy person, who provides information in an unbiased, honest manner? If not, why is that the case? Can you start building greater trustworthiness?

4. Do others regard you as an effective communicator? Are you comfortable speaking in public? Can you speak off the cuff, with minimal notes? If not, are you motivated to improve your oratorical skills?

5. Can you identify distal followers who can help you persuade—or put pressure on—proximate followers, if necessary?

6. Which persuasive leaders do you recognize in your own professional and/or personal environment? How do you relate to their style of leadership?

7. Are you able to hide your ulterior intentions when required?

8. Have you used appeals to self-interest in persuading others? Did that work?

9. What feedback have you ever received that portrayed you as a persuasive leader?

10. In what situation(s) have you been in where being a "persuasive leader" would have been most effective? What did you actually do and with what results?

PART THREE

DIRECTIVE LEADERSHIP – DEFINE THE MARCHING ORDERS

8

CORTÉS SCUTTLES HIS SHIPS

"We unanimously answered him that we would
do as he ordered."
—BERNAL DÍAZ DEL CASTILLO, SPANISH CONQUISTADOR AND
SOLDIER IN CORTÉS'S ARMY

Leadership Dilemma: How could Cortés get his men to follow him in the face of overwhelming dangers?

CONTEXT

In the twenty-five years after Columbus first reached the New World, Spanish exploration was largely confined to the Caribbean. From the home base of Hispaniola (present-day Haiti and the Dominican Republic), Spaniards made sporadic ventures to the north and south. In the south, from 1509 onward, they made contact with the indigenous population of the mainland. Vasco Núñez de Balboa crossed the Isthmus of Panama to the Pacific Ocean in 1513, becoming the first European to see the Pacific. This established beyond doubt that the Americas were a separate continent. In the north, the Spanish settled other Caribbean islands and made contact with the mainland of Mexico, but made only limited inroads there. In 1517, the Mayas in the Yucatán peninsula successfully repelled a Spanish expeditionary force. However, the expedition brought back gold, which fueled continued interest in the region.[1]

Unknown to the Spaniards, there existed a large, powerful Aztec Empire that controlled much of present-day Mexico and Central America (Figure 8.1).[2] Its capital was the great city of Tenochtitlán.

Ruled by Montezuma II, the ninth semi-divine emperor of a devout people, the Aztecs possessed elaborate and accurate calendars, efficient irrigation systems for their various year-round crops, zoos and botanical gardens, clean city streets with waste-management methods, astounding arts and jewelry, state-run education, and a vast trade and tribute network.[3] The Aztecs adhered to a highly evolved and ritualized religion, worshipping

Figure 8.1 Aztec Empire

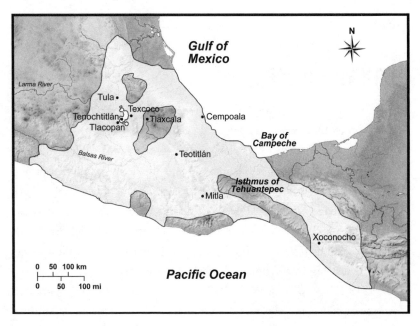

a pantheon of deities in elaborate ceremonies. A key element of their religion was human sacrifice. A victim (often, but not always, a prisoner of war)
would be taken to the top of a great pyramid and laid down over a sacrificial
stone. A priest would stand over him, holding a knife with a blade of vol-
canic glass. That blade would come down upon the victim's chest and break
it open, and the priest would tear out his still-beating heart, holding it up
high for all to see. The flesh from the body could be consumed by humans.
The Aztecs believed that human sacrifices appeased the gods and ensured
rains for their crops, healthy harvests, victories in battle, and even the daily
rising of the sun.[4]

The Aztec Empire was a formidable military power, able to muster
hundreds of thousands of warriors. It continuously waged war upon its
neighbors to obtain prisoners of war, required for their sacrifices. The Aztec
warriors were fearsome, brave, and well trained. But it was an empire ruled
by fear. Many of the subjugated people chafed under the Aztecs' domination and continuous requirements for human sacrifices. A determined
conqueror might have a fighting chance against the Aztecs, but who would
dare this? How could this person even get his men to follow him in the face
of such danger?

HERNAN CORTÉS

Hernán Cortés was born in 1485 in Medellín, Spain, the son of a minor
noble. As a child, Cortés was pale and sickly.[5] He went to the University
of Salamanca at the age of fourteen, but returned home after two years.
However, those two years at Salamanca—plus his long period of training
and experience as a notary, first in Spain and later in Hispaniola—gave
Cortés knowledge of the legal codes of Castile (Spain) that he would use
to justify his unauthorized conquest of Mexico.[6] In 1504 he left Spain for
Hispaniola. He held various positions in the Spanish colonial administration in the Caribbean and amassed substantial wealth.

In 1518 Diego Velázquez de Cuéllar, the governor of Cuba, appointed
Cortés as captain-general of an expedition to explore and secure the interior

of Mexico for colonization. At the last minute, due to a disagreement over an old argument between the two, Velázquez changed his mind and revoked Cortés's charter. Cortés ignored the orders and, in an act of open mutiny, went on his expedition anyway in February 1519. From then on, Cortés placed himself directly under the auspices of the Holy Roman Emperor Charles V, who was also King Charles I of Spain. This was disingenuous— the emperor was not even aware of Cortés's existence. Not everybody was happy with Cortés's decision to ignore Velázquez's orders; some soldiers were still loyal to the governor of Cuba.

SCUTTLING THE FLEET AND THE AFTERMATH

Cortés's force consisted of 11 ships, 110 sailors, 552 soldiers (including 13 musketeers and 32 crossbowmen), 16 cannons, and 16 horses.[7] The expedition disembarked on the Mexican shore on April 21, 1519. The Spaniards remained near the coast for a while, gathering information, and founding Veracruz as a secure harbor to maintain communications with the Spanish Empire in the Caribbean. Here, Cortés learned that various tribes on the coast and inland were unwilling subjects of Montezuma II. They had to pay exorbitant tributes and supply large numbers of victims for his human sacrifices. Importantly, one particularly warlike inland tribe, the Tlaxcalans, was in active revolt and had never surrendered to Montezuma II.[8]

Before long, Aztec ambassadors visited the Spanish camp. Cortés learned more about the powerful Aztec Empire and its magnificent capital. The emissaries brought generous gifts of precious stones and objects of solid gold, as well as specific instructions from their emperor: "Under no circumstances could they venture through the mountains to visit him [Montezuma II] . . . The Spaniards were to take his gifts as gestures of good faith and evidence of his wealth and power—and leave. They must leave."[9] From the Aztec perspective, opulent gifts were indications of wealth and power and meant to show how unassailable their emperor was.

Unbeknownst to them, these gifts had the exact opposite effect on Cortés. Clearly, a realm that could give such unsolicited gifts had much more to offer. More than ever, Cortés was determined to visit Montezuma II in Tenochtitlán and take stock of the situation there. However, his followers had different ideas. The Velázquez loyalists suggested that they take their easily won spoils and return to Cuba. Others were frightened by the enormous odds against them, now that it had become clear that this empire they were previously unaware of could field hundreds of warriors for every Spanish soldier. Mutiny hung in the air. The stage was set for a showdown between Cortés and the disaffected.

Cortés realized that, as long as there was a way back, he might face a mutiny every instance the expedition ran into difficulties. And he certainly expected that there would be plenty. So, in an act of incredible daring, he ordered his trusted shipmasters to bore holes in the bottoms of the ships. Before his men realized what was happening, his ships were beyond saving. As the last of his magnificent ships disappeared to the bottom of the Gulf of Mexico, he stood with his men.

He staked everything on the future. He gave his men no choice—it was physically impossible to turn back. Cortés told his army that they should be ready for battle and see it through to the end because "should we be put to the rout in whatever place, we would not be able to recover, being so few, and we had no help or aid but God's—because we now had no ships to return to Cuba—save our good fighting and strong hearts."[10] There were only two options: "win the land or die in the attempt."[11]

Proceeding inland (see Figure 8.2), the Spaniards encountered fierce resistance from the Tlaxcalans, who, being aware of the visit by the Aztec ambassadors, suspected that Cortés had made common cause with their archenemies, the Aztecs. Several hard-fought battles ensued over a three-week period in September 1519, culminating in a battle in which the Spanish army of around 500 men defeated a massive Tlaxcalan army of 40,000 warriors. The combination of outstanding Spanish discipline, cavalry, and superior weapons (steel blades, cuirasses, and helmets, as well as guns, harquebuses, and crossbows) proved irresistible. It was neither the first nor the last time that this combination would be decisive. The Tlaxcalans now assembled an even larger army of 100,000 troops. Undaunted, Cortés used the carrot-and-stick approach, giving them the following stern message: "We come as your allies and brothers, but if we are further impeded, we will annihilate everything in our path."[12] These words persuaded the Tlaxcalans that Cortés was not allied with the Aztecs, and they decided to join forces with the Spaniards.

The Spaniards and their Tlaxcalan allies then advanced to Cholula, where Montezuma II had planned a surprise attack. However, Cortés, who had obtained advance information of the Aztecs' intentions, struck first, and thousands of unarmed Cholulans were massacred. This subdued Cholula and ensured a safe supply route to Veracruz. It also sent shock waves throughout the region. Everyone now understood that the Spaniards were ruthless, a psychological advantage of inestimable value given that the enemy was so much stronger in manpower. Cortés and his army then

Figure 8.2 Route of Cortés

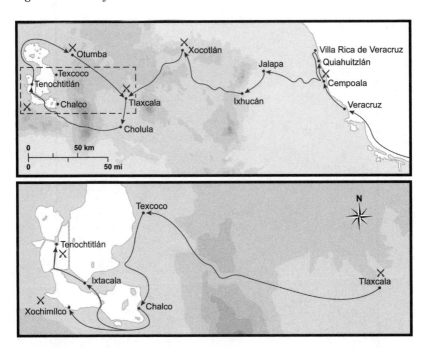

Note: Top panel shows Cortés's route from the coast to Tenochtitlán and withdrawal to Tlaxcala. The bottom panel shows Cortés's return route to Tenochtitlán.

advanced toward the Valley of Mexico (Figure 8.3) and, on November 8, 1519, entered Tenochtitlán without opposition. When the Spaniards arrived, they wondered whether they were seeing a mirage.[13] They had never seen such a place. Built on raised islets in Lake Texcoco, the city was connected to the mainland via three causeways. With more than 250,000 inhabitants, it was one of the largest cities in the world at the time, much larger than Paris, London, or Rome.

Cortés was soon able to capture and imprison Montezuma II, whom he made a puppet. It looked as though the conquest was complete. But then

Figure 8.3 The Valley of Mexico

another Spanish force, sent by Governor Velázquez, and led by his lieutenant Pánfilo de Narváez, arrived on the coast with orders to arrest Cortés.
Cortés left some of his forces in Tenochtitlán and hastily led the rest of his
troops back to the coast. There, he defeated this Spanish force and persuaded the survivors to join him. They returned to Tenochtitlán on June 24,
1520, only to find chaos. Incensed by ongoing large-scale human sacrifices,
Pedro de Alvarado, whom Cortés had left in charge of the soldiers in
Tenochtitlán, ordered a massacre of assembled Aztec nobles. Heavy fighting raged in Tenochtitlán, and Montezuma II was killed (either by Aztecs
or on orders of Cortés—the sources are conflicting). Seeing that the situation was hopeless, Cortés decided his army should flee while the northern
causeway was still open. On June 30, 1520 (*La Noche Triste*—The Sad
Night), the Spaniards withdrew under the cover of darkness, but their
retreat was discovered. In the ensuing bitter fighting on the causeway, being
attacked from all sides, Cortés lost over half his force, many horses, all cannons, most of their gunpowder, and almost all the treasure.

The Spaniards' retreat was blocked at the town of Otumba by an enormous Aztec army. Given their scant numbers and dire condition, Cortés
believed they were doomed. Nevertheless, he once again gave a rousing
speech, appealing to his soldiers' sense of duty and honor, and to their love
of the Crown and the Cross. Against all odds, the few remaining warhorses
and the strict defensive discipline of the Spaniards proved decisive.[14] It
turned out to be the last best chance the Aztecs would have to save their
empire. The Spaniards retreated to Tlaxcala to prepare for the next attack
on Tenochtitlán.

These preparations took some eight months. Cortés gave first priority to
replenishing his sorely depleted forces. He achieved this thanks to men and
supplies that arrived at Veracruz in subsequent weeks from the Caribbean
and Spain. He built thirteen brigantines (small sailing ships), equipped with
cannons, with which to wrest control of Lake Texcoco from the Aztec fleet
of canoes. Together with his Tlaxcalan allies, he carried out raids on neighboring towns and brought them over to the Spanish camp. By the end of
April 1521, Tenochtitlán stood alone, and the siege began on May 22, 1521.
By now, Cortés had gathered a vast army of native allied warriors, whereas
the Aztecs were cut off from outside help. Nevertheless, the Aztecs resisted

their attackers for nearly three months and won some notable, albeit short-lived, victories. The desperate fighting cost countless lives and impelled Cortés to destroy the city systematically, one block at a time, as the only way of reducing the defenders. Tenochtitlán fell on August 13, 1521.[15]

After that, Spanish control of Mexico was reasonably secure, although Cortés had to spend some time "pacifying" outlying regions. Cortés rebuilt Tenochtitlán and renamed it Mexico City, which became the capital of the Spanish colony of New Spain. It is now one of the largest cities in the world. The Spanish Empire in the New World was to last for three hundred years, shaping Latin America's culture, religion, institutions, and language well into the twenty-first century.[16] Emperor Charles V appointed Cortés as governor of the newly conquered territory and made him a marquis. In subsequent years, however, Cortés quarreled with the emperor and with Spanish rivals, and he was involved in many lawsuits. Heavily in debt, he died in Seville, Spain, in 1547, on his way back to Mexico, an embittered man.

LESSONS

When I told a friend of mine, who is of Spanish descent and the dean of a major Mexican business school, that I would include Cortés in this book, her first reaction was: "He was not a nice man." Indeed, not even his most ardent admirers would describe Cortés as a nice man. Integrity was also not his strong suit. Cortés was cunning, manipulative, and a master of deception, right from the beginning. He knowingly disobeyed the orders of Velázquez and created the fiction that he acted under the auspices of Charles V. Scuttling the fleet and so presenting his men with a life-or-death fait accompli (and for many, it would be death) was duplicitous, to say the least. One could also consider him hypocritical. While he sincerely abhorred human sacrifices and cannibalism, the massacre of thousands of Cholulans and other native inhabitants did not seem to unduly trouble him.

Yet there is no denying that Cortés was a supremely effective leader who conquered a powerful empire against all odds. Cortés achieved immortal fame and became a folk hero in his own lifetime, not only in Spain but also around Europe.[17] He was an eagle. As a true hedgehog, he never wavered in his goal—to conquer the Aztec Empire. However, he possessed fox-like sensitivity to the surroundings, adapting his means to achieve his high aspirations, from scuttling one fleet to building another one. In contrast, Montezuma II was a hapless ostrich. He lacked a sense of direction, not knowing how to deal with Cortés, wavering between enmity and friendship, with disastrous results for him and his people. At the same time, he was ineffective in leveraging the huge means at his disposal. Montezuma II was apparently oblivious to the threat the Spaniards posed to him when he allowed them to enter Tenochtitlán. He even let himself be arrested in his own palace and subsequently told his nobles he was held by the Spaniards by his own will and they should not be alarmed. This understandably bewildered his followers.[18]

What can we learn from Cortés's leadership (without resorting to his methods)? A lot, actually. While Cortés (sometimes) listened to the opinions of others, it was he, and he alone, who set out the marching orders. At every instance, he was in command. For example, the tide had swung against the Spaniards after suffering heavy losses in early July 1521; ironically, this was the consequence of him acquiescing, for once, to the demands of his captains. Many of his Indian allies deserted from his army, while others that were away from the Spanish forces were vigorously attacked by Aztec allies and appealed for help. Cortés agreed to send help to his allies despite strenuous opposition from senior captains who claimed he would destroy them all by reducing their forces in Tenochtitlán. In the end, his decision to go ahead anyway was crucial in stopping the hemorrhaging of allied support.[19]

The one quality Cortés possessed above all others was determination. His determination to go to Tenochtitlán was the reason he decided to scuttle his ships. This decision was crucial. Without this, it is unlikely that he would have been able to get his men to take on one of the greatest empires in the world. Sometimes, you should lead by not giving your followers a choice. Research has shown that people who have no backup plan associated with their primary goal perform better than those who have a backup plan.[20]

Cortés's determination showed up in countless other instances as well, but perhaps best in his decision to build a fleet of brigantines. These ships were built from scratch in Tlaxcala and were transported piece by piece by 50,000 workers some fifty miles over the mountains and down to Texcoco (Figure 8.3), where they were assembled. An army of local workers dug a mile-long canal so they could launch the ships from a safe and defensible distance from the lakeshore. It still ranks among the largest landlocked naval operations ever conducted in history.[21]

Cortés had other qualities. He was courageous and able to inspire his followers. He led by example, saw opportunities where others saw problems, looked forward rather than backward, and learned from experience. Any leader covets such qualities. Time and again, he was in the thick of the actual fighting, rather than supervising the battle from a distance. Twice, he was caught by the Aztecs, only to be saved at the last moment by his men. This made his directive leadership style more acceptable. When he scuttled the ships, Cortés was facing the same consequences as his followers were. This behavior, as well as his oratory, inspired his men. After the Spaniards were victorious in the Battle of Otumba, many of his followers had had enough. They were exhausted and wanted to return to Veracruz, criticizing him for his "insatiable thirst for glory and authority."[22] He responded with "stirring and patriotic oratory of a man born to lead men."[23] He argued, "What nation of those who have ruled the world has not once been defeated? . . . Victories are not won by the many but by the valiant . . . Never before in these Indies of the New World have Spaniards been seen to turn back through fear."[24]

Cortés rarely dwelled on the past. He showed an amazing resilience in the face of the countless setbacks he experienced. The morning following the disastrous *Noche Triste*, despite bleeding from many wounds and grieving for the huge human and material losses (including the gold), he was already thinking about the future. He looked around to find the master carpenter and shipbuilder. Why? Because an audacious idea for reconquest was already germinating in his mind—to build brigantines to wrest control over the lake from the Aztecs.[25]

While Cortés did not dwell on the past, he excelled in the ability to learn from past experiences. One example is his decision to use brigantines the second time around. From his first time in Tenochtitlán, he learned the hard way that the city could not be taken without control of the causeways, which, in turn, was impossible without control of the lake. The Aztecs retained the advantage there; they possessed thousands of canoes with the ability to hit both flanks of the causeways at the same time. The brigantines were a brilliant solution to this challenge.

Returning to the observation of my Mexican friend that Cortés was not a nice man, there are plenty of examples of business and political leaders who would fit that label too—think about John D. Rockefeller, Henry Ford, Steve Jobs, Martha Stewart, U.S. president Lyndon B. Johnson, Turkey's president Recep Erdogan, or Russia's Vladimir Putin. They share other characteristics with Cortés: being directive, if not (borderline) dictatorial and manipulative, and wanting everything done their way. Yet, they all had considerable success during their time at the helm of their organization or country.[26]

A final note on Montezuma II's puzzling behavior while in captivity for seven months. He gave in to almost all of Cortés's demands. Montezuma II even refused Cortés's offer of freedom (which may or may not have been genuine). In the process, he caused irreparable harm to the Aztec Empire, where power was concentrated in the semi-divine emperor. Contemporaries could not understand this behavior. With the benefit of hindsight, it was an early instance of what we now call Stockholm syndrome. Stockholm syndrome is a condition in which the captive develops a psychological alliance with and ultimately identifies with their captor (initially out of fear) as a survival strategy during captivity.[27]

CHAPTER TAKEAWAYS

- Cortés was an eagle while Montezuma II was an ostrich.

- Cortés was always in command, directing his often fearful soldiers with an iron will.

- Cortés saw opportunities where others saw dangers. Even in adversity he was already planning his next moves. This gave him an edge over the vastly more powerful Aztecs, who were mainly reactive.

- Cortés was dictatorial, controlling, and manipulative. He shares these traits with many successful political and business leaders.

- Cortés's positive leadership qualities include determination, a towering motivation to succeed, courage, and ability to inspire his (reluctant) followers.

- Montezuma II's puzzling behavior while in captivity is an early instance of Stockholm syndrome.

- Cortés's life highlights several directive leadership principles:

    ° Sometimes, you have to lead by giving your followers no choice.

    ° You can keep reluctant followers on board through inspired directive leadership.

    ° Stay resilient in the face of setbacks.

    ° Learn from mistakes without dwelling on the past; new opportunities are always beckoning if you have the willingness to see them.

    ° Leading by example makes directive leadership more acceptable.

THATCHER
CLOSES A PIT

**"I don't mind how much my ministers talk,
as long as they do what I say."**
—MARGARET THATCHER

Leadership Dilemma: How could Thatcher rejuvenate Great Britain when previous administrations had failed miserably?

CONTEXT

In 1945, Great Britain emerged as one of the Big Three victors of the Second World War. But appearances were deceiving; the battle of life and death with the Axis powers left Britain economically exhausted. Even the fact that most of its industry infrastructure was still intact was a curse in disguise. With U.S. aid (the Marshall Plan), Continental European states rebuilt their industries with the latest machinery, and British manufacturing steadily lost competitiveness. In 1950, German labor productivity was half that of Britain's, but it surpassed Britain's during the 1960s.[1]

The first postwar government, headed by Labour Party Prime Minister Clement Attlee, nationalized over 20 percent of the nation's industry. There was a great extension of publicly financed social welfare. But in the ensuing decades, with lagging productivity, the public sector became a millstone around Britain's neck.[2] In 1967 the country had to devalue the pound by a hitherto unimaginable 14 percent. In 1976 another financial crisis forced Britain to borrow $3.9 billion from the International Monetary Fund—at the time, the largest loan ever requested from the IMF.[3] The 1970s found Britain in a demoralized, chaotic, and confused state. It was rightly called "the sick man of Europe." No leading politician appeared to know how to cure the sickness. Successive Conservative and Labour governments tried and failed at this task. The endemic problems of high inflation, low productivity, lack of managerial decisiveness, and unsustainable levels of public expenditure had shattered national self-confidence.

Looming over all these ailments was the power and militancy of the trade (labor) unions. Trade unions enjoyed many legal and customary rights in Britain, including the statutory right to "peaceful" picketing, immunity against damages caused during a strike, and closed shops.[4] As the economic malaise intensified, trade-union militancy increased. In late 1973 Great Britain was hit by widespread industrial action, spearheaded by the militant National Union of Mineworkers, Britain's most powerful trade union. Without coal, the workweek was reduced to three days to save fuel. Shops were lit by candles and industries were shutting down. Edward Heath's Conservative government called an election over the issue of "Who Governs Britain?" in February 1974. The answer was clear: The Conservatives lost the election and Labour returned to power.

Large-scale labor unrest returned in full force in the winter of 1978–1979 (the "winter of discontent"). Various unions—from truck drivers, train operators, and waste collectors to health care workers and grave diggers—went on strike. By January 1979, the country was in chaos. Lack of fuel deliveries meant power cuts at a time of extreme cold. Unable to have goods delivered in or out by road transport, many businesses shut down. Schools closed. Hospitals accepted only emergency cases. Scenes of violent picketing outside factories, docks, and power plants shocked the nation's television viewers. The face of trade-union militancy had never looked uglier as the excesses spread toward anarchy.[5] The government's reaction to such events was one of impotence, and it fell in March 1979. New elections were called in which the Labour Party, under Prime Minister James Callaghan, faced the Conservative Party, led by its untried head and the first female leader of a major U.K. party, Margaret Thatcher.

MARGARET THATCHER

Margaret Thatcher (née Roberts) was born on October 13, 1925, in Grantham, a small town in Lincolnshire, 100 miles north of London. Her father was a grocer and active in local politics. The Robertses were reasonably well-to-do, but certainly not rich, and hard work, thrift, and living within one's means were values they instilled in the young Margaret. Asked about her father, she would say, "he gave me integrity."[6] During World War II, Thatcher studied chemistry at Oxford. She was a good, but not brilliant, student, relying on hard work to succeed.

After university, she worked for several years at a plastics company. She applied to another company, where she was rejected with the following verdict from the personnel department: "This woman is headstrong, obstinate and dangerously self-opinionated."[7] Not often has a personnel assessment been more correct (although lopsided). She married Denis Thatcher, a wealthy businessman who was some ten years older than she was, in 1951. Denis would be her closest confidant and steadfast supporter throughout her life. His support would be both private and public. If he felt a speech was not going well, he would sit at the back of the hall and clap and shout his agreement. Others would follow suit and the atmosphere of the meeting would be changed.[8]

During her days at Oxford, Thatcher was elected president of the Oxford University Conservative Association. This brought her in contact with prominent Conservative politicians at a young age. She was elected as a member of parliament (MP) in 1959, a position she held until 1992. She steadily rose in prominence. In October 1961, Prime Minister Harold

Macmillan promoted her to the frontbench as undersecretary at the Ministry of Pensions and National Insurance. After the Labour Party came to power in 1964, she held various positions as a member of the shadow cabinet. The Conservative Party returned to power in 1970, and she was appointed education secretary in the Heath administration.

Heath's dismal performance during the elections in 1974 led to calls for his resignation as leader of the Conservative Party. Thatcher announced her candidacy after several other heavyweights refused to stand against their leader. She defeated Heath, and on February 11, 1975, she became the party's leader.

Her years as Leader of the Opposition were difficult.[9] The Conservative MPs did not unite behind her, and her shadow cabinet simmered with divisions and discontent. In parliamentary debates, she was generally outmaneuvered by the wily Harold Wilson (Labour prime minister between 1974 and 1976) and the fatherly and condescending James Callaghan (1976–1979). Yet, the general population became increasingly receptive to her ideas about how to tackle Britain's decline.

In the 1979 election campaign, she was uncharacteristically nonconfrontational. Counseled by her image consultant Gordon Reece, the emphasis in her schedule was on soft photo opportunities rather than provocative speeches. The party's manifesto promised some limits on union activity, but they were nowhere near as radical an agenda as the one she really wanted to pursue on union reform.[10] One other aspect of the 1979 election deserves mentioning. In the 1970s, it was still unusual for political parties to rely on advertising agencies to "sell" their message to the population. But Margaret Thatcher decided to hire Tim Bell, managing director of Saatchi & Saatchi—at the time a small advertising agency. Bell suggested a strategy that consisted of appealing to voters' instincts with emotional messages, and hitting Labour hard by going on the attack. Its most famous ad was a billboard showing a dole line, tailing off into the distance. The slogan read in a screaming font, "LABOUR ISN'T WORKING." The poster would become a legend both in political and marketing history. It worked—the Conservative Party won the election handily, and Margaret Thatcher became the first elected woman leader of a major Western democracy. But would the National Union of Mineworkers let the Conservatives govern?

Figure 9.1 Margaret Thatcher, 1983

Source: Nationaal Archief

TAKING ON THE NATIONAL UNION OF MINEWORKERS

PRELUDE

Thatcher's first administration (1979–1983) passed restrictive legislation on trade unions. For example, trade unions became liable for civil damages if they committed unlawful acts, and it was made easier for employers to dismiss persistent troublemakers. Many in the cabinet resisted this legislation, but their voices were crushed by Thatcher, who vigorously supported her employment secretary, Norman Tebbit.[11] At the same time, labor unrest was rising. Steelworkers went on strike in 1980, demanding a 20 percent wage increase, which British Steel Corporation (a nationalized firm) could not possibly pay. In the past, the government would foot the bill for such wage increases, and Secretary of Industry Keith Joseph tried three times to get Thatcher to agree on a compromise. Her response was, "Don't wobble, Keith." Her iron determination won the day.

After thirteen weeks, the strike was broken, the first time in over twenty years this had happened to a major British union strike.[12] Yet, the Conservative Party was rattled by the social unrest, and many urged Thatcher to adopt a softer approach. She responded to her critics at the annual conference of her party on October 10, 1980, with a defiant speech in which she declared, "The lady's not for turning." Her speech made a deep impression on the delegates and the country. I vividly remember seeing it on the Dutch evening news.

Thatcher announces she will stay the course at the 1980 annual conference of the Conservative Party.

https://www.margaretthatcher.org/document/112661

In these early years of her administration, strikes by train drivers and health care workers—both nationalized industries—also ended in stale-mate or in humiliation for the unions. One union, however, stood proud and tall: the National Union of Mineworkers (NUM). In the first eighteen months of the Thatcher administration, the NUM won pay raises of 30 percent, which was unsustainable. In the winter of 1981, the National Coal Board (another nationalized entity) announced it would close twenty-three uneconomic pits with a loss of some 10,000 jobs. The NUM threatened to strike. Thatcher had to make a swift and humiliating U-turn. Why? She discovered that coal stocks at power stations would last for only six weeks before Britain would return to the conditions that toppled the govern-ments of Heath and Callaghan. The NUM was ecstatic that it had won so easily, and elected as its new president Arthur Scargill, to succeed the "moderate" Joe Gormley. Scargill was "a Marxist militant whose skill as a rabble-rousing orator was equaled by his determination to overthrow the elected [Conservative] government."[13]

THE MINERS' STRIKE OF 1984–1985

In the national elections held on June 9, 1983, Thatcher won a landslide victory, benefiting from a surge in popularity after winning the Falklands War against Argentina in 1982. This strengthened her hand politically; now was the moment for a final showdown with the NUM. The challenge was daunting. In the words of the home secretary, "The miners' union was considered as unstoppable as the rain."[14] Thatcher prepared carefully and gave instructions to build up huge stocks of coal at pit heads and power stations around the country.

Scargill did not hide his disdain for democratic government. On May 12, 1983, in response to being questioned on how he would respond if the Conservatives were reelected in the upcoming general election (which they were), Scargill replied, "My attitude would be the same as the attitude of the working class in Germany when the Nazis came to power. It does not mean that because at some stage you elect a government that you tolerate its existence."[15]

Scargill's position was that no pit should ever be closed for economic reasons, but only if its seams were exhausted or unsafe.[16] Thus, when the National Coal Board announced on March 6, 1984, that it would close twenty uneconomic pits, it was clear to everyone that a fight was at hand. However, Scargill was unsure whether he could get the required 55 percent majority, as per NUM rules, to call a national strike. So he orchestrated the strike without a national ballot. He persuaded miners at the most militant coalfields (e.g., Yorkshire) to walk out and then to send mass pickets to other regions to coerce them into joining the chain of action. Many miners, especially in Nottinghamshire, who did not want to join the strike were prevented from going to their pits by aggressive picketing from NUM militants.

Scargill felt invulnerable. Who was going to stop his tough miners? But he underestimated the iron determination of Thatcher. She directed the chief constable of Nottingham to uphold the lawful right of working men to go to work. Thatcher's orders changed everything. Her private secretary, Andrew Turnbull, said,

> Had she not given that signal, history would have been completely different. She realized at once that the battle she had been expecting had begun. Up to then, the police were being cautious. But when they were told their duty, they did it. And from then on at [Downing Street] No. 10 [the residence of the prime minister] we were on a war footing.[17]

Apart from the moral case to protect miners willing to work, Thatcher understood the importance of keeping coal moving from the Nottingham pits to the power plants. If this supply line could be increased, Scargill would be defeated; if it was broken, coal stocks might run out before the strike was ended. Thatcher also directed the organization of mobile police units so that forces from outside the strike areas could neutralize efforts by flying (mobile) pickets to stop the transport of coal to power stations.[18]

The strike was marred by violence. Brutal intimidation of working miners—vandalizing their cars and pelting them with stones, paint, or brake fluid—was not uncommon. Their families were not spared either. For example, the wife of a working miner was held down by youths while others scraped her face with a Brillo steel wool pad (to remove the "scab"). Bloody battles took place between pickets and police, horrifying law-abiding citizens. The worst instance happened on June 18, 1984, in South Yorkshire. Scargill had organized mass picketing to prevent coke being moved from the British Steel works. For several hours, between 5,000 and 10,000 pickets and 5,000 riot police fought pitched battles of a size and ferocity not seen since the English Civil War of the seventeenth century.[19]

The trade-union legislation introduced in Thatcher's first administration was crucially important in defeating the strike. The High Court ruled that the NUM had breached its own constitution by calling a national strike without holding a national ballot. Thus, as per the 1982 Employment Act, the NUM could not claim immunity for damages. Sequestration of NUM assets was ordered for contempt of court because of this breach of the law. It was one of the turning points in the dispute.[20] As the conflict dragged on, more and more strikers were reduced to poverty and decided to go back to work.

The strike was "the most bitter industrial dispute in British history."[21] At its height, the strike involved 142,000 mineworkers, and over 26 million work days were lost.[22] The strike ended on March 3, 1985, with a total defeat of the NUM.

AFTERMATH

The importance of Thatcher's victory over the NUM far superseded the breaking of the strike per se. It ended an era of strong trade unionism, which had lasted for a century. While trade unions in earlier times had been a progressive movement focused on improving working conditions, they had increasingly become a retrogressive force, hindering efforts to improve labor productivity and introduction of new technologies. After Thatcher's victory, the business climate changed, and trade union power steadily declined.

However, the social costs were high. Bitter divisions between working miners and striking miners remain to this day. In fact, as late as December 2019, at a Christmas party in Chapel Hill, I talked to the wife of the president of Executive Development of our business school about my book. Being from Yorkshire, she hoped I did not include Thatcher because she still hated her with a vengeance. Communities where pits were the only significant economic activity sunk into poverty after their closure. Jobs vanished in the tens of thousands, suicide rates increased, and a whole way of life going back sometimes for two centuries disappeared in many parts of Britain.

Thatcher's victory over the unions was keenly noted by unions on the Continent, who became more amenable to realistic solutions to economic problems facing Europe at the time, in order to pre-empt tough legislation. Her victory also was crucial in ending what has been called the "post-war consensus," consisting of heavy regulation, interventionist poli-cies ("Keynesianism"), nationalization of key industries, strong trade unions, high taxes, and a generous welfare state.[23] Her successes gave credibility to an alternative point of view—privatization, lower taxes, and reduction of absurdly generous social benefits. It encouraged an entire generation of young Europeans, including myself, not to rely on the state, but on their own hard work.

The economic and legal infrastructure that Thatcher built became so deeply embedded in British society that it largely remained in place when the Labour Party returned to power in 1997. In 2019, Labour under Jeremy Corbyn veered to the extreme left again. Its election manifesto called for a return to many of the socialist policies of the 1970s. The population wanted none of it. In the general election of December 12 of that year, Labour suf-fered its worst electoral defeat since the 1930s.

LESSONS

When Thatcher rose to prominence, Great Britain was the "sick man of Europe." When she left, the country was in far better shape. She brought the country back from the precipice of economic ruin, albeit at high social costs. What were some of the key elements of her leadership style?

Thatcher's one most outstanding leadership quality was her determi-nation to succeed. Time and again, she persevered against unfavorable odds. She had to overcome the pervasive sexism of the time, which was strong among Conservative grandees. Her determination is best shown by quoting her: "I had said at the beginning of the Government 'Give me six strong men and true, I will get through.' Very rarely did I have as many as six."[24] Yet, she got through. There is no doubt that it was her determination to fight until the end that led to victory in the miners' strike. The trade-union legislation introduced in her first administration could not have happened without Thatcher's strong and unequivocal sup-port, against the wishes of most of her cabinet. It was she who concluded that Employment Secretary Jim Prior had to go. Prior held that history showed unions could defeat any legislation if they wanted to; hence, the government should go slow and not rock the boat. She strongly disagreed. In her opinion, governments in the past had failed the nation through lack of nerve. She replaced Prior with the tough Norman Tebbit. How did she quickly know she made the right choice? Because, in her words, "The fact that the Left howled disapproval confirmed that he was just the right man for the job. He was someone they feared."[25] An interesting litmus test, also for today's leaders.

Thatcher was determined and strong-willed, but not rash. Indeed, contrary to what many believe, often she behaved with caution. In the years leading up to the 1979 election, she was rather circumspect about her true beliefs and radical new policies, lest she scare off the voters. After becoming prime minister, according to biographer Jonathan Aitken, "The surprise of her first cabinet appointments lay in their caution."[26] There was no tilt to the right, yet; she understood her position was too weak to rock the boat. She was also cautious not to alienate the other unions in her fight with the NUM.

At first sight, one might assume that extreme self-confidence was also one of her qualities. Her entire life, she appeared convinced of the correctness of her ideas (recall what the personnel department wrote about her in the late 1940s). Yet, beneath her outer shell of self-belief, there lay an inner level of insecurity and vulnerability. In a class-conscious society, as a grocer's daughter, she did not have the "natural" self-assuredness that comes with blue blood. Another area of insecurity was her self-perceived intellectual inadequacy. Thatcher felt she had a good brain but not a brilliant mind. To survive in the cutthroat world of British politics, she hid her insecurities to all but her most trusted inner circle.[27]

Courage was another outstanding quality of Thatcher's. As leader of the opposition, she was a passionate opponent of détente with the Soviet Union when it was bon ton in the West. She also spoke about the taboo subject of immigration. Many Britons were concerned about the number of immigrants from countries with very different cultures entering the country every year. Both Labour and Conservative politicians were afraid to discuss the subject out of fear of being labeled racist. Not so Thatcher. In a TV interview she said,

> People are really rather afraid that this country might be rather
> swamped by people with a different culture . . . [I]f there is any
> fear that it might be swamped, people are going to react and
> be rather hostile to those coming in. So, if you want good race
> relations, you have got to allay people's fears on numbers . . . So,
> we do have to hold out the prospect of an end to immigration
> except, of course, for compassionate cases.[28]

Regardless of one's own opinion on the topic, it took courage to speak
out like that. This and other speeches on immigration played unfavorably
in the shadow cabinet, where her position was not strong in the first
place; however, the public reacted much more favorably.[29] This highlights
another quality of Thatcher—her intuition. Time and again, she followed
her instinct rather than received wisdom and mostly she was right, at
least until the last years of her premiership. Her championship of self-
reliance, a smaller state, and the right to be better rewarded for hard work
were anathema to the political elites of Western Europe. Take Britain's
top income tax rate in 1978 of 83 percent. Thatcher not only believed
this was morally wrong, but instinctively knew that many Britons felt the
same way.

One glaring weakness of Thatcher's leadership style was her limited relationship-building skill. Telling is what her policy advisor John Hoskyns wrote
to her early in her premiership in an unusually blunt memo: "You break every
rule of good man-management. You bully weaker colleagues. You criticise
colleagues in front of each other and in front of their officials . . . You give little
praise or credit, and are too ready to blame others when things go wrong."[30]
Well, you might think that Thatcher was extreme; that this is not common
among leaders. Actually, such rude behavior is more common than you might
think. GE's Jack Welch was famous for his "public hangings." One of Welch's
famous quotes is: "Public hangings are teaching moments. Every company
has to do it. A teaching moment is worth a thousand CEO speeches."[31] In
December 2019, Steph Korey, co-founder of the direct-to-consumer luggage
brand Away, had to step down as CEO after an investigation highlighted
the company's toxic culture. Korey was infamous for tearing into employees

in public on the chat app Slack, which was used for intra-organizational communication.[32]

One of my friends is a senior manager at a large industrial company. His boss exhibited a near-dictatorial degree of directive leadership. He had the habit of dressing down his direct reports in the presence of colleagues and CEOs of contractor firms. This practice created a climate of fear. Nobody dared to voice their opinion; keeping your mouth shut became the survival strategy. The boss's directive leadership style improved operational performance significantly, but there was limited buy-in from his staff. It worked well for him, though. After four years, he moved to an even higher position, because he was the go-to guy who apparently delivered the results. However, as we shall see later, directive leadership style has a limited shelf life. He was let go less than two years later, after top management became aware of his bullying leadership style.

Until the mid-1980s, Thatcher could be characterized as an eagle. Almost everything Thatcher did as leader of the opposition and as prime minister was directed by her single central vision to cure Britain of its sickness—to make Britain strong politically and economically. However, she overlaid that hedgehog vision (which was always the more dominant dimension) with a fox-like flexibility in the means necessary to achieve this vision. For example, in April 1984, her government dropped its plan to have union members opt in rather than opt out of paying a membership contribution to the Labour Party because she wanted to avoid anything that might encourage other union leaders to make common cause with Scargill. More generally, her determined efforts to break the power of the unions were essentially one element of her goal to make Britain strong again, complemented by the privatization of state industries, cutting of taxes, and business regulation, as well as an assertive foreign policy. Her chief opponent, Scargill, was a hedgehog. At every twist and turn, his intransigence—no compromise, no pits to be closed—made things easier for the government.

However, after she won the third national election in 1987, Thatcher evolved into a pure hedgehog. She lost the tactical flexibility of the fox, and the relationship with her Conservative MPs—the one leadership resource no prime minister can ever do without—started to unravel. The Conservative Party fared badly in the local elections of May 1990, and a growing number of Conservative MPs began to panic that they might lose their jobs in the next national election.

People started to whisper it was time for Thatcher to go. The final straw came from the European Union, about which she had gradually become increasingly critical. The EU was pushing for more political integration and a common currency. She wanted none of this, but key members in her cabinet were much more positive. In exasperation, two erstwhile trusted lieutenants, Nigel Lawson (chancellor of the exchequer) and Geoffrey Howe (foreign secretary), resigned. Howe's resignation speech was a devastating attack on Thatcher's policies. He identified her categorical rejection of the common currency as a "tragic" mistake. Ironically, anybody who has followed the travails of the euro in the last two decades will probably conclude that Thatcher rather than Howe was right.

The Conservative Party had had enough of her and her domineering leadership style. In November 1990, she was forced to resign as prime minister. This final episode in her distinguished political career showed the danger of great success based on directive leadership. People may accept your directive leadership style as long as you can deliver the goodies (in this case electoral success). If that stops, your days are numbered.

CHAPTER TAKEAWAYS

- Thatcher started out as an exceptionally strong-willed eagle who led the country out of economic calamity. Later in her premiership, Thatcher became increasingly rigid in her thinking and morphed into a hedgehog. Her adversary Scargill was a hedgehog throughout.

- Thatcher was able to pursue many goals at the same time, while never losing sight of her overarching goal to make Britain strong again.

- Thatcher showed an exceptional degree of determination in all she did. One reason for this was that she had to overcome pervasive sexism—she had to show she was tougher than her male colleagues.

- Thatcher showed considerably more caution than people give her credit for.

- Thatcher possessed unparalleled political intuition, at least until late in her career.

- Thatcher was weak in relationship-building skills. That made her vulnerable when things no longer went her way.

- Thatcher's life highlights several directive leadership principles:

  ○ Determination and courage are qualities of a directive leader.

  ○ Being strong-willed and determined can be combined with being cautious.

  ○ Resistance to directive leadership is likely to rapidly increase if you can no longer deliver the goodies.

  ○ There is danger that continued success will calcify your initially fox-like (flexible) directive mind.

REFLECTIONS ON DIRECTIVE LEADERSHIP

DIRECTIVE LEADERS INITIATE the structure within which their followers are expected to operate. A directive leader sets clear standards of performance and makes the rules of the game clear to their followers. At first sight, the blood-stained leadership of the Spanish conquistador Hernán Cortés has little in common with that of the thrice–democratically elected British prime minister Margaret Thatcher. Yet there are instructive parallels in their lives, which can further our insight into directive leadership. They both (1) had a high need for control; (2) led from the front; (3) stiffened the spine of wobbly followers; (4) were action-oriented; but also (5) outwore their welcome.

1. NEED FOR CONTROL

Directive leaders have a general desire for control over events and situations, expressed by directing others as to what they should and should not do. Not everybody is comfortable doing that. For example, my wife has a very low desire for control. As a consequence, she has been less successful in mentoring PhD students where detailed directions of what to do are essential. On the other hand, she has been eminently successful working with people at her own level of seniority where directive leadership would generally be unacceptable. Cortés and Thatcher had no such qualms. They both were very comfortable giving orders to their followers, while they themselves hated to be controlled by others (these two traits often go hand in hand). For example, Cortés ignored the orders of Governor Velázquez not to go to Mexico. As leader of the opposition, Thatcher was not taking her personal policies from the shadow cabinet. As she saw it, she was a trailblazer establishing her followers rather than a spokesperson for a united front.[1]

2. LEAD FROM THE FRONT

Compared to adaptive and persuasive leadership, directive leadership puts a greater emphasis on leading not from behind but in front of your followers. Otherwise, your credibility suffers. Cortés and Thatcher certainly led from the front, either physically (Cortés) or politically (Thatcher). Leading from the front is tough because you get the blame when people are unhappy about changes or when things go wrong. Be prepared for that.

Academic articles are peer-reviewed, and getting an article in the *International Journal of Marketing*, the flagship journal of the European Marketing Academy, is a make-or-break issue for academic careers in Europe and beyond. When I became editor of *IJRM*, I decided to desk reject any paper that had little chance of making it through the review process. That is, I did not send these papers out for review, and thus I could not "hide" behind anonymous review reports. As a consequence, I sent out far fewer papers to the editorial review board members, who, in return, were expected to give their best time and effort to the papers that were not desk rejected. This led to a substantially improved and faster review process, but it also made me a bête noire among those colleagues who believed I did not value their research.

3. STIFFEN THE RESOLVE OF WOBBLY FOLLOWERS

Particularly in leadership situations where much is at stake, a leader may have to deal with followers who get scared and want to throw in the towel. This certainly was a situation faced by Cortés and Thatcher. Cortés had to take drastic measures—scuttling his fleet—to stiffen the resolve of his followers, but he faced near rebellions by discouraged and fearful ranks then and later. Thatcher faced strong pressure from within her cabinet and her Conservative Party to change course. Early in her premiership, she was already under pressure to moderate her efforts to liberalize the economy. Her response became legendary: "You turn if you want to. The lady's not for turning."

4. BE ACTION-ORIENTED

Another commonality between Cortés and Thatcher is that they both had a high action orientation. Whenever Cortés faced a crisis, he immediately launched into action. For example, after he heard that Pánfilo de Narváez had landed at Veracruz to arrest him, he divided his already small army and marched to the coast to confront him.[2] Thatcher is described as "brisk and businesslike, displaying an impatience to take and implement decisions."[3] Directive leadership means that things have to be accomplished, and once you see what needs to be done, dithering may very well undermine your credibility among your followers.

Both leaders also knew *when* to act. Directive leaders can generally expect stronger resistance than adaptive or persuasive leaders. This requires directive leaders to bide their time until the situation is right—which can be a challenge to them. For example, Cortés sent away a large contingent of Velázquez loyalists on a reconnaissance mission before implementing his legal coup of putting himself directly under the Crown rather than under Cuban governor Velázquez.[4] Thatcher's ability to bide her time is powerfully illustrated by giving in to the National Union of Mineworkers in 1981, when she knew her hand was weak.

5. DO NOT OVERSTAY YOUR WELCOME

It is instructive that Cortés's and Thatcher's careers as directive leaders were cut short. Cortés was accused of abuse of power and was deposed as governor of New Spain. Thatcher increasingly became a one-woman band who did not care about or even listen to the opinions of others, and she was forced to resign by her own Conservative members of parliament. While the specific reasons for the end of their directive leadership careers differed between Cortés and Thatcher, at some point, their followers got tired of following marching orders. As long as the leader continues to bring home the bacon (e.g., gold or electoral success), followers have a vested interest in remaining loyal, but if the leader is no longer able to do that, support can crumble fast. It remains to be seen how long directive leaders like Turkey's president Recep Erdogan or Russia's president Vladimir Putin remain in power (at least through democratic means) once they fail to deliver to their followers. And why is the leadership of China so obsessed with economic growth? Because they realize that the population might acquiesce to their directive leadership as long as China's citizens experience a steady increase in income. Once that stops, unrest becomes a distinct possibility.

For an example in an entirely different domain, consider the career of José Mourinho, one of the most successful soccer coaches of all time. He has won titles with five of Europe's most storied soccer clubs: Porto, Chelsea, Inter Milan, Real Madrid, and Manchester United. He is a brilliant coach, yet he hardly ever manages to stay with any club for even three years. Almost any sports coach must have a healthy dose of directive leadership, but Mourinho is exceptional in this regard. After about two years, the players become tired of his hectoring style and increasingly resent his criticism, often uttered in public, on them not carrying out his orders. This leads to a breakdown in Mourinho's relationship with key players, and team performance declines dramatically. He is fired and the cycle is repeated at the next club.[5] The last time he was sacked was in December 2018 by Manchester United, which cost the club over $25 million. As I was writing this chapter, Tottenham Hotspur announced it had hired Mourinho, on a contract of 3.5 years. Will the Spurs be any different? Or will they prove the saying: "Only a fool does the same thing again and expects a different outcome"?

To assess whether directive leadership is a style that suits you, consider the following questions.

1. Do you like control over events? How comfortable are you setting the directions for your followers?

2. Are you able to clearly articulate what you want to your followers? What evidence do you have that your intentions are accurately understood by others?

3. Are you comfortable leading from the front? Or does that create too much anxiety?

4. Have you had experience with situations where you had to encourage others and stiffen their resolve? How successful were you in these efforts?

5. Do others regard you as a person of action? Can you give examples of when you took charge and were able to lead change?

6. Which directive leaders do you recognize in your own professional and/ or personal environment? How do you relate to their style of leadership?

7. What feedback have you ever received that portrayed you as a directive leader?

8. In what situation(s) have you been where being a "directive leader" would have been most effective? What did you actually do and with which results?

PART FOUR

DISRUPTIVE LEADERSHIP — BREAK WITH THE PAST

ST. PETER DISCARDS ONE THOUSAND YEARS OF RELIGIOUS DOCTRINE

"Whatever you bind on earth will be bound in heaven, and whatever you loose on earth will be loosed in heaven."
—JESUS CHRIST TO ST. PETER

Leadership Dilemma: Should Peter require Gentile Christians to follow the Mosaic Law?

CONTEXT

Jesus Christ was born in c. 4 B.C. in Bethlehem, a town in Judea, which was part of the Roman Empire.[1] He was crucified in Jerusalem in c. 29 A.D. After his death, his work was continued by his closest associates, the apostles.[2] The apostles called upon their fellow Jews to repent and embrace Jesus as their Lord. Important for this chapter is that Jesus's followers were uncertain about a crucial question: For whom was Jesus's message intended? Who, in marketing terminology, was the target market? Was his message for Jews only, or for the entire world? If it was for the entire world, how should one square this with the strict laws of Judaism? Did non-Jews have to follow the Mosaic Law in order to be saved?

In the early years after Jesus's death, this was of little relevance, as the apostles focused on areas solely inhabited by Jews: Jerusalem and Judea. The religious authorities initially took little note of the apostles' activity, thinking that the matter was settled after Jesus's crucifixion. But as the number of Jewish converts grew, the authorities started to persecute Christians. Many fled to other parts of Palestine, but for the time being, the apostles stayed in Jerusalem.[3]

Thus, the religious authorities inadvertently helped to spread the new faith. Christians established communities in many other towns and villages in Palestine, then in Syria—most notably Antioch. Antioch, called the "Queen of the East," was the third-largest city in the Roman Empire. It was a cosmopolitan place in which many different nationalities and religions lived in close vicinity. In Antioch, the term "Christians" (meaning "follower of Christ") was used for the first time.[4]

Christianity entered a new phase with the conversion of Paul, a highly educated Jew who was born in Tarsus (present-day Turkey). He was a Roman citizen, fluent in Greek (the lingua franca of the eastern part of the Roman Empire), and had been trained by the best rabbis in Jerusalem.[5] Thus, his theological knowledge was formidable. While the original apostles were focused on making converts in Palestine, Paul's emphasis was to bring the new faith to the much larger, Greek-speaking part of the Roman Empire.

In 46 A.D., Paul and a fellow apostle named Barnabas set out on a missionary trip to Turkey. Once entering a new city there, they would start to preach in the synagogue, but were usually met with resistance from orthodox Jews.[6] This then led Paul and Barnabas to reach out to the non-Jewish

("Gentile") population in that city, who were usually more receptive to their message. They established a church in each city they visited and appointed elders. After two years, Paul and Barnabas returned to Antioch and reported to the Christian community there about their success with the Gentiles—news that was received with great enthusiasm.

The two apostles got pushback, however, when orthodox Jewish Christians from Jerusalem visited Antioch. The issue was whether it was necessary for Gentile Christians to observe the Mosaic Law to be saved (e.g., be circumcised, honor the strict Sabbath rules, and adhere to many dietary restrictions). In other words, was it necessary to become a Jew if you wanted to become a Christian? This led to a sharp dispute between orthodox Jewish Christians and Paul and Barnabas. The importance of this question facing the early Church cannot be overstated. At stake was the overarching vision on Christianity—was it a Jewish sect or a new faith? This required a judgment call by the Church's highest echelon, and its leader, Peter.

PETER

Peter was born in c. 1 A.D. He was of humble origin, a fisherman from Bethsaida in Galilee. Originally, he was called Simon, but Jesus gave him the Aramaic name Kepha, or Petrus in Latin, meaning "rock." Peter was one of the first followers of Christ, who called Peter and his brother Andrew with the words: "Come, follow me and I will make you fishers of men."[7] Peter had a unique position among the twelve apostles. He is always mentioned first among the apostles in the Gospels and in the book of *Acts*. Jesus singled him out as the leader of the future church with the following momentous words:

> I tell you that you are Peter, and on this rock I will build my church, and the gates of Hades will not overcome it. I will give you the keys of the kingdom of heaven; whatever you bind on earth will be bound in heaven, and whatever you loose on earth will be loosed in heaven.[8]

An abbreviated version of these words is written in Latin on the inside of the magnificent dome of St. Peter's Basilica in Rome: *Tu es Petrus et super hanc petram aedificabo ecclesiam mean et tibi dabo claves regni caelorum* ("You are 'Rock' and on this rock I will build my Church, to you I will give the keys of the kingdom of heaven"). Jesus reiterated Peter's special position after the Resurrection by commanding him, "Take care of my sheep."[9]

After Jesus's death, Peter became the leader of the fledgling church. According to the New Testament book *Acts of the Apostles*, he took the lead in selecting the replacement for the traitor Judas Iscariot, gave the "coming out" sermon on Pentecost, and rendered judgment upon the deceitful Ananias and Sapphira, among others. Peter left Jerusalem after King Herod Agrippa tried to kill him (c. 44 A.D.), and James the Just became the leader ("bishop") of the Jerusalem church. James the Just was respected by the orthodox Jewish Christians for his austere and devoted lifestyle. He was vegetarian, wore no sandals, drank no alcohol, and spent hours every day in the temple praying.[10]

There is little information about which areas and places Peter went to, but it is certain that he visited different parts of Palestine, Antioch, and Rome. He was the first pope (bishop of the congregation in Rome) and was martyred in Rome under the emperor Nero (c. 64 or 68 A.D.). The legitimacy of all subsequent bishops of Rome to lead the Church is based on the claim that Peter's powers to bind and loose were inherited by them.[11] Peter would have to ultimately rule on the dispute between Paul and the orthodox Jewish Christians.

COUNCIL OF JERUSALEM AND THE AFTERMATH

During his travels in Palestine in the early 40s A.D., Peter had a vision, described in *Acts of the Apostles* (Figure 10.1).[12] In his vision, heaven opened and something like a large sheet was let down to earth. It contained various four-footed animals, as well as reptiles and birds—all forbidden foods under Jewish Law. According to *Acts*,

Figure 10.1 Peter's Vision

Source: Illustration from Henry Davenport Northrop, "Treasures of the Bible," published 1894

Then a voice told him, "Get up, Peter. Kill and eat." "Surely not, Lord!" Peter replied. "I have never eaten anything impure or unclean." The voice spoke to him a second and third time, "Do not call anything impure that God has made clean."

While Peter was contemplating the meaning of this vision, three men came to him on behalf of a Roman army centurion, a Gentile named Cornelius. The men asked Peter to visit Cornelius in Caesarea. Peter went to Caesarea, entered Cornelius's house, had dinner with him, and baptized him. All of this was against the Mosaic Law. So, when Peter went up to Jerusalem, he was sharply criticized by the orthodox Jewish Christians. He defended himself by explaining that he interpreted the vision to convey the message that God accepts people from every nation. The Jerusalem community appeared to accept this, at least for the time being, probably regarding it as an isolated case.[13] Things came to a head some years later due to Paul's success in converting Gentiles to

Christianity. Now, the question of whether Gentile Christians should adhere to the Mosaic Law could no longer be ignored. A meeting was called in Jerusalem in the fall of 48 A.D. to try to resolve the issue.[14]

Three groups of people attended the Council of Jerusalem: the apostles, the elders of the church in Jerusalem, and members of the Jerusalem congregation.[15] Unlike the church in cosmopolitan Antioch, which was the bastion of Gentile Christianity, the Jerusalem congregation was dominated by orthodox Jewish Christians. The atmosphere was tense. Paul and Barnabas defended their actions, but the orthodox stuck to the position that "the Gentiles must be circumcised and required to keep the Law of Moses."[16] It proved impossible to reach a solution. This is understandable— at stake was how to deal with one thousand years of divinely ordained laws. The meeting was adjourned. In the meantime, Paul had separate conversations with Peter, John, and James the Just.

The next day, discussions continued until Peter intervened, and this proved decisive. Referring to his vision and his earlier visit to Cornelius, he argued that God apparently made no distinction between Jews and Gentiles and that the church leadership should not burden Gentiles with the "yoke" of the Mosaic Law.[17] For the orthodox Jewish Christians, James the Just was their last hope, but he agreed with Peter. However, he proposed as a face-saving measure a compromise that Gentile Christians abstain from food sacrificed to idols, from the meat of strangled animals, and from sexual immorality. Peter's decision, together with James's requirements, was accepted by the council. It seemed the matter was settled.

Not so fast. First, nothing had been decided about what was required of Jewish Christians. Did they still have to follow the Mosaic Law or not?[18] If this were the case, for all practical purposes there would be two types of Christians: Jews who would have been held to a higher standard because they followed the Mosaic Law, and Gentiles, who would be some kind of lesser Christians, as they would have been held to a lower standard.

Second, it became increasingly clear that the orthodox Jewish Christians saw the decision more as a temporary defeat than as a fait accompli.[19] They continued to be unwilling to have unfettered social intercourse with Gentile Christians, as that was not allowed under the Mosaic Law.

Illustrative of the unresolved tension is what happened some time later

(c. 49 A.D.) in Antioch.[20] Peter was there at the time and freely and enthusiastically shared meals with the Gentile Christians. But when orthodox Jewish Christians arrived from Jerusalem and refused to mingle with the Gentiles, Peter also separated himself from the Gentile Christians. He did this so as not to offend the orthodox group, but it signaled that, indeed, there were two types of Christians. Other Jewish Christians, including even Barnabas, followed the example of their leader. This confused and dismayed the Gentiles. Paul intervened and publicly confronted Peter about the inappropriateness of his behavior, and Peter conceded that he was wrong.

Although it was not obvious at the time, and despite his temporary relapse in Antioch, Peter's decision forced a decisive breach with Judaism. Perhaps Jewish religious leaders might have accepted orthodox Jewish Christians as a particular sect within Judaism—after all, at the time, there were many Jewish sects. However, they would never accept uncircumcised people who did not obey the Law of Moses. After the Council of Jerusalem, there was no going back. It meant that devout orthodox Jewish Christians at some point had to choose between Christianity and the Mosaic Law. Most chose the millennium-old precedent of the Law, and Christianity in Palestine gradually disappeared. The process was accelerated by the destruction wrought by two failed revolts against mighty Rome (in 66–73 A.D. and 132–136 A.D.).

Leaving aside theological considerations, let us look at the practical import of Peter's decision. Of the approximately 65 million inhabitants of the Roman Empire, 1 million were Jews living in Palestine and a few million Jews were living elsewhere in the empire. According to sociologist Rodney Stark, "The Law set Jews apart as fully in the first century as in the nineteenth and prevented them from full participation in civic life. In both eras, the Jews were in the unstable and uncomfortable position of social marginality."[21] Peter's decision broke Christianity out of this cultural-social niche. At the "expense" of forgoing a target market of a few million at most, Christianity could reach out to a much larger target market of over 60 million Gentiles.[22]

The outcome was spectacular. Despite initial struggles and persecutions, in 350 A.D. there were around 30 million Christians in the Roman Empire (about 50 percent of the population),[23] and, in 380 A.D., Emperor

Theodosius I made it the empire's sole authorized religion. By that time, Christianity had also spread beyond the empire to Germanic tribes, who would overrun the western part of the empire in the next century. In the twenty-first century, Christianity is the world's largest religion, with around 2.2 billion believers.

LESSONS

In my opinion, Peter was an eagle. From the moment he became the leader of the young Christian sect, his overarching goal was to spread the Gospel of Jesus Christ.[24] While he wavered and searched how best to achieve this, it was this mission that animated all of his actions, and for which he was prepared to die. We have limited information on his flexibility regarding the means he employed to achieve this life goal, with one major exception, which is the topic of this chapter. Peter undoubtedly started out with the assumption that being—or becoming—Jewish was one indispensable means to become a Christian.

We can be confident that Peter would regard himself as a servant leader rather than as a disruptive leader. Yet, I discuss him under disruptive leadership because the decision he made in response to the dilemma of what to do with Gentile Christians was one momentous historical disruption that lifted the world out of one groove and set it in another. How did Peter achieve disruptive change? He did not have wealth or the deep knowledge of somebody like Paul. Jewish leaders described him as "unschooled."[25] His brain was characterized as slow but steady, and his speech as clumsy.[26] Several times in his life, he backed away when he received strong pushback. After an emphatic promise of loyalty to Jesus ("I will lay down my life for you"), he denied knowing Jesus three times on that same night to save his own life.[27] In Antioch, he backed away from Gentiles when he felt the opprobrium of the orthodox Christian Jews.

But Peter also had significant strengths. He had positional power as leader of the Church to bind and loosen, although there is no hard evidence that he used this to force a decision at the Council of Jerusalem.[28]

Peter was a warm and enthusiastic person, and he had great integrity. Despite claims that he was a clumsy speaker, he was able to appeal to large groups of people who appreciated his forthright speech.[29] And over the course of his life—notwithstanding episodes of backing away under pressure—he exhibited great firmness. He was arrested twice by the authorities in Jerusalem, but refused to budge from spreading the Gospel. He bore the ultimate responsibility to jettison a millennium of divinely revealed tradition. It is difficult to imagine the anguish he must have felt when breaking with the system of norms and rituals that constituted his world.[30] What leaders have the courage to make such a break with their own or their organization's roots? For example, it took Unilever's leadership decades before they decided in 2017 to sell the (underperforming) margarine unit. Why? It was one of the two businesses that stood at the basis of the firm. And that is just margarine.[31]

Peter could also draw upon his life experiences. In fact, his biggest failure—like Roosevelt's polio, a crucible, using the terminology of Warren Bennis (see chapter 7)—turned out to be his biggest gain. Earlier in life, Peter exhibited rash and self-confident truculence, boasting about his supreme love for Jesus.[32] Peter's fall—denying Christ when the going got tough—taught him profound humility. From then on, he was willing to listen to the arguments of others, accept criticism, and change his ways if he was proven wrong, including in Antioch. About what transpired in Antioch, Cardinal Johannes de Jong wrote, "It is not clear what to admire more: the prescience of the Teacher of the Gentiles [Paul] or the humility of the Prince of the Apostles [Peter]."[33]

Humility does not imply low self-esteem, but rather a keen understanding of one's own cognitive and emotional limitations. The best definition of humility, in my view, is: not thinking less of yourself, but thinking of yourself less.[34] Many disruptive leaders may have such high self-confidence and towering ego (see next chapter for an example) that they are simply not open to seeing, let alone acknowledging, that they are wrong. If anything, humility is even more important if you are a disruptive leader in a nonprofit organization. These organizations rely on large groups of volunteers who can simply leave the organization at little cost to themselves if they do not like radical changes. Disruptive changes in such organizations can only be achieved by changing people's hearts and minds. This requires lengthy discussions involving many people, led by a leader who is willing to listen. If the leader relies on their institutional position to push through disruptive change, the results are likely going to be counterproductive. And, even then, there will be fallout. Ultimately, Peter and his successors were not able to keep the orthodox Jewish Christians on board.[35] Even with the best of intentions, organizational casualties are an unavoidable corollary of disruptive decisions.

My brother Paulus is a member of an evangelical church in Gouda (the Netherlands). After lengthy discussions and consultations, the board of elders decided that women and men were to be given exactly the same opportunities. Initially, nothing changed, as there were no female elders yet, and when a female gave a sermon, opponents discreetly did not attend. Things came to a head when, a year later, proposed candidates for the new board of elders included women. The opponents now became very vocal in their opposition, but after another heated debate, in which some elders who were getting wobbly had to be reminded of their earlier support for this position, the board of elders stuck by its earlier decision. Ultimately, a much smaller percentage of the members left the church than feared, and the church never regretted the disruptive decision.

In chapter 6, we have seen that Campbell-Bannerman is an example of a "Level 5 leader." Recall that Level 5 leaders blend deep personal humility with intense professional will.[36] Peter is another example. Interestingly, Peter's very names combine these two qualities. His Hebrew name, Simon, means "listen," while Peter denotes firmness (rock), pointing to the steely side of his character. Simon Peter disrupted the world—and set his organization on the path to greatness—with humility, firmness, courage, integrity, warmth, enthusiasm, and life experiences garnered from overcoming failure. There are great secular disruptive leaders who share many of these qualities. Abraham Lincoln comes to mind. Now, that is an encouraging message for those of us who do not have the abrasive brilliance of an Elon Musk or a Steve Jobs.

CHAPTER TAKEAWAYS

- Peter was a (reluctant) eagle. He combined his life goal of spreading the Gospel of Jesus Christ with a willingness to discard the greatest barrier to its success in the Roman world.

- Peter's character was formed by his failures, most notably the denial of Jesus. In the terminology of leadership theorist Warren Bennis, this transformative event was a "crucible." It taught him humility and willingness to listen to others.

- Peter exhibited great courage—both in body (physical harm, persecution) and in doctrine. Note that religious doctrine has been a matter of (eternal) life and death since time immemorial.

- Peter is an example of a Level 5 leader—exhibiting the paradoxical combination of deep personal humility and strong professional courage and firmness.

- Peter regarded himself as a servant leader, not a disruptive leader. Yet, his disruptive decision changed world history.

- Peter's life highlights several disruptive leadership principles, especially for nonprofit organizations:

  ° Humility as leadership quality to push through disruptive change

  ° The importance of extensive discussions before disruptive change

  ° The need to resist temptation to use positional power to push through disruptive change

  ° The need to stay the course in the face of resistance that can be expected to be fierce

  ° Willingness to accept that you cannot keep everybody "on board"— expect some followers to leave the organization

FISHER LAUNCHES A SHIP

"Big risks bring big success!"
—ADMIRAL JOHN ARBUTHNOT FISHER

Leadership Dilemma: Should the Royal Navy wipe out with one stroke its overwhelming strategic advantage, on which the safety of the country and its empire rested?

CONTEXT

When Queen Victoria celebrated her Diamond Jubilee on June 26, 1897, with a naval review involving 165 British warships, Great Britain appeared at the zenith of its power.[1] It accounted for nearly 20 percent of world manufacturing output, and its per capita level of industrialization was 50 percent higher than that of the United States and twice that of Germany.[2] London was the financial capital of the world, with pound sterling the anchor of the global financial system, comparable to what the dollar is today. Britain both imported and exported more than any other country, and its merchant marine was the world's largest by far. And then there was the British Empire, on which the sun never set, comprising one-quarter of the world's land surface. It was a sea empire, scattered around the globe, its territories connected to each other and the mother country by sea lanes and protected by a string of naval bases. It was won, held, and protected by sea power. Indeed, ever since Admiral Horatio Nelson smashed the combined French-Spanish fleet at Trafalgar on October 21, 1805, without losing a single ship, Britain ruled the waves.

Britain knew, and all its rivals knew, that without the Royal Navy Britain was very vulnerable. The country had to import much of its food and, in the words of Germany's Emperor Wilhelm II, it had "a contemptible small army."[3] On the other hand, as long as the Royal Navy maintained absolute naval supremacy, no foreign power could touch the British Isles, while Britain could do largely what it wanted. Consequently, in the nineteenth century, the Royal Navy was oftentimes larger than all other navies in the world combined.

But Britain's strategic situation was deteriorating. Other nations, especially the United States and Germany, were rapidly closing the manufacturing lead Britain had enjoyed since the dawn of the Industrial Revolution. Between 1880 and 1900, Britain's share of world manufacturing output decreased from 22.9 percent to 18.5 percent, while Germany's increased from 8.5 percent to 13.2 percent and America's, from 14.7 percent to 23.6 percent.[4] War with the United States seemed unlikely, but tensions with Germany were rising. The key problem was that Great Britain was satisfied with the status quo, while an increasingly assertive German Reich wanted its own place "under the sun." Germany felt constrained geographically—no ship could reach Germany without passing the British Isles—and harbored global ambitions. But as long as Britain ruled the waves, it could bottle up German ships in harbor and seize German colonies. This was unacceptable for a proud, rising, and rapidly industrializing power.

Germany sought to rectify this situation by building a powerful navy of its own, with the goal of frightening Britain into an alliance. This proved a catastrophic misunderstanding. For Britain, command of the sea was a greater necessity than any Continental alliance.[5] Starting with Germany's Second Naval Law in 1900, the Anglo-German naval arms race began in earnest. Britain had a large lead, but the Germans were catching up.

At the same time, not all was well in the Royal Navy. The victory at Trafalgar had been so overwhelming that a culture of complacency and conservatism had crept into the organization. Weapons and tactics in naval warfare were changing rapidly, but many senior officers preferred not to notice. According to historian Robert Massie, "Anything new was suspicious and potentially dangerous." For example, when torpedoes were being developed and tested, the First Sea Lord's[6] reaction was that "there were no torpedoes when he came to sea and he did not see why the devil there should be any of the beastly things now."[7] By getting out of step, one might make a mistake; by remaining in step, one eventually reached the top. For instance, when a good idea was submitted to the Admiralty, one of its members scribbled across the paper: "On what authority does this lieutenant put forward such a proposal?" Even gunnery, the hallmark of the fleet under Admiral Nelson, left much to be desired. In 1881, the Royal Navy fired 3,000 rounds at the fortresses protecting Egypt's harbor city of Alexandria and made . . . ten hits![8]

In short, the Royal Navy was stuck in the past while Germany was making rapid advances. Although many inside and outside the navy refused to recognize this, Great Britain urgently needed somebody to disrupt the so-called senior service in the British military. That person was Admiral Jacky Fisher.

JACKY FISHER

John Arbuthnot Fisher, commonly known as Jacky Fisher, was born on January 25, 1841, in the British colony of Ceylon (present-day Sri Lanka). His father was an officer in the 78th Highlanders who decided to become a coffee planter. This enterprise failed miserably, which left the family in dire financial circumstances. To lessen the financial burden, Jacky was sent back to England at the age of six to live with his maternal grandparents.

Although penniless, he was able to enter the Royal Navy as a cadet at age thirteen via family connections. In those days, boys who were accepted by the navy went directly to sea to learn by doing. Over the next two decades, Fisher served on different ships that were stationed in various places around the world. He also did four tours of duty at the navy's elite gunnery school near Portsmouth, where he studied and taught gunnery and torpedoes. Fisher possessed an inexorable energy and a towering self-confidence. He was also very competent. When Fisher took his lieutenant's examination, he received top grades in seamanship and gunnery, and achieved the highest score ever for navigation.[9]

Fisher steadily rose through the ranks, and in 1899 he became commander in chief of the Mediterranean fleet, Britain's principal battle fleet at the time. This fleet guarded the all-important shipping route to India—the jewel in the crown of the British Empire. As with previous assignments, he found the state of readiness and gunnery skills grossly deficient, but within three years he whipped the fleet into superb fighting shape. The culture change was profound. Before he arrived, conversations in the officers' messes were mainly confined to trivialities. After a year of Fisher's regime, conversations were about controversies on tactics, strategy, torpedo warfare, or blockades.

In 1902 he took the appointment as Second Sea Lord in charge of personnel, then, in 1904, Fisher was appointed First Sea Lord. The penniless boy had arrived at the top of the British naval establishment. His career success was not due to money, relations, or playing it safe. In fact, he was outspoken, if not blunt. He ignored seniority and railed against bureaucracy. Fisher stood for change, reform, efficiency, and readiness. And as First Sea Lord, Fisher revolutionized the navy, instituting many disruptive reforms.[10] He broke down the traditional barriers of social class that plagued the navy. All cadets, regardless of social origins, would from then on receive the same education in seamanship and engineering (the latter being seen as "unworthy" for upper-class cadets). He drastically reduced the number of ships by striking 154 old and—in his view—useless ships off the active list. He redeployed the Royal Navy to home waters to counter the growing German threat. He introduced two new types of ships: the destroyer and the battlecruiser.

Yet, his most important decision was to engage in creative destruction by building an entirely new type of battleship, the HMS *Dreadnought*.[11] Coined by the economist Joseph Schumpeter, "creative destruction" dictates an organization must be willing to introduce a new product or business model that destroys the basis of its current success in order to remain viable in the future.

Figure 11.1 Jacky Fisher, 1915

CREATIVE DESTRUCTION: BUILDING THE *DREADNOUGHT*

In 1900, the backbone of each major navy was the battleship—a floating gun platform designed to destroy enemy ships at a distance. Naval strength was assessed by the number of battleships a country had. Standard battleships in all major navies had four 12-inch guns, supported by various guns of smaller caliber. From the turn of the century onward, Fisher started discussions with navy designers to develop a new type of fast, all-big-gun battleship. Earlier than others in the Royal Navy, he sensed where naval technology was going. In 1903, an article appeared in *Jane's Fighting Ships*, proposing an all-big-gun ship.[12] He was aware that U.S. and Japanese navies were also becoming interested in faster, heavier-gunned ships. Although it was not obvious at the time what would come of their efforts, Fisher decided to take the initiative.

In December 1904, he created a Committee on Designs to develop the blueprint for a new battleship with a uniform armament of 12-inch guns and 21 knots of speed, which was 50 percent faster than existing battleships. The members on the committee were young, exceptionally able, and eager to embrace new ideas. While most were Fisher protégés, they were by no means his puppets. Fisher gave them considerable leeway in coming up with a blueprint. After seven weeks of deliberation, they submitted their report. Figure 11.2 provides the overall diagram.

The resulting ship carried ten 12-inch guns. This made the HMS *Dreadnought* the equivalent of two or three (dependent on the fire line) earlier battleships. To arrive at a speed of 21 knots, the standard reciprocating steam engines would not suffice. The solution was to use a new, essentially untried system of steam turbine engines. The committee hesitated, given the enormous risks involved. The die was cast when the navy's chief designer and committee member, Sir Philip Watts, said that if they were fitted with reciprocating engines, these ships would be out of date within five years.

Fisher wanted to make the *Dreadnought* unsinkable. On existing ships, each compartment was sealed off by watertight doors. These doors were closed when action was imminent, but when disaster struck unexpectedly (think of a mine or torpedo), it was often too late to close the doors. Fisher's solution was true to form—that is, radical. Each compartment in the hull

Figure 11.2 Diagram of the HMS Dreadnought

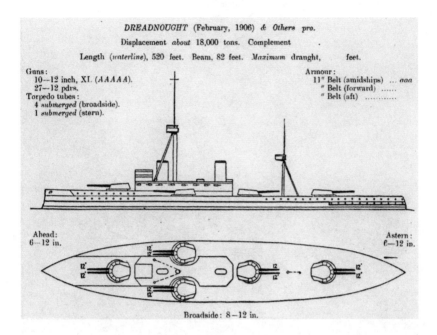

DREADNOUGHT (February, 1906) & Others pro.

Displacement *about* 18,000 tons. Complement

Length (*waterline*), 520 feet. Beam, 82 feet. *Maximum* draught,   feet.

Guns:
  10--12 inch, XI. (*A A A A A*).
  27--12 pdrs.
Torpedo tubes:
  4 *submerged* (broadside).
  1 *submerged* (stern).

Armour:
  11" Belt (amidships) ... *aaa*
  " Belt (forward) ......
  " Belt (aft) ....

Ahead:
6--12 in.

Astern:
6--12 in.

Broadside: 8--12 in.

of the *Dreadnought* was a self-contained unit with no horizontal access at all. Men could only enter these spaces on ladders from a hatch on the main deck. If the hull of a particular compartment were to rip open, the men in that compartment would drown, but the rest of the ship would survive.

Standardized components, a first in the Royal Navy, helped to cut construction time from a previous record of thirty-one months to twelve months. Instead of having each of the ship's great steel plates cut individually, Fisher ordered them in advance by the dozen in standard sizes and had them piled up ready in the dockyard. The *Dreadnought*'s very short construction time was intended to demonstrate to foreign powers that Britain could build an unassailable lead with this new type of battleship.[13] Standardization also helped to drive down costs, which made it easier for Prime Minister Arthur Balfour to get it approved by Parliament. In fact, for an increase of only 10 percent in costs, Fisher was equipping the navy with a ship two to three times as powerful. On October 1, 1906, one year from the laying of her keel, the *Dreadnought* went to sea and performed admirably. It became the flagship of the Royal Navy's massive Home Fleet in 1907.

Figure 11.3 HMS Dreadnought *at Sea*

The *Dreadnought* sent shock waves around the world. It was obvious that the ship was so revolutionary it made all existing battleships obsolete. This was also the reason why Fisher was heavily attacked by colleagues in the Admiralty, members of Parliament, and the press. Critics regarded the building of the *Dreadnought* as a horrendous blunder because it threw away the Royal Navy's overwhelming superiority in existing (quickly dubbed pre-dreadnought) battleships. Admiral Frederick Richards, who was First Sea Lord from 1893 to 1899, expressed the outrage of many: "The whole British Fleet was . . . morally scrapped and labeled obsolete at the moment when it was at the zenith of its efficiency and equal not to two but practically to all the fleets in the world combined."[14]

Yet, after the introduction of the *Dreadnought*, there was no turning back. Something close to a panic ensued in Berlin. The German navy was in the process of launching multiple battleships that would be obsolete upon arrival. Before it was able to switch to dreadnought-class ships, nine additional dreadnought ships were already under construction for the Royal Navy. The Kiel

Canal, the waterway by which the German navy shuttled safely between the North Sea and the Baltic, was too shallow to accommodate dreadnought-size ships. Deepening the canal required years of effort and tremendous expenditure, money that otherwise could have been spent on warships.[15]

When World War I (1914–1918) started, Britain had twenty-nine dreadnought-type battleships versus Germany's seventeen. On the outbreak of the war, Britain established a naval blockade of Germany. Like Britain, Germany relied heavily on imports from overseas to feed its population and supply its war industry. The only way to escape the stranglehold was to defeat the Grand Fleet (the Royal Navy's fleet in home waters) in a "mother of all sea battles." Winston Churchill, who was secretary of the navy at the time, summarized what was at stake when he said that the commander of the Grand Fleet was the only man on either side who could lose the war in an afternoon. That afternoon happened on May 31, 1916, near Jutland (Denmark), when the world's two biggest navies clashed in one of the largest naval battles in history. Although the German navy acquitted itself well, the Royal Navy's numerical supcriority—twenty-eight dreadnoughts and nine battlecruisers versus Germany's sixteen and five, respectively—allowed it to retain the upper hand.

The Royal Navy's blockade continued unabated, slowly strangling Germany. If not for Britain's naval superiority, there is little doubt that Germany would have won the war. In World War II, the Germans did not even make a serious effort to challenge Britain's naval mastery.

LESSONS

Fisher was a true eagle. The survival and success of the Royal Navy was the overriding goal of Fisher's life, animating his actions over a fifty-year career. To achieve this goal he would use any means necessary. For example, Fisher did not like torpedoes any more than his peers did, but while they wrote them off as "cowardly" and "un-English," Fisher realized that, in the hands of the Royal Navy, they could be used to send enemy battleships to the bottom of the ocean. Building the *Dreadnought* is the greatest example of how Fisher developed new means to reach his goal.

I have told the *Dreadnought* story to a multitude of audiences, ranging from executive MBAs and executives to the cadets at West Point. In
business terms, Fisher was the CEO of a huge, complex organization with
interests around the world. During his time as "CEO" (1904–1910), he—

- Pushed through a complete restructuring of the organization

- Cut countless serviceable business lines (scrapped many ships)

- Pulled off creative destruction by introducing a new product in its main
  product line that destroyed its existing business, where it had a commanding lead over its competitors (HMS *Dreadnought*)

- Accomplished all this against fierce resistance both from within the
  organization and from outside stakeholders

In this case, however, Fisher was not merely the CEO of a company
but the head of the immensely powerful Royal Navy. And at stake was
not a company, but the security and very survival of a country and its
empire—the largest empire the world had ever seen—against the threat
of a new entrant in the "market": Germany. So, what does the case study
on Fisher tell us about what it takes to be a disruptive leader? I single out
five key qualities: continuously challenge, analyze, and learn; prioritize
long-term over short-term; ensure top-level support; maintain unrelenting focus; and have a thick skin.

CONTINUOUSLY CHALLENGE, ANALYZE, AND LEARN

According to Tom Santora, chief marketing officer of Omni Hotels &
Resorts, disruptive leaders are intellectually curious and proactively inves-
tigate new things, identify and solve never-seen-before problems, and
apply new ways of doing business.[16] Starting early in his career, Fisher
was always thinking about new (potential) threats to his organization and
how they might be addressed using new thinking and solutions. Fisher
was among the first to demand reforms in technology, in human resource

management, in tactics and strategy at sea. Yet, Fisher was not on a wild goose chase. Rather, his change was purposeful—founded on careful thinking and learning about trends in the organization and the environment, and on experimenting with possible solutions before committing himself. Too many managers have suffered leaders who change for the wrong reasons, often because they want to make their own mark on the organization or seek to undo the efforts of their predecessor.

Like Fisher, you should not wait until you have reached the top of your organization to develop a challenging, analyzing, and learning mindset. The earlier you start, the better. As a young captain taking command of an infantry company, Todd Woodruff—now colonel, and Director, West Point Leadership Center at the United States Military Academy at West Point— was thinking about how his team could make a substantial and enduring difference. This is not unique; most new commanders want to have an impact and implement changes, often to the dismay of the soldiers. He approached it differently. He thought about major environmental changes that would affect any conflicts the U.S. Army might face in the future. His analysis revealed that urbanization was rapidly increasing and that more conflicts were occurring in urban areas, meaning that U.S. soldiers were more likely to find themselves fighting in cities—a skill for which they were not well prepared (neither Vietnam nor the First Gulf War were heavy on urban warfare). After getting buy-in from his own commander, he explained his reasoning to his soldiers and told them that under his leadership they would become the best urban fighters in the army. That not only happened, but their success also led to their selection to develop urban warfare tactics and procedures for their parent unit, as well as test new tactics for the army. As it turned out, this skill was sorely needed in Iraq after 2003.

PRIORITIZE LONG-TERM OVER SHORT-TERM

Fisher did not need Admiral Richards to point out that the *Dreadnought* threw away Britain's commanding lead over any other nation in the number of existing battleships. In Fisher's words, "Only a congenital idiot with criminal tendencies would permit any tampering with the maintenance of our naval supremacy." However, unlike Richards, Fisher understood that naval supremacy cannot be based on old technology. He recognized that as the leading maritime power of the day, Britain should lead—not follow—in naval innovation. Fisher saw that Britain's lead in battleships was a short-term advantage. If you do not move first, others will.

Fisher's decision to launch the *Dreadnought* is an example of creative destruction. Creative destruction creates an innovator's dilemma— conflict between (1) continuing to allocate resources to tweak and incrementally improve products, and (2) allocating resources to develop new products that will radically disrupt and possibly make obsolete the current operation.[17] Fisher believed that the second option was the right thing to do, although it would cannibalize the installed base of battle- ships. Apple and Amazon also went for the second option. For example, Apple introduced the iPhone even though it was well aware it would destroy its iPod business, and it introduced the iPad, which would eat into its Mac business. Apple's CEO Tim Cook explained the compa- ny's philosophy: "We don't fear cannibalization as long as it's another Apple product that's doing the cannibalizing."[18] Amazon introduced the Kindle e-reader, although that would heavily cannibalize its mainstay, physical books. In contrast, under Steve Ballmer, Microsoft followed the first option—incrementally improving its immensely profitable Windows and Office products while repeatedly killing promising proj- ects that threatened to cannibalize these products until it was nearly too late. Only after Ballmer was replaced as CEO by Satya Nadella did the company change its strategy. Nadella pushed Microsoft faster beyond its old, Windows-centric business model, in which all its other businesses once supported the PC operating system. That included a version of its database software to run on the rival Linux—an open-source operating system once described by former CEO Steve Ballmer as a "cancer" on the software industry.[19]

The marketing and management literatures have identified ten orga- nizational inhibitors to cannibalizing existing products.[20] Seven of these inhibitors are applicable to military organizations as well. Fisher's ability to pull off creative destruction is especially noteworthy considering that *all seven inhibitors* operated in his situation. These are as follows:

- The trap of high market share—the Royal Navy had overwhelming might over its rivals.

- Large investments in underappreciated assets—the Royal Navy had a large installed base of functioning battleships.

- The lack of creative destruction mindset—as the case made clear, most senior naval officers were conservative in their mindset.

- Risk-averse resource allocation—the appetite for risk taking in the Royal Navy was low. One "wrong" decision could wreck your career.

- Insufficient recognition of employees for breakthrough products—the promotion system of the Royal Navy favored not standing out. Radical ideas were frowned upon.

- Copying, tweaking, and slow imitation dominate—previous new classes of battleships were all incremental improvements on earlier classes.

- Hierarchically organized, bureaucratic organization—this characterized the Royal Navy (and most of today's military organizations).

ENSURE TOP-LEVEL SUPPORT

How was Fisher nevertheless able to push through the building of the *Dreadnought* against all these organizational inhibitors? A key factor was that he built a small support network consisting of three key people, King Edward VII—a navy enthusiast who appreciated Fisher's vision and knowledge—Prime Minister Arthur Balfour, and Navy Secretary Lord Selborne. Fisher did two things right. First, his naval reforms, especially the scrapping of many old ships, saved a lot of money, something Balfour appreciated given spiraling expenditures on the navy. Second, Fisher spent much time explaining the rationale for his reforms to these three over-lords and only went ahead once they were on board. With this small, but powerful, coalition, his back was secure, and he could move forward and build *Dreadnought*.

MAINTAIN UNRELENTING FOCUS

Fisher was single-minded, obsessive, ruthless, tenacious, and fanatical in the pursuit of his goal to prepare the Royal Navy for any conflict.[21] Interestingly, many of these characteristics can also be found in Walter Isaacson's biography of Apple founder and disruptive CEO *par excellence*, Steve Jobs.[22] At various times, Fisher was offered top positions at private companies where he could earn much more and would not have to deal with organizational resistance. He was tempted, but never made the switch. He could not abandon his life's mission for the sake of money.

To achieve this overarching goal, over the course of his career Fisher pursued more specific (lower-level) goals, such as measures to improve the navy's efficiency, modernize its organization, increase its readiness, and revolutionize its tactics. He applied himself to every task with complete focus. For example, when he moved from the gunnery school to the torpedo school, he explained his attitude to his student officers: "If you are a gunnery man, you must believe and teach that the world is saved by gunnery, and will only be saved by gunnery. If you are a torpedo man, you must lecture and teach the same thing about torpedoes . . . The man who doubts, or who is half-hearted, never does anything for himself or his country. You are missionaries; show the earnestness—if need be, the fanaticism—of missionaries."

HAVE A THICK SKIN

As I alluded to earlier, opposition to Fisher's reforms was fierce. By 1907, it had found its spokesman in Admiral Lord Charles Beresford, a charismatic leader who was enormously popular both with officers and men, and who had many friends in society, the press, and Parliament. His wealth allowed him to entertain on a lavish scale, and he used his position as a member of Parliament to attack everything Fisher stood for. At the same time, Fisher's position was severely weakened by a change in government. At the end of 1905, the Conservative government of Balfour was replaced by a Liberal government under Henry Campbell-Bannerman (see chapter 6), and after Campbell-Bannerman's death in early 1908, led by H. H. Asquith. Fisher's new political overlords were weak and indecisive, at least in naval matters. A Committee of Inquiry was created (often a bad sign). There was no precedent in the history of the Royal Navy that a First Sea Lord had to account for his actions on the basis of the charges of a subordinate. Not wanting to antagonize Beresford, the Committee's overall conclusion was critical of both antagonists. Fisher was bitterly disappointed and called the committee members great cowards—which they were. The damage to Fisher's reputation was such that he was obliged to retire slightly early, in 1910.

Fisher claimed to have the skin of a rhinoceros that poisoned darts could not pierce, yet it was tough on him. He told a friend that were he to write his reminiscences, he would title them "Hell. By One Who Has Been There."

CHAPTER TAKEAWAYS

- Fisher was an eagle. His entire life was devoted to increasing the efficiency of the Royal Navy and preparing it for war. To achieve this goal, he used a variety of means, including building the *Dreadnought*.

- Building the *Dreadnought* is a prime example of creative destruction when the stakes could not have been higher. At stake was not the future of a company but of a country and its huge empire.

- Building the *Dreadnought* was especially noteworthy because all organizational inhibitors worked against creative destruction in the Royal Navy.

- A crucial factor in Fisher's ability to push through disruptive change was that he had the strong support of the country's three topmost decision makers—the king, the prime minister, and the navy secretary.

- Fisher experimented with solutions before committing himself to a new course of action. He was a calculated risk taker.

- Fisher understood that as "market leader," the Royal Navy had to lead in innovation, not to follow.

- Fisher encountered vehement resistance to his disruptive leadership, yet persevered.

- Fisher's reforms prepared the Royal Navy for the two great challenges it was to face since the Napoleonic Wars—World Wars I and II.

- Fisher's life highlights several disruptive leadership principles:

  ° A mindset of incessant challenging, analyzing, and learning, nurtured from early on in his career. Do not wait to develop this mindset until you have reached the top of your organization. In fact, by that time, it may be too late.

  ° A willingness to accept assured short-term pain for uncertain long-term gain.

  ° The importance of getting the strong support of your superiors before initiating disruptive change.

  ° A degree of single-mindedness, tenacity, and ruthlessness.

  ° A thick skin.

  ° The great risks you run as disruptive leader. If there is a change of guard in the organization's leadership, you may be fatally exposed.

REFLECTIONS ON DISRUPTIVE LEADERSHIP

DISRUPTIVE LEADERSHIP SEEMS a contradiction in terms. According to the Oxford Dictionary, the verb "disrupt" comes from the Latin verb *disrumpere*, which means "to break apart." Why should leaders be called to break apart something? Because competitive pressures, changes in the environment, new technologies, new business models, and new competitors are disrupting established ways of organizational conduct—whether it is in business, nonprofits, the military, or other types of organizations. Two examples illustrate the point.

The Catholic Church faces strong competitive pressures (e.g., rapid rise of evangelical churches, especially in Latin America) and changes in its followers (e.g., reduced interest in celibacy). As a consequence, ordination of new priests is declining rapidly, while more priests are needed (to counter the loss of market share). The Church is rethinking its centuries-old rule of celibacy. If celibacy were to be abolished, it will be the most disruptive change in centuries, and we can expect fierce resistance from traditionalists.

Turning to business, entire industries—from cell phones, computing, entertainment, and book publishing to photography, grocery retailing, and health care—have recently experienced dramatic change.[1] Leaders of incumbent firms need to shake their organizations to avoid the fate of former industry leaders like BlackBerry, Blockbuster, Borders, Nokia, and Kodak. They all missed opportunities to leapfrog to the next big thing. At the same time, companies like Apple and Netflix rose to dominate their industries. Interestingly, they disrupted themselves repeatedly. By introducing the iPhone, Steve Jobs killed Apple's own lucrative iPod line. In 2007, Reed Hastings disrupted Netflix's own DVD-by-mail rental business by starting subscription-based streaming video.

Leaders today must acknowledge and embrace a life of continuous ambiguity and uncertainty as they navigate through disruptive change and create breakthroughs that leapfrog existing ways of doing business.[2] What can we learn from the lives of St. Peter and Admiral Jacky Fisher about essential elements of successful disruptive leadership? First, some good news. People with entirely different personalities can be disruptive leaders. Peter was diplomatic, humble, and keenly aware of his faults. In contrast, Fisher had a towering ego, a burning ambition, and was abrasive and hectoring. Yet, they were both successful. How is that possible? One key factor is that they were heading radically different organizations. Peter led a nonprofit, all-volunteer organization, where disruption cannot easily be forced through by autocratic means. On the other hand, the Royal Navy is a hierarchical organization where the norm is to obey orders. It is unlikely that Fisher's style of disruptive leadership would be successful in egalitarian or nonprofit organizations, while it is not obvious that Peter's leadership style would work to push through disruptive innovations in hierarchical organizations.

However, there are similarities in the lives of Peter and Fisher, which point to four qualities that are essential for disruptive leadership across almost any organization: (1) nurture a disruptive mindset; (2) display courage; (3) be deeply convinced about the righteousness of your cause; and (4) build a guiding coalition.

1. NURTURE A DISRUPTIVE MINDSET

A disruptive mindset approaches the world with the intent of changing the game: creating or doing something radically new or different that produces a significant leap forward. You need to be able to envisage an entirely different future—different products, services, policies, ideas, or business processes. What are markers of a disruptive mindset? You need to have high tolerance for ambiguity and risk, and be comfortable with unstructured situations, which should be regarded as an opportunity rather than a threat. Not everybody can do that. One friend of mine is extremely smart and highly educated. He is also very structured—even his private life is planned to the minute—and ambiguity makes him anxious. Not surprisingly, he is not a disruptive leader—but he is a successful directive leader.

Both Peter and Fisher had a disruptive mindset. Peter saw a different future when he decided to follow an unknown rabbi from the obscure town of Nazareth. The New Testament shows that Peter was typically the first among the apostles to see an opportunity. Fisher was cut from the same cloth. It was easier for them to see opportunities because they were essentially outsiders. Peter was not part of the Jewish establishment, and Fisher was promoted on performance rather than by leveraging the clubbish network that was (and still is) so characteristic of Britain's establishment. Thus, they had less to lose by disrupting the (for insiders) comfortable status quo. Neither owed anything to the powers-that-be, which made it easier to disrupt the system. In my consulting work, I think my most important contribution is to challenge managers as to why they do things in a particular way. The answer usually is that either they never thought about it doing in any other way, or they do not want to rock the boat.

2. DISPLAY COURAGE

While courage benefits any leader, it is crucial for disruptive leaders, because followers who resist change are usually more numerous and more vehement in their opposition than those in favor of change. This important principle was first identified by the Florentine political philosopher Niccolò Machiavelli, who wrote in *Il Principe* (*The Prince*),

> It must be considered that there is nothing more difficult to carry out nor more doubtful of success nor more dangerous to handle than to initiate a new order of things; for the reformer has enemies in all those who profit by the old order, and only lukewarm defenders in all those who would profit by the new order; this lukewarmness arising partly from the

incredulity of mankind who does not truly believe in anything new until they actually have experience of it.[3]

Until his death, Peter's decision to discard Jewish tradition was bitterly
opposed by groups within the Church, as evident from the letters written
by Paul. Yet he stayed the course. Fisher faced fierce opposition from within
and outside the Royal Navy. In his conflict with Beresford, he was virtually
alone, being deserted by political masters who feared Beresford's popularity
in Parliament and society. Like Peter, he went through hell but persevered.

3. BE DEEPLY CONVINCED ABOUT THE RIGHTEOUSNESS OF YOUR CAUSE

It matters a great deal whether you are deeply convinced that disruption
is the right thing to do. Both Peter and Fisher not only believed they were
right, but also that it was their duty to introduce the disruptive idea—this
strengthened their resolve to ultimately overcome, rather than yield to, the
opposition. If you believe passionately in the disruptive idea, if you believe
that not doing this is somehow morally wrong, you are in a better position
to take the abuse that will be heaped upon you. Take the building of the
Dreadnought. Fisher's inner conviction is well expressed in the words of one
of his protégés:

> Knowing what we did that the Dreadnought was the best type
> to build, should we knowingly have built the second-best ship?
> What would have been the verdict of the country if Germany
> had . . . built a Dreadnought while we were building Lord
> Nelsons [pre-dreadnoughts], and then forced a war on us and
> beaten our fleet? What would have been the verdict of the
> country if . . . the Admiralty had deliberately recommended
> the building of second-class ships?[4]

4. BUILD A GUIDING COALITION

Even the profoundly cynical Machiavelli acknowledged that an organization may have some followers who favor change. To succeed, the disruptive leader needs to motivate those pockets of people with the right mindset to act in ways to support their goals.[5] Leadership thinker John Kotter calls this building a "guiding coalition."[6] How can the disruptive leader accomplish this? By leveraging the four I's, proposed by another leadership scholar, Bernard Bass.[7]

Individualized consideration. Listen carefully to the individual ideas of your followers. By all accounts, Peter was a good listener. In Fisher's case, as commander in chief of the Mediterranean fleet, he accorded free access to all officers, junior and senior. When one lieutenant brought him a carefully worked-out plan for defending the fleet against a torpedo attack, Fisher ordered his captains to practice these tactics at sea the following week.[8]

Intellectual stimulation. Encourage your followers to be creative and innovative and to challenge their own beliefs. Peter challenged his followers to change their beliefs, after explaining the baptism of the Roman centurion Cornelius with the words, "So if God gave them the same gift as He gave us, who was I to think that I would oppose God?"[9] (And by implication, this applied to his followers.) When Fisher was commander in chief of the North Atlantic and West Indies station, he regularly asked a group of junior officers ashore to join him and his wife for the weekend. He invited them to talk freely and share their ideas. He welcomed it when they stood up to him (an uncommon situation in such a hierarchical organization), provided their arguments were sound.

Inspirational motivation. Inspire and motivate your followers through having a vision and presenting that vision. In his "coming out" speech as leader of the Church on Pentecost, Peter presented a vision of the new word, which apparently was so inspiring that the young Church gained three thousand followers that day.[10] During his stints at the navy's elite research institutes, Fisher developed a coterie of younger officers who shared his sense of alarm and urgency about improving the offensive capabilities of the fleet.

Idealized influence. Act as a strong role model for your followers. Peter chose the martyr death, which encouraged his followers then, and in the following centuries of persecution, to keep the faith. The fact that he was martyred as bishop of Rome was one of the turning points in human history. It was the basis for the future bishops of Rome to be the head of the Church—a claim that has shaped the world and Christianity up to today. Fisher's drive, his ruthless search for efficiency, energy, and remorseless hounding of the inefficient, inspired and awed his junior officers and bound them to him. He was an electrifying speaker whose fiery language, wit, and sly digs at naval tradition kept his audience spellbound.

To assess whether disruptive leadership is a style that suits you, consider the following questions.

1. Are you comfortable with ambiguity, uncertainty, and lack of structure?

2. Would you say you have a disruptive mindset—always thinking how to do things differently? What evidence can you give?

3. How strong are your ties to your organization? Are you willing to make personal sacrifices for its future success?

4. How often have you voiced opinions that went against received opinion in your organization?

5. Are you generally a person who can weather a storm of opposition or do you tend to fold? Can you give examples? What can you learn from this?

6. Have you built a guiding coalition in your organization? If so, who are they, how strong is their loyalty, and how influential are they? If not, can you build such a network?

7. Which disruptive leaders do you recognize in your own professional and/or personal environment? How do you relate to their style of leadership?

8. What feedback have you ever received that portrayed you as a disruptive leader?

9. Have you ever been in a situation where being a "disruptive leader" would have been most effective? What did you actually do and with which results?

PART FIVE

AUTHENTIC LEADERSHIP — SET THE EXAMPLE

12

WASHINGTON STOPS, TWICE

"The greatest character in the world."
—KING GEORGE III ABOUT GEORGE WASHINGTON

Leadership Dilemma: How could Washington avoid the fate of previous revolutions that all ended in dictatorship?

CONTEXT

The last decades of the eighteenth century were a period of unprecedented political ferment in the Western world. The two epochal events were the French Revolution, along with the subsequent failure of republican government, and the American Revolution, along with the subsequent success of republican government. My focus is on the American Revolution and why it succeeded—which is due in no small part to one of world history's most authentic leaders, George Washington.

The root cause of the American Revolution was whether Great Britain had the right to tax its colonial subjects without their approval. The decade preceding the Declaration of Independence witnessed an increasingly vicious cycle: unilateral imposition of a tax on Britain's American subjects, fierce resistance, withdrawal of the tax, imposition of a new tax, and so on. British political incompetence—its attempts to impose taxes were criticized even at the time by leading British politicians[1]—created an ever-widening gap between the mother country and its colonial subjects, culminating in the famous Declaration of Independence of July 4, 1776.

Against all odds, the American Continental Army, with the help of the French, defeated Great Britain in the Revolutionary War that followed, and in 1783, Britain granted the United States full independence. But having won their independence, Americans needed to determine what sort of government would—or should—emerge. Thus far, the new nation was a confederation of thirteen loosely linked states governed under the Articles of Confederation. There was no real executive branch, just a few departments; no independent judiciary; and only an ineffective Congress.[2] This political structure could not adequately deal with the myriad of domestic and foreign challenges the fledgling nation faced. To address these problems, a Constitutional Convention was called in 1787. The convention adopted a new political structure, governed by the Constitution of the United States, which endures today. Federal authority was divided between the legislative, judicial, and executive branches of government. Under the Constitution of this new federal republic, the president is the head of the executive branch and wields significant power. The first elections under this new Constitution were held in November 1788, and the first president was inaugurated in April 1789. Since the Constitution left many details unspecified, the first president would have to set many precedents that would guide the behavior of future presidents.

In sum, in a span of a mere twenty-five years, the United States (1) won a war against the superpower of the day; (2) developed a radically new system of government based on the will of the people, which, according to received wisdom at the time, was bound to lead either to anarchy or dictatorship (the French Revolution would bear out both); and (3) created a powerful presidency, whose occupant was expected to agree to a peaceful transition to a successor, not being his oldest son (as in monarchies). There was no historical precedent for any of this, and the temptation to grab, and hold on to, power would tax the ability of almost any man. According to historian Joseph Ellis, there was a consensus at the time, and since confirmed for all time, that "no one . . . could have performed these elemental tasks as well, and perhaps that no one could have performed them at all—except for one man, George Washington."[3]

GEORGE WASHINGTON

George Washington was born on February 22, 1732, in the British colony of Virginia, the son of a moderately wealthy tobacco planter. He received the modern equivalent of a grade-school education but was never exposed to the classical curriculum or attended college, a deficiency that haunted him throughout his career. As an adult, he had a commanding presence due to his height of six feet two inches; this made him a head taller than the average male of the time. According to Ellis, "he was the epitome of a man's man: physically strong, mentally enigmatic, emotionally restrained."[4]

Helped by influential relations, Washington was appointed major in the Virginia militia in 1753, despite having neither military experience nor formal military training. In the French and Indian War of 1754–1763, he made some serious tactical mistakes but also distinguished himself by conspicuous bravery: In one battle he had two horses shot from under him, and his hat and coat were bullet-pierced. As an aide on the staff of British general Edward Braddock, he also gave sound advice that was ignored. What would a militarily unschooled colonial have to say that would be of value to a British general? Washington's advice was "vindicated" by the subsequent defeat of Braddock's army.[5]

Washington resigned his commission in December 1758, with his military reputation much enhanced, and married Martha Custis the month after. Her huge dowry immediately catapulted Washington into the top tier of Virginia's (slave-holding) planter class, and the next sixteen years would be largely devoted to managing and enlarging his estate at Mount Vernon. From 1758 to 1775, he also was a member of the Virginia House of Burgesses (Virginia's colonial parliament), but he was not a particularly remarkable delegate.

The successive British efforts to impose taxes on the American colonists weakened Washington's allegiance to the motherland. Punitive laws passed by the British parliament in 1774 after the Boston Tea Party (the so-called Intolerable Acts) radicalized him. For the first time, he detected what he saw as a full-blooded conspiracy against American liberty.[6] Washington was elected as a member of the Continental Congress, a convention of delegates from the thirteen colonies that started meeting in the fall of 1774 in Philadelphia. Britain proved unwilling to redress their grievances, and fighting at Lexington and Concord in April 1775 released the "shot heard round the world." The Continental Congress decided to create the Continental Army, and on June 15, 1775, one year before the colonies declared their independence, Washington was unanimously elected as its commander in chief.

Figure 12.1 George Washington as Commander in Chief of the Continental Army

Source: Painting by Charles Wilson Peale

Why was Washington chosen?[7] Because he was the only delegate to attend the Continental Congress in military uniform; he was tall; he exuded martial dignity, self-control, and reserve; and he was the most qualified Virginian. At the time, Virginia was the most populous and wealthiest colony. Moreover, Virginia was in the South, while the fighting up to then was confined to New England. If a New Englander had been chosen as supreme commander, the Southern colonies could have seen the fighting as a Northern affair.

The active phase of the Revolutionary War ended after a large British army under Lord Charles Cornwallis surrendered to the combined American-French army led by Washington and Comte de Rochambeau at Yorktown on October 19, 1781. The peace treaty (the Peace of Paris) was signed on September 3, 1783, and Washington resigned as commander in chief in December 1783. He intended to spend the rest of his life in happy retirement with his wife, whom he had scarcely seen in the preceding eight years.

His respite would be brief. In 1787 he was called upon to preside over the aforementioned Constitutional Convention as the only person who was universally acceptable to all states. Washington was reserved during the constitutional debates and voting, lending his prestige to the goodwill and work of the other delegates. His support convinced many state delegates to vote for ratification of the Constitution. The delegates to the Constitutional Convention designed the presidency with Washington in mind, allowing him to define the office once elected. However, this also meant that he could not refuse the job, and the Electoral College unanimously elected him as America's first president. He assembled a team of giants around him, including Alexander Hamilton, John Jay, and four people who were destined to become America's next four presidents: John Adams, Thomas Jefferson, James Madison, and James Monroe.

Although the Electoral College unanimously reelected him in 1793, his second term was less happy—foreshadowing what would become a common occurrence in U.S. presidencies. The government and Congress were increasingly divided between a group around Hamilton (Federalists) and a group around Jefferson and Madison (Democratic-Republicans). The Federalists advocated for a strong federal government, a national bank (a proto Federal Reserve), the promotion of commerce and industry, and closer relations with Britain. The Democratic-Republicans championed limited government and states' rights, opposed a national bank, emphasized agricultural interests, and favored close ties with Revolutionary France. The Democratic-Republicans launched increasingly bitter attacks on Washington, whom they regarded as being much too inclined toward Federalist ideas.

Washington relinquished office at the end of his second term in 1797. He died shortly after, in 1799. General Henry Lee delivered his famous oration, in which he praised Washington as "first in war, first in peace, and first in the hearts of his countrymen." Washington's death brought tributes even from the British. Royal Navy battleships blockading the French harbor Brest lowered their colors to half-mast, and *The London Morning Chronicle* opined that "the whole range of history does not present to our view a character upon which we can dwell with such entire and unmixed admiration."[8]

Figure 12.2 Apotheosis of Washington

Source: Metropolitan Museum of Art

Almost immediately, Washington became a larger-than-life figure. He was compared to Moses, and popular prints showed him ascending to heaven in the presence of angels (see Figure 12.2). Hagiographic biographies, including one by John Marshall, one of America's most consequential chief justices, extolled his virtues and manufactured enduring myths like Washington refusing to lie about chopping down a cherry tree.

Why did he receive such fulsome praise? Many things Washington did would have a profound influence on U.S. history, but his greatest moments were when, like a modern Odysseus, he withstood the siren call of unlimited power and stepped down. But unlike the original Odysseus, who had to be tied to a mast because he would not be able to restrain himself, Washington did it voluntarily. And he did it not once, but twice. Only the greatest among the great can resist such temptation.

WASHINGTON RELINQUISHES POWER—TWICE

Washington resigned first as commander in chief of the Continental Army of the United States, and second as president. Seen from the perspective of the twenty-first century, neither of the two seems out of the ordinary, but at the time, they were—and proved crucial for the survival of the republican experiment that was taking place.

RESIGNING AS COMMANDER IN CHIEF OF THE CONTINENTAL ARMY

Stepping down as commander in chief was, from a historical perspective, arguably the most amazing of his two resignation decisions. Almost every revolution in the history of the world, however idealistically begun, has ended in tyranny. The military dictatorships of Julius Caesar and Oliver Cromwell destroyed the Roman and English republics, respectively. Just a few years after the French Revolution, Napoleon grabbed power in 1799. In the twentieth century, this pattern would be repeated in Russia, Cambodia, North Korea, and China, to name but a few.

In the early 1780s, the situation in the nascent United States resembled the chaos in ancient Rome at the time of Caesar, or in France in the late 1790s. The Continental Congress was weak and unable to raise money to pay debts incurred during the Revolutionary War. Many soldiers and officers doubted whether they would ever receive years of back pay, let alone that Congress would honor its pledge to provide veterans with a pension. Washington was keenly aware of this. He said to one general, "The army, as usual, are without pay and a great part of the soldiery without shirts. And though the patience of them is threadbare, the states seem perfectly indifferent to their cries." To another general, Washington observed that his men were "soured by penury and what they call the ingratitude of the public, involved in debts, without a farthing of money to carry them home."[9] As long as the army kept together, they remained a force to be reckoned with. If disbanded, many risked being thrown in debtors' prison. This was no way to honor the men who had given everything for the cause of freedom.

Congress also owed large debts to civilians for war supplies. The fact that the army and prominent businessmen were similarly defrauded created a highly dangerous situation.[10] Military officers and leading financers met and agreed that the only protection for creditors, whether civilians or soldiers, was the strength of the army. In fact, the army was the only well-functioning national organization. If Congress proved unable or unwilling to honor its debts, military force should be used as a temporary expedient—as any military dictatorship in world history invariably has claimed.

The big question was whether Washington could be persuaded to join the emerging insurrection. Alexander Hamilton, a former aide-de-camp to Washington and now a newly minted member of Congress, took this task upon himself.[11] This is telling. This was no conspiracy of extremists like France's Maximilien de Robespierre. Hamilton was one of the Founding Fathers of the United States. He would become Washington's first secretary of the treasury, as well as the author of many of the immensely influential Federalist Papers.

In a letter to Washington dated February 13, 1783,[12] Hamilton argued that Congress is "a body not governed by reason [or] foresight but by circumstances"—a disturbing admission by one of its own members. Hamilton proposed that an army revolt could help spur Congress to action. However, he was also concerned that such a coup might get out of hand, noting "the difficulty will be to keep a *complaining* and *suffering army* within the bounds of moderation" (emphasis in the original). According to Hamilton, this undesirable outcome could be avoided if Washington would put himself at the helm of this movement, not for his own sake, but for the sake of the country. This same old argument has been used time and again, from Caesar to today's strongmen like Egypt's president, General Abdel Fattah el-Sisi. Under Washington's benign control, justice would be achieved.[13]

In his written response to Hamilton, dated March 4, 1783,[14] Washington first indicated the many areas of agreement. Washington lamented, "The sufferings of a complaining army on one hand, and the inability of Congress and tardiness of the States on the other, are the forebodings of evil." He also felt that Congress should receive enlarged powers. He was in favor of a strong national government. However, he argued that it would be "impolitic" to involve the army as party in the legislative process, which might only "bring on its concomitants." How prescient of Washington. Countries such as Argentina, Egypt, and Pakistan, to name a few, might have fared better if they had taken his warning to heart rather than expecting salvation from military intervention. Washington urged Hamilton to keep faith in civilian leaders, who, he believed, could not be so devoid of common sense and honesty as to refuse to aid the soldiers, once the facts had been laid out in Congress. In short, Washington refused to become the leader of the coup and make himself a military dictator. He would not encroach upon the prerogatives of Congress, even though he agreed with the army's grievances.

But Washington realized that he had to do more to persuade his fellow officers to banish the very idea of army intervention from their minds. Anonymous letters poisoned the atmosphere at the headquarters of the Continental Army at Newburgh, New York. Washington needed to get ahead of the curve. He called a meeting of all officers on March 15 (interestingly, the anniversary of the assassination of Julius Caesar, the world's most famous military dictator) at Newburgh.[15] Historian James Flexner called it "probably the most important single gathering ever held in the United States."[16] The atmosphere was grim. Washington addressed the officers with a nine-page speech that sympathized with their demands but denounced the methods by which they proposed to achieve them.[17] He did not elevate himself above his officers but portrayed himself as a friend and peer. He argued that any attempted coup was simultaneously a repudiation of the ideals for which they fought and an assault on his own integrity.[18] However, his speech failed to sway the resentful officer corps.

Then something happened. To reassure the officers of congressional good faith, he pulled out a supportive letter from a congressman, but stumbled over the first few sentences. He seemed confused, staring at the paper helplessly. He then pulled from his pocket a pair of new reading glasses, which came as a surprise to his officers, who had never seen him wearing glasses. He said, "Gentlemen, you will permit me to put on my spectacles, for I have grown not only gray, but almost blind in the service of my country."[19] This heartfelt, simple act did what lofty words failed to achieve—it moved his angry, battle-hardened officers to tears. It reminded them of the many sacrifices their commander in chief had made for his country. The so-called Newburgh conspiracy was over. There would be no military coup.

The final act of this saga occurred in December 1783. Washington went before Congress and said, "Having finished the work assigned to me, I retire from the great theater of action . . . I here offer my Commission and take leave of all the enjoyments of public life."[20] The words and symbolism were profound. Congress had commissioned him as military leader eight years earlier, and, to Congress, Washington returned his commission. The republic would be led by civilians, and the armed forces—like any other group in society—were subject to civilian control.

RESIGNING AS PRESIDENT

Washington did not expect it at the time he resigned his commission, but he was not yet done providing shining examples to the young nation. After the country called him to be its first president, he was reelected in 1792.

What about 1796? While it is true that he had become increasingly tired with the job, that has hardly ever stopped a leader from continuing in power.

Few doubted that he would have won another election handily.[21] There was no historical precedent for stepping down. Kings and dictators ruled until their death or forced removal. John Jay, the country's first chief justice and, at the time, governor of New York, exhorted him to "remain with us at least while the storm lasts and until you can retire like the sun in a calm, unclouded evening." Many Americans could not imagine another president and assumed he would stay in his office until his death.[22]

For Washington, stepping down after two terms served a higher purpose. He felt that he might not live to serve out a third term, and he regarded the election of a new president as a powerful demonstration to the world that republican institutions were viable. The establishment of the vice presidency permitted succession in a monarchical manner. The president could be reelected again and again, and, upon his death, be succeeded by his hand-picked heir.[23] In fact, some delegates to the Constitutional Convention had advocated a lifetime appointment for presidents. Washington felt that a final use of his immense prestige was to show how succession in the new republic had to take place—by the ballot box. If he stepped down voluntarily, it set a powerful precedent for a free, peaceful, democratic change of guard. According to historian Flexner, "This would be the culmination of his own career, his final gift to the world."[24] All subsequent presidents felt compelled to follow this precedent—who could claim to be greater than the Father of the Country?—until it was breached by Franklin Roosevelt (due to the exceptional circumstances of World War II; see chapter 7). The two-term limit was then added to the Constitution as Amendment XXII in 1951.

Washington's resignation represented another milestone in the democratic experiment that was the United States. The highest praise came from an unexpected quarter. According to his erstwhile nemesis, King George III of Great Britain, by giving up power twice, Washington stood out as "the greatest character in the world."[25]

LESSONS

Washington was an eagle. From the beginnings of the American Revolution, his overriding vision was to establish an independent republic of the people, by the people. This republic was not about any individual person but about all Americans. But he overlaid his hedgehog-like vision with flexibility in means, both as general and as president. For example, he was keenly aware—after some initial mistakes—that the U.S. army would struggle in a set battle against British veteran soldiers. Hence, he waged a war of maneuvers and avoided decisive battles until his forces were strengthened with highly trained French soldiers.

Yet, being an eagle is not enough to make Washington, in the words of Flexner, "The Indispensable Man." Why was he indispensable in the process that created the United States in the period from 1775 to 1800? Because he possessed a degree of authentic leadership seldom seen in leaders. Time and again, he set a new, unselfish example with personal conduct for his followers. His stepping down from the pinnacle of power twice is the most important example of his authentic leadership, but there are many more. For instance, by agreeing to become commander in chief of a (nonexistent) army before the colonies had even declared independence, he made a personal pledge to the cause of freedom before anybody else. If he failed to assemble an army, or if the Declaration of Independence was never promulgated, his estate and his life would surely be forfeited. As commander in chief, he refused pay, for eight long years, lest anyone think he was in it for the money. Even his critics acknowledged that Washington could not be bribed, corrupted, or compromised—in an age where that was quite common (Benedict Arnold comes to mind).[26] He stayed in the field for the entire war, until the Peace of Paris was signed. It took great efforts to convince him to become president of the Constitutional Convention, and later, president of the United States, because he had promised, when he resigned his military commission, to leave public life for good. He also proposed to serve as president of the United States without pay.

He did not shirk from danger, either. Time and again, he was in the midst of his men where the fighting was going on. Here is just one example (there are too many to recount). At the victorious Battle of Princeton in January 1777, his army was in danger of breaking up, until Washington appeared at the front lines. While men on both sides of him were falling, Washington remained atop his horse—making him an easy target—urging his officers to bring up the troops.[27]

It is noteworthy that the quality of Washington's authentic leadership overcame certain weaknesses that would have proved fatal for other generals or politicians. His record as general was decidedly mixed, racking up more defeats than victories.[28] His decisive victory at Yorktown was largely due to his French allies.[29] He was distant, hardly smiled, and delivered praise sparingly.[30] He was not a noted orator or debater, or a composer of political treatises like Hamilton, Madison, or Jefferson.[31] Nevertheless, people followed him through thick and thin because they trusted his integrity.

While Washington's outstanding personality trait was integrity, his outstanding competency was learning from experience. Compared to his contemporaries, Washington had received little or no schooling in political or military theory, but he exhibited a great capacity to teach himself from experience. As president, he was in uncharted territory and had to learn on the job, while being well aware that everything he did would set a precedent. According to Flexner, "[H]is preeminence was achieved through a Darwinian adaptation to environment. It was a triumph of a man who knows to learn, not in a narrow sense of studying other people's conceptions, but in the transcendent sense of making a synthesis from the totality of experience."[32]

I want to single out one other outstanding feature of Washington's leadership: ironclad control over his emotions.[33] Washington had to deal with scheming rivals who attempted to discredit and depose him as commander in chief.[34] As president, he was exposed to malicious slander that would render today's political climate a kindergarten. The man who had given everything was called a traitor, a hypocrite, an apostate, and an imposter.[35] Editorials in Democratic-Republican newspapers depicted him as a senile accomplice or willing co-conspirator in Hamiltonian plots to establish a monarchy, and accused him of having been a sellout to the British like the hated Benedict Arnold. After his resignation as president, hostile editorials described Washington as a "tyrannical monster" and his farewell address as "the loathings of a sick mind."[36] All the scheming, plotting, and slandering hurt Washington—biographer Ron Chernov called

Washington "thin-skinned." But he refused to respond to his detractors, which rendered him dignified, circumspect, and upright, whereas his enemies seemed petty and skulking.[37] Might this hold a lesson for today's political leaders?

Washington's decision to quit after two terms in office offers an example for other leaders. Too often, as time passes, leaders start to see themselves as indispensable and lose their edge. Some examples of leaders who did not know when to stop include Helmut Kohl (Germany), Leonid Brezhnev (Soviet Union), Hosni Mubarak (Egypt), and Robert Mugabe (Zimbabwe). Business leaders also routinely stay on too long. According to the *Financial Times*: "Like political lives, many executives' careers end in failure. Those who over-extend their tenure are often prone to stumble in their last years in office."[38] In 2017, departing-CEO tenure at S&P 500 companies was the highest recorded since 2002, at nearly eleven years.[39] There comes a point when almost every long-serving leader starts to get complacent. The boss carries on with a strategy that worked once but is outdated; seeks advice from a clique of obsequious insiders, all of whom owe him their jobs; and steadily becomes more isolated from the company's customers and suppliers.[40]

CHAPTER TAKEAWAYS

- Washington was an eagle. His life was devoted to a free, independent, and democratic republic. To achieve these goals, he used a variety of means.

- Washington is one of the most authentic leaders in history. Time and again he set the example for his followers.

- As commander in chief of the Continental Army, Washington persevered against overwhelming odds.

- While Washington's military record is mixed, he exhibited a great capacity to learn from experience. For much of the war, he fought an unconventional war for which there was little precedent.

- Washington's authentic leadership carried the day in what is perhaps the greatest crisis ever faced by the United States, the Newburgh Conspiracy.

- Washington was offered absolute power and declined it, not once, but twice. This made him the greatest character of his time.

- Washington's life highlights several authentic leadership principles:

  ○ Integrity, courage, and learning from experience as leadership qualities

  ○ The importance of ironclad control over your emotions

  ○ Authentic leadership can overcome weaknesses that would be fatal otherwise

  ○ The wisdom of *not* responding to plotting and slandering—a lesson for today's leaders?

  ○ Stepping down before you have worn out your welcome

MANDELA GOES TO A MATCH

"As I walked out the door toward the gate that would lead to my freedom, I knew if I didn't leave my bitterness and hatred behind, I'd still be in prison."
—NELSON MANDELA

Leadership Dilemma: How could Mandela achieve the impossible—reconciliation of Afrikaners and blacks?

CONTEXT

As we saw in chapter 6, the rights of the black majority were not part of the agreement between the Afrikaners and the British government of Campbell-Bannerman. In his speech in the House of Commons, Churchill presciently said that "We may regret that decision."[1] He was right. Ever since the Union of South Africa was founded in 1910, blacks enjoyed limited rights at best. However, segregation accelerated dramatically after 1948 when the Nasionale Party (National Party) won the elections on the doctrine of apartheid, with warnings against the "black peril." Apartheid (separateness) was the philosophy of extreme segregation between South Africa's races.[2] In descending order of privilege, the four "race groups" were: whites (20 percent of the population in 1948), coloureds (mixed race), Indians (together with coloureds, 10 percent), and blacks (70 percent).

All political and economic power was held by the white minority, and they were the only ones who could vote in elections. The whites consisted of two groups. The Afrikaners (formerly known as Boers—see chapter 6) made up around 65 percent of South Africa's white population in 1948. Their language, called Afrikaans, is closely related to Dutch. When I visit South Africa, I can understand Afrikaners with little difficulty. The other 35 percent spoke English at home and were mostly of British descent. English speakers were dominant in the business world, but in terms of political power, the Afrikaners reigned supreme. They ran the public sector, including the government and the vast security apparatus. They farmed (Boer means "farmer" in Afrikaans/Dutch) on land that often had been grabbed from the blacks without compensation. The Afrikaners were apartheid's lords and protectors.[3]

The National Party would remain in power until 1994. In the 1950s and 1960s, successive governments would impose ever stricter racial segregation. Entire neighborhoods in urban areas were bulldozed, and some 3.5 million nonwhite South Africans were removed from their homes and forced into segregated townships on the urban periphery. It was one of the largest mass evictions in modern history.

The African National Congress (ANC) was founded in 1912. Its primary mission was to obtain voting rights for all South Africans, and from 1948 on, their goal was to end the hated apartheid system. The ANC originally espoused nonviolent protests, but in the wake of the massacre of sixty-nine black protestors at Sharpeville in 1960, the ANC resorted to violence as well.

As the years passed, South Africa faced increasing isolation in the community of nations. By the 1980s, anti-apartheid boycotts gained momentum, campaigns for disinvestment and sanctions were biting, and foreign loans were called in. As a consequence, South Africa's formerly fast-growing economy deteriorated sharply, and ethnic unrest and violence increased dramatically. Yet, the ANC's armed struggle met with limited success against the crushing might of the South African security apparatus.[4] The ANC's alignment with the South African Communist Party helped the government. Western countries were concerned that if white minority rule collapsed, the communists would take over this strategically vital country. After all, this had happened before in Angola and Mozambique after the Portuguese left in 1975. The key event that would change the landscape for South Africa's liberation struggle was the fall of the Berlin Wall on November 9, 1989, signaling the collapse of communism in Eastern Europe. South African president F. W. de Klerk saw the writing on the wall (pun intended).

But would the ANC be ready to negotiate a peaceful transition after a century of injustice, assassinations, deprivations, and torture? Building a nonracial society would require a partnership with an ANC led by an authentic leader who had the moral authority to persuade blacks to forgo retribution *and* was able to assuage white fears about their future in the post-apartheid society. In a country of 43 million, there was only one person who could pull this off: Nelson Mandela, a convicted activist, who had not been seen or heard from by the South African population for twenty-seven years.

NELSON MANDELA

Nelson Rolihlahla Mandela was born on July 18, 1918, to the Thembu royal family in what is now the Eastern Cape province. He studied law at the University of Fort Hare (a tiny black university) and the University of Witwatersrand (which, at the time, admitted a handful of black students). He began working as a lawyer in Johannesburg in 1952, opening South Africa's first black law firm with Oliver Tambo, the future ANC president.

Mandela joined the ANC in 1944. Over the next two decades, he steadily rose in its ranks. He was involved in protests against apartheid legislation and was arrested, imprisoned, and banned from visiting certain areas in South Africa. Following the Sharpeville Massacre, he was asked to lead the armed struggle and co-founded "Spear of the Nation"—the armed wing of the ANC. The first bombings by Spear of the Nation occurred on December 16, 1961, causing a national furor. Many more acts of sabotage would follow. In 1962, Mandela traveled around Africa to receive military training and to gain support for the armed struggle. The brutality of apartheid transformed Mandela from ANC activist to ANC militant and into South Africa's most wanted man. He returned to South Africa in July 1962, and within a month he was arrested in a police roadblock.

Mandela and several other ANC leaders stood trial for sabotage and attempting to violently overthrow the government in what became known as the Rivonia Trial. Under the Sabotage Act of 1962, they could face the death penalty. The high point of the trial was Mandela's four-hour "Speech from the Dock" on April 20, 1964. Mandela argued that his cooperation with the hated communists could be compared with Churchill's cooperation with Stalin in World War II. He further noted that the communists were the only political group who were prepared to treat blacks as human beings and equals. He finished with these famous words, which electrified world opinion:

> I have fought against white domination, and I have fought against black domination. I have cherished the ideal of a democratic and free society in which all persons live together in harmony and with equal opportunities. It is an ideal which I hope to live for and to achieve. But if needs be, it is an ideal for which I am prepared to die.[5]

According to biographer Anthony Sampson, it was the most effective speech of Mandela's career.[6] It identified him clearly as the leader not just of the ANC, but of multiracial opposition to apartheid. International support helped save Mandela's life, but that was the only clemency he would receive. On June 12, 1964, Mandela and other ANC leaders were sentenced to life imprisonment and sent to the notorious Robben Island prison, South Africa's Alcatraz.

Prisoner 466/64 would remain in prison for twenty-seven years, of which he spent eighteen years on Robben Island. The first ten years were the worst. In a 1990 TV interview, Mandela described their treatment as "very harsh and even brutal." Mandela and his ANC colleagues worked in the lime quarry, where the sun's glare reflected on the white stone and burned their eyes. For three years, they were refused dark glasses. Mandela's eyes never recovered; for the rest of his life, he read with difficulty.[7] The inmates were humiliated on purpose. In those first years, they were required to wear shorts to remind them that they were "boys."[8]

International interest in Mandela subsided soon after the Rivonia Trial. Out of sight and out of mind, forgotten and abandoned, was the government's cunning strategy.[9] The South African economy was booming, which led to a dramatic reduction in ethnic unrest. According to Mandela, "During the harsh days of the early 1970s, when the ANC seemed to sink into the shadows, we had to force ourselves not to give in to despair."[10] This situation, propitious for the regime, ended in the mid-1970s. The South African economy started to deteriorate, and, following an uprising in the massive township of Soweto in June 1976, ethnic unrest increased once more. Mandela was thrust back into the limelight, never to leave it again. In the 1980s, while violence in South Africa mounted and many townships became virtually ungovernable, the international campaign to release Mandela gathered momentum. Mandela was moved to Pollsmoor prison near Cape Town, where he was treated much better.

In the late 1980s, Mandela took the initiative to reach out to the government for secret talks. His biographer Anthony Sampson called it "the loneliest stretch of Mandela's ordeal."[11] He was facing the government alone, unable to closely coordinate with the ANC leadership in exile. While these talks did not achieve a breakthrough, they allowed government leaders, including President de Klerk, to get to know Mandela and vice versa. Finally, on February 11, 1990, de Klerk released Mandela unconditionally and lifted the prohibitions on the ANC, the South African Communist Party, and many other banned organizations. De Klerk announced, "The time for negotiations has arrived." His interlocutor would be the man he had just released, Nelson Mandela.

Figure 13.1 Nelson Mandela, 1993

Source: National Archives and Records Administration

In the ensuing four years, the ANC negotiated with the government amid ever greater violence in which thousands of people were brutally slaughtered. Nearly all violence pitted blacks from different ethnic groups against each other, but was facilitated (if not instigated) by hard-line apartheid supporters in the government and the security forces (the so-called Third Force), who sought to sabotage the negotiations. Mandela suspected that de Klerk was somehow involved in fomenting the violence or, at least, did little to stop the massacres, something de Klerk has always vehemently denied.

According to Mandela, de Klerk had allowed the slaughter of inno-cent people because they were black. De Klerk, on his side, was convinced Mandela was overwhelmingly responsible for the vitriolic attacks on himself.[12] In June 1992, the violence culminated in the massacre of forty-five people in Boipathong at the hands of some three hundred machete-wielding men allegedly aligned to the Third Force. De Klerk tried to visit Boipathong to show sympathy, but protesters would not let him exit his car. Mandela visited the site and promised to hold the government accountable, but even these assurances were not enough. With the country descending quickly into chaos, de Klerk had no option but to ask Mandela to speak to the country on national TV. The violence ceased and it was clear to everyone that de Klerk had lost control over the country.

At the negotiating table, Mandela and de Klerk repaired their working relationship in order to reach a settlement and set a date for elections. For this settlement, Mandela and de Klerk received the Nobel Peace Prize in 1993. The ANC won the first democratic elections, and on May 10, 1994, Mandela was inaugurated as president in a ceremony watched by hundreds of millions around the world (including me). A new nonracial constitution was written that contained a robust and detailed Bill of Rights. Mandela also launched the Truth and Reconciliation Commission (TRC), headed by Archbishop Desmond Tutu. Its goal was to forgive the crimes without forgetting them. The TRC had quasi-judicial powers to grant individual amnesties, but only when applicants came out with the full truth. The TRC was able to reveal a detailed and credible picture of torturers, murderers, and victims, which has helped heal South Africa.[13]

Yet, many blacks remained deeply angry about the past, while many Afrikaners had not made their peace with the new South Africa. Mandela understood that the Afrikaners had nowhere to go (unlike many whites of British descent), and that they were tough, heavily armed, military veterans. A nightmarish scenario would be a prolonged guerrilla war against highly trained Afrikaner fighters. Mandela was keenly aware of what their ancestors had accomplished in the Boer War (chapter 6). He also realized South Africa sorely needed the cooperation and goodwill of Afrikaners in the reconstruction of the country.[14] Reconciliation between the two sworn enemies, blacks and Afrikaners, required more than a new constitution. It required a change in the hearts of the people. Mandela was looking for a dramatic symbolic gesture. He found that in an unlikely corner: rugby.

MANDELA USES RUGBY TO RECONCILE A NATION WITH ITSELF

Few things are as symbolic as sports. Sports bring people together and create national unity. Even in a country like the Netherlands, which rejects most symbols of nationalism, when Orange (the name of the Dutch national soccer team) plays in the FIFA World Cup tournament, the entire country is decked out with orange flags. During matches, you can picnic on the street if you belong to the 1 percent who does not watch.

In South Africa, there was no unifying sport.[15] The one team sport in which South Africa excelled was rugby, akin to American football. However, at the time, rugby was played by whites, while blacks favored soccer. White South Africans, and especially Afrikaners, were crazy about rugby. It was their secular religion. For blacks, rugby, more than any other sport, was associated with apartheid, and with Afrikaner thuggery toward blacks.[16] The national team, called the Springboks, was seen as a symbol of apartheid oppression as repellent as the old white national anthem (*"Die Stem van Suid-Afrika"*—"The Call of South Africa") and the old flag (based on the seventeenth-century Dutch flag). Whenever the Springboks played against another country, the few black people in the stadium were loudly cheering every point scored by the other side.

Due to international sanctions, South Africa was excluded from the first two Rugby World Cups in 1987 and 1991. But after the negotiated settlement in South Africa, international bans were lifted, and the third Rugby World Cup tournament would be held in South Africa in 1995. Early in his presidency, Mandela saw the possibility that the Rugby World Cup might present him with the opportunity to win the hearts of the Afrikaners—to show them he was serious about reconciliation and that the Springboks were the team of all South Africans. His challenge was to win over the Afrikaners without losing his black followers.

Mandela argued forcefully at meetings with the ANC for using rugby as an instrument of political reconciliation. Initial reactions were very negative. At one rally, his supporters booed him down when he said that the Springboks were now their team, too. One activist summarized the revulsion: "These Afrikaner rugby people, they were the ones that treated us worst. These were the guys who kicked us off the pavements onto the street, who said, 'Give way, kaffir.'"[17] Mandela persevered and argued that nation building required that they all had to pay a price. The whites had to open sports to black people, and blacks must embrace the rugby team. After much effort, and drawing on his immense moral authority and leveraging the trust his followers had in him, he was able to persuade his people to acquiesce. Mandela also blocked efforts to eliminate the very name of Springboks and their distinctive green jerseys.

Mandela began his efforts to win the hearts of the Afrikaners barely a month after his inauguration. He invited François Pienaar, the captain of the Springboks team, for tea at his office in Pretoria, and to woo him ("I felt like a wide-eyed kid listening to an old man telling stories," Pienaar said later).[18] Mandela was keenly involved with the preparations for the tournament. He worked closely with Morné du Plessis, the Springboks' manager, who presented several ideas to make the Springboks more palatable to blacks. Du Plessis came up with the slogan "One Team, One Country." It was a powerful one-liner that conveyed Mandela's broader purpose to perfection. He also proposed teaching the teammates to sing the "black" half of the new national anthem (the other half still being "*Die Stem*"), "*Nkosi Sikelel' iAfrika*" ("God Bless Africa"), which was the old liberation protest song.

On May 25, 1995, the Springboks played their first match, against reigning world champion Australia, in Cape Town. Mandela visited the players the day before. He told them, "You now have the opportunity of serving South Africa and uniting our people . . . Just remember, all of us, black and white, are behind you."[19] He chatted with the players, who were stunned when he greeted each of them by name. He won them over completely. Now, they would be playing not only for glory, but also for their country and their president. Before the match, Mandela appeared on the field in the stadium wearing the cap he received the day before from one of the players.

Invigorated by the rising tide of support among all South Africans, the Springboks defeated one team after another, until they reached the final, in which they opposed the legendary New Zealand All Blacks, one of rugby's best teams ever. By now, the entire country—blacks and whites—was rooting for the Springboks. The streets were deserted. The match was played at Ellis Park in Johannesburg, the center of South Africa's economy and symbol of former white power. Of the 62,000 in the stadium, many could have come right from an Afrikaner defiance rally. It was a security nightmare. What would Mandela's reception be?

Minutes before kickoff, Mandela stepped out onto the field, wearing the Springboks cap and jersey. The crowd gasped, went dead still, and then exploded in a thundering roar: "Nel-son! Nel-son! Nel-son!" Du Plessis spoke for millions of Afrikaners when he said, "It was the moment when I realized that there really was a chance this country could work. This man was showing that he could forgive, totally, and now they—white South Africa, rugby white South Africa—they showed in that response to him that they too wanted to give back."[20]

Against all odds, the Springboks defeated the All Blacks in overtime, and the country exploded. Mandela emerged again, still in his green jersey and to even louder cries of "Nel-son! Nel-son!," walking onto the pitch to shake the hand of Springboks' captain Pienaar. As he prepared to hand over the Webb Ellis Cup to the captain, he said, "François, thank you for what you have done for our country." The Afrikaner Pienaar replied, "No, Mr. President. Thank *you* for what you have done for our country."[21] In his acceptance speech, Pienaar made it clear that the team had won the trophy not just for the 62,000 fans at Ellis Park, but for all 43 million South Africans.

A short video of that day at Ellis Park. Note that the fans wave the new post-apartheid flag.

https://www.youtube.com/watch?v=G7E4KGJFTek

The image of a beaming Mandela wearing the Springbok rugby jersey at the victorious end of the Rugby World Cup became the graphic symbol for reconciliation and transformation.[22] It was widely seen as a major step in the reconciliation of white and black South Africans; as de Klerk put it,

"Mandela won the hearts of millions of white rugby fans."[23] Kobie Coetsee, the former minister of justice and prisons, regarded the moment as comparable to the creation of the United States, and called it "Mandela's greatest achievement."[24] Archbishop Desmond Tutu, the winner of the 1984 Nobel Peace Prize, understood the emotive power of what had happened that day. He concluded that Mandela's genuine and authentic leadership did for South Africans what speeches and rational arguments could not. It made the people realize that it is actually possible for blacks and whites to be on the same side.[25] Jani (Engelbrecht) Brown, an Afrikaner and now a program assistant at the Kenan-Flagler Business School, told me her experience, which is worth recounting in full:

> I was in high school when Mandela became president. Not having known anything other than apartheid, it was scary. Will they retaliate? How bad will it be? It was a big change and my whole family was very afraid of what is to come. There was Mandela . . . the man who will make all the mayhem and destruction possible. Him and what he is taking away invoked fear in the hearts of Afrikaners. A few tense months into the "new South Africa" came the Rugby World Cup, still a "white man's" sport. A huge triumph as we as a country had not competed in sport on an international level for many years because of apartheid sanctions. Here we are, in the finals of the World Cup, the first year we compete. I will never forget the day my family and friends gathered to watch that Rugby World Cup game. Filled with excitement and anticipation, we tuned in only to see Mandela wearing the green and gold Springbok jersey. That was a shock. That was the first day my family quietly started to believe, this man might bring unity and a brighter future for this country. And he did. By the end of that game I remember how we [cheered] Mandela, as well as our winning champions. He replaced fear with hope in one single moment. Our unlikely hero.

Recognizing a powerful story when it sees it, Hollywood made a movie of the events, called *Invictus*, after Mandela's beloved poem (see the next section). The movie featured Morgan Freeman as Mandela and Matt Damon as Pienaar, who both earned Oscar nominations. While the film takes some liberties, it is remarkably accurate.

Although the 1996 constitution allowed the president to serve two consecutive five-year terms, Mandela resigned after one term in 1999. He had never planned to stand for a second term in office. While much remains to be done before the consequences of centuries of oppression are rectified, it is largely due to Nelson Mandela's authentic leadership that South Africa did not drown in seas of blood in the 1990s. Mandela died on December 5, 2013. The memorial service on December 10 was one of the largest gatherings of world leaders ever, attended by America's own first black president, Barack Obama, among others. On November 2, 2019, the Springboks won their third Rugby World Cup, with a multiracial team and a black player as its captain.

LESSONS

Mandela started his career as a hedgehog, animated by his vision to overthrow the hated apartheid regime through military action. Over time, he became a soaring eagle. Two things happened. First, his vision changed to a multiracial, democratic South Africa where there was a place for all races, including the Afrikaners. Second, he became much more flexible in the use of his means. He came to see that the ANC's military means were simply no match for the power of the South African security apparatus. While he did not give up on armed resistance, he came to use it as just one tool to keep pressure on the government, while he negotiated with them to reach a settlement. Mandela's new vision required that he achieve reconciliation between the races. He understood that he could not possibly achieve reconciliation between blacks and Afrikaners unless he could convince them that he was sincere. In this, he faced a daunting challenge: changing himself.

The leadership thinkers David Rooke and William Torbert distinguish between seven action logics—how leaders interpret their surroundings and react when their power or safety is challenged. The highest form of action logic is called "alchemist." Alchemists have an extraordinary capacity to deal simultaneously with many situations at multiple levels. They can talk with heads of state and with people in townships. They excel in the ability to reinvent themselves, and their organizations, in historically significant ways. Mandela clearly exhibited this highest form of action logic.[26]

But how did Mandela reinvent himself as a reconciler between the races? In his autobiography, *Long Walk to Freedom*, Mandela described the internal struggles before he was able to forgive his enemies. For many years in prison, Mandela survived on his hatred. But one day, he realized that the government could take everything away from him except his mind and his heart. If his mind and heart would be filled with hate, then the regime would own him completely. In his words, "I wanted to be free. And so I let it go."[27] This insight proved key to his ability to heal a nation. Where did he find his inspiration? For one, he was deeply inspired by the life of Martin Luther King (see chapter 15). But unlike King, for whom the Christian faith was the key source of inspiration, Mandela was not a particularly religious man. He found inspiration in the poem "Invictus" ("Unconquered"), by the nineteenth-century English poet William Ernest Henley. It is worth quoting it in full:

Out of the night that covers me,
Black as the pit from pole to pole,
I thank whatever gods may be
For my unconquerable soul.

In the fell clutch of circumstance
I have not winced nor cried aloud.
Under the bludgeonings of chance
My head is bloody, but unbowed.

Beyond this place of wrath and tears
Looms but the Horror of the shade,
And yet the menace of the years
Finds and shall find me unafraid.

It matters not how strait the gate,
How charged with punishments the scroll,
I am the master of my fate,
I am the captain of my soul.

Having transformed himself, he was well placed to address the dual challenges of reaching out to his enemies while keeping his followers on board. Let us first look at his strategy to win over the Afrikaners. Two elements stand out.

First, he got to know the enemy. He learned Afrikaans in prison and read Afrikaans literature and history books. This helped him understand the Afrikaners' psyche, their complex of feeling threatened by others—first by condescending English South Africans, now by the overwhelming majority of blacks.[28] Knowing your enemy is a first step toward disarming them. Time and again, Mandela impressed Afrikaner leaders by speaking their language. It showed respect for their heritage and created a tentative bond he could leverage.

An anecdote from the Netherlands highlights the power of communicating with people in their own language. When the Dutch Crown Prince (now King) Willem Alexander announced his intention to marry Máxima Zorreguieta, it caused a furor in the Netherlands because her father was a minister in the bloodthirsty Argentinian regime of General Videla in the late 1970s. But when Máxima was interviewed for the first time on Dutch television, the population was blown away by her command of their language—which is neither globally important nor beautiful (many Dutch would agree with me that that honor goes to French). National sentiment changed dramatically (admittedly, mine too), her father was forgotten, and Queen Máxima is now the most popular member of the royal family.

Alternatively, it will already pay big dividends if you know something about the home countries of your team members. They will see this as a sign of respect for their heritage, just as the Afrikaners did. In my experience, before visiting another country in a professional capacity, studying some of its history, culture, and politics invariably opens doors, especially during the dinner afterward.

Second, Mandela consciously communicated his commitment to embracing Afrikaners by symbolic gestures, all aimed to convey the message that he was their president, too. His appearance at Ellis Park in a Springboks outfit was the most dramatic one. Jani Brown testified as to its impact. One Afrikaner who was present at Ellis Park said, "You should have seen the faces of these Boers all around me. I was looking at one of them and there were tears rolling down his face and he kept saying: *'Dit is my president'* ['That is my president'].'' Mandela made many other symbolic gestures. At his inauguration, three of his erstwhile prison guards were given a place of honor. He had lunch with Percy Yutar, the hectoring and vindictive prosecutor at the Rivonia trial.[29] He visited former president P. W. Botha after he had a stroke. Botha was a decidedly unpleasant character—his nickname *Die Groot Krokodil* (The Big Crocodile) says enough. He visited Betsy Verwoerd, the widow of the hated chief architect of apartheid, Dr. Hendrik Verwoerd. She read a demand for an Afrikaner homeland, something that Mandela absolutely disagreed with. Yet, when the ninety-four-year-old widow struggled with the text, he helped her read it, in Afrikaans! None of these behaviors were necessarily expected of President Mandela, but they sent a compelling signal to Afrikaners about his sincerity.

Mandela needed to reach out to Afrikaners without losing his followers. In *Long Walk to Freedom*, Mandela explained his view on how to do this: "There are times when a leader must move out ahead of the flock, go off in a new direction, confident that he is leading his people in the right way."[30] His challenge was to lead the flock without losing them. As a lone ranger, his political career would have been short-lived, ending like Mikhail Gorbachev's, the Soviet Union's last leader. He avoided this by repeated strong public statements that he was a loyal servant of the ANC. Said one of his fellow prisoners and ANC leaders, "The 'I' [Mandela] never supplanted the organization."[31] He never made it about himself. After his release from prison, Mandela said, "They [the ANC] may say: well you are a man of seventy-one, you require a pension; or, look, we don't like your face, please go. *I will obey them*" (emphasis added).[32] By declaring his total loyalty to the movement, he reassured others that, even if he did things they disagreed with, they could still trust him.[33] He did not even forget his black followers during the rugby event. Mandela walked onto the pitch wearing the Springboks' jersey so hated by black South Africans, at the same time giving the clenched fist salute of the ANC, thereby appealing, almost impossibly, both to black and white South Africans.[34]

Finally, consider Mandela's outstanding ability to forge relationships with others, both with his followers and his enemies. His relationships with fellow ANC leaders proved crucial when he engaged in the exploratory talks with the government prior to his release from prison. Many in the ANC were suspicious that he might sell out the organization, but ANC president Oliver Tambo kept faith in him. Mandela's ability to relate to others helped him win the hearts and minds of a long list of Afrikaner leaders.

CHAPTER TAKEAWAYS

- Mandela started as a hedgehog, who over time became a soaring eagle. His vision for the country changed, to a multiracial, democratic South Africa, and he learned to become more flexible in the use of his means.

- Despite being tortured and imprisoned, Mandela came to the realization that only by letting go of hatred would he become "the master of his fate, the captain of his soul." This set him on the path of authentic leadership to reconcile the races of South Africa.

- Mandela is an example of the highest form of action logic—an alchemist.

- He won over the Afrikaners by working hard to understand where they were coming from and by highly visible gestures.

- Mandela made sure he did not "lose" the blacks by swearing absolute loyalty to the ANC and never made it about himself. He emphasized repeatedly that his career, his negotiations, and his fame were due to the ANC.

- Mandela's parting gift was to resign after one term. It set a shining example for democratic change in South Africa and beyond.

- Mandela's life highlights several authentic leadership principles:

    ° Authentic leadership may require that you change yourself.

    ° The need for integrity in all strands of life—private and public.

    ° Symbolic, emotional gestures captivate hearts more than logical reasoning. For most people, heart trumps mind.

    ° If you go against the beliefs of your followers for the greater good, counter the negative effects by emphasizing that you are still one of them. This is made easier if you exhibit strong relationship-building skills.

REFLECTIONS ON AUTHENTIC LEADERSHIP

AUTHENTICITY AS AN ideal dates back to the ancient Greeks, as captured by their timeless admonition that people be "true to themselves."[1] Authentic leadership is an attractive type of leadership. In today's culture, being authentic is clearly seen as highly positive. According to *Forbes* contributor Kevin Kruse, though, many leaders attempt to be one way at work, while their true personality emerges outside of work. He noted that one CEO reminded him that "leadership is acting." And these same leaders seem shocked or confused when their employees do not trust them.[2]

Truly excelling on authentic leadership—as opposed to demonstrating a "normal" level of integrity and honesty in one's behavior—requires particular qualities that may not be for everyone. According to Bill George, one of the founding fathers of authentic leadership theory, authentic leaders (1) develop strong values about the right thing to do, (2) show integrity consistently across all spheres of life, (3) exercise self-discipline, (4) are willing to sacrifice for their values, and (5) establish meaningful relationships with followers.[3] Let us evaluate the lives of George Washington and Nelson Mandela on these common themes.

1. DEVELOP STRONG VALUES ABOUT THE RIGHT THING TO DO

Authentic leadership requires a strong inner compass. Authentic leaders know, in the terminology of Bill George, their "True North."[4] They have a clear idea of what is the right thing to do. They do not make it about

themselves, but about what they stand for. While Americans strongly identified the nation with Washington and blacks put their faith in Mandela,
both leaders emphasized that it was the cause—independence and democracy—that mattered. Given the adoration and praise showered upon them,
it truly takes strong values not to be corrupted.

Burma's Nobel Peace Prize–winning dissident Aung San Suu Kyi provides a sobering lesson. For decades, she led the Burmese people in resistance
to the military dictatorship by her moral authority and courageous behavior.
After she became the country's civilian leader, her erstwhile supporters have
since accused her of betraying her values. The most egregious instance was
her staunch defense of the military's brutality against the country's ethnic Rohingya Muslim minority. When she was still a dissident, she wrote
that it is not power that corrupts, but fear of losing power that corrupts
those who wield it. According to the U.N. High Commissioner for Human
Rights, "she has proved she is no exception to that rule."[5]

2. SHOW CONSISTENT INTEGRITY ACROSS ALL SPHERES OF LIFE

Integrity across time and situations is key to authentic leadership. Nothing
undermines authenticity more than (perceived) hypocrisy. In 2019, the
Duke and Duchess of Sussex (Harry and Meghan) announced that they
would have no more than two children because of humans' environmental
imprint. However, shortly thereafter, it was revealed that they used private
jets for their travel. The outcry was tremendous. Their behavior was seen as
hypocritical. Such arguably hypocritical behavior cannot be found in the
lives of Washington and Mandela.

Washington and Mandela could not be bribed, corrupted, or compromised, despite repeated attempts by their adversaries. Their "true"
personality did not emerge outside of work—their private personas were
aligned with their public personas. Near the end of the Revolutionary
War, a British warship was anchored near Washington's beloved estate at
Mount Vernon, presumably to ravage his property. His cousin, who was

the steward of the estate during the war, bought off the British captain with a boatload of provisions. Washington berated him: "It would have been a less painful circumstance to me, to have heard, that in consequence of your non-compliance with their request, they had burnt my House, and laid the Plantation in ruins."[6]

Mandela's outreach to Afrikaners did not "just" appear in front of the camera. My friend Steve Burgess served as a member of the South African five-person mission team to the United States in June 1994. He told me about a meeting he had shortly after Mandela's election as president. One of the people present made light of a meeting with de Klerk's outgoing team the next day. Mandela asked if he had slept well the night before. Then Mandela asked if he thought de Klerk and his team had slept as soundly, naming them one by one. Mandela reminded the people in the meeting that nonracial democracy was fragile and the former government negotiators took risks that had not been abated by his election. Thus, each of them should be considered a freedom fighter for their own cause, and treated with respect in the negotiations.

Washington and Mandela exhibited integrity right until the end; that is, they made the ultimate sacrifice many leaders find so difficult to make—to leave before their due date. Authentic leaders resign their position while their followers are loath to see them leave. Despite the admiration of their followers, both leaders purposely wanted to signal that they were not indispensable. Washington resigned as president after two terms, Mandela after one term. In both cases, this was unusual. In Washington's case, there was no precedent for stepping down at all. In Mandela's case, fellow African leaders like Robert Mugabe (Zimbabwe), Yoweri Museveni (Uganda), Hosni Mubarak (Egypt), Muammar Gaddafi (Libya), and José Eduardo dos Santos (Angola) were in power long before Mandela became president, and stayed in power long after. By relinquishing power, Mandela set the example for the peaceful and democratic transfer of power from one leader to the next leader.

3. EXERCISE SELF-DISCIPLINE

Self-discipline gives leaders focus and determination. When leaders establish objectives and set standards of excellence, self-discipline helps them reach these goals and helps keep them and their followers accountable. In stressful times, self-discipline allows authentic leaders to remain cool, calm, and consistent in their words and actions. Because authentic leadership is leading by example, everything the leader does or says matters. Both Washington and Mandela possessed an iron control over their emotions. According to biographer Joseph Ellis, "Washington became the most notorious model of self-control in all of American history."[7] In victory and defeat (of which there were many), Washington maintained his stoical composure.[8] While Mandela did express anger at the failure of the government to stop the widespread killing and violence in the early 1990s, this authentic anger was controlled, as he realized that if he let his emotions spin out of control—not unreasonable, given the horrific massacres—the effect on his followers would be terrible. Anthony Lewis of *The New York Times* wrote, "like George Washington, Mandela was a man of strong emotions who suppressed them in the interest of creating a nation."[9]

4. BE WILLING TO PAY THE PRICE

Authentic leaders are willing to pay a high price for achieving their purpose. Mandela longed to be reunited with his family. Nevertheless, he refused three times an offer of release from his lifelong prison sentence because it came with conditions, which he saw as prejudicing the cause of freedom. While in prison, he told his followers at a mass meeting (via his daughter), "I cherish my freedom dearly, but I care even more for your freedom . . . I am not less life-loving than you are. But I [am not] prepared to sell the birthright of the people to be free."[10] Washington was also separated from his family for many years during the Revolutionary War. He did not want to be president, and his wife did not want him to be president either.

5. ESTABLISH MEANINGFUL RELATIONSHIPS WITH FOLLOWERS

According to leadership theorist Bill George, a fifth characteristic of authentic leaders is that they establish meaningful relationships with followers. While this characteristic fully applies to Mandela, Washington was socially rather distant. He inspired tremendous respect but did not really forge deep personal relations with his followers. The implications are intriguing. While Mandela started out with fierce enemies, he was able to reconcile Afrikaners with the new South Africa. As a result, he ended his presidency with vastly more followers than when he was inaugurated. On the other hand, Washington's presidency started out in reasonable harmony, but he could not bridge the emerging gap between two rival views on government. Perhaps nobody could have done that. Yet, it is hard to see that Federalists and Democratic-Republicans were farther apart than blacks and Afrikaners. As a result, Washington ended with many fewer followers than when he began. This shows that even seminal leaders cannot have it all.

To assess whether authentic leadership is a style that suits you, consider the following questions.

1. Do others generally regard you as a person of high integrity, or is this not one of the traits that come to mind first when they think about you? Be honest. Remember, if this is not the case, that does not mean you lack integrity!

2. Are you comfortable leading by example, covering all spheres of your life? Is your public persona aligned with, or different from, your private persona?

3. Do you have a tight grip on your emotions, or are you a person who experiences and expresses emotions as they bubble up?

4. Do you have a strong long-term, guiding purpose in your professional life that supersedes self-interest, for which you are willing to pay a high price, if required?

5. Are you strong on relationship-building skills? Do you enjoy networking or is it a chore?

6. Which authentic leaders do you recognize in your own professional and/or personal environment? How do you relate to their style of leadership?

7. Have there been situations where you set a clear example, and, consequently, people followed your lead?

8. In what situation(s) have you been in where being an "authentic leader" would have been most effective? What did you actually do and with which results?

PART SIX

SERVANT LEADERSHIP — PUT FOLLOWERS FIRST

14

NIGHTINGALE CARRIES A LAMP

"N is Miss Nightingale, with her fair band; Who
solaced our sick in a far distant land . . ."
—THE PANORAMIC ALPHABET OF PEACE (1856)

Leadership Dilemma: Should Florence Nightingale accept the poisoned
chalice of head of nursing operations in Turkey?

CONTEXT

In the early nineteenth century, medical science was in dismal shape.
Bleeding of sick patients was a common "remedy." Wounds were not
thoroughly cleaned and wrapped with fresh bandages. There was no understanding of how diseases spread from one patient to the other. Hospitals
were dirty, overcrowded places that even poor people avoided if they could.
Patient care in hospitals was rudimentary at best, and nurses who worked

in hospitals had no training and commanded little respect.[1] They were recruited from the lower classes, where addiction to alcohol was endemic. Many were victims of sexual harassment from patients and doctors.[2]

The care situation was particularly grim for soldiers. In the eighteenth and nineteenth centuries, the lethality of warfare had increased steadily, and following the French Revolution (1789–1799), European armies swelled dramatically in size. As a result, the number of wounded in the series of wars that swept over Europe between 1792 and 1815 (the French Revolutionary and Napoleonic Wars) increased exponentially, leading to overcrowded field hospitals and a vastly increased death rate. After the final defeat of Napoleon in 1815, Europe experienced four decades of peace, and hospital reform—never a priority anyway—receded into the background. This changed with the advent of the Crimean War (1853–1856), which was fought between Russia and a coalition of Great Britain, France, the Ottoman (Turkish) Empire, and Sardinia.

Allied forces landed on the Crimean peninsula in September 1854 to capture Russia's main naval base at Sevastopol. It was a human disaster from start to finish. The fighting was only noted for its "notoriously incompetent butchery."[3] Turkish barracks in Scutari (near Istanbul) were retrofitted into a hospital for wounded British soldiers. Conditions were terrible. Beds were crammed within eighteen inches of each other. There was a lack of bandages, medical supplies, food, clothing, and blankets. Infection, typhus, typhoid, dysentery, pneumonia, and cholera killed thousands of wounded soldiers. Eighty-two percent of patients who underwent an amputation died in postoperative care. Soldiers who were hastily operated upon in the battlefield stood a statistically much better chance of survival.[4]

Yet, the Barrack Hospital was not uniquely bad among military hospitals. What was unique, though, was that its conditions attracted the attention of the *London Times* newspaper, which reported extensively on the hospital's horrible conditions. This was made possible by the recent invention of the telegraph. A public uproar threatened to bring down the government.

Something had to be done urgently to rectify the situation. Secretary of War Sir Sidney Herbert spun into action. According to him, "There is but one person in England that I know of, who would be capable of organizing & superintending such a scheme."[5] That person was Florence Nightingale, a thirty-four-year-old, physically fragile woman with little formal training in nursing, but with a keen intellect and sharp observational faculties.

FLORENCE NIGHTINGALE

Florence Nightingale was born on May 12, 1820, into a wealthy, socially well-connected family, the second child of William and Fanny Nightingale. Her father insisted that she and her sister, Parthenope, receive an education far beyond what was typical for British girls. William Nightingale was ahead of his time, when many people thought a girl lacked a boy's intelligence and that too much study would make her unladylike.[6] The sisters could hardly have been more different. Parthenope cared for fun, parties, and fashion, while Florence liked to read and was self-absorbed, thoughtful, neat, and methodical. She exhibited great interest in learning foreign languages as well as the sciences, especially mathematics.[7]

In her teenage years, Nightingale became increasingly aware of the sickness and poverty that was rampant in neighboring villages. She started to attend to the patients' needs, often spending hours with the sick and dying. In the next decade, attending to the sick gave meaning to Nightingale, who chafed at prevailing conventions that expected gentlewomen to marry, bear children, and spend their days in leisure—a life so well described in Jane Austen novels. On journeys with her family to the Continent, she often took detours from tourist paths to visit hospitals, prisons, and charitable institutions. In Paris, she befriended Mary Clarke, an English expatriate who was to have a great influence on Nightingale's thinking. Clarke lived independently, was a prolific writer, and advocated for women's rights. She provided a role model for Nightingale, showing her the possibilities for a Victorian-era lady if she had the courage to defy social norms and carve her own destiny.[8]

Nightingale asked herself what an individual could do to alleviate the suffering of the poor and helpless, and by the age of twenty-four she knew that the answer for her was to pursue nursing. In December 1845, she shared her intentions with her family, who could not believe their ears. Her mother and sister were especially vehement in their objections, accusing her of being selfish, displaying vanity, and wanting to mingle with lower classes where she might hear indecent words and be exposed to vulgar behavior.[9]

After a second attempt one month later also failed to persuade her family, Nightingale adopted a different strategy. During normal hours, she played the dutiful daughter, focused on home and family; but in the early morning and late at night, when she was alone, she studied reports on hospitals and health care, tabulating information. She learned that experts were beginning to suspect that the high death rates from diseases like typhus and smallpox arose from unclean living conditions.[10] Still, Nightingale felt unfulfilled and she sank into depression. Help came from friends of the family, the Bracebridges, who invited her on an extended trip to Rome in the winter of 1848. In Rome, she met, and became friends with, Sidney and Elizabeth Herbert. According to her biographer Mark Bostridge, "the encounter can only be described as momentous."[11] Herbert was a rising star in the Conservative Party and would become a steadfast supporter of her.

Nightingale returned home to find nothing had changed. Her family stubbornly opposed her nursing plans until they finally relented in 1851— after five years!—worried about her depressed and possibly suicidal state of mind, and persuaded by trends in society that saw some women of standing starting to enter the nursing profession.[12] Nightingale was allowed to spend three months at the nursing institute at Kaiserwerth, Germany. At the time, Kaiserwerth was probably the most advanced place in the world to train nurses. Her time there rejuvenated Nightingale; gone were feelings of boredom, despondency, and aimlessness that had dragged her down all those years. She worked in all sections of the institute, made copious notes, and paid close attention to how the female superintendent ran the hospital. Her time there gave her invaluable clinical experience. She dressed wounds, practiced bandaging, prepared and issued medicines, and assisted in operations.[13] Her parents finally, and against their best instincts, reluctantly acquiesced to her nursing ambitions.[14]

In 1853, Nightingale was appointed as the new superintendent of a small charitable institution for sick gentlewomen in London. She had her freedom at last. She applied lessons learned from her study of hospitals on the Continent and developed management skills that would prove crucial during the Crimean War.[15] She completely reorganized the institution, cleaning the rat-infested place, making new linens from old cloth, reorganizing the food supply, and cutting costs wherever possible to redirect those monies to other purposes. After about a year, in August 1854, with the hospital running smoothly, she needed a bigger challenge and she resigned. That challenge came soon, and it was vastly bigger than anything she could have imagined.

On October 12, 1854, the *London Times* printed a shocking report on the conditions at the Barrack Hospital at Scutari, and on October 18, with the unanimous approval of the cabinet, her friend, Secretary of War Herbert, appointed her "Superintendent of the female nursing establishment in the English General Military Hospitals in Turkey." She would have complete authority over nursing operations in Turkey and over the nurses she would hire to help with her task. Her hour of destiny had finally arrived. Yet, many would consider it a poisoned gift. Not being of strong health, in a farewell letter she admitted that she little expected to see Britain again.[16]

Figure 14.1 Florence Nightingale, 1858

Source: Goodman

THE LADY WITH THE LAMP

The Barrack Hospital in Scutari made J.R.R. Tolkien's Mordor look like a spa. This is how one of the nurses described the place: "It was like a huge slaughter-house . . . wounded men lying with mangled limbs on the open pavements . . . Most of them, even apart from wounds, were half-dead with cold and exposure. Some had been six weeks in the trenches, with their flesh frozen to their clothes."[17] Bandages, clothing, blankets, medications, and food were in short supply, or absent. The hospital was unventilated. There was no kitchen or laundry room.

With no time to lose, Nightingale took action. The most urgent task was to improve sanitation. She understood the relationship between sanitation and health, which at the time was not yet a widely accepted notion (Louis Pasteur's groundbreaking work on germs lay in the future). Many of her actions are considered to be common sense now, but not then. She and her team of thirty-eight hand-picked female nurses set to work bathing the wounded, washing and changing their bedsheets, and insisting on using a clean cloth for each patient (until then, it was common to use the same cloth to clean multiple patients). She commanded that windows be installed to allow the circulation of fresh air. Human waste was removed from the patients, and she used her own money to buy better food. These basic measures led to a significant decrease in the mortality rate.

Nightingale had to operate with caution and needed to keep close control over her team because of organizational resistance. Many in the army's medical staff, particularly the older and more senior doctors, resented any intrusion into their territory—especially if it came from a woman. She ensured that neither she nor her team could be accused of infringing on army regulations and lines of authority. Her close surveillance of the nurses reflected her well-founded concern that any indiscretion or sign of disobedience could jeopardize the whole operation. Nurses who were deemed incompetent or who had been caught drunk were summarily sent home.

A crisis of authority emerged in December 1854 when Secretary of War Herbert authorized sending a second party of forty-six nurses to Scutari under Mary Stanley, an old acquaintance of Nightingale's. This was in direct violation of the agreement with Nightingale that no more nurses would be sent until she specifically requested them. She lashed out at Herbert in an angry letter. Nightingale had sound practical objections: She doubted she could properly supervise over eighty nurses, she did not know their qualifications, and she lacked space to house the extra nurses. But underlying this was that Nightingale resented Stanley's intrusion on her authority. Two captains on one ship never make for smooth sailing; so, when Stanley and her team arrived, Nightingale announced she would resign and requested that Stanley take her place. This was a bluff—she did not want to resign at all—but it worked. Terrified at being in charge of such a large team in such difficult circumstances, Stanley resigned on the spot and Nightingale's authority was confirmed.[18]

Nightingale could work as much as twenty hours a day. At night, when others were fast asleep, she patrolled the cavernous hospital, carrying an oil lamp to light her way in the dark, checking the wounds of some and speaking words of comfort to others. The first appearance of the iconic image of the "Lady with the Lamp" appeared in the *Illustrated London News* on February 24, 1855.

The iconic image of the "Lady with the Lamp" as it appeared in the *Illustrated London News*

https://www.npg.org.uk/collections/search/portrait/mw39734/Florence-Nightingale?LinkID=mp03298&wPage=1&role=sit&rNo=29

The portrayal of Nightingale with her lamp, on her nighttime vigil in the wards at Scutari, became part of her personal mythology and remains one of the most enduring and iconic images of the modern age. This is what John Macdonald wrote in the *London Times* after returning from visiting Scutari:

> She is a "ministering angel" without any exaggeration in these hospitals, and as her slender form glides quietly along each corridor, every poor fellow's face softens with gratitude at the

sight of her. When all the medical officers have retired for the night and silence and darkness have settled down upon those miles of prostrate sick, she may be observed alone, with a little lamp in her hand, making her solitary rounds.

The government promoted the image of Nightingale as a heroine in a conflict that lacked military giants of the ilk of Wellington or Nelson, and to deflect attention from their own incompetence.

Once the Scutari hospitals were running well, Nightingale expanded the scope of her activities. For example, patients would spend much of their money on alcohol. She banned all sales and consumption of alcohol at Scutari, but, since time immemorial, idle soldiers always find a way to get booze. What to do about this? She devised a three-pronged strategy. First, offer an alternative—she established the Inkerman Café where the men could get coffee and food. Second, relieve boredom—she established reading rooms and schools to occupy the mind. Third, relieve them of their money—if soldiers could send money home, they could not squander it on booze. Capitalizing on the trust they had in her (there were enough financial swindlers around—not much has changed over time here, either), every Saturday afternoon she collected money from the men that they wished to send home to support their families.[19]

Long before it became common practice in the armed forces, Nightingale included the soldiers' families in her care, answering inquiries about the missing and seriously ill, and writing letters of condolence. Here is an excerpt of a letter, typical of many others. It informed a Mrs. Maria Hunt of the death of her son:

I grieve to be obliged to inform you that your son died in this Hospital on Sunday last . . . His complaint was Chronic Dysentery—he sank gradually from weakness, without much suffering . . . when there was anything he had a fancy for, it was taken to him immediately . . . [H]e spoke much of his Mother, & gave us the direction to you in his last

moments . . . He died peacefully & sorrowful as this news is
for his bereaved Mother.[20]

The attention to detail and the care to soften a mother's grief by emphasizing that his last moments were as comfortable as could be, with his
mother being on his mind, are exemplary. Few trained bereavement coun-
selors could do a better job.

Nightingale was only given control over the appointment and allocation of female nurses in Turkey. But due to her successful work in Turkey,
women had also moved into military hospitals in the Crimea. This frustrated
Nightingale, as she strove to maintain uniform high standards. In May 1855,
she journeyed to the Crimea to lay claim to what she considered to be her
rightful domain. The soldiers received her with warm cheers, but she encountered fierce resistance from Dr. John Hall, the army's chief medical officer.
Hall objected to change in almost any form. For example, he refused the use
of chloroform, a relatively new drug widely favored by younger surgeons, in
amputations. Through his contacts, Hall threw up one bureaucratic obstacle
after the other. One of his associates wrote a report in which Nightingale's
nurses were accused of lax discipline, insubordination, and drunkenness, while
nurses that were not under her authority received fulsome praise. Nightingale
defended herself with gusto, writing an even longer rebuttal report and calling upon the war department to order the army medical officers to no longer
oppose her. After considerable governmental dithering, she achieved victory.
On March 16, 1856, she became superintendent of every nurse in every army
hospital in the war zone.[21] It made no difference anymore—two weeks later,
the war was over—but a precedent was set.

Nightingale's success was bought at high personal cost. During her first
stay in the Crimea, she contracted brucellosis, a bacterial illness caused
by consuming milk or meat from infected goats. For much of the rest of
her life, Nightingale would be plagued by chronic pain, fever, exhaustion,
depression, and nervous irritability. She often would not even be able to
leave the house because of illness. Yet, from her chaise longue, she used her
celebrity status, dubbed "Nightingale Power," experience, and network of

contacts in high places—including Queen Victoria—to further the cause of health care for the next fifty years.

Her work in the ensuing decades ensured that what she started in Turkey would change health care forever. Drawing on the careful notes she had kept while in Scutari, she wrote a report on improving patient care in the army hospitals. Her 800-page report was full of statistics, numerical tables, and graphs that conveyed the message more powerfully than dry numbers would. Her innovative use of statistics earned her admission to the Royal Statistical Society in 1858, making her the first woman to receive that honor. Although implementing her recommendations took some time, largely due to resistance by the bureaucracy in the war office and the army, her suggestions would lead to an extraordinary improvement in the health of the British army. The peacetime mortality rate among soldiers in Britain declined from 2 percent per year before the Crimean War to 0.5 percent a decade later.

In 1860 Nightingale established the world's first secular nursing school for women: the Nightingale School of Nursing. It became a model for many similar training schools throughout the United Kingdom, its empire, and other countries. It continues to be one of the best nursing schools in the world. The association between nursing and women became so strong that, in the 2018 movie *On the Basis of Sex*, the young Ruth Bader Ginsburg (played by Felicity Jones) had to fight the generally accepted wisdom that nurses were women. While from today's perspective this is sexist, we should not forget that when Nightingale entered the profession, it was the reverse. She broke the sexist barrier so successfully that nursing became one of the few "respectable" occupations for women for many decades.

In 1863 she published a 2,028-page report on better sanitation of the British army in India. It contained massive amounts of statistics and information collected in surveys. One decade later, the mortality rate had declined from 6.9 percent to 1.8 percent as a direct result of her recommendations.[22] Subsequently, she broadened her scope to the oppressed, poverty-stricken, huge Indian peasant population. Understanding that keeping people clean when they are dying of starvation made little sense, in a series of papers and pamphlets she advocated a program of irrigation, land tenancy reform, and sanitation that was far ahead of her time. Sadly, there was little follow-up.

Nightingale's legacy was further cemented by an outpouring of writings. Two of her books, *Notes on Hospitals* (1859) and *Notes on Nursing* (1860), became particularly influential. Nightingale practiced an early form of market segmentation for *Notes on Nursing*. The initial version was written for middle-class women who were caring for the sick at home. Subsequently, she released adapted versions targeting professional hospital nurses and working-class women. These books ignited reforms in hospital design and health care all across the world.

When she died on August 13, 1910, in London, thousands of mourners gathered to pay their respects. *The New York Times* wrote: "Perhaps the greatest good that has resulted from her noble life has been the setting in motion of a force which has led thousands of women to devote themselves to systematic care of the sick and wounded."[23] In 1912, the International Committee of the Red Cross instituted the Florence Nightingale Medal, the highest international distinction a nurse can achieve. Since 1965, International Nurses Day is celebrated on her birthday, May 12.

LESSONS

While several of the leaders discussed in this book changed history by killing people, Nightingale changed history by keeping people alive. Her lasting contribution has been her role in founding the modern nursing profession, which would save millions of lives in the cataclysmic wars that were to come. Nightingale was a hedgehog. The central goal in her life was to improve health care for the sick, primarily through nursing. She was dogmatic about the means through which that should be achieved—nursing, hygiene, fresh air. She had a low regard for doctors, and it took her a long time to embrace germ theory. Her hedgehog qualities might have been necessary to fight and overcome endless bureaucratic obstacles. Yet, the struggle was tough on her. Her frustration comes out clearly in a letter she wrote to the war office in her bid to unify all nurses in the war theater under her command:

> If the War Department desire me to continue to exercise these functions entrusted to me by themselves, I must request that they will support me . . . by notifying to the Inspector General of Hospitals [Dr. John Hall] that he is to second & not to oppose me in the performance of my duties. The incessant difficulties arising from the want of such support consume my time & strength to the impediment of my work.[24]

Note that when she wrote this letter, she was not receiving any salary, often paid for food and books for the wounded out of her own pocket, had already saved thousands of lives, and had ruined her own health. Most other people would have given up. She persevered because she believed she served the wounded soldiers who had come to adore her. Nightingale relied on concepts like duty and a desire to serve. What can we learn from her servant leadership? I single out two things: self-effacement, and the challenges to serving both the needs of distal and immediate followers.

Despite all her accomplishments, Nightingale exhibited a great degree of self-effacement. This was not because she had low self-esteem, but because she did not want to make it about her—she only wanted the focus to be about her mission, the cause of helping the sick and improving health care. She did not crave the adoration of the masses. To avoid a grand welcome, she returned from Scutari incognito, under the name of Miss Smith. She was the famous "lady with the lamp" to everybody but herself. While she was a prolific writer under her own name, she also wrote many articles about the state of health care and gave them to other writers and journalists. If they put their own names on them and took the critical acclaim, that was fine as long as her ideas were spread.[25] When Herbert wanted to mention her efforts for army health in his plans, her reaction was telling: "Whatever information your own judgement has accepted from me will come with far greater force from yourself . . . I had much rather therefore that any mention of my late occupations were left out—not from any modesty or candour, but simply from a feeling what is best for the troops."[26]

Nightingale had two groups of followers: *proximate* followers (her team of nurses and, later, associates who helped her with research and crafting papers) and *distal* followers (patients).

Proximate followers support the leader in serving distal followers, which provide the raison d'être for the organization (think about the staff of a nonprofit or a church, versus the nonprofit's members or the church's congregation). The needs of these two groups are not necessarily aligned and can easily create tensions for the servant leader. Servant leader gurus such as Robert Greenleaf advise managers to put the needs of their immediate followers ahead of themselves and their organization,[27] but what if some team members are mediocre, let alone incompetent or lazy? Should you spend your efforts trying to build them up in the—possibly vain—hope you will succeed? Servant leaders need to consider the economic principle of opportunity costs—the loss of potential gain from other alternatives when one alternative is chosen. Any time you spend on building up your proximate followers is not spent on catering to the needs of your distal followers, who, at the same time, are also underserved by these underperforming team members. When should you call it a day and fire the underperformer?

I have seen organizations struggle with this dilemma. In fact, this dilemma is relevant for all times. An early instance is provided in the New Testament book *Acts of the Apostles.* As we saw in chapter 10, Paul and Barnabas co-led a missionary journey to (present-day) Turkey in 46 to 48 A.D. One of their team members, Mark, deserted them along the way, daunted by the very real physical dangers ahead. When Paul and Barnabas were planning their second journey to revisit the churches they founded on their first trip, Barnabas (which aptly means "son of encouragement")[28] wanted to give Mark a chance to redeem himself by including him in their team. Paul objected and the ensuing disagreement was so sharp that they parted company. Barnabas's focus was on building up an immediate follower while Paul's emphasis was on catering to the needs of distal followers (Christian congregations in Turkey). Paul believed while they needed all the help they could get, he could not trust Mark to stay with them.[29]

Nightingale was never able to fully balance the needs of these two groups of followers. She considered the needs of her distal followers paramount. At the Barrack Hospital, she expected the nurses to obey her without question, and she considered it a waste of time to give them explanations. She had "no time for such trifles."[30] In her defense, the needs of the distal followers were overwhelming—she had thirty-eight nurses to care for four miles of beds.[31] Yet we will never know whether spending more time encouraging her nurses would have led to better outcomes for her distal followers.

What about your organization? Do you have the resources (time, money) to build up your immediate followers? Perhaps you can improve their game by extensive counseling and training, but might this occur at the expense of your distal followers? There may be no Goldilocks solution. For Nightingale, the choice was clear which group of followers was her priority. What about you?

CHAPTER TAKEAWAYS

- Nightingale was a hedgehog. Her life goal was improving health care for the sick, and she was quite dogmatic about the means to achieve this.

- Nightingale had to fight sexism through much of her life, starting with her own mother and sister.

- Although Nightingale was not good at relation building in general, she was able to assemble a coterie of devoted supporters, most importantly, Secretary of War Sidney Herbert.

- Nightingale was a lifelong learner—she acquired and continuously improved her statistical, medical, and administrative skills.

- Nightingale was not able (or particularly interested) to balance the needs of proximate followers (e.g., her team of nurses) and distal followers (e.g., patients in Scutari). Her zeal to serve her distal followers meant she was often harsh and unfeeling toward her proximate followers.

- Nightingale practiced an early form of market segmentation—she adapted her writings to specific target audiences, thus increasing their impact.

- Nightingale's life highlights several servant leadership principles:
  - ° Persevere: even when the only thing you want is to help others.
  - ° Self-effacement: make it about the cause, not yourself.
  - ° Standing ground: as a servant leader, you may need to be tough as a nail, especially when you operate from a weak position.
  - ° Be prepared for frustration: you may be passionate about the people you want to serve, but others may not share your passion, or may even see it as a threat to their position.

KING GOES MIA

"Like anybody, I would like to live a long life. But I'm not concerned about that now . . . I've seen the promised land. I may not get there with you. But I want you to know tonight, that we, as a people, will get to the promised land."

—DR. MARTIN LUTHER KING JR. ON THE NIGHT BEFORE HE WAS ASSASSINATED

Leadership Dilemma: How could King achieve justice for his people in the face of racism and oppression?

CONTEXT

The U.S. Declaration of Independence states: "We hold these truths to be self-evident, that all men are created equal." Noble words, but they did not extend to African-Americans in the Southern states where they were slaves—euphemistically referred to as "those bound to Service for a Term of

Years" in Article 1 of the U.S. Constitution. The issue of slavery was a festering wound in the fledgling United States, and, for all practical purposes, the cause of the Civil War. After the Civil War, the Thirteenth Amendment to the Constitution abolished slavery, the Fourteenth Amendment granted the former slaves citizenship and equal protection of the laws, and the Fifteenth Amendment prohibited states from disenfranchising voters on account of race, color, or previous condition of servitude.

While these amendments looked good on paper, from the late 1870s on, the reality on the ground in the former Confederate States became increasingly grim for blacks. The white elite that was the backbone of the Confederacy returned to power in the Southern state legislatures and passed laws (commonly known as "Jim Crow" laws) requiring segregation of whites and blacks.[1] Segregation invaded all spheres of life, from public transportation, schools, and restrooms to parks, water fountains, cemeteries, theaters, and restaurants in an effort to prevent any contact between blacks and whites as equals. Marriage between whites and blacks was forbidden in many states. Segregation got a tremendous boost when, in 1896, the U.S. Supreme Court issued its infamous "separate but equal" decision (*Plessy v. Ferguson*). It gave constitutional sanction to laws designed to achieve racial segregation by means of separate and supposedly equal public facilities and services for African-Americans and whites.[2] The "separate" part of the decision was pursued with gusto by Southern authorities, while the "equal" part was conveniently forgotten. Regardless of the fact that separate can never be equal, black facilities were invariably far inferior to those of whites.

Segregation was perpetuated by a warped electoral system that disenfranchised the vast majority of blacks in the South. Unintentionally, the Fourteenth Amendment left open the possibility that states could institute voter qualifications equally to all races. Confederate states took advantage of this provision to employ warped literacy and comprehension tests to exclude blacks from voter registration. As a result, in the early 1960s only 20 percent of voting-age blacks in Alabama were registered to vote. In Mississippi, it was even lower: 5 percent.[3]

Most blacks were mired in poverty. Many accepted their plight with apathy and thought of themselves as inferior to whites.[4] Yet there were others who wanted change. In the decade after World War II, discontent was growing, but people did not know how to break down the white bastion. What blacks needed was a leader who would take the initiative, who had the courage—with the Ku Klux Klan roaming about on nightly rides—to serve his community and wrest change from the hands of an unwilling local elite. Could this be achieved through peaceful means, or was armed struggle required? A twenty-six-year-old Baptist pastor, Dr. Martin Luther King Jr., would show the way.

MARTIN LUTHER KING JR.

Martin Luther King Jr. was born on January 15, 1929, in Atlanta, Georgia. Two years later, his father, Martin Luther King Sr., succeeded his father-in-law as pastor of Ebenezer Baptist Church in that same city. King Sr. was active in the civil rights movement. In those days, pastors were natural leaders in the black community. People looked up to them; many pastors had attended college, and the church occupied a central place in the community. It was the only place where black people could feel free. Here, they could be spiritually reborn, encouraged, and uplifted.[5]

The young King grew up in relative comfort as Ebenezer Church flourished under his father's leadership. King Jr., though, would soon experience the ugly realities of segregation. In his preschool years, his best friend was a white boy. Upon entering racially segregated elementary schools, the parents of his friend told the young Martin that he could no longer play with their son "because we are white and you are colored."[6] King did well at academics and finished high school when he was only fifteen years old. He had a phenomenal memory and won a prize at an oratorical contest on "The Negro and the Constitution." After high school, he entered Morehouse College, a black liberal arts college in Atlanta, where he majored in sociology. One book he read for a class assignment that made a deep impact on him was Henry David Thoreau's *On Civil Disobedience*, which introduced King to the idea of nonviolent resistance and noncooperation with evil.[7]

In early 1948, the nineteen-year-old King was ordained as associate minister in his father's church. During summer breaks from Morehouse, he worked as a manual laborer in Atlanta to pay for some of his expenses. Although King Sr. offered to arrange a respectable job at any black-owned business, his son wanted to find out what life was like for the underprivileged, to "learn their plight and feel their feelings."[8] It would help him, coming from a comparatively privileged background, to empathize with the plight of his downtrodden (future) followers.

In 1948, King was admitted to Crozer Theological Seminary in Chester, Pennsylvania. There, in his own words, he began "a serious intellectual quest for the method to eliminate social evil."[9] He studied the great philosophers, from Plato to Nietzsche, as well as communism, which he rejected upon careful examination. He wrestled with the tension between the Christian ethic of love and his strong desire to solve social problems, especially segregation, which he thought could only be abolished through armed revolt. He could not see how the ethic of love could work in social conflict. His philosophical breakthrough occurred on a Sunday morning in the spring of 1950, when he attended a lecture on the life and teachings of Mahatma Gandhi. According to his own testimony, it was an "electrifying" event. Gandhi's concept of nonviolent resistance—in the form of strikes, boycotts, and protest marches—all predicated on love for the oppressor, provided a viable alternative to armed struggle to force social change. Gandhi's goal had not been to defeat the British in India, but to redeem them through love so as to avoid a legacy of bitterness. Gandhi called this *satyagraha* (*satya* is "truth" which equals "love," and *agraha* is "force"). It reconciled love and force in a single, operational concept. *Satyagraha* would be the principle that would guide King's thoughts and behavior for the remainder of his life.[10]

After receiving his bachelor's degree in divinity from Crozer in 1951, he entered Boston University's School of Theology, where he received his doctorate in systematic theology in 1955. During his time in Boston he met Coretta Scott, and they married in 1953 in Marion, Alabama. Since there were no bridal suites for blacks in the South, the Kings spent their wedding night in the home of a Scott family friend. Throughout the rest of his life, Coretta would be his invaluable pillar and strongest supporter.

After his course work was completed in early 1954, King decided to look for employment and finish his thesis on the job. Although an academic career beckoned, he felt it would be better to have several years of practical experience as a pastor.[11] Now, the Kings had to make a monumental decision: Should it be a church in the South or in the North? By accepting a pulpit in the North, he "had a chance to escape from the long night of segregation."[12] Going back to the South meant being subjected to all the inequities of Jim Crow. And what about raising children in such a society? After much soul searching, the Kings concluded that "in spite of the disadvantages and inevitable sacrifices, our greatest *service* could be rendered in our native South . . . we had something of a moral obligation to return" (emphasis added).[13] He intended to stay in the South for a few years before moving into academia.

In April 1954, King accepted the offer to become pastor of Dexter Avenue Baptist Church in Montgomery, Alabama, a place that could not

Figure 15.1 Martin Luther King Jr., 1963

Source: United States Library of Congress

have been more Jim Crow–like. The city had served as the first capital of the Confederate States in 1861. King's biographer Stephen B. Oates described the scene the Kings saw when they toured Montgomery: "With falling hearts, they saw black people riding in the backs of buses and realized that Coretta would have to sit there too, if she wanted to shop while he had the car. Coretta, who had wanted badly to remain in the North, tried to be brave, [saying,] 'If this is what you want, I'll make myself happy in Montgomery.'"[14] Little would they know what was in store.

King quickly earned a reputation as a social activist and was elected to the executive committee of the Montgomery chapter of the National Association for the Advancement of Colored People (NAACP). The first year was relatively calm—the proverbial quiet before the storm, which would burst on December 1, 1955.

KING LEADS THE MIA BUS BOYCOTT

City buses were the only means of transportation for many of Montgomery's fifty thousand blacks. But like everything else, they were strictly segregated. The first four rows were for whites only. If all these seats were taken and more whites entered the bus, blacks in the unreserved section had to turn their seats over to them. If a white passenger took a seat beside a black passenger, the latter had to stand because regulations prohibited white and black people from sitting next to each other.

On Thursday, December 1, 1955, Rosa Parks, who was black, got on a bus and took a seat in the unreserved section. When all the whites-only seats were taken, the driver ordered her to stand so that a white man (!) could sit down. She was tired and refused to move, and was arrested for her "crime." It was the spark that ignited the proverbial powder keg. Some fifty ministers and civic leaders gathered at King's church and decided to call for a boycott of the buses, to be launched the following Monday, December 5. Ministers alerted their congregations on Sunday, and King and his secretary produced seven thousand leaflets that were distributed throughout the black neighborhoods in Montgomery. The city's black taxi companies were persuaded to offer transportation to black people for the bus fare of ten cents.

King was concerned that his people were too apathetic or too frightened to participate in the boycott. He need not have worried—the participation rate on that historic Monday was almost 100 percent. That afternoon, the black leaders met again. Where to go from here? They decided to set up a permanent organization to run the boycott and handle future racial issues with the authorities. They called it the Montgomery Improvement Association, or MIA, to stress the positive, uplifting approach of the movement. The next point on the agenda was to elect its president.

King was proposed and elected unanimously. This took him by surprise. Only three weeks before, he had turned down the opportunity to run for the Montgomery NAACP presidency because he had just become a father and he felt he needed to devote more time to his church work. He asked for time to think it over, but his fellow leaders would have none of it. King relented: "Somebody has to do it, and if you think I can, I will *serve*" (emphasis added).[15]

That evening, King gave what he called "the most decisive speech in my life" to a packed audience at Holt Street Church. He found the right balance between being militant enough to keep his people aroused to positive action, and yet moderate enough to keep this fervor within the Christian doctrine of love—in other words, he made his first major *satyagraha* speech. It received a rapturous response, and the community agreed to continue the boycott until segregation in buses was abolished and the city agreed to hire black bus drivers.

The problem of transportation required King and his team's immediate attention. The police commissioner informed the MIA that the flat taxi rate of ten cents was against a local law that limited taxis to a minimum fare of forty-five cents. In response, King and his team came up with the idea to set up a pool of voluntary drivers, who transported people to and from work in their own cars. Later, the MIA added a fleet of station wagons, registered as church property.

Some on the MIA executive board and the wider community advocated a modicum of violence to signal to whites that they meant business, but King pushed back and kept them in line. King later opined that most of his followers probably did not believe in nonviolence as a way of life, but, because of their confidence in their leaders, they were willing to use it as a technique.[16]

Negotiations with the authorities went nowhere, and, with the carpool a success, the authorities resorted to psychological warfare. Malicious rumors were spread that King was pocketing MIA money. Prominent white citizens visited older black ministers to urge them to replace the young upstart, who was not even from Montgomery, with "older" and "wiser" men. Some ministers were receptive to these arguments, having become jealous of King.[17] The stress took a heavy toll on him. He offered his resignation as MIA leader, but that was unanimously rejected. His fellow leaders said they would follow his leadership to the end.[18] After the authorities' tactics failed to break the boycott, they planted fake news in the local newspaper, announcing that they had worked out a settlement with a group of senior black ministers. Many African-Americans therefore thought the boycott was over. However, the MIA struck back decisively to rectify the misinformation by making announcements in all the black churches, as well as King making a tour of black bars (a first in his life).

Desperate by now, the city commissioners resorted to the oldest script in the Jim Crow book: repression. They arrested King and many other leaders, as well as carpool drivers, for minor or fake traffic violations. Afraid of the consequences, many drivers dropped out of the carpool. Having been raised with respect for the law, King felt intellectually confused to be jailed, until he remembered what Thoreau wrote in *On Civil Disobedience*: "Under a government which imprisons any unjustly, the true place for a just man is also in prison."[19]

By late January 1956, King was receiving dozens of hate letters and threatening phone calls *per day*. Some callers threatened to not only murder King, but his wife and infant daughter, too. King admitted that he was scared to death for himself and his family, and worn down by the "freezing and paralyzing effect of fear."[20] Threats were followed by action. On January 30, his house was bombed. Miraculously, nobody was hurt. Yet, he did not quit. On his shattered porch, he admonished his angry followers who had violence on their minds: "We cannot solve this problem through retaliatory violence . . . We must love our white brothers, no matter what they do to us . . . We must meet hate with love."[21]

The authorities tightened the screws further by invoking an obscure state anti-labor law, which prohibited boycotts. An all-white grand jury indicted eighty-nine leaders, including twenty-four ministers, and all the drivers in the carpool.[22] King happened to be out of town, but, despite the pleas of his parents, he returned to Montgomery and promptly went to the jail, to be arrested. He joined many others who voluntarily turned themselves in, in an unprecedented sign of defiance and solidarity. According to King, "a once fear-ridden people had been transformed."[23] King was found guilty of leading the illegal boycott, but the case was appealed. King's arrest and trial made the boycott national front-page news. It brought reporters from all over the country and overseas streaming into Montgomery to cover this unprecedented black mass movement.

This was not exactly what the local authorities had in mind. They went to court to enjoin the carpool as a private enterprise operating without license. The request was granted on November 13, 1956, which meant that blacks would all have to walk. King felt hopeless; his people were tired and there appeared no end in sight. But the segregationists' time was finally up. On that same day, the U.S. Supreme Court came to the rescue by ruling in *Browder v. Gayle* that Alabama's state and local laws requiring segregation on buses were unconstitutional.

The Montgomery bus boycott marked the turning point for African-Americans in their struggle for equality. It was the first time that organized, nonviolent mass resistance overcame the power of Jim Crow. It gave blacks a new self-confidence and a hope for a better future. However, it was not the beginning of the end, only the end of the beginning. The forces of racism remained strong, both in the South as well as in Congress. President Eisenhower remained disengaged from the civil rights debate. Therefore, King called 115 black leaders to Montgomery in August 1957. The delegates formed the Southern Christian Leadership Conference (SCLC), with King as president. In the ensuing years, the SCLC would expand "the Montgomery way" of nonviolent, grassroots movements across the South. Under King's leadership, the SCLC would fight against segregation in all areas of life—such as employment, schools, restaurants, and public facilities—and lead voter-registration drives. In August 1963 he would lead a march on Washington, where he addressed over a quarter of a million people, galvanizing them, and the world, with his "I Have a Dream" speech.

King's "I Have a Dream," one of the seminal speeches of the twentieth century.

https://www.youtube.com/watch?v=_RsKxzopTN0

King received the Nobel Peace Prize in 1964, and Congress passed the Civil Rights Act. In 1965 he spearheaded the voting-rights campaign in Selma, Alabama, where only 333 out of 15,000 voting-age blacks were registered voters. The savage repression and violence, immortalized in the 2014 Hollywood drama *Selma*, forced President Lyndon Johnson to act. The result was the seminal Voting Rights Act, forced through Congress against the fierce opposition of Southern Democrats.

After the passage of the Voting Rights Act, King shifted his focus to the crowded ghettoes of the North. There, segregation was de facto rather than de jure. Most blacks in the North lived in slums, characterized by substandard housing, unequal job opportunities, racist real-estate practices, poverty, and de facto school segregation. In 1966, King moved temporarily to the black ghetto of Lawndale in Chicago to organize a movement to force the city to improve conditions in the slums. However, his time in Chicago was by and large a failure, not least because he was deftly outmaneuvered by the wily Chicago mayor, Richard Daley.[24]

In 1968, King planned to lead a march on Washington, D.C., at the head of a poor-people's army of all ethnicities to force Congress to grant poor people "an Economic Bill of Rights," which bore some resemblance to the economic part of the Green New Deal proposed in 2019 by U.S. representative Alexandria Ocasio-Cortez. It would not happen. On April 4, 1968, King was assassinated in Memphis, Tennessee, by James Ray, an escaped convict. The world came to a standstill. Back in the Netherlands, I was only eight years old, but I can still remember that day. The night before, with eerie premonition, he said: "I may not get there with you. But it really doesn't matter with me now, because I've been to the mountaintop." He paid the ultimate price for the sake of his people. He was only thirty-nine years old. Up to this day, it is still not clear whether King's murderer acted on his own or was part of a conspiracy.[25] While there is still plenty of racism in societies around the world today, there is no doubt that King's servant leadership has made the world a better, more just place.

LESSONS

I could have discussed King's life and work as an example of charismatic leadership. King was undoubtedly a supremely charismatic leader who could get his followers to do—or not do—things because of their belief in him. One anecdote illustrates this. The day after the buses in Montgomery were integrated, a white man slapped a black woman because she refused to vacate her seat. She refused to slap back. Why? She explained: "I could have broken the little fellow's neck all by myself but I left the mass meeting last night determined to do what Reverend King asked."[26] However, I decided to discuss King under servant leadership because he was willing to give up everything: family life, freedom, high income,[27] and, ultimately, his life. Two months before he was assassinated, King delivered a moving message to his flock at Ebenezer Church, Atlanta. He said,

> Every now and then I think about my own death . . . Every now and then I ask myself, "What is it that I would want said?" . . . Tell them not to mention that I have a Nobel Peace Prize. That isn't important . . . I'd like somebody to mention that day that Martin Luther King Jr. tried to give his life serving others.[28]

True to the tenets of servant leadership, King put his followers ahead of himself. He was put behind bars nineteen times, and the FBI recorded more than fifty death threats against him. He survived multiple bombings, and he was placed under continuous surveillance—and even blackmailed—by J. Edgar Hoover's FBI. Despite his frequent disappointments and despondency, enduring growing criticism by more militant members of the civil rights movement, he built up his followers, giving them self-esteem and the confidence that they could take their lives into their own hands. King's message and methods channeled a great deal of pent-up rage in the black population into nonviolent action. In workshops, his team trained countless followers to become leaders in nonviolent combat.[29]

With the notable exception of Albany police chief Laurie Pritchett (described shortly), King's opponents were hedgehogs. They had one immutable overriding vision: white supremacy. They did not realize that the times, and therefore, the adequacy of their tried means, were changing. Most African nations had recently gained independence. How could one defend that a black person could freely vote in Nigeria but not in the United States? Modern media, especially TV, made it increasingly difficult to use the traditional means of violence and intimidation to keep blacks down. The segregationists simply were unwilling to show flexibility. As a consequence, they dug an ever deeper hole for themselves—the classic dysfunctionality of hedgehogs gone awry.

On the other hand, King was an eagle. His overarching vision was a society where people would not be judged by the color of their skin, but by the content of their character. Right from the beginning as president of the MIA, he was flexible in the means that he employed. Over his career, he used boycotts, marches, protests by children and clergy, open letters, refusing or accepting bail, flooding jails with arrests, using black gangs as parade marshals to keep them from violence during marches, building relationships with Presidents Kennedy and Johnson (he and Eisenhower never got very far), even trying to flatter Hoover.[30] However, there was one constant in his means, and that was nonviolence. Nonviolence was deeply rooted in his Christian convictions and his embrace of Gandhian *satyagraha*. Yet even in his deeply held dogma of nonviolence, he had a *Realpolitik*, fox-like quality. He believed that violent resistance was doomed to fail. There were ten whites for every black in the United States, and he had learned from history that violent revolutions only succeed if the government had already lost the allegiance of the military and most of the people. In King's words, "anyone in his right mind knows that this will not happen in the United States."[31]

From the mid-1960s onward, King's strict adherence to nonviolence caused a widening rift with younger, more militant black leaders who were disappointed with the pace of change toward racial equality, rejected reconciliation with whites, and regarded King as too soft and too accommodating. King tried to reason with more activist followers, but he was met with increasing opposition. He was even booed in some meetings. Some followers warned King that if he refused to change his views on nonviolence, he would lose touch with the people in the ghetto and be out of step with the times.[32] His response gives us additional insight into his leadership philosophy:

> I would not be interested in being a consensus leader. I refuse to determine what is right by taking a Gallup poll of the trends of the time . . . Ultimately, a genuine leader is not a searcher for consensus but a molder of consensus . . . I would rather be a man of conviction than a man of conformity.[33]

King illustrates that effective servant leaders need not be saintlike and unworldly in their behavior. Indeed, King was an astute leader. He understood that he could accelerate change if people around the country would see images of savage police brutality. A corollary of this insight was that, if the police behaved courteously, King was inclined to shift his protests to another city. The desegregation campaign in Albany, Georgia, in early 1962, failed because there, quite exceptionally, Chief of Police Laurie Pritchett did not behave like a hedgehog. He had studied King's Gandhian speeches and methods. He overcame nonviolent protest with nonviolent law enforcement. There was little that was sensational to report, and reporters lost interest.

On the first day of the Selma campaign, Selma sheriff Jim Clark managed to restrain himself. According to biographer Oates, that night King and his staff were "frankly disappointed that Clark had behaved himself that day."[34] But a hedgehog like Clark could not restrain himself for more than one day. The ensuing police brutality so shocked the nation that it led to the Voting Rights Act of 1965. The liberal magazine *The Nation* proclaimed King "the finest tactician the South has produced since Robert E. Lee."[35]

King was also a superb orator. Unlike Florence Nightingale, King had the ability to inspire and move masses by the sheer force of his words. Another difference with Nightingale was his relationship with his immediate team. While Nightingale felt no compunction firing nurses who did not perform, King was reluctant to hurt anybody. When faced with a staff member caught for stealing SCLC funds, his reaction was, "we are supposed to be a church. So do you throw a man out of the church? Or do you try to keep him in the church and right his wrong?"[36] Nightingale was more like St. Paul, and King more like Barnabas. Just like in the Paul/Barnabas case, it is difficult to say which approach is "right."

CHAPTER TAKEAWAYS

- King was an eagle. He pursued his life goal with a variety of means, already evident in the Montgomery bus boycott. Almost all his opponents were hedgehogs.

- King learned much from Gandhi's example and teachings, especially the concept of *satyagraha.*

- King saw himself as a man of conviction, not of conformity.

- King used his opponents' rigidity to further his cause (e.g., by banking on violent repression and having child protestors).

- King knew that his emphasis on nonviolent action was causing a widening rift with more militant followers, yet he refused to lead by "taking a Gallup poll." Such principled leadership is a beacon for all ages.

- King astutely leveraged the power of the press to spread his message as well as the brutality of his opponents to the wider U.S. public.

- King was well aware that his servant leadership might cost him his life, yet he refused to give up.

- King's life highlights several servant leadership principles:

    ° Relationship building and oratorical skills as leadership qualities

    ° Perseverance if you believe your cause is right, even against overwhelming odds

    ° The need to be politically and tactically astute, to use (almost) any peaceful means to reach your goals

    ° The difference between being a consensus seeker vs. consensus builder

REFLECTIONS ON SERVANT LEADERSHIP

SERVANT LEADERSHIP IS the only style discussed in this book that frames the leadership process around the principle of caring for others. It emphasizes that leaders put their followers first, nurturing, empowering, and helping them develop their full potential. Perhaps without realizing it, many academics practice servant leadership when they are mentoring PhD students. The servant-leader academic puts the students' interests first, and spends countless hours mentoring them and nurturing them as independent researchers. Unfortunately, it also happens that supervisors abuse their power by appropriating the work of the PhD student for their own publications or requiring that their names be listed as co-authors on papers to which they contributed little or nothing.[1]

Service leadership is among the most popular leadership topics in management development and training programs.[2] Organizations such as Southwest Airlines, Wegmans, Costco, and the U.S. military have embraced servant leadership.[3] A hard-and-fast rule in the U.S. military is "Officers eat last." Servant leadership can create a serving culture among employees, which, in turn, can enhance business performance.[4] A word of caution is warranted, though. My many conversations with managers reveal substantial skepticism about the realism of servant leadership. They are not always convinced (to put it mildly) that servant leadership as a corporate principle survives declining sales and margins, investor dissatisfaction, acquisition by another company, or a change in top leadership.

As an economist by training, I believe that money talks. A simple litmus test of whether your organization truly practices servant leadership (as opposed to paying lip service to a fashionable idea) is to compare the compensation of the CEO with the remuneration of the median employee.

A benchmark, which I adapted from Peter Drucker, is that, for servant leadership to be credible as an organizational practice, the CEO should be paid no more than forty times the median worker, including bonuses.[5] While one may quibble about the exact cutoff, the reality in the United States is that in 2018, CEO pay at an S&P 500 firm was on average 287 times that of the median employee.[6] Wegmans and the U.S. military meet this benchmark, but Southwest and Costco fail it by a wide degree.[7]

Like any other leadership style, servant leadership is a personal decision. With that in mind, what can *you* learn from the case studies of Florence Nightingale and Dr. Martin Luther King Jr.? Their lives illustrate five key principles of servant leadership: (1) put followers' interests above your self-interest; (2) behave ethically; (3) engage in emotional healing; (4) create value for the community; and (5) deprioritize institutional power and control in favor of expert power.[8]

1. PUT FOLLOWERS' INTERESTS ABOVE YOUR SELF-INTEREST

This is *the* defining characteristic of service leadership. When there is a conflict between your interests and those of your followers, you place their interests first. This is a radical notion. Ever since Adam Smith explored the economic effects of self-interest in his seminal book *The Wealth of Nations* (1776), it has been broadly accepted that individuals act in their own self- interest. Yet, Nightingale continued to nurse the sick, even after she contracted brucellosis. In Turkey, she established reading rooms and schools to provide education for the convalescing soldiers, often covering expenses out of her own pocket. By going back to the segregated South in 1954, something he and his wife dreaded, King put his followers ahead of himself. From then on, he tirelessly worked to improve the conditions of African-Americans, first in the South, and later in the entire country.

The CEO of a software company who practices servant leadership contrasted servant leadership scholar Ken Blanchard's idealistic view of servant leadership versus what he believes is the reality (Table SL.1).[9] As an ex-Marine, he talks a lot about the mission, but the thrust is clear. Servant leaders face tough choices, like any other leader, between accomplishing their goals (or mission) and serving others. We can expect in real life that servant leaders give more weight to serving others than other leaders will do, but that is not an absolute.

Table SL.1 Servant Leadership in Theory versus in Practice

Theory	Practice
Servant leaders serve others - not themselves.	Servant leaders serve the mission first.
Servant leaders commit to their employees' professional and personal growth.	Servant leaders will commit their employees' well-being to accomplishing the mission, even if sacrificially, but will also invest heavily in their employees' personal growth and mission-readiness.
The fundamental principle of servant leadership is to place others first.	The fundamental principle of servant leadership is to place the mission first and others second, and to successfully reconcile the tension between the two over the long term.
Servant leaders work to make the world better for everyone.	Servant leaders work to change the world, usually for the better, but often fail.
Servant leaders are persuasive and visionary community builders.	Servant leaders are persuasive, but command when necessary and must be both visionary and execution focused.
Servant leaders are responsible stewards.	Servant leaders waste what is plentiful to preserve what is scarce. It often looks nothing like stewardship.

Source: CEO of U.S. software company (and ex-Marine).

2. BEHAVE ETHICALLY

Behaving ethically is obviously commendable for any type of leader, but it is a *conditio sine qua non* for servant leaders. This creates special challenges. Since putting others' interests ahead of our own is not "normal" human behavior, we tend to put real servant leaders on a pedestal.

However, any person put on a pedestal receives more scrutiny arising from, what Machiavelli in *The Prince* called, "the incredulity of mankind." If a servant leader's behavior falls short, the fall can be steep. You may remember televangelists Jimmy Swaggart and Jim Baker. They were adored by many, until sex scandals in the late 1980s brought them down—scandals that would hardly create a stir for Donald Trump. But then, Swaggart and Baker were put on a moral pedestal, while even Trump's most ardent admirers would not see him as a paragon of sexual virtue. The late evangelist Billy Graham made it a habit never to be alone with a woman other than his wife for the express reason of avoiding any suggestion (or false accusation) of misbehavior.

To understand how this works, I turn to the marketing theory of expectation-disconfirmation (Figure SL.1). According to this theory, disconfirmation occurs when there is a discrepancy between our prior expectations of a leader's attitudes and behavior and their actual attitudes and behavior ("performance"). If performance exceeds expectations, positive disconfirmation results, which leads to a modest improvement in the leader's reputation. If expectations and performance are aligned, nothing much changes. However, if performance is lower than expected, the result is negative disconfirmation, disappointment, and a disproportionate decline in the leader's reputation. Thus, there is a fundamental asymmetry in the effects—the adverse effect of negative disconfirmation is stronger than the beneficial effect of positive disconfirmation.[10] Since people's expectations about the saintlike attitudes and behavior of servant leaders are so high, negative information, which would cause, say, adaptive or persuasive leaders little harm, creates negative disconfirmation with a concomitant drop in reputation.

Nightingale's reputation was hurt posthumously when information about her less commendable leadership qualities became known. Irked by the image of the plaster saint, Lytton Strachey in the popular book *Eminent Victorians*, first published in 1918, paints a picture of Nightingale as a manipulator who treats people as objects, a megalomaniac and a bird of prey, subject to fury, terrible rage, and demoniac frenzy.[11] The pendulum has continued to swing back and forth between the reductive extremes of saint and sinner ever since. A middle ground appears hard to find, because high expectations continue to be so deeply ingrained.[12]

Figure SL.1 Expectation-Disconfirmation Theory Applied to Servant Leadership

```
┌──────────────┐                              ┌──────────────────┐
│ Expectations │                              │ Servant leader's │
│ about servant│              ┌──────────────►│reputation improves│
│ leader (E)   │              │               │    somewhat      │
└──────┬───────┘       ┌──────┴──────────┐    └──────────────────┘
       │               │  Positive: P > E │
       │    Disconfir- ├─────────────────┤    ┌──────────────────┐
       └───────────────┤  Neutral: P = E  ├───►│ Servant leader's │
       ┌───────────────┤─────────────────┤    │   reputation     │
       │    mation      │  Negative: E > P │    │   unchanged      │
┌──────┴───────┐       └──────┬──────────┘    └──────────────────┘
│ Performance  │              │
│ of servant   │              │               ┌──────────────────┐
│ leader (P)   │              └──────────────►│ Servant leader's │
└──────────────┘                              │reputation deteriorates│
                                              │   substantially   │
                                              └──────────────────┘
```

During King's life, numerous attempts were made to discredit him. They had little effect, in part because, in those times, many newspapers refused to publish salacious materials, as they respected a person's privacy to a greater degree.[13] In May 2019, the American historian David Garrow published an article in which he made serious allegations of sexual misconduct by King. Garrow maintained that this new information obtained from summaries of FBI audiotapes "poses so fundamental a challenge to his historical stature as to require the most complete and extensive historical review possible."[14] Whether this is true and to what extent this affects King's reputation will only become apparent after the complete FBI tapes on King are unsealed in 2027.

For Nightingale, the negative fallout occurred posthumously, and King was shielded by media reticence and "benefited" from his death as a martyr for a noble cause. These are unusual circumstances. In today's hyperconnected world, servant leaders should be prepared to deal with near-instantaneous disconfirmation during their lives. How to do that? Well, if you reduce expectations, the potential for disconfirmation and the associated shift toward a negative opinion is reduced. You can manage expectations by making yourself a little vulnerable, by being open about your weaknesses and struggles, and by asking your followers to help you grow.[15]

3. ENGAGE IN EMOTIONAL HEALING

Servant leaders are sensitive to the personal concerns and well-being of others. This includes recognizing others' problems and being willing to take the time to address them.[16] Nightingale went far beyond physical healing. She spent countless hours walking from bed to bed, speaking words of comfort to as many as she could. She wrote sensitive letters of condolences to grieving parents. Her care reduced soldiers' anxiety. One soldier, an ex-patient from Scutari, was overheard in the trenches before Sevastopol telling his fellow soldiers that they no longer needed to fear being wounded or falling sick because Florence Nightingale was there to care for them. Officers were amazed to see her treating their men as if they were human.

Likewise, King gave hope to millions of African-Americans. He showed them a way forward out of a situation where many had come to regard themselves as second-class citizens who were not as good as whites—which was the result of a century of segregation. His soaring rhetoric, combined with his courageous behavior, gave them renewed self-esteem. Anybody who reads King's "I Have a Dream" address, even today, cannot but feel energized and more hopeful.

4. CREATE VALUE FOR THE COMMUNITY

Servant leaders consciously and intentionally give back to the community. Due to Nightingale's recommendations, hospital designs were changed all over the world. She empowered women around the word. King's leadership was the impetus behind the monumental civil rights legislation of the mid-1960s, which remains as relevant today as it was back then. He improved every community, from Montgomery to Chicago, where he lived, preached, and worked.

5. DEPRIORITIZE INSTITUTIONAL POWER FOR EXPERT POWER

The management and marketing literatures commonly distinguish between five bases of power that leaders can draw on to influence their followers. These are *coercive* power (forcing followers to do something, possibly against their will), *reward* power (doling out or withholding various rewards), *legitimate* power (using one's position in the organization), *referent* power (being a role model), and *expert* power (deep knowledge and expertise).[17] The first three are traditional power bases, rooted in institutional power and control. Both Nightingale and King used them to some degree. Take coercion. Nightingale coerced Mary Stanley to resign her position by offering her own resignation. She also coerced the government into appointing a Royal Commission by informing them that otherwise, she would publish her own findings. When King faced opposition within the MIA, he offered his resignation. His colleagues were aware that the people would not follow anybody else. Hence, even if some of them had other thoughts, they had to express their unanimous support for him. Machiavelli himself would have approved of such behaviors.

Nevertheless, servant leadership calls for drastic deprioritization of traditional power sources in favor of influencing one's followers through referent and expert power. Referent power can be helpful, especially if the person has, like King, high charisma. Nightingale did not have such charisma, but could still draw on the image of the "Lady with the Lamp." Nightingale also knew much more than her followers (or the army's medical staff) about sanitation and hospital design. She collected massive amounts of statistical information on mortality, conducted surveys, and interviewed people. This enabled her to convince others, despite deep-seated sexism. King was admired by his followers for his extensive knowledge of theology, philosophy, and history. This greatly encouraged his followers who saw that one of their own could best their adversaries. One example is what happened when he was jailed in Birmingham, Alabama. Eight learned white clergymen attacked his campaign in an open letter. He responded with an open letter of his own, called "Letter from a Birmingham Jail," in which King methodically debunked every argument by drawing on scholars such as Socrates, St. Augustine, and Niebuhr. Few black men had done that before him.[18]

To assess whether servant leadership is a style that suits you, consider the following questions.

1. Are you truly willing to prioritize the interests of your followers, even if it is at your own expense? Can you give examples of such behavior?

2. Do you hold strong ethical principles or are you more of a moral relativist? Be honest! Can you give examples of when you refused to compromise on your ethical principles in order to achieve success? What were the consequences?

3. Are you generally a person who has a genuine interest in the personal concerns and well-being of your followers? When you notice that a follower is in distress, do you avoid the issue, or do you proactively reach out to help?

4. Do you feel it is important to give back to the local or wider community? Are you involved in community activities? Do you encourage your followers to volunteer for community service? To the extent possible, are you willing to devote some of your organization's resources to their efforts (e.g., time off)?

5. Are you comfortable eschewing traditional power sources—coercive, reward, and legitimate power? Can you lead with referent or expert power? If not, can you build this?

6. What feedback have you ever received that portrayed you as a servant leader?

7. Have you ever been in a situation where being a "servant leader" would have been most effective? What did you actually do and with which results?

PART SEVEN

CHARISMATIC LEADERSHIP – BUY INTO THE LEADER, THEN FOLLOW THEIR VISION

ALEXANDER THE GREAT SAYS NO

"He magnetized all who came in contact with him."
—GENERAL J.F.C. FULLER, MILITARY HISTORIAN

Leadership Dilemma: Should Alexander the Great accept the Persian King Darius's buy-off of immense riches, or should he play all-or-nothing?

CONTEXT

After the destruction of the Persian navy in 480 B.C. at Salamis (see chapter 5), and the Persian army the following year at Plataea, Greece entered a golden age, flourishing militarily, economically, and culturally. However, by 350 B.C., this was a distant memory. Incessant fighting between the Greek city-states had weakened and impoverished the country. The Persian Empire had regained dominance in the Eastern Mediterranean, interfering in Greek affairs and playing one Greek state against the other with bribes and threats. The political and social distress pushed fourth-century B.C. thinkers like Gorgias and Isocrates to propose the Panhellenic program. They urged Greek states to come together and wage a war of revenge for the devastation caused by the Persian armies during their invasion of 480-479 B.C. They hoped that the riches of Asia Minor (present-day Turkey) would solve the poverty of Greece, which was the root of all internecine disputes.[1] Over time, though, Isocrates and others realized that the Greek states were hopelessly divided and would never arrive at an internal peace. Therefore, they began to look around the fringes of the region for political and military leadership. They put their hope on Macedon, a kingdom on the northern edge of the Greek world, and its king, Philip II. In 346 B.C., Isocrates wrote an open letter to Philip, urging him to execute his Panhellenic program. Philip was happy to oblige.

During his reign (359–336 B.C.), Philip transformed a weak, barbarous kingdom into Greece's most powerful state. He reorganized the Macedonian army and made it the best professional fighting force of its day. Its three key strengths were the heavy-armed Companion cavalry, the phalanx (heavy infantry with a long pike, called *sarissa*), and the light-armed elite infantry (*hypaspists*), who acted as a link between the faster-moving cavalry and the slower-moving phalanx.[2] During his reign, Philip vastly expanded Macedon, which brought him into conflict with various Greek states. A decisive event was the Battle of Chaeronea (338 B.C.), in which the Macedonian army crushed the combined army of Thebes and Athens. After this victory, a peace conference was held in Corinth. A Panhellenic League was formed involving Macedon and all Greek states except Sparta. Philip was elected as the captain-general (*Hegemon*) of the league and was tasked to lead a Panhellenic war on Persia. But just before Philip was about to embark on the invasion of Asia Minor, he was assassinated, in October 336 B.C. Everyone thought this was the end of the Panhellenic League. Neither the Greek states nor the Persian Empire gave much thought to the twenty-year-old new king, Alexander III. They had no idea what would be coming. If Philip was a tropical storm, Alexander was a category 5 hurricane.

ALEXANDER THE GREAT

Alexander was born in 356 B.C. in the Macedonian capital of Pella.[3] He received perhaps the best education relative to his contemporaries of any leader discussed in this book, being tutored by nobody less than Aristotle between the ages of thirteen and sixteen. They remained in contact throughout Alexander's life. Aristotle inspired a passionate love for Greek culture, literature, and art, and made Alexander wholly Greek in intellect. Because of Aristotle's teachings, he acquired a keen interest in the natural sciences. However, on one important issue Alexander deviated from his tutor. Aristotle taught that Greeks were superior to non-Greeks, and favored despotic control over the latter, while Alexander's career would move toward concord and reconciliation.

When Alexander was sixteen, Philip started to give him administrative and military responsibilities, and Alexander commanded the Companion cavalry in the battle at Chaeronea. After Philip's assassination, Alexander was proclaimed king. According to the treaty of the Panhellenic League, he also should have become its captain-general, but that was conveniently ignored by the Greek states. There were uprisings everywhere. Alexander reacted with lightning speed. He secured the kingdom's western and northern frontiers and extended the kingdom to the Danube River. Incited by Persia, there was a dangerous uprising in Greece centered in Thebes. Efforts to bring the city back into the league without bloodshed failed, so, after a short siege, Alexander's army broke into the city. A massacre took place and the city was destroyed. Most of the atrocities were not committed by the Macedonians, but by Alexander's Greek allies, who had long been oppressed by Thebes. In late 335 B.C., peace in Greece was restored.

With his home base secure, Alexander crossed the Hellespont in the spring of 334 B.C. at the same place where Xerxes crossed the Narrows 150 years earlier (Figure 16.1). With a Macedonian-Greek army of some thirty thousand infantry and five thousand cavalry, he intended to take on the mightiest empire the world had seen to date.[4] The Persians woefully underestimated the threat and thought it could be dealt with at the provincial level. In the ensuing battle at the Granicus River, Alexander destroyed the provincial army of about equal size. The Greek cities in Asia Minor were liberated and incorporated in the Panhellenic League. He was greeted as a

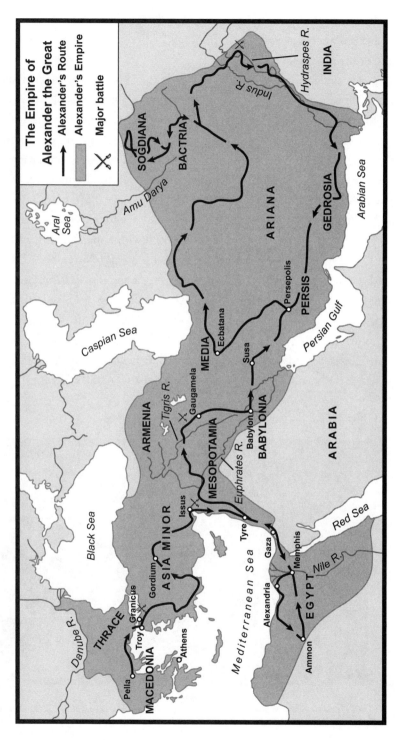

Figure 16.1 Empire of Alexander the Great

liberator almost everywhere in Ionia, and, where resistance was offered, he took the town by force.

Alexander's fleet was vastly inferior to the Persian navy, which allowed the Persians to attack his supply lines and to stir up trouble in Greece. However, warships at the time could not carry enough stores to feed their crews for long; they had to constantly put in for water and food. Alexander solved the navy problem in a novel way—by occupying the entire coast of Asia Minor. Without secure bases, the Persian fleet had to withdraw ever farther.

After conquering Asia Minor, Alexander entered Syria, where the Persian king Darius III was waiting for him with a massive army of some 100,000 men. The two armies met at Issus, in early November 333 B.C. Alexander won a brilliant victory, as always, leading the decisive heavy cavalry charge himself (Figure 16.2). Darius fled the field and his army crumbled. An immense treasure, along with Darius's wife, daughters, and mother, fell into Alexander's hands.

Alexander resisted the temptation to pursue Darius. He was well aware that the Phoenician coast (today's Lebanon) was still in Persian hands,

Figure 16.2 Battle at Issus

Source: Detail of the famous mosaic representing the battle of Alexander the Great (left) against Darius III (right) at Issus; Naples National Archaeological Museum.

which gave the Persians a launch pad to attack his newly conquered territories. Thus, he went on to secure the coast first. Most harbor cities surrendered without a fight, but not so the most important one: the island city of Tyre. Tyre had withstood countless previous sieges, including one lasting for thirteen years. To everybody's astonishment, Alexander took the city after a siege of merely seven months by building a causeway from the mainland to the island.

In late 332 B.C., Alexander moved on to Egypt, where the population received him as a liberator. When he visited the oasis of Siwa he was hailed as son of the god Zeus-Ammon. Ammon is usually shown with the horns of a ram, which would later become a common way to depict Alexander.

While in Egypt, Alexander founded Alexandria, destined to become one of the most important cities in the world for one thousand years. Today, it is Egypt's second-largest city, still carrying the same name. In the summer of 331 B.C., he returned to Syria and entered Mesopotamia to confront Darius, who was amassing an even larger army in Babylon. While Alexander was besieging Tyre, Darius had written him a letter. Alexander's response would determine the course of history.

ALEXANDER REFUSES AN OFFER

In the letter, Darius offered a large ransom for his family: the hand of one of his daughters, a treaty of friendship and alliance, and the surrender of all the area west of the Euphrates. Alexander presented the letter to the council of his senior officers. His senior general Parmenio said that, if he were Alexander, he would be happy to end the war on such terms. Alexander answered, "So would I if I were Parmenio."[5] According to Alexander's biographer Ulrich Wilcken, if his father Philip had ever advanced so far, he would certainly have accepted the offer. Alexander, on the other hand, had begun to see himself as "King of Asia" and saw no reason to share that with Darius.[6] Here is how Wilcken described the importance of Alexander's refusal:

It was a fateful moment for the ancient world. If Alexander
had been satisfied with this empire up to the Euphrates, the
whole subsequent evolution of ancient civilisation would
have been totally different; the after-effects of this decision,
indeed, stretch through the Middle Ages down to our own
day, in the East as in the West . . . [T]here never could have
been that world-wide culture, whose effects can be traced to
India and even to China . . . At any rate, we see here most
clearly what a decisive effect the will of Alexander had on the
subsequent history of the world.[7]

Upon deeper reflection, Alexander's decision made eminent strategic
sense. A strong Persian kingdom beyond the Euphrates, which could draw
upon its vast financial resources and the warlike peoples of Iran (encompassing present-day Iran, Afghanistan, and the Central Asian countries),
would be a permanent threat to Alexander's empire. The later experience of
the Roman Empire, with its vastly greater manpower than Alexander had
at his disposal, showed how hard it was to hold the Euphrates line against
a hostile Persian kingdom. An undefeated and deep-pocketed Persia could
continue to stir up trouble in Greece and stretch Macedon's limited manpower resources to the breaking point.

With Alexander refusing Darius's offer, the fate of the world would be
decided on the battlefield. On October 1, 331 B.C., the final showdown
took place on the plain of Gaugamela, in today's Iraq. Military historian
J.F.C. Fuller called this "the epoch-most making of all the decisive battles
of the western world."[8] With 47,000 men, Alexander faced an army of at
least a quarter of a million men—the largest army ever assembled west
of the Himalayas until Napoleon's *Grande Armée*. When seeing 100,000
campfires before them, terror struck the Macedonians, but not their
king.[9] He devised a new kind of battle plan, anchored on a grand hollow
square, which remains the textbook solution to how a smaller army can
face a much more numerous enemy. Gaugamela also saw the first use of
a strategic reserve force of soldiers in a major engagement. Alexander
explained his strategy to his generals, and went to sleep. In a brilliant

piece of psychology, he overslept and had to be awakened. The preter-
natural calmness of their king had the desired effect on his men. Led by
Alexander, who was, as always, spearheading the decisive cavalry attack,
the Macedonian army crushed the Persian army.

Darius fled again and was assassinated the year after by his dwindling
band of followers. Alexander conquered the eastern part of the Persian
Empire (Afghanistan and Central Asia), which was accomplished by 327
B.C. In this campaign, he led his army over the icy heights of the Hindu
Kush, a feat of leadership that far surpasses Hannibal's celebrated crossing
of the Alps in 218 B.C. The time it took Alexander to subdue Afghanistan
should have cautioned future would-be conquerors of that country. When
an American friend asked me in the early 2000s how long it would take the
U.S. forces to pacify Afghanistan, I was pessimistic. I observed that it took
Alexander as long to subdue that region as for all the rest of the Persian
Empire, and he was the greatest military genius of all time. It turned out to
become the longest war in U.S. history, longer than the Revolutionary War,
the Civil War, or the War in Vietnam.

In 326 B.C., Alexander invaded the Punjab and won another brilliant
battle, this time at the Hydaspes River against a large Indian army with as
many as two hundred war elephants, led by King Porus. This battle would
become a textbook example of how to mislead the enemy and how to use a
holding force together with a turning force to strategically immobilize the
enemy.[10] However, by that time, his troops had had enough and refused to
go any farther. Even Alexander's charisma could no longer convince the
weary soldiers, and they returned to Mesopotamia by 324 B.C. There, he
reorganized his empire and initiated new plans for exploration, commerce,
and conquest. They would never be executed. His health had been undermined by countless wounds sustained in battles and sieges, and he fell ill
and died on June 10, 323 B.C. He was only thirty-two years old. He had
said earlier, "I would rather live a short life of glory than a long one of
obscurity." He certainly lived up to that.

Since he died without an (adult) heir—his wife Roxane was pregnant,
but it would prove too late to make a difference—his generals quarreled
over the future of his massive empire, which, by 300 B.C., was broken up
into four main kingdoms (Figure 16.3). In the ensuing Hellenistic period

(323–31 B.C.), the area conquered by Alexander experienced a surge in prosperity, the arts, literature, architecture, music, mathematics, philosophy, astronomy, engineering, and medicine.[11] Greek cities were founded across the empire, and Greek became the Near East's lingua franca. The economy was greatly boosted by Alexander's policy of putting the hoarded wealth of Persia into circulation, minting the gold and silver into coin of a uniform standard. The Hellenistic period witnessed the emergence of the world's first proto-capitalist, market economy.

The Hellenistic culture was absorbed by, and profoundly transformed, the Roman culture.[12] Alexander, therefore, was the original architect of the Greco-Roman civilization, which constitutes the bedrock of Western civilization up until today. Deeply influenced by practices of this Greco-Roman civilization, Hellenistic Judaism, Christianity, and Islam were born. It is no coincidence that the entire Biblical New Testament was written in Greek, which greatly facilitated its diffusion in the Roman Empire. Biographer Guy Rogers concludes that today's four billion "people of the book" (Christians, Muslims, and Jews) worldwide owe more than a little to the ambitions of a Macedon king who refused to say no.[13]

Figure 16.3 Successor (Diadochi) Kingdoms in 301 B.C.

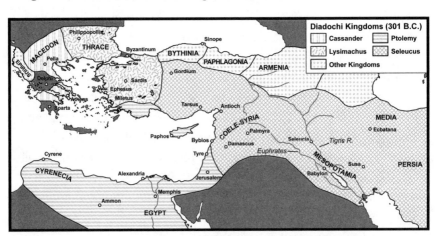

Note: Seleucus's kingdom stretched to the Indus River.

LESSONS

Alexander the Great is a larger-than-life figure. The Old Testament prophet Daniel (sixth century B.C.) prophesized Alexander:

> A goat with a prominent horn between its eyes came from the west, crossing the whole earth without touching the ground. It came toward the two-horned ram I had seen standing beside the canal and charged at it in great rage. I saw it attack the ram furiously, striking the ram and shattering its two horns . . . The goat became very great, but at the height of its power the large horn was broken off, and in its place four prominent horns grew up toward the four winds of heaven.[14]

Alexander appears in the Koran as Dhul-Qarnayn (He of the Two Horns), who travels to the east and west and erects a wall to protect mankind from the evil forces Gog and Magog.[15] Elsewhere, the Koran tells how the end of the world would be signaled by the release of Gog and Magog, who break through the wall made by Alexander. When Julius Caesar saw Alexander's statue in Spain, he burst into tears, realizing that, at his age, Alexander had conquered the world while Caesar had done nothing noteworthy.[16] Mythical stories about Alexander can be found in medieval European and Arabic texts. Chieftains in Central Asia still seek in him their ancestry.[17] Even today, he remains one of the most recognized secular leaders of all time.

We can be confident that most of his followers would have been perfectly happy if Alexander had accepted Darius's offer in 333 B.C. Nevertheless, his soldiers followed him for another 10,000 miles and countless battles, skirmishes, and sieges before they finally had enough. Several of his generals, all proud Macedonian nobles, would become strong rulers in their own right after Alexander's empire broke up. However, as long as he was alive, they were fiercely loyal. What can we learn from Alexander's charismatic leadership? Three things stand out: his ability to combine an overarching vision with great flexibility, his ability to forge a truly reciprocal relationship with his followers, and his moral outlook.

COMBINE VISION WITH FLEXIBILITY

Alexander the Great was one of the greatest eagles of all time. Like a true hedgehog, his life was guided by one overarching vision, albeit that vision did expand over time. His initial goal was to defeat Persia, although, until the victory at Issus, it is unclear whether that goal was to "merely" wrestle Asia Minor from Persian control—the goal of the Panhellenic League— or the conquest of the entire Persian Empire.[18] After Gaugamela, his goal was to be king of Asia. This later morphed into his final overarching goal, to establish a world empire, but his premature death prevented him from putting this into action.

In achieving his (evolving) overarching vision, he exhibited extraordinary fox-like qualities. To the Greeks, he behaved as captain-general of the league, to the Persians as "Great King," and to the Macedonians as "one of them." After the conquest of Asia, he faced the daunting problem of how to reconcile the independent Greek city-states—who hated kingship—with their captain-general being king of Asia. He resolved this by asking the city-states to grant him divine honors. This would put him above the city-states, not as king, but as a semi-deity. This sounds strange, if not megalomaniac, in our eyes, but in the Greek world there was no ironclad divide between the divine and the human. Alexander's pragmatism shines through in that he never pushed the divine honors idea upon Macedonians or Persians, to whom this was uncommon. If he were a megalomaniac tyrant, he certainly would have done that.[19]

His strategy to forgo a naval battle and occupy the Mediterranean coast instead was brilliant. He had exemplary toleration for the traditions and gods of foreign peoples. In Egypt, he sacrificed to the sacred bull, Apis, that was reportedly slain by the Persian conqueror Cambyses. In Babylon, he ordered the rebuilding of temples destroyed by the Persians. On the other hand, in India, he showed much less religious flexibility—baffled by Hindus, Buddhists, and Jains—and resistance, led by Brahmin priests, was fierce.[20]

Alexander experimented with different administrative arrangements, and he had no hesitation in canceling what did not work well in practice. He separated civil administration from military control. The former, he often handed over to representatives of the conquered people, and the latter he placed in the hands of one of his trusted Macedonians. In large parts of the empire, he made a separate office for finance and taxation, which he bestowed on a special officer not subordinate to the governor or military commander of the province. This meant a considerable limitation on provincial leaders' abilities to operate independently of Alexander's wishes.[21]

A common pitfall for hedgehogs is their failure to establish a proper relation between ends and means—in other words, their overarching goal exceeds the means at their disposal. Alexander understood that, as his vision expanded, he needed to increase his means. Even his unsurpassed military genius—only Napoleon and Caesar might come close—would not suffice. There were simply not enough Macedonian soldiers to hold Asia. He consciously began to draft Persians and peoples of the eastern part of his empire into his army. As a result, the army with which he invaded India had increased to some 120,000 men. However, he remained realistic—nearly all the senior officers were Macedonians.

FORGE A TRULY RECIPROCAL RELATIONSHIP WITH YOUR FOLLOWERS

Charismatic leaders engender an unusually high degree of loyalty—if not adulation—among their followers, which motivates their followers to do things they would not normally do. Alexander's Macedonians performed feats of courage and endurance that they could not have imagined. However, such adulation can easily be a one-way street—the followers give their devotion to their leader. In Alexander's case, their devotion to him was fully reciprocated by his devotion to them. He was deeply loyal to his followers, he shared in all their hardships, and he let them share fully in his successes.

LOYALTY TO—AND FAITH IN—YOUR FOLLOWERS

Alexander's charismatic leadership was characterized by a reciprocal loyalty to—and faith in—his followers. One telling example is an episode that happened in the summer of 333 B.C., a few months before the victory at Issus. After having bathed in a river, Alexander fell ill. His doctor, Philip, was about to give him a potion when a letter arrived from Parmenio informing

Alexander that Darius had bribed the doctor to poison him. Alexander handed Philip the letter, and, while Philip read it, drank the potion. When the doctor looked up in horror, he saw "Alexander's looks were cheerful and open, to show his kindness to and confidence in his physician."[22] The potion was indeed healing rather than poisonous.

On one's deathbed, all pretenses are stripped away and the true person is revealed. When Alexander was dying, his soldiers wanted to see him. On his orders, they were let inside his chamber, where they passed through in a single file. It was here that Alexander held his last parade. As the first man entered, Alexander turned himself with utmost exertion toward him, and held himself there until the last man had gone by. Not one of them went without acknowledgment; he greeted them all, lifting his head, though with difficulty, and acknowledging each with his eyes.[23]

SHARE FULLY IN YOUR FOLLOWERS' HARDSHIPS

Alexander showed himself to be a great leader of men by participating in all the dangers and exertions of his soldiers. Reckless with his own life, he was never wasteful of theirs, a fact well known to them and highly valued.[24] He was the first into danger and the last to take comfort when conditions were rough. In battles, he exhibited extreme personal bravery. After battles, he visited the wounded and made them individually display their wounds and relate how they got them. On the march, there were no toils he did not share. In sieges, he took a hand in constructing ramparts and could be the first one to enter a city. In short, Alexander teaches us that charismatic leaders share their followers' privations.

LET YOUR FOLLOWERS FULLY SHARE IN YOUR SUCCESS

According to Plutarch, Alexander "was naturally most munificent."[25] He shared the Persian treasure with his followers, and so all his followers were vastly better off because of their king's largesse. In one anecdote, a common soldier was driving a mule laden with some of Alexander's treasure. The soldier noticed that the beast was tired, and he took the treasure upon his back. Alexander saw the man struggling with this heavy load and asked what was the matter. When the soldier explained what had happened, Alexander responded, "Do not faint now but finish the journey, and carry what you have there to your own tent for yourself."[26] These and other stories swirled around the camp and tied his soldiers close to him. Compare Alexander's attitude to the wage disparity that is prevalent in U.S. and international corporations. As mentioned in "Reflections on Servant Leadership," CEO pay at an S&P 500 firm is on average 287 times that of the median employee.[27] It is difficult to have your workers follow you through thick and thin if, obviously, you take much better care of yourself than you do of your followers.

Alexander used sharing hardships and spreading wealth to full effect when he faced his worse crisis: the mutiny at Opis in Mesopotamia in 324 B.C. The trigger was the decommissioning of ten thousand soldiers who were all past service. Each soldier would receive a huge bonus, roughly equivalent to nine years' pay of a skilled worker. Nevertheless, the Macedonians strongly resented being decommissioned. They suspected that his aim was to oust them in favor of the Persians, whom he had recruited into his army. His policy of reconciliation with the Persians was never popular among the rank-and-file. Discontent led to mutiny by the whole army.

In response, Alexander gave a powerful speech in which he reminded the soldiers that "no one can point to treasure of mine apart from all this which you yourself either possess, or have in safe keeping for your future use." Alexander went on to compare privations: "Come now—if you are wounded, strip down and show your wounds, and I will show mine. There is no part of my body but my back which has not a scar; not a weapon a man may grasp or fling the mark of which I do not carry upon me." His soldiers were stunned and begged the king to forgive them. The mutiny was over.[28]

MORAL OUTLOOK

According to historian Fuller, "it was his [Alexander's] moral outlook which, above all his qualities, distinguished him from his contemporaries."[29] There are countless examples of Alexander showing compassion to others, and this in an age in which such behavior was considered to be unmanly. After the Battle of Issus, he showed compassion for the

Theban ambassadors, partly out of pity for Thebes—although being found in Darius's entourage, they were traitors according to the Panhellenic League. At the siege of Miletus, some of the besieged soldiers took refuge on an island. Seeing they had nowhere to go, Alexander "felt compassion for them," according to the second-century A.D. historian Arrian, and made terms with them.

Even more noteworthy was his treatment of women, considered legitimate spoils of the soldier. Alexander treated them with great respect and held in abhorrence rape and violence toward them, which was unheard of. On one occasion, having heard that some soldiers of Parmenio's regiment had violated women, he ordered them to be tried and, if convicted, to be put to death like wild beasts.[30] As mentioned earlier, Darius's family was captured after Issus, but was treated with great respect. When Darius's wife died in captivity, Alexander grieved sincerely and buried her with all due funeral ornaments. When Darius heard of this, he could not understand it: "How is it possible a young man as he is, should treat the wife of his opponent with so much distinction?" Darius beseeched the gods that if ruin was to come to the Persian monarchy that the gods "grant that no other man but Alexander may sit upon the throne of Cyrus."[31]

Alexander made grave errors, such as the killing, in a drunken rage, of Cleitus, a Macedonian commander who had saved his life at the Granicus River. This did not commend him compared to other leaders of his time, who might have done the same. What did commend Alexander, though, was that he repented. *That* was totally unheard of. Kings did not repent. His behavior was noted even in antiquity. Arrian wrote, "I do indeed know that Alexander, of all the monarchs of old, was the only one who had the nobility of heart to be sorry for his mistakes."[32]

All this hardly makes Alexander a saint. Yet, it is important here to consider Alexander's moral outlook relative to what was the norm of his time. I agree with biographer Mary Renault, who observed, "It is as foolish to apply anachronistic moral standards to this as it would be to condemn Hippocrates for not teaching septic surgery."[33] His moral outlook, unique for his day and age, contributed to the awe in which his men held him.

LIMITS TO WHAT CHARISMA CAN ACHIEVE

There were limits, though, to how far his charisma could carry even Alexander. After Gaugamela, Alexander ever more strongly strove for reconciliation between Macedonians and Persians. To this end, he incorporated many Persians in his army and appointed others to high administrative positions. Yet, despite his best efforts, this created serious tensions with his Macedonians, who regarded themselves as conquerors and the Persians as the conquered. It was the root cause of the Opis mutiny. Alexander's view was of unprecedented radicalness. Since time immemorial, the spoils went to the victors, and the vanquished had to submit or be killed. To complicate things for Alexander, prevailing customs and values differed widely between the two peoples. To illustrate Alexander's challenge, let us look at one important sticking point: court ceremonial. In Persia, *proskynesis*, or prostration, before the king was considered perfectly normal, while this was seen as utterly contemptible to the Macedonians. To signal the equal position of Persians with Macedonians, Alexander tried to introduce *proskynesis* as common court ceremonial, but he had to abandon that plan due to fierce resistance.[34]

Alexander's problems on how to reconcile radically different values within one empire foreshadowed a challenge that faces multinational corporations— what to do if the values in the home and host country clash.[35] For example, PayPal takes a strong, inclusive public stance on LGTBQ issues in the United States, but at the same time, its international headquarters are in Singapore, where homosexual activity is punishable by up to two years in jail.[36] IKEA airbrushed women out of the Saudi Arabian edition of its furniture catalogue. Adil Khan of advertising giant Saatchi & Saatchi explained the challenge: "It's an extremely difficult position for a global brand to be in. On the one hand, they have their value system as a global brand, but then on the other they have to be aware of local market sensitivities."[37] There was no easy solution for Alexander, and there is no easy solution now, either.

PLANNING

I conclude by highlighting one quality in Alexander's leadership that in itself has little to do with charismatic leadership per se, but is nevertheless worth examining—his ability to think ahead and to plan his actions care-fully. Campaigns were meticulously planned, far in advance of execution, right down to the smallest logistical detail. In marketing terminology, Alexander (1) conducted extensive research before entering a market, and (2) understood the importance of having control over his supply lines.

Before entering an area, Alexander sent out spies to inform him about its topography, peoples, and political structures. This allowed him to plot his moves well in advance, and consequently he was rarely caught off guard. Sounds obvious, no? Actually, it is less common than you might think. The marketing literature is replete with examples of companies that made big blunders because, apparently, they did not do even the most elementary market research. In 2018, Coca-Cola introduced a new slogan, "*Kia ora, mate,*" in New Zealand that combined English and Maori. The result was not what they hoped for—in Maori, the entire slogan means "Greetings, death."[38] In that same year, the Italian luxury fashion brand Dolce & Gabbana launched three short videos on Chinese social media, which were culturally so insensitive (racist) that it created a firestorm.[39] In 2017, the personal care brand Dove had to apologize for an ad showing a black woman turning into a white one after using their product.[40] If they, like Alexander, would have just done a little market research, these mis-steps would not have happened.

Alexander also carefully planned logistics.[41] He took special care to keep the supply lines to the homeland open by manning key fortress cities and establishing depots for troops that were sent on their way to him. It is an astonishing accomplishment that he received reinforcements from the homeland while he was in Central Asia—a distance of thousands of miles. Compare this with the logistical mess Napoleon and Hitler made when invading Russia. If they had had Alexander's logistical skills, things might have gone very differently.

CHAPTER TAKEAWAYS

- Alexander is the only secular person who appears in the Bible as well as in the Koran.

- Alexander was one of history's greatest eagles. He combined a sky-high overarching and evolving vision with an ability to expand the means to reach that vision.

- Alexander's followers accomplished things they could never have dreamed of because of their trust in him.

- Alexander never gave up (until the Indus River).

- Alexander's policy of reconciliation between Macedonians and Persians was unprecedented. However, despite his best efforts, he was unable to bridge the wide gap in values and customs between Macedonians and Persians. His policy of reconciliation was largely abandoned after his death.

- Alexander excelled in thinking ahead and planning his actions carefully.

- Alexander's life highlights several charismatic leadership principles:

    ○ The power of charismatic leadership to get your followers to do things they would not dream of

    ○ How to forge a two-sided relationship in charismatic leadership by showing great loyalty to your followers, fully sharing in their hardships, and generously doling out benefits

    ○ The role of moral outlook in charismatic leadership

    ○ The challenge of pursuing goals that are too far removed from those of your followers. Even the most charismatic leader may be unable to bridge the gap—during your leadership and even more certainly after you step down.

DE GAULLE UNDERSTANDS THE *PIEDS-NOIRS*

"All my life I have had a certain idea of France."
—GENERAL CHARLES DE GAULLE

Leadership Dilemma: Should de Gaulle align with the military and the populace and keep French Algeria, or sever those ties to regenerate France?

CONTEXT

When World War II in Europe ended in May 1945, France was acknowledged as one of the four victors, together with Great Britain, the United States, and the Soviet Union. It acquired a zone of occupation in Germany and a permanent seat on the United Nations Security Council. Even so,

France was morally and economically bankrupt. It had suffered an ignominious defeat against the German war machine in 1940. Many Frenchmen
had collaborated with the Germans, including Marshal Philippe Pétain, the
hero of World War I, who had led the collaborationist Vichy regime.

Post-war France faced a series of daunting challenges, including rebuilding and modernizing the economy, persistent high inflation and budget
deficits, chronic political instability, a strong communist party, and how to
deal with independence movements in its huge colonial empire in Africa
and Indochina. Between 1946 and 1958, it had twenty-one different governments. Nevertheless, considerable economic progress was made, aided
by massive amounts of Marshall Aid that allowed France to modernize its
industrial apparatus. This period also witnessed the creation of the European
Economic Community, the predecessor of today's European Union.

France was considerably less successful in dealing with its overseas empire.
It tried to hold on to Indochina, but after suffering a crushing defeat at Dien
Bien Phu in 1954, it was forced to grant Vietnam independence. Algeria
was an even bigger problem, as it was administered as part of France. Algeria
had become a destination for hundreds of thousands of European immigrants, who became known as *pieds-noirs*, literally "black feet," a name given
to early French settlers by native inhabitants because of the shoes they wore.
The *pieds-noirs* constituted around 10 percent of the Algerian population and
were fiercely attached to metropolitan (European) France.

After World War II, dissatisfaction with French rule grew rapidly
among the native Algerian populace. The Algerian War of Independence
started in November 1954, when the *Front de Libération Nationale* (FLN;
National Liberation Front) attacked targets throughout Algeria. France had
just lost Indochina and was determined not to lose Algeria, too. The socialist
minister of the interior (and future French president), François Mitterrand,
spoke for the political class when he said, "The only negotiation is war.
Algeria is France." Premier Pierre Mendès France echoed this sentiment:
"The Algerian departments are . . . irrevocably French. Between them and
metropolitan France there can be no conceivable secession."[1] French forces
in Algeria swelled to nearly 500,000 troops—about the same number of
soldiers the United States would deploy in Vietnam, albeit France's population was only one-quarter that of the U.S.

The Algerian War was characterized by extraordinary brutality and atrocities on both sides, radicalizing the natives and the French army. Hundreds of thousands of people would be killed, imprisoned, or tortured. By 1958, the French army had regained control of most of the country, but the savagery of the fighting undermined the will of French politicians to continue the conflict. Sensing this, an army junta under General Jacques Massu seized power in Algiers on May 13, 1958, and demanded that General Charles de Gaulle be named to head a government of national unity invested with extraordinary powers to prevent the "abandonment of Algeria." French paratroopers from the Algerian corps seized control of the island of Corsica. Airborne landings in the mainland were planned. In desperation, France's President René Coty appealed to de Gaulle to save the country, again.

CHARLES DE GAULLE

EARLY LIFE

Charles de Gaulle was born on November 22, 1890. His father, Henri de Gaulle, was a teacher of Latin, philosophy, and literature at a highly reputed Jesuit college in Paris. His parents instilled in him traditional, Catholic, and patriotic values. Later in life, when asked to name the person who had most influenced him, de Gaulle would unhesitatingly mention his father.[2] In 1898, British and French forces collided with each other at Fashoda, in Sudan. War threatened, but Britain won the battle of wills, forcing the unconditional French withdrawal from Fashoda. This event made a lasting impression on young Charles, who would retain a lifelong distrust of Britain.[3]

De Gaulle decided to pursue a military career, and he graduated from Saint-Cyr, France's elite military academy, in 1912. He did well, but did not stand out in any way except for his height. At six feet four inches, he was a foot taller than the average Frenchman at the time. He fought bravely in World War I, was wounded three times, and was promoted to the rank of captain. De Gaulle was taken prisoner at the Battle of Verdun in 1916 after passing out from the effects of poison gas. During his captivity, he honed his oratorical skills, giving numerous lectures to his fellow inmates. The ideas sketched out in these lectures—the nature of leadership, the importance of contingency in war and in politics, the relationship between civil and military power—were developed in more detail in the four books he wrote in the inter-war years. In that sense, de Gaulle's period in prison contributed greatly to his intellectual formation.[4]

In 1934, his book *Vers l'Armée de Métier* (*Towards a Professional Army*) was published. Here, de Gaulle argued that tank formations should be deployed autonomously instead of supporting the infantry, the latter being the official view of the French army brass. Unfortunately, the German, rather than the French, army decided to adopt that strategy, with devastating effect (*Blitzkrieg*). French troops found a copy of the German translation with some approving annotations by Adolf Hitler himself in the Führer's retreat in Berchtesgaden in 1945.[5]

WORLD WAR II

World War II started in September 1939. When German tank formations broke through the Allied lines in northeast France in May 1940, Colonel de Gaulle was one of the few officers who tried to stop them, but it was too little too late. Nevertheless, for his initiative he was promoted to brigadier general, and, on June 5, Prime Minister Paul Reynaud appointed de Gaulle under-secretary of war. De Gaulle urged the government to fight on, but the French military leadership believed the situation was hopeless. Reynaud resigned on June 16, 1940, and Marshal Pétain, as the new prime minister, reached out to the Germans to seek an armistice. De Gaulle refused to accept this and escaped to Britain.

On June 18, 1940, in a radio broadcast in London, de Gaulle called upon all the French who wanted to remain free to listen and follow him.[6] It was an act of great courage—or of amazing presumption. At that same moment, the legitimate government of France was seeking an armistice with Germany, while de Gaulle urged France to fight on. He had never been elected to any post and had held a junior government position for just twelve days. Hardly any Frenchman had ever heard of him, let alone knew how he looked. He was utterly alone. Nobody of importance had followed him to Britain.

But de Gaulle had one great asset: the support of Churchill. For the British, the immediate priority was to find a Frenchman who would continue the fight outside France. Churchill was an excellent reader of people. The first time he had met de Gaulle was on June 13, 1940, in Tours, France, after which Churchill uttered the prophetic words, "*l'homme du destin*" ("the man of destiny"). Over the next five years, the two men would have a love-hate relationship. Churchill was exasperated by de Gaulle's arrogant intransigence and self-righteousness, which is best

Figure 17.1 Frenemies—Churchill and de Gaulle, 1944

Source: Imperial War Museums

described by quoting de Gaulle: "When I am right, I get angry. Churchill gets angry when he is wrong. We are angry at each other much of the time."

While U.S. president Franklin D. Roosevelt (the subject of chapter 7) would dismiss the general as an unbalanced crypto-dictator and an egotist who took himself for Joan of Arc, Churchill swung between extremes, admiring de Gaulle's "massive strength" and hailing him as "perhaps the last survivor of a warrior race," but then threatening to have him clapped in chains because he was so impossible to deal with. But Churchill saw no alternative (although he tried to find one) and, better than Roosevelt, he understood the importance of having France as an ally during and after the war. After much maneuvering, a provisional government was formed with de Gaulle as its prime minister and recognized by the Allies as the legitimate representation of France in 1944.

After the invasion of Normandy, and the liberation of most of France in the fall of 1944, de Gaulle returned to France, where he was greeted by delirious crowds. He ordered the French forces under General Leclerc to race ahead and liberate Paris ahead of the U.S. forces. Before the city was fully secure, de Gaulle entered Paris and gave an impassioned speech to the crowd: "Paris . . . Liberated by itself, liberated by its people with the help of the French armies, with the support and the help of all of France, of the France that fights, of the only France, of the real France, of the eternal France." The Allied contribution was only mentioned in passing. De Gaulle's purpose was to restore France to the place among nations that, he firmly believed, was its due. For that, the French needed to banish the memories of its ignominious defeat and to embrace the myth that it had played a key role in defeating Nazi Germany.

SELF-IMPOSED EXILE

After the war was over, politics as usual along party lines reemerged. De Gaulle was temperamentally not well suited for the jostling of parliamentary politics. Legislators complained that de Gaulle did not value their opinions (which was true). Everyone agreed that a new constitutional form had to be adopted to replace the discredited Third Republic.[7] But what should come in its place? De Gaulle favored a strong executive presidency (akin to the U.S. model), while many legislators preferred a system with a largely ceremonial president, elected by parliament, which was to rule supreme (similar to the post-World War II German model). Many feared the presidential system as a precursor to dictatorship. Tired of all the infighting, de Gaulle resigned as prime minister in early 1946 and withdrew to his house in Colombey-les-Deux-Églises, some 125 miles from Paris. That same year, a new constitution was approved in a referendum, which vested power in parliament. The Fourth Republic had begun.

For the next twelve years, de Gaulle lived in self-imposed exile from governmental affairs, although he made occasional forays into politics. During that time, he also wrote his war memoirs, which were a commercial success. His memoirs start with the famous sentence, "*Toute ma vie, je me suis fait une certaine idée de la France*" ("All my life I have had a certain idea of France"). Politics moved on without him until the problems facing the Fourth Republic became unbearable. On May 29, 1958, a message from President Coty was read in parliament, which said that France was on the brink of civil war. According to Coty, there was only one man who could save the country. He was therefore sending for General de Gaulle, who would be tasked to form a government of national safety within the existing legal framework and to propose reforms of France's institutions.[8] On June 1, parliament voted de Gaulle into office as prime minister by a decisive majority, the main holdout being the large contingent of communist deputies. Parliament suspended itself for six months, which gave the general vital breathing space.

BACK IN OFFICE

In his first six months in office, de Gaulle moved with lightning speed. Within three months, he presented a new constitution to the population, which created a strong presidency with powers that exceeded even those of the U.S. president. The Fifth Republic was approved on September 29, 1958, in a referendum by an overwhelming majority of 78 percent of the votes cast. Next came elections for a new National Assembly (akin to the House of

Representatives). The supporters of de Gaulle, together with their allies, won the majority of the seats. Finally, on December 21, de Gaulle was elected the first president of the Fifth Republic.

De Gaulle understood the importance of a sound economy for achieving his overarching vision to restore France's *grandeur* ("glory and greatness"). In these six months, he pushed through a series of reforms against the opposition of a reluctant cabinet. De Gaulle went on television to announce the measures, and he linked them to the need to restore France's *grandeur*. Sacrifices were needed to escape from mediocrity, he told the nation.[9]

On September 14, 1958, he invited West German Chancellor Konrad Adenauer to his house in Colombey-les-Deux-Églises, the only foreign statesman ever invited there. They understood that a free Europe could not be built without Franco-German understanding. There, the idea of a unified Europe led by a politically strong, self-assured France and an economically powerful Germany was born. The Franco-German alliance has been the engine of the European Union ever since.[10]

De Gaulle accomplished more in these first six months in office than almost any other politician would accomplish in a lifetime. Yet, there was still this most Gordian of all knots: Algeria. The generals there, commanding huge forces, could still take him—and the Fifth Republic—down, if he did not do their bidding.

DE GAULLE CUTS THE ALGERIAN KNOT

Three days after taking office, de Gaulle flew to Algiers, where he was greeted by huge crowds. He appeared on the balcony of the Palais d'Été, raised his arms in his familiar V gesture, and shouted, "*Je vous ai compris*" ("I have understood you"). The crowd went berserk. As people are prone to do, they interpreted the words as what they wanted them to be—that he understood their cause and would keep Algeria French. He had said no such thing. His Delphic utterance could mean anything. In fact, de Gaulle had begun to understand that Algerian independence was inevitable, not for the sake of Algeria, but for the sake of France. He regarded Algeria as a cancer that was destroying

A video of de Gaulle's speech on June 4, 1958, in which he says he has understood the *pieds-noirs*. Focus on the first thirty seconds and listen to the reaction of the masses.

https://www.youtube.com/watch?v=vzm0APfrflkRsKxzopTN0

the French state from within. Since de Gaulle's overarching objective was to restore the *grandeur* of France, the question was how to cut out this cancer. An ignominious withdrawal after the trauma of Indochina was unthinkable.

Therefore, de Gaulle would first step up the war against the FLN to gain the upper hand at the negotiating table. However, this was solely a tactical maneuver to prepare for ultimate withdrawal, hopefully in conjunction with some kind of federal scheme tying France and Algeria together. Pulling this off would require all his genius for ambiguity, duplicity, and improvisation, his ability to impose abrupt changes of policy, and his capacity for rallying popular support, when the majority of Frenchmen favored *Algérie française*. If he failed, his entire project to regenerate France would be in jeopardy, and a putsch led by the generals in Algeria a realistic possibility, if not a certainty.[11]

De Gaulle's first move was to separate military and civilian command in Algeria. In late 1958, he replaced the staunchly *Algérie française* general Raoul Salan, who held both military and civilian positions, with the loyal Gaullist General Maurice Challe and a newly appointed civil representative, Paul Delouvrier. De Gaulle gave full support to Challe's military operations, which proved to be remarkably successful. Encouraged by the improving military situation, and mindful of the growing criticism of France's war in Algeria on the international stage, de Gaulle took the next major step. In a televised address on September 16, 1959, he announced that, after peace was restored, the people of Algeria would be offered the chance to decide their own future in a referendum on self-determination. The words "self-determination" were crucial; a taboo was broken. The *pieds-noirs* became increasingly suspicious.

In January 1960 the successful army commander of Algiers, General Massu, expressed his worries in an interview with a German newspaper, lamenting that "General de Gaulle has become a man of the left."[12] De Gaulle promptly relieved Massu of his command, but widespread violence erupted in Algiers and barricades went up on January 24. For five days, chaos reigned. According to one observer, "During these five days, nothing existed any more . . . there remained only one man—and a man alone."[13] Then, this man, General de Gaulle, intervened in a televised speech, appearing in uniform and adopting a tone not of persuasion but of command. He assured the *pieds-noirs* that France would never leave Algeria and hand it over to the rebels (which was a lie). He praised the army for its service while reminding the army that its duty was to serve the state. Who was the state? Echoing the Sun King, Louis XIV, who famously said, *"l'état, c'est moi"* ("I am the State"), General de Gaulle said, "I am the person responsible for the destiny of the nation. I must be obeyed by all French soldiers."[14] The insurrection collapsed. For the first time ever in the long crisis over Algeria, the government had gained the upper hand. De Gaulle's popularity soared.

In yet another television address on Algeria on November 4, 1960, after his usual praise for the army's successes, he dropped a bombshell—de Gaulle used the words "the government of the Algerian Republic" to describe a future situation. Shortly thereafter, he visited Algeria for the eighth—and last—time since returning to power. There was nothing left of the exuberant enthusiasm with which he was greeted less than three years before. Yet, while the *pieds-noirs* were disillusioned, some 75 percent of the French electorate approved of de Gaulle's Algerian policy in a referendum held on January 8, 1961.

At a press conference on April 11, 1961, he dismissed Algeria with almost callous indifference: "France has no interest in keeping Algeria under her laws or dependent on her . . . Algeria costs us more than it brings us . . . That is why today France would contemplate with the greatest sang-froid a solution by which Algeria would cease to belong to her."[15] Now it was clear to everyone what the endgame would be. The response was ferocious. On April 22, 1961, elite regiments seized key buildings in Algiers and the Gaullist (!) General Challe announced that the army had taken control. He said, "*Algérie française* is not dead . . . There is not, and will never be an independent Algeria."[16] Panic gripped the French capital. There was a plane ready at an airfield outside Paris to whisk de Gaulle away if the Elysée Palace were attacked. He handed his will to one of his aides in a sealed envelope.

Yet, it was again de Gaulle who turned the tide. At 8 p.m. on April 23, de Gaulle appeared on television, again in full uniform, announcing he was taking emergency powers under Article 16 of the Constitution. He spoke contemptuously of the coup leaders, referring to them as "a small bunch [he used the word *quarteron*, a dismissive term] of retired generals" and "a group of fanatical, ambitious and partisan officers." De Gaulle went on to say, "I forbid any Frenchman, and in the first place any soldier, to execute any of their orders."[17] The effect was electrifying. Thousands of conscripts who made up the bulk of the army in Algeria heard this on their transistor radios. The attempted coup was over. De Gaulle was not some weak leader of the Fourth Republic—here spoke the man who personified France. Many conscripts might not have been sympathetic to the cause of *L'Algérie libre* (independent Algeria), but they had faith in their leader to do what was right for France.

Negotiations with the Algerian Provisional Government started in May 1961 in Evian, Switzerland, and on March 18, 1962, the treaty (Evian Accords) was signed. The Evian Accords were approved in a referendum in April by 91 percent of the French electorate, and on July 5, 1962, Algeria became independent. The Evian Accords guaranteed the rights of French settlers, but the (not unrealistic) perception that they would not be respected led to the exodus of some 700,000 *pieds-noirs* back to France before the end of the year. In the negotiations, de Gaulle abandoned almost every position he had held in May 1961. As he explained, "[W]e had to extricate France from a crisis that brought her only misfortunes . . . As for France, she has to move on to other things."[18]

De Gaulle was reelected in December 1965, but there were signs the population was getting tired of him. In 1968, societal unrest swept over the Western world. France appeared to be on the brink of revolution. De Gaulle initially wavered, but was able to rise to the occasion one last time. On May 30, he addressed the French on the radio, because the state television service was on strike. He announced he had dissolved parliament and practically accused the communists of plotting a revolution (which was not true). It worked. Hundreds of thousands of Frenchmen joined a demonstration in support of the constitutional order, and in the parliamentary elections of June 1968, the Gaullists won a resounding majority. It would be de Gaulle's swan song. People voted more for the Gaullist party to support the established order than because of its leader, who was now seen by many as too old (seventy-seven years), a man of the past, and out of touch with their problems.

De Gaulle resigned on April 28, 1969, after having lost an unimportant referendum, and he died on November 9, 1970. His successor Georges Pompidou informed the nation on television: "*Françaises, Français, Général de Gaulle est mort. La France est veuve*" ("French women, Frenchmen, General de Gaulle is dead. France is a widow").

LESSONS

According to biographer Jonathan Fenby, "Charles de Gaulle poses an enormous problem for those who deny that history is shaped by great human beings."[19] Indeed, de Gaulle is one of France's most consequential leaders, saving this venerable nation not once, but twice. His legacy lives on. The institutions created by de Gaulle still function, have survived presidents from the left and the right, and accommodated a divided government (*cohabitation*). It is easy to discern the Gaullist strands in the current French president, Emmanuel Macron, who is a keen student of the general.[20]

De Gaulle was definitely a hedgehog. His actions were motivated by a single overarching vision: to restore France to its former *grandeur*. He sincerely believed that France was a great and glorious nation, probably the greatest nation on earth, but had been slipping in power and influence in the world. Was he also a fox? At first sight, he was not. That was certainly the view of Churchill and Roosevelt. De Gaulle was often obstinate and refused to compromise. But upon closer examination, de Gaulle is more fox-like than he seemed. According to biographer Julian Jackson, "De Gaulle had always emphasized the need to adapt to circumstances, and the need for a policy that respected realities."[21] Take his intransigence in World War II. There was a strategy behind de Gaulle's often insufferable behavior. De Gaulle told his spokesman that intransigence was the one weapon he had, and one which served his campaign to establish leadership of the French. Churchill understood this: "He had to be rude with the British to prove to French eyes that he was not a British puppet."[22]

De Gaulle also exhibited great tactical acumen in dealing with the Algerian problem, deftly maneuvering to neutralize the threat of a putsch and taking into account French and international public opinion, as well as the international political climate. De Gaulle reformed the economy because he understood that great power claims require a strong economy.

Was de Gaulle therefore an eagle? To some degree, yes. He did restore France's reputation and made it again a major political power on the world stage. As recent as 2019, following the European elections, France played the determinant role in the appointment of all senior international positions held by Europeans—from the presidents of the European Central Bank, European Commission, and European Council to the managing director of the International Monetary Fund.

Yet, de Gaulle's ultimate vision of *grandeur* is, in principle, without limitations.[23] He saw France striding the globe as a colossus, a power that could somehow create a new East-West equilibrium with France in the central position, a country that could radically reform the global monetary system centered on the United States and reintroduce the gold standard. He made lengthy trips to Latin America to urge its countries to stand up for themselves and distance themselves from Washington. All these attempts were ultimately futile.[24] As the 1960s progressed, it became ever clearer that all of this was well beyond France's means. De Gaulle also increasingly lost touch with the desires and concerns of the French population, who were getting tired of his anti-Americanism and getting less interested in his dreams of *grandeur*. Thus, like Thatcher two decades later (chapter 9), during his long time in office, de Gaulle gradually moved from an unusually strong-willed eagle to a stubborn hedgehog.

De Gaulle was undoubtedly a charismatic leader. When nobody believed in the cause of French freedom after the country lay prostate in 1940, he stood alone and provided hope to millions who listened to his radio addresses. In late 1940, Agnès Humbert joined one of France's first resistance groups and distributed tracts in support of de Gaulle, albeit she had little idea who he was:

> How bizarre it all is! Here we are, most of us on the wrong side of forty, careering along like students all fired up with passion and fervor, in the wake of a leader of whom we know absolutely nothing, of whom none of us has even seen a photograph. In the whole course of human history, has there ever been anything quite like it? Thousands upon thousands of people, fired by blind faith, following an unknown figure. Perhaps this strange anonymity is even an asset: the mystery of the unknown![25]

The French population approved the constitution of the Fifth Republic by an overwhelming majority, although half of those who voted yes told pollsters they had not read any of it. Why? They trusted the general to do what was right for them.[26] It was his charisma, talking directly to the nation, that quelled two uprisings in Algeria. Understanding de Gaulle's strand of charismatic leadership is facilitated by the fact that he laid out many of his ideas long before he could put them in practice in his book *Le fil de l'épée* (*The Edge of the Sword*), published in 1932. His leadership philosophy rested on four elements: inner strength, public restraint, myth making, and emotional power.[27] All these elements can be acquired, or at least improved, if the aspiring charismatic leader makes an effort.

INNER STRENGTH

In *Le fil de l'épée*, de Gaulle drew a prescient picture of a "man of character," characterized by inner strength, willing to bear the burden no other can. This person is waiting to assume the role of a national savior, exalting the leader to whom people would turn in a crisis "as iron toward the magnet":

> When the crisis comes, it is he who is followed, it is he who raises the burden with his own arms, though they may break in doing so, and carries it on his shoulders, though they may crack under it . . . As soon as the matters grow serious and the danger urgent, as soon as the safety of the nation requires immediate initiative . . . a kind of tidal wave sweeps the man of character to the forefront.[28]

While de Gaulle's typology of a man of character is perhaps somewhat unusual, I have seen how the inner strength of the cadets is built at the U.S. Military Academy at West Point. In general, adversity, if overcome, builds inner strength. In the words of Friedrich Nietzsche, "What doesn't kill you makes you stronger."[29]

PUBLIC RESTRAINT

According to de Gaulle, charisma requires public restraint from leaders. The Soviet dictator Joseph Stalin also followed this principle. De Gaulle's "man of character" is isolated from others, renouncing the joys of relaxation, familiarity, and friendship. This sounds pretty grim, but it is aligned with what resistance fighter Agnès Humbert said previously: "Perhaps this strange anonymity is even an asset: the mystery of the unknown!" As charisma involves an element of mystery, according to de Gaulle, leaders must maintain a distance between themselves and their public. They should restrict public appearances and carefully assess the impact of each appearance before committing themselves in public. This is more difficult to pull off in today's era of hyperconnectivity, but one may wonder whether some of today's leaders might not benefit from maintaining a greater distance from their followers, rather than being on social media every moment of the day.

MYTH MAKING

According to de Gaulle, followers need to feel that their leader transcends their own limitations, weaknesses, and selfishness. De Gaulle's charisma was animated by his genuine belief that he incarnated France, and that he alone had the strength to raise this nation to the status he believed with all his heart and all his mind it deserved.[30] According to Fenby, "He would embrace reverses and difficulties as the spur to action like the mythical hero he imagined himself to be."[31] De Gaulle saw himself as some kind of reincarnation of Joan of Arc, the savior of France in the fifteenth century, and often spoke about himself in the third-person singular.

Numerous events, small and large, built his myth. After World War II, he rejected a ministerial suggestion that his rank should be raised to the status of marshal. What could be more tempting for an officer? Yet, de Gaulle opined that his two stars were enough for the war years, and to change it would be inappropriate.[32] In one of the many attempts on his life, the (apparently unarmored) presidential car was hit by fourteen bullets. Nevertheless, he continued to the air base he was scheduled to visit and reviewed the guard of honor as if nothing had happened. Incidentally, this particular attack was the inspiration for Frederick Forsyth's (1971) gripping best seller *The Day of the Jackal* and the eponymous 1973 movie. As president, de Gaulle gave press conferences—that he turned into "high masses"—which, according to the editor of the French newspaper *Le Monde*, were "the absolute weapon of the regime."[33]

Richard Branson, the founder of the Virgin Group, is an example of a businessman who has thrived by building a myth around himself. He has created an image of somebody who flaunts the rules, has an outrageous sense of humor, and is an underdog willing to attack the establishment. Branson is well known for his attempts to break world records, including multiple balloon flights and the fastest crossing of the Atlantic by ship. Regardless of whether the attempt was successful or not, it built the Branson myth. His personal myth is a key element of the equity of the Virgin brand, which spans many industries, from music (Virgin Records) to space travel (Virgin Galactic).

EMOTIONAL POWER

De Gaulle clearly grasped that the highest form of power was not vested in one's organizational position (a remarkable insight for an army officer) but in emotions, in the hearts of one's followers. In his view, leaders need to establish a personal, emotional relationship between themselves and their distal followers because the masses do not obey impersonal power.[34]

De Gaulle connected with his distal followers in two ways. First, his frequent recourse to the referendum gave power directly to his distal followers—effectively bypassing parliament, which was populated by his proximate followers as well as his opponents. Second, his communication skills were legendary. He had great command of the French language and spoke with conviction and self-confidence. He augmented his verbal skills with non-verbal forms of communication. According to Fenby, "His appearances [on television] became huge events, and he knew how to milk them for all they were worth, with his mobile facial expressions, his gesticulations and the mining of the recesses of the French language for the precise words he needed to announce a policy change or vilify opponents in the rhetorical equivalent of a tank attack he had championed in the 1930s."[35]

De Gaulle announces on television that the Evian Accords were signed. You do not need to understand French to get his intonation, facial expressions, and gesticulations.

https://www.youtube.com/watch?v=uG-rKmcdo9U

A soaring vision, compelling oratory, inner strength, avoidance of public overexposure, creation of a myth, and power vested in emotions rather than position—these principles remain as relevant today as they were in de Gaulle's time. His view of a charismatic leader drawing followers by carrying the burden in difficult times for the sake of the organization or country will continue to resonate. De Gaulle showed how this can be done and how to amass great power without letting it corrupt you. That is an encouraging lesson for today, as well.

CHAPTER TAKEAWAYS

- De Gaulle started out as an unusually strong-willed eagle who, at the end of his life, had morphed into a hedgehog. His opponents, the French generals in Algeria and the *pieds-noirs*, were pure hedgehogs.

- De Gaulle saw himself as a larger-than-life figure, a twentieth-century version of Joan of Arc.

- De Gaulle's intransigence in World War II was a conscious strategy to hide his weak position and signal to the French he was no puppet of the Allies.

- De Gaulle understood that cutting Algeria loose was necessary for France to thrive. He outfoxed his hedgehog-like opponents at every step. To achieve this, he used ambiguity, duplicity, and improvisation, and abrupt changes of policy.

- Repeatedly, de Gaulle astutely relied upon distal followers (the electorate) to circumvent proximate followers and opponents (politicians).

- Like Thatcher, de Gaulle stayed in office too long.

- De Gaulle's life highlights several charismatic leadership principles:

  ○ Self-confidence is a key quality for charismatic leadership.

  ○ A soaring vision can rally your followers.

° Inner strength—willingness to carry any burden—draws followers to you.

° Avoid public overexposure to strengthen your appeal.

° Myth making is an element of charismatic leadership.

° The highest form of power is in the emotional relationship the leader has with their followers.

° Charismatic leaders are not above duplicity to achieve their goals.

REFLECTIONS ON CHARISMATIC LEADERSHIP

CHARISMATIC LEADERS EXCEL in their ability to formulate and articulate an inspirational vision, and by behaviors and actions signal to followers that they—and by inference their mission—are exceptional. Individuals choose to follow charismatic leaders, not primarily because of any formal authority the leader may have, but because of perceptions of extraordinariness. Charismatic leaders make their followers part of something larger than themselves. In marketing, this idea is used in "purpose branding"—how a brand can change the world for the better. The role of purpose branding is to unite the firm's employees and brand customers in the pursuit of that higher vision. Take ice-cream brand Ben & Jerry's. It has benefited enormously from employees and consumers acting as brand ambassadors, who rave on social media about the brand's advocacy of social causes. Incidentally, this has also made Ben & Jerry's one of the world's best-selling ice-cream brands.[1]

Management scholars Jay Conger and Rabindra Kanungo introduced a framework for charismatic leadership, which I use to reflect on the case studies of Alexander the Great and General Charles de Gaulle.[2] Based on their work, I identify five key components of effective charismatic leadership: (1) great desire to change the status quo; (2) define and communicate an idealized vision, which is highly discrepant from the status quo; (3) show exemplary acts of great personal risk and sacrifice; (4) create a deep emotional bond with followers; and (5) mind your lifespan.

1. GREAT DESIRE TO CHANGE THE STATUS QUO

Charismatic leaders are essentially opposed to the status quo and strive to change it. They share this characteristic with disruptive leaders. The difference is that the locus of power for disruptive leadership is usually institutional (based on coercion, rewards, or one's position in the organization), while the main source of power of charismatic leaders is the person's qualities (referent power). According to German sociologist Max Weber, who introduced the concept of charismatic leadership, "Men do not obey [the charismatic leader] by virtue of tradition or statute, but because they believe in him."[3]

Alexander the Great and de Gaulle both exhibited a great desire to change the status quo. Alexander was not satisfied with merely being king of Macedon, or even king of the western part of the Persian Empire. He also was not satisfied with the "normal" role of being the victor that lords over the defeated. De Gaulle refused to accept the "new world order" imposed by Nazi Germany and accepted by the legitimate French government in 1940. He was also unwilling to accept the Fourth Republic—which was essentially a continuation of the ineffective Third Republic—or the situation in Algeria.

2. DEFINE AND COMMUNICATE THE DISCREPANT, IDEALIZED VISION

Leadership author John Kotter identifies the creation of a vision for change and communication of the change vision as the third and fourth steps in his model for effective change management.[4] Charismatic leaders excel in the ability to formulate a new, idealized vision, which is highly discrepant from the status quo, and is attainable only because of the exceptional qualities of the leader. Alexander's vision of a world empire, governed jointly by the Macedonians and the Persians, was totally new to the world. De Gaulle's vision of France, free and restored to its former *grandeur*, was highly discrepant from its actual situation in World War II, and later again in the late

1950s. In 1946, people did not want to follow his vision and he resigned, waiting in the wings until he was needed again.

Ingvar Kamprad, the charismatic founder of Ikea, built the company on a highly discrepant, idealized vision, laid out in his "Testament of a Furniture Retailer." In this document, he contrasted his vision with the prevailing industry practice of marketing high-priced furniture that was out of reach of most people. His vision was—

> To create a better everyday life for the many people by offering a wide range of well-designed, functional home furnishing products at prices so low that as many people as possible will be able to afford them. We have decided once and for all to side with the many . . . In our line of business, far too many of the fine designs and new ideas are reserved for a small circle of the affluent. That situation has influenced the formulation of our objective . . . we will be able to make a valuable contribution to the process of democratisation.[5]

It is not enough if charismatic leaders are able to *define* a new vision; they should also be able to *communicate* their vision in an inspirational manner to the mass of their followers. Inspirational communication builds the necessary emotional bonds with followers that give charismatic leadership its unique strength. From the ancient sources, a picture emerges of Alexander as a highly inspirational communicator, able to articulate his vision, and accessible to every Macedonian soldier. De Gaulle was a supremely effective (verbal and nonverbal) communicator of his ideas, who used the media to connect with the French people.

3. SHOW EXEMPLARY ACTS OF GREAT PERSONAL RISK AND SACRIFICE

Charismatic leaders engage in exemplary acts that involve great personal risk and sacrifice. They do not only talk the talk but also walk the walk. This behavior inspires and emotionally arouses their followers. It shows their sincerity and binds their followers more strongly to them. Ideally, stories about their risk and sacrifice lead to myths.

Alexander the Great never asked his soldiers to do something he did not do himself. He was wounded eight times, and in all four major battles he personally led the cavalry charge, at obvious great personal risk. One celebrated instance of sacrifice occurred when Alexander led part of the army through the Gedrosian desert (present-day Baluchistan in Pakistan). The army suffered terribly because of lack of water. When some soldiers found some water, they offered it to Alexander in a helmet (by itself telling, that they did not drink it themselves). He praised them but poured the water into the sand. He would not drink if his men could not drink. Alexander lived on in countless legends, told in Europe and Asia, about fantastic journeys and romantic adventures.[6]

De Gaulle gave up a comfortable life for the sake of his vision. He was sentenced to death by the Vichy regime, and he survived more than thirty assassination attempts. Like Alexander, he did not claim privileges that others did not have. He was incorruptible. After he resigned in 1946, he refused to use his position to acquire additional food ration coupons and supplies that were sometimes tight. The de Gaulles even paid the telephone and electricity bills for their apartment in the Élysée Palace. When their grandchildren were unable to go on a winter sports holiday because they could get no seats on the train, de Gaulle refused to pull rank. When he passed away in 1970, he left behind a very modest inheritance. Such behaviors stand in sharp contrast to the entitlement behaviors we can witness in some of today's business and political leaders.

4. CREATE A DEEP EMOTIONAL BOND WITH YOUR FOLLOWERS

Ultimately, the power of charismatic leaders does not reside in their institutional position but in the hearts of their followers. Alexander the Great had a close bond not only with his officers but also with the common soldiers. They followed him because they loved him. De Gaulle, too, excelled in creating an emotional bond with his followers. But he did it in a different way. While Alexander was accessible to even the lowest soldier, de Gaulle was top-down, through myth making and dramatic television appearances.

Oprah Winfrey is a very successful and charismatic businesswoman. Her devoted followers describe her as inspirational, brilliant, but also highly personable. She is considered a sister by many of her employees, who are willing to work long hours because of their love for her.[7]

5. MIND YOUR LIFESPAN

Charismatic leaders engage in innovative behaviors that run counter to the established norms of their organizations, industries, and/or societies. Their plans and strategies to achieve change, their exemplary acts of heroism involving personal risks, and their self-sacrificing behaviors must be novel, unconventional, and out of the ordinary. This has two important implications.

First, the potential for charismatic leadership is greatest when the organization—or society—experiences significant tribulation; think about a corporate bankruptcy or national crisis. In Alexander's time, Greece was impoverished and in desperate need of change to alleviate this condition. De Gaulle's France faced two existential crises: defeat by Germany and the Algerian War.

Second, charismatic leadership is essentially unstable and transitory. Once the new order is institutionalized, charisma fades because the need for radical change has disappeared.[8] This creates a problem when the charismatic leader does not (want to) perceive this, and rather views themselves as indispensable and the only one in whose hands the organization's (or country's) destiny can be trusted. It is possible that the mutiny at Opis was an indication that Alexander's charisma was slipping away, although how he handled this—and the response of his soldiers—casts doubt on this idea. We will never know, as he died soon thereafter. Yet, there is little doubt that Alexander's reputation benefited greatly from his early death.

De Gaulle lived much longer, and his case illustrates that the lifespan of charismatic leadership is finite. Gradually, as the 1960s progressed, and memories of the instability of the Fourth Republic and the Algerian War faded away, the French grew tired of de Gaulle and his antics and authoritarian behavior, which they did not object to when they were in dire need. He increasingly lost the connection with his followers, and in the end, he was more or less forced to resign.

Carlos Ghosn, the once-hallowed boss of the Renault-Nissan-Mitsubishi Alliance, started out as the savior of Nissan, whose employees were mesmerized by his charisma. Ghosn's drive inspired those around him who had lost faith in the viability of the company. Initially, his leadership style was open and transparent, and he was an excellent listener. Over time, and especially after he was also appointed CEO of Renault, he became increasingly autocratic. According to insiders, there emerged a personality cult around him. He became a business leader whose long years at the top had made it difficult to tell where his dreams for his companies ended and his personal ambitions began. In November 2018, he was ousted and arrested, accused of financial misconduct. On December 29, 2019, he escaped his house arrest and fled to his native Lebanon. His mistake was to ignore the advice he had given himself when talking to investors in the early 2000s: that every CEO should step down within five years.[9]

THE EVIL SIDE OF CHARISMATIC LEADERSHIP

Charismatic business leaders are often heralded as corporate heroes by orchestrating turnarounds, launching new enterprises, engaging in organizational renewal or change, and obtaining extraordinary performances from individuals. The story of Carlos Ghosn shows that, while there is truth to that, over time, the negatives associated with charismatic leadership can easily outweigh the positives unless the leader knows when it is time to step down. As I discussed in chapter 1, each leadership type has its potential dark side, but the danger is especially pertinent for charismatic leadership. History shows that charismatic leadership can have an evil side.

Charismatic leaders engender a degree of adulation among their followers, which is a much more powerful bond than one vested in traditional, institutional bases of coercion, reward, and position. They can motivate their followers to do things they would not normally do. If the mission of the leader is evil though, the consequences will be, too. It is no coincidence that many of the great villains in history were charismatic leaders—think about Adolf Hitler, Joseph Stalin, Mao Zedong, Charles Manson, Saddam Hussein, Pol Pot, Kim Il-sung, Osama bin Laden, Jim Jones (Peoples Temple cult), or Abu Bakr al-Baghdadi (Islamic State). They were all able to get their followers to commit unspeakable crimes.

Of course, a charismatic leader does not have to go to the extremes of a Manson, let alone Hitler, to have a negative effect on their organization. There are many shades of gray in between. That is why it is important that organizations set their own ethical standards, and develop procedures to instill and maintain these ethical standards in their managers, especially, but of course not limited to, those with charismatic qualities. Procedures should include having a strong and credible (words are cheap) top management commitment to a clearly stated code of ethical conduct; recruiting, selecting, and promoting managers with high moral standards as shown in their behaviors; training in ethical leadership; and celebrating (political, historical, business) heroes who exemplify ethical conduct.[10] Royal Dutch Shell has had its "Shell General Business Principles" for several decades, and it comes with an associated strong Code of Conduct. Every employee is trained, and periodically retrained, on this Code of Conduct, and violating the Code can typically result in sanctions and even termination of employment. This is no window dressing, as not a year passes without staff dismissals for these reasons.

To assess whether charismatic leadership is a style that suits you, consider the following questions.

1. Are you comfortable with breaking the status quo? Can you give examples where you advocated major change in your current organization or earlier in life?

2. Are you generally seen by others as a very inspiring person? As a person who can make others fiercely loyal to you, regardless of your position?

3. Are you able to formulate a radically new vision for your organization? Can you give examples in your life when you have done that?

4. Have you had experience in successfully articulating your vision to others?

5. Are you ready to engage in acts involving significant personal risk and sacrifice to make your vision a reality? Have you done that in the past? How did you feel about this?

6. Have you created deep emotional bonds with your followers? Are they willing to go through the fire for you? If not, why not?

7. Which charismatic leaders do you recognize in your own professional and/or personal environment? How do you relate to their style of leadership?

8. What feedback have you ever received that portrayed you as a charismatic leader?

9. Are you confident you can handle admiration, if not adulation, of followers without it getting to your head?

WHERE DO *YOU* GO FROM HERE?

IN THIS BOOK, we have looked at sixteen leaders who exemplify seven leadership styles, separated from each other across geography, gender, race, social status, and 2,500 years of history. Now, you may wonder, "Where do I go from here? Can I use this book for reviewing and possibly improving my own leadership skills?" I think you can. To help you do this, I organize my recommendations around four questions:

- How gritty are you?
- What is your animal metaphor?
- What is your dominant leadership style?
- When is it time for you to go?

HOW GRITTY ARE YOU?

The case studies reveal a remarkable variation in the personal qualities of the leaders, all of whom were sufficiently effective in changing history. Some leaders were highly intelligent (e.g., Alexander the Great), others not particularly so (e.g., Campbell-Bannerman). Some had exemplary integrity (Mandela), others decidedly not (Clovis). Some excelled in humility (St. Peter), others not at all (de Gaulle). Some were highly educated (King), others received little formal education (Washington). Some were very sociable and good at building relations (Themistocles), others not so much (Nightingale). However, all these leaders had one thing in common: grit.

Recall that grit is the courage and determination that makes it possible for somebody to continue doing something difficult or unpleasant (see chapter 1). Gritty leaders have focus, self-confidence, motivation to succeed (overcoming obstacles, persistence), and resilience (rebounding from setbacks, weathering criticism, performing under pressure). Grit is the common denominator that ties together the lives of Themistocles and Thatcher, of King Clovis and Martin Luther King.

How gritty are you? To answer that question, Appendix A provides the Grit Scale. If you score very high, congratulations! You have the grit to (potentially) be a great leader. If you score below 90, and definitely if you score below 80, there is significant room to increase your grit. To help you identify which area(s) offer the greatest upward potential, look at your score on each of the four grit components—focus, self-confidence, motivation to succeed, and resilience. If you score low on a particular component, here is what you can do.

- **Focus.** If you have difficulty focusing, you might want to reread the chapter on Bismarck. While his adversaries like Napoleon III pursued many different interests, Bismarck never lost sight of what he wanted to achieve. You could further enrich your insights by reading chapters 4 and 5 of Henry Kissinger's masterpiece, *Diplomacy* (1994). If you want to delve deeper into Bismarck's fascinating life, Jonathan Steinberg's *Bismarck* (2011) is the ultimate resource.

- **Self-confidence.** If you score low on self-confidence, you may want to turn again to the chapter on de Gaulle—a leader with no particularly distinguished record until 1940, and yet he single-handedly saved France, twice, drawing on his self-confidence. If you are looking for more, I recommend Julian Jackson's biography *De Gaulle* (2018).

- **Motivation to succeed.** Almost all leaders discussed in this book had a great motivation to succeed, but even in this august group, Cortés stands out as a leader who persevered against overwhelming odds. For him, it truly was not over until it was over. Read chapter 8 again. Buddy Levy's *Conquistador* (2009) is also highly readable.

- **Resilience.** Ever since I read a biography on Roosevelt when I was a pre-teenager, I have been inspired by his resilience in facing polio at a time when his future was so bright. Chapters 10 and 11 in Ted Morgan's *FDR* (1985) are an excellent source.

In addition, if you want to learn more about the concept of grit, I recommend Angela Duckworth's *Grit* (2016). It talks about grit in all spheres of life.

WHAT IS YOUR ANIMAL METAPHOR?

I did not choose the case studies on the basis of where they would fall in the hedgehog-like versus fox-like chart developed in chapter 1 (Figure 1.1). However, as it turns out, with the exception of Campbell-Bannerman, all the leaders examined in this book exhibited strong hedgehog qualities— they were guided by an overarching vision.

Moreover, most leaders were so effective because they were able to align means with goals. In sum, most leaders were eagles. What are you? Are you a hedgehog, a fox, an eagle, or (dare to face the truth) an ostrich? I encourage you to turn to Appendix B and fill out the Hedgefox Scale. You might even be different than you think.

If you are a hedgehog, you are in good company. Most gurus are hedgehogs. If you aspire, though, to become an eagle, consider modifying your vision to bring it in line with your means, and show more flexibility in the means you employ. Mandela did that with tremendous effect. A good starting point for your journey would be to reread chapter 13 and then move on to Mandela's compelling autobiography, *Long Walk to Freedom* (1994). This impressive book will not fail to touch and inspire you.

If you are a fox, you are in good company too. There are many foxes who have risen to high and impactful leadership positions. Think of Germany's chancellor Angela Merkel, U.S. president Bill Clinton, Dutch premier Mark Rutte, European Commission president Ursula von der Leyen, and many others. Especially in European politics, you probably need to be a fox because your peers will be suspicious if you have a strong vision. You can find many foxes in the top leadership of large corporations, too. But if you aspire to become an eagle, you have to set a clear goal in your life. You need to identify where you are heading, so to speak.

To do this, it may be helpful to adopt the intellectual method, called "tower perspective," developed by Austria's chancellor Klemens von Metternich (1773–1859), whom we encountered briefly in chapter 3. Metternich discovered this method when he was visiting Brussels with some companions in 1792.[1] Metternich found out that there are two ways to survey a city: from a high tower or by walking the streets. While his fellow travelers walked the streets, Metternich climbed the highest tower in Brussels. Within minutes he understood the layout of the city better than his companions achieved in hours. He never forgot the lesson, which he subsequently applied to his hugely successful professional life. When called upon to solve the big problems of state (of which there were many), he first distanced himself from all the details; he sought an observational highpoint, so to speak. That allowed him to discern where he wanted to go ("vision"), unencumbered by confusing complexities ("means"). Only then did he plunge into the fray to achieve this vision. Because he had first seen the problem from "above," he always knew where he was going. Can you do the same? Can you step back and survey the landscape of your career from above, and determine your endpoint?

Somebody who, probably without realizing it, adopted Metternich's so-called tower perspective was Deng Xiaoping. Given the immense complexity of the tasks he faced, he had to pursue many goals but was able to achieve this by stretching them out over time, while always keeping the overall overview of where he wanted to go. You might want to read chapter 4 on Deng again. For more on Deng, I recommend Pantsov and Levine's *Deng Xiaoping* (2015).

Now, if you possess neither clear fox-like nor hedgehog-like qualities, a deeper self-assessment is called for, as being in that category is typically not helpful for impactful leadership. Turn to Figure 1.1 and study the characteristics of the fox and the hedgehog. You can focus on either acquiring one type of qualities or the other, or develop both. One role model to help you is Nightingale. She broke out of Victorian conventions and found her mission. Over time, she systematically acquired the means (nursing expertise, organizational skills, statistical knowledge, political contacts) that prepared her for the ordeal of the Barrack Hospital and life thereafter. If you still want more after reading chapter 14 again, I recommend Mark Bostridge's *Florence Nightingale* (2008). Another role model is Campbell-Bannerman, who started out as an ostrich. Over time, he developed fox-like qualities, and in the last years of his life he found his true mission in South Africa. It ensured his place in history. John Wilson's *CB* (1973) is a great resource if you are looking for more. Or, for a quick fix, turn to Roy Hattersley's much shorter *Campbell-Bannerman* (2006).

WHAT IS YOUR DOMINANT LEADERSHIP STYLE?

As the case studies in this book document, none of the leadership styles are, by their very nature, effective or ineffective. Regardless of what any particular leadership guru may claim, there is not a single universally effective leadership strategy.[2] To assess to what extent you exhibit each of the seven leadership styles discussed in this book, Appendix C provides the Steenkamp Assessment Instrument for Leadership Styles, or SAILS.

SAILS was informed by the common themes distilled from the case studies pertaining to each leadership style as detailed in the "Reflections" chapters, the leadership literature, and feedback from leadership scholars and business, nonprofit, and military leaders. SAILS consists of two parts:

Part I deals with *actual* leadership, and Part II with *aspirational* leadership. SAILS was developed for four groups of people.

- **Seasoned leaders:** People who have many years of leadership experience and want to assess their current leadership style and look for role models and inspiration to further strengthen their dominant leadership style(s). If that applies to you, fill out Part I (actual leadership) of SAILS.

- **Starting leaders:** People who have little, if any, leadership experience. If you are in this group, you are typically in an early career stage. Now is the time to assess the kind of leader you aspire to be. By planning this in advance, you get a leg up on others. I recommend you fill out Part II (leadership aspirations).

- **Developing leaders:** Leaders with significant experience who want to further develop their leadership skills in specific areas where their actual behavior falls short of what they really aspire to be. If that applies to you, you may want to fill out both Part I (actual) and Part II (aspirational).

- **360 Leaders:** Leaders who want to conduct a full-fledged, 360-degree feedback on their leadership. If you are interested in this, Parts I (actual) and II (aspirational) should be filled out by yourself, your boss, and a representative sample of the people who work for you.

WHEN IS IT TIME FOR YOU TO GO?

Themistocles, Cortés, Thatcher, and de Gaulle—and some would argue, Roosevelt—stayed in the job too long. If they had resigned their position when they were still at the top of their game, if anything, their reputation would have been (even) higher. Take what the biographer Jonathan Aiken wrote about Margaret Thatcher: "If she had retired, as Denis [her husband] wanted her to do, after ten years as Prime Minister, she would have departed at a level of public acclaim unequalled by any other previous occupant of No. 10 [Downing Street]."[3] Themistocles, Cortés, Thatcher, and de Gaulle had come to see themselves as indispensable, and may also have loved the trappings that come with high office too much. They are not the only ones, though.

While I was writing this chapter, Bolivia's president Evo Morales was forced out of office after having engineered an unconstitutional fourth electoral victory marred by allegations that his government rigged the elections. One former supporter said, "He has been sucking on the teat of power for 14 years . . . He has forgotten what he was— a man of the people."[4] Business leaders also routinely outlive their usefulness.[5] Jeff Immelt, General Electric's CEO from 2001 to 2017, is one such example. Telling is that the share price jumped 4 percent when his resignation was announced. In October 2019, Under Armour announced that Kevin Planck would resign as its CEO after twenty-four years. The company, which had been struggling in recent years, was being investigated by U.S. authorities over its accounting practices, and Planck was criticized for presiding over a "frathouse" corporate culture, including adult entertainment and gambling.[6]

What are warning signs that you should seriously consider stepping down from your leadership role? Here are seven qualitative markers.

1. Are you starting to regard your position as your "right," as the natural condition? This is something that plagued Cortés in the years after his great success.

2. Are you becoming less patient with your followers? One example is Thatcher, who indeed became ever more impatient with her colleagues the longer she was prime minister.

3. Looking backward, do you see significant changes in your style of leadership? Are there signs of hubris? Are you becoming more directive (even autocratic) than you used to be? Do you have a diminished appetite for being questioned or challenged by your followers? De Gaulle was never low on hubris, but it became worse in the last years of his presidency.

4. Are you as involved and motivated doing your job as you were early in your tenure? Or is your leadership slipping? Are things happening now that did not happen before? Especially in the last year of his presidency, Roosevelt's leadership was slipping, albeit his rapidly deteriorating health was one key contributing factor.

5. Are you losing trusted advisors at a faster rate than you acquire new

ones? This certainly applied to Thatcher, who, in the last year of her premiership, lost even erstwhile trusted lieutenants such as Nigel Lawson and Geoffrey Howe.

6. Do you see yourself as indispensable? The only person who can really do the job? Are you setting up your organization to succeed without you, or are you setting it up to fail without you? Remember, only in exceptional cases is somebody truly indispensable. Washington should certainly rate high on this aspect and, according to his own judgment, he was not indispensable. Neither was Themistocles, but he failed to see that.

7. If you step down now, would your followers be truly sorry to see you go? Or would they be relieved? Most people were not sorry to see de Gaulle or Thatcher go, despite everything they had done for their countries.

If your answers to these questions give you pause to wonder whether it is time to step down from your present leadership position, I recommend you reread the chapters on Washington and Mandela. They provide shining examples of leaders who knew to step down before their time was up.

CONCLUDING COMMENTS

In the Preface, I quoted Niccolò Machiavelli, who wrote in *The Prince* that his most prized possession was "a knowledge of the actions of great men." In this book, I presented sixteen case studies of great men and women whose accomplishments have stood the test of time. All of them faced a daunting dilemma that called for a decision, which decisively affected the lives of their followers, and the course of history. Indeed, the effects of their leadership can be still be felt today.

Their leadership does reveal two silver bullets. First, they all exhibited grit. You can build your grit, too. Second, they all had an overarching goal that guided their lives—that is, they all possessed hedgehog qualities—even if that overarching goal was sometimes formulated only late(r) in their lives.

What is the overarching goal in your career? If you do not have one, take some time to think about what you really want to achieve in life.

The fact that these sixteen leaders were all people of flesh and blood, with more than their share of weaknesses, coming from different strands of life, race, gender, country, and time, and exhibiting different leadership styles, is a message of hope for any reader who wants to make a difference in their company, nonprofit organization, or public service. If this book has helped you in any of this, I have achieved my objective.

APPENDICES:

LEADERSHIP ASSESSMENT TOOLS

APPENDIX A

GRIT SCALE

INSTRUCTIONS: This questionnaire contains statements that assess how gritty you arc.[1] There are no right or wrong answers. Do not overthink the statements. Instead, ask yourself how you compare not just with your co-workers, friends, or family, but to "most people." In filling out the questionnaire, be sure to focus on the labels above the columns as well as the numbers, because sometimes the scale goes from 5 to 1 instead of from 1 to 5.

Compared to most people:	Not at all like me	Not much like me	Some- what like me	Mostly like me	Very much like me
1. I have the patience and discipline to direct my efforts to achieve my goals.	1	2	3	4	5
2. My inner confidence makes me believe I can achieve anything I set my mind to.	1	2	3	4	5
3. I fully subscribe to the phrase, "It's not over until it's over."	1	2	3	4	5
4. Adversity makes me stronger.	1	2	3	4	5
5. My long-term goals are not structured or planned.	5	4	3	2	1
6. I believe I can push through any obstacle people put in my way.	1	2	3	4	5
7. I exhibit a consistently high degree of persistence in reaching my career goals.	1	2	3	4	5
8. In stressful performance situations, my anxiety sometimes overwhelms me.	5	4	3	2	1
9. I get easily distracted in my work.	5	4	3	2	1
10. I am convinced I can take on and beat the best in the world.	1	2	3	4	5
11. I finish what I begin.	1	2	3	4	5
12. I have difficulty performing under intense pressure.	5	4	3	2	1
13. I am totally committed to my career goals.	1	2	3	4	5
14. I have a killer instinct to capital-ize on the moment.	1	2	3	4	5
15. I have overcome setbacks to conquer important challenges.	1	2	3	4	5
16. I dislike facing resistance to my plans or goals.	5	4	3	2	1
17. I stay focused on my goals despite obstacles.	1	2	3	4	5
18. I sometimes doubt my abilities.	5	4	3	2	1
19. When an obstacle is in my way, I tend to back away.	5	4	3	2	1
20. I handle criticism well.	1	2	3	4	5

To calculate your score on the four grit components and your total grit score, use the worksheet below.

Grit component	Statements in Grit Scale	Sum score
Focus	1, 5, 9, 13, 17	
Self-confidence	2, 6, 10, 14, 18	
Motivation to succeed	3, 7, 11, 15, 19	
Resilience	4, 8, 12, 16, 20	
Total grit score	Sum of scores on four components	

Scoring interpretation: The maximum total grit score is 100 (extremely gritty), the lowest possible score is 20 (not at all gritty). You can interpret your grittiness using the following guidelines: very high = 90–100, high = 80–89, medium = 70–79, low = 20–69.

The maximum score on each grit component is 25. A sum score below 20 indicates that this is an area where there is significant room for improvement.

APPENDIX B

HEDGEFOX SCALE

INSTRUCTIONS: This questionnaire contains statements to measure to what degree you are a hedgehog or a fox.[2] There are no right or wrong answers, and your first reaction is important. Circle Y for Yes and N for No.

1. I easily see the big picture in what I do.	Y	N
2. I believe in best practices.	Y	N
3. Having clear rules and order at work is essential for success.	Y	N
4. I start with a belief and then look for information to support it.	Y	N
5. It is annoying to listen to people who cannot seem to make up their minds.	Y	N
6. I usually make important decisions quickly and confidently.	Y	N
7. If there is one thing I would like to change about myself, it would be to be more flexible.	Y	N
8. People sometimes criticize me for sticking with a position even when the data don't support it.	Y	N
9. Others usually regard me as strongly opinionated when I know a subject.	Y	N

10. My career is guided by a single central long-term vision.	Y	N
11. I am someone who tends to focus on the trees rather than the forest.	Y	N
12. My philosophy of career development is that it is best to reinvent myself regularly.	Y	N
13. Even after I have made up my mind about something, I am always eager to consider a different opinion.	Y	N
14. My learning interests tend to be scattered or widely diversified.	Y	N
15. If someone asks me how to solve a problem, I struggle to identify the best single approach.	Y	N
16. I like questions that can be answered in many different ways.	Y	N
17. When considering most conflict situations, I can usually see both points of view.	Y	N
18. When I encounter organizational constraints, my first reaction is to conform to them.	Y	N
19. I like interacting with people whose opinions are very different from my own.	Y	N
20. I am generally regarded as a "details" person.	Y	N

To assess what you are, use the following figure:

Statements 11-20 Yes: 6-10 times	Fox	Eagle
Yes: 0-5 times	Ostrich	Hedgehog
	Yes: 0-5 times	Yes: 6-10 times

Statements 1-10

APPENDIX C

STEENKAMP ASSESSMENT INSTRUMENT FOR LEADERSHIP STYLES (SAILS)

The SAILS instrument measures the extent to which you exhibit each of the seven leadership styles discussed in the book, with five character-istic statements.[3] SAILS is broadly applicable across a wide spectrum of organizations. The assessment consists of two parts. The first part involves thirty-five statements designed to measure your *actual leadership styles in a particular organization of your choosing*. The second part consists of a matching set of thirty-five statements designed to measure your *leader-ship aspirations*. As this book has clearly shown, there is no one universally preferable leadership style. Not everyone will need to complete all parts of SAILS. In chapter 18, I identified four groups of users.

Here are the guidelines:

- **Seasoned leaders:** Fill out Part I (actual leadership).

- **Starting leaders:** Fill out Part II (leadership aspirations).

- **Developing leaders:** Fill out Parts I and II.

- **360 Leaders:** Fill out Parts I and II by yourself, then have your supervi-sor and followers fill them out.

SAILS QUESTIONNAIRE

PART I: ACTUAL LEADERSHIP PROFILE

INSTRUCTIONS: People often have leadership roles in different organizations. Your specific behaviors may vary across the organizations. First choose one organization for which you want to assess your actual leadership styles. Most often, that will be your workplace, but it can also be a non-governmental organization, church, volunteer organization, school board, political party, or some other organization. Fill out the actual leadership profile with that particular organization in mind. If you feel a statement absolutely does not describe your leadership in your organization, circle the number 1. If you feel a statement absolutely describes your leadership, circle the number 9. If your feelings are at neither extreme, circle the number in between that best represents your actual profile. Answer *who you are*, not *who you would like to be*. Answer truthfully. Remember, according to the renowned psychologist Daniel Goleman, realistic self-awareness is a hallmark of emotional intelligence.

PART I: YOUR ACTUAL LEADERSHIP PROFILE IN ORGANIZATION X

	Completely Disagree				Neutral				Completely Agree
1. In my work at this organization, I believe it is more important to be open-minded than to be loyal to my ideals and principles.	1	2	3	4	5	6	7	8	9
2. I am good at identifying tangible benefits to which my followers can relate.	1	2	3	4	5	6	7	8	9
3. I usually take charge in a team project rather than letting somebody else take the leadership role.	1	2	3	4	5	6	7	8	9
4. I am always looking for ways to disrupt the status quo or normal way of doing things in my organization.	1	2	3	4	5	6	7	8	9

	Completely Disagree				Neutral			Completely Agree	
5. My behaviors in this organization always reflect my core values.	1	2	3	4	5	6	7	8	9
6. My followers seek help from me if they have personal problems.	1	2	3	4	5	6	7	8	9
7. My followers regard me as an exciting and motivational speaker.	1	2	3	4	5	6	7	8	9
8. I seriously consider different points of view brought up by my followers even if I disagree with them.	1	2	3	4	5	6	7	8	9
9. I change my followers instead of changing myself.	1	2	3	4	5	6	7	8	9
10. I give detailed directions to my followers about what they need to do and how it needs to be done.	1	2	3	4	5	6	7	8	9
11. I often advocate nonconventional courses of action to achieve my organization's goals.	1	2	3	4	5	6	7	8	9
12. My followers know where I stand on issues that are controversial in this organization.	1	2	3	4	5	6	7	8	9
13. I prioritize my followers' career development over my own career development.	1	2	3	4	5	6	7	8	9
14. My followers see me as an inspirational leader.	1	2	3	4	5	6	7	8	9
15. Even when I have made up my mind, I am open to changing my opinion.	1	2	3	4	5	6	7	8	9
16. I identify competing alternatives beforehand and take care to eliminate or neutralize them when presenting my case to my followers.	1	2	3	4	5	6	7	8	9
17. I enjoy being able to direct the actions of my followers.	1	2	3	4	5	6	7	8	9
18. I am regarded by my followers as an out-of-the-box thinker.	1	2	3	4	5	6	7	8	9
19. My morals always guide what I do as leader in this organization.	1	2	3	4	5	6	7	8	9
20. My followers feel I work for them, not they for me.	1	2	3	4	5	6	7	8	9

	Completely Disagree				Neutral				Completely Agree
21. I have formulated a new, idealized vision for (parts of) this organization that widely deviates from the status quo.	1	2	3	4	5	6	7	8	9
22. I excel in the ability to adapt my behavior according to circumstances to achieve maximum success.	1	2	3	4	5	6	7	8	9
23. I am supremely gifted in convincing my followers of my point of view.	1	2	3	4	5	6	7	8	9
24. I usually set out the detailed direction for the team rather than let the team decide upon the best course of action.	1	2	3	4	5	6	7	8	9
25. I am not really bothered by organizational opposition to my radical plans or goals.	1	2	3	4	5	6	7	8	9
26. I have tight control over everything I say and do and how I express my emotions.	1	2	3	4	5	6	7	8	9
27. I encourage my followers to volunteer in the community and facilitate this with organizational resources to the extent possible (e.g., time, money, work schedule).	1	2	3	4	5	6	7	8	9
28. I engage in activities involving considerable self-sacrifice and personal risk to achieve my vision for this organization.	1	2	3	4	5	6	7	8	9
29. I change myself instead of changing my followers.	1	2	3	4	5	6	7	8	9
30. I hide my ulterior intentions from my followers.	1	2	3	4	5	6	7	8	9
31. I tend to act without consulting my followers.	1	2	3	4	5	6	7	8	9
32. I have the courage to push through big changes in the face of resistance.	1	2	3	4	5	6	7	8	9
33. I do not allow group pressure to control me.	1	2	3	4	5	6	7	8	9
34. I always adhere to the highest ethical standards even when it interferes with organizational success.	1	2	3	4	5	6	7	8	9
35. I am regarded by my followers as an extraordinarily gifted leader.	1	2	3	4	5	6	7	8	9

PART II: ASPIRATIONAL LEADERSHIP PROFILE

INSTRUCTIONS: This questionnaire contains statements about different leadership attitudes and behaviors. Based on your self-insight about the kind of person you are and your life experience, think about the kind of leader you would like to be in the organization that you currently work for. That is *your aspirational level.* There are no right or wrong answers. If you absolutely do not aspire to be the kind of person described in the statement, circle the number 1. If you aspire very much to be the kind of person described in the statement, circle the number 9. If your aspiration level is somewhere in between, circle the number that best represents your level. Provide a realistic answer. Remember, as mentioned earlier, realistic self-awareness is a hallmark of emotional intelligence.

PART II: YOUR ASPIRATIONAL LEADERSHIP PROFILE FOR ORGANIZATION X

	I do not at all aspire to this				Neutral			I aspire to this very much	
1. Being open-minded rather than being loyal to my ideals and principles	1	2	3	4	5	6	7	8	9
2. Being good at identifying tangible benefits to which my followers can relate	1	2	3	4	5	6	7	8	9
3. Being in charge in a group project rather than letting somebody else take the leadership role	1	2	3	4	5	6	7	8	9
4. Always looking for ways to disrupt the status quo or normal way of doing things	1	2	3	4	5	6	7	8	9
5. Having my behavior reflect my core values in my personal and professional life	1	2	3	4	5	6	7	8	9
6. Having followers come to me for help if they have personal problems	1	2	3	4	5	6	7	8	9
7. Being an exciting and motivational public speaker	1	2	3	4	5	6	7	8	9
8. Being truly open to different points of view, even if I disagree with them	1	2	3	4	5	6	7	8	9

	I do not at all aspire to this				Neutral			I aspire to this very much	
9. Changing my followers instead of changing myself	1	2	3	4	5	6	7	8	9
10. Giving detailed directions to followers on what they need to do and how it needs to be done	1	2	3	4	5	6	7	8	9
11. Advocating nonconventional courses of action to achieve organizational goals	1	2	3	4	5	6	7	8	9
12. Letting my followers know where I stand on controversial issues	1	2	3	4	5	6	7	8	9
13. Prioritizing my followers' career development over my own career development	1	2	3	4	5	6	7	8	9
14. Having followers see me as an inspirational leader	1	2	3	4	5	6	7	8	9
15. Even when I have made up my mind, being open to change my opinion	1	2	3	4	5	6	7	8	9
16. Being able to identify competing alternatives beforehand and take care to eliminate or neutralize them when presenting my case	1	2	3	4	5	6	7	8	9
17. Enjoying being able to direct the actions of followers	1	2	3	4	5	6	7	8	9
18. Being an out-of-the-box thinker	1	2	3	4	5	6	7	8	9
19. Having my morals guide me always in whatever I do as leader	1	2	3	4	5	6	7	8	9
20. Having followers feel I work for them, not they for me	1	2	3	4	5	6	7	8	9
21. Being able to formulate a new, idealized vision that widely deviates from the status quo	1	2	3	4	5	6	7	8	9
22. Excelling in the ability to adapt my behavior according to circumstances to achieve maximum success	1	2	3	4	5	6	7	8	9
23. Being supremely gifted in convincing my followers of my point of view	1	2	3	4	5	6	7	8	9
24. Setting the detailed direction for the team rather than letting the team decide upon the course of action	1	2	3	4	5	6	7	8	9

	I do not at all aspire to this				Neutral			I aspire to this very much	
25. Being at ease with organizational opposition to my radical plans or goals	1	2	3	4	5	6	7	8	9
26. Having tight control over everything I say and do and how I express my emotions	1	2	3	4	5	6	7	8	9
27. Encouraging my followers to volunteer in the community and facilitate this with organizational resources (e.g., time, money, work schedule)	1	2	3	4	5	6	7	8	9
28. Engaging in activities involving considerable self-sacrifice and personal risk to achieve my vision	1	2	3	4	5	6	7	8	9
29. Changing myself rather than trying to change my followers	1	2	3	4	5	6	7	8	9
30. Hiding my ulterior intentions from my followers	1	2	3	4	5	6	7	8	9
31. Acting without consulting my followers	1	2	3	4	5	6	7	8	9
32. Having the courage to push through big changes in the face of resistance	1	2	3	4	5	6	7	8	9
33. Not allowing group pressure to control me	1	2	3	4	5	6	7	8	9
34. Always adhering to the highest ethical standards, even when it interferes with organizational success	1	2	3	4	5	6	7	8	9
35. Being regarded by my followers as an extraordinarily gifted leader	1	2	3	4	5	6	7	8	9

USING SAILS

SAILS WORKSHEET

All user groups—seasoned leaders, starting leaders, developing leaders, and 360 leaders—will use either part or the entire worksheet, as explained below.

SAILS WORKSHEET

Leadership Style	Statements in SAILS (both Part I and II)	Sum score on Part I ("Actual")	Sum Score on Part II ("Aspirational")	GAP Score = Actual Score - Aspirational Score
Adaptive	1, 8, 15, 22, 29			
Persuasive	2, 9, 16, 23, 30			
Directive	3, 10, 17, 24, 31			
Disruptive	4, 11, 18, 25, 32			
Authentic	5, 12, 19, 26, 33			
Servant	6, 13, 20, 27, 34			
Charismatic	7, 14, 21, 28, 35			

1. SEASONED LEADERS WHO ASSESS THEIR CURRENT LEADERSHIP STYLE

Calculate your actual leadership score for each leadership style separately by adding your scores on the five statements pertaining to the leadership style in question (see the worksheet). For each leadership style, your score can range between 5 and 45. You can interpret your sum scores using the following guidelines:

- **High range:** A score between 36 and 45 indicates you strongly exhibit this leadership style.

- **Moderate range:** A score between 26 and 35 indicates you exhibit this leadership style to some degree.

- **Low range:** A score between 5 and 25 means you do not really exhibit this leadership style.

For the leadership styles for which are you in the high range (36–45), you may want to revisit the relevant part(s) of the book. Even though you are an experienced leader, it is unlikely that you cannot learn new things from the leaders discussed in this book who excelled on the leadership style that you use a lot. To quote *The Economist*, "Those [historical leaders] who have passed through the fire surely have something to teach modern-day managers."[4] If you have time, you can next revisit the chapters on the leadership styles that you exhibit to a medium degree.

2. STARTING LEADERS

Calculate your aspirational leadership score for each leadership style separately. Add up your scores on the five statements pertaining to the leadership style in question (see the worksheet). The interpretation of low (5–25), medium (26–35), and high (36–45) is the same as for actual leadership. For the leadership styles for which are you in the high range (36–45), you may want to revisit the relevant part(s) of the book. What did those leaders do—and not do? This allows you to learn from the best. Revisit the qualitative questions posed in the "Reflections" chapter at the end of the leadership style in question. Are there areas where you are still somewhat lacking? How can you develop yourself further?

3. DEVELOPING LEADERS

The key issue here is to what extent your aspirations and your actual leadership are aligned. Areas where your actual behavior falls short of your aspirations are primary areas to work on.

For this, you need to fill out both Parts I and II. Next, calculate the GAP score for each leadership style as *the actual score minus the aspirational score* (see the worksheet).

Positive scores indicate that your actual level exceeds your aspirational current level. You exhibit this leadership style to a greater degree than you aspire. This may be fine. Or, alternatively, do you feel compelled to behave in a way you really do not want? Are you misreading the situation? Something else?

A more common situation is a negative score—you perform below aspirations. A GAP score lower than −10 calls for the most immediate attention. There is a large discrepancy between what you do and what you aspire to do. In that case, do the following:

- Delve into the GAP scores for each of the five SAILS statements tapping into that leadership style. Are there particular aspects (questions) that drive the GAP score? Can you do something about them?

- Are the organizational conditions such that you cannot exhibit your leadership style to the extent you want to? Are you in the right position? Is it a matter of lack of organizational commitment on your side? Are your aspirations perhaps unrealistically high?

- Revisit the chapters that deal with this leadership style. What did those leaders do that you do not do? Do you have the leadership qualities that facilitate that leadership style? If so, what can you do to build those?

If you have no GAP score lower than −10, turn your attention to leadership styles for which you have a GAP score between −5 and −10.

4. 360 LEADERS

If you wish to perform a 360-degree feedback of your leadership, Parts I and II should be filled out by yourself, your boss, and (a representative sample of) the people who work for you. The statements will have to be slightly modified for followers and supervisors, and the scale for the aspirational leadership part should range from "I do not wish [Y=you] to do this at all" (=1) to "I wish [Y] to do this very much" (=9). With these data, you can drill deep and examine seven gaps (Figure A.1).[5]

- **GAP 1:** Your own leadership gap (see previous)

- **GAP 2:** Follower perception gap—on which leadership styles is there a large discrepancy between what you believe you do and how your followers perceive your behavior?

- **GAP 3:** Follower aspiration gap—on which leadership styles is there a large discrepancy between your aspirations for yourself and your followers' aspirations for you?

- **GAP 4:** Follower performance gap—on which leadership styles do your followers think you fall short on (or exceed) your followers' aspirations?

- **GAP 5:** Supervisor perception gap—on which leadership styles is there a large discrepancy between what you believe you do and how your supervisor perceives your behavior?

- **GAP 6:** Supervisor aspiration gap—on which leadership styles is there a large discrepancy between your aspirations for yourself and your supervisor's aspirations for you?

- **GAP 7:** Supervisor performance gap—on which leadership styles does your superior think you fall short on (or exceed) your supervisor's aspirations?

Of some interest is the gap between follower/supervisor aspirations and your actual behavior. As Figure A.1 shows, it is the sum of the perception and performance gaps. This discrepancy can be due to others

Figure A.1. Using SAILS for 360-Degree Feedback

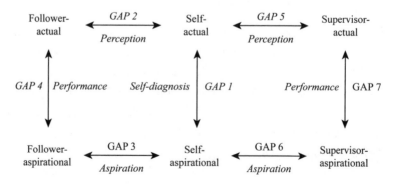

"misinterpreting" your behavior, and/or your behavior, as seen by them, falling short of their aspirations.

Use the GAP analyses to initiate discussions with your followers and supervisor and develop strategies to bring your actual and/or aspired leadership more in line with that of your followers and supervisor, where this would be desirable and/or necessary.

NOTES

CHAPTER 1

1. McNeill, J.R., and William H. McNeill (2003), *The Human Web: A Bird's-Eye View of World History*, New York: Norton.
2. House, Robert J. et al. (2004), *Culture, Leadership, and Organizations*, Thousand Oaks, CA: Sage; and Locke, Edwin A. (1991), *The Essence of Leadership*, New York: Lexington Books. Discussion of the components of this definition is based on Locke (pp. 2–3) and Northouse, Peter G. (2016), *Leadership: Theory and Practice*, Los Angeles, CA: Sage, pp. 6–7; Kotter, John (1990), "What Leaders Really Do," *Harvard Business Review* 68 (3), pp. 103–111.
3. Cohen, Allan R., and David L. Bradford (2005), "The Influence Model: Using Reciprocity and Exchange to Get What You Need," *Journal of Organizational Excellence*, Winter, pp. 57–80.
4. Kotter, op. cit., p. 104.
5. https://www.oxfordlearnersdictionaries.com/us/definition/english/grit_1.
6. https://www.youtube.com/watch?v=-n3sUWR4FV4.
7. Berlin, Isaiah (1953), *The Hedgehog and the Fox: An Essay on Tolstoy's View of History*, edited by Henry Hardy, Princeton, NJ: Princeton University Press, 2nd ed., p. 1. Berlin did not include "smaller" (or "little") in the quote but that seems to be an oversight. See p. 113.
8. Berlin, op. cit. p. 2.
9. Herodotus, *The Histories*, transl. by Aubrey de Sélincourt, published in 2003 by Penguin Books, New York, 7:50.
10. Gaddis, John L. (2018), *On Grand Strategy*, New York: Penguin Press, p. 14.
11. Geyer, Michael (1986), "German Strategy in the Age of Machine Warfare, 1914–1945," in Peter Paret (ed.), *Makers of Modern Strategy*, Princeton, NJ: Princeton University Press, pp. 527–597; especially pp. 575–584.
12. Gaddis, op. cit., pp. 13–14.

13. Odendahl, Christian (2019), "Dogma and Complacency Put the German Economy at Risk," *Financial Times*, August 16.
14. Tetlock, Philip E. (2005), *Expert Political Judgment*, Princeton, NJ: Princeton University Press.
15. Berlin, op. cit., p. 101; Gaddis, op. cit., p. 15.
16. Gaddis, op. cit., p. 15.
17. Ibid., p. 16.
18. https://www.independent.co.uk/voices/theresa-may-resigns-how-long-prime-minister-ranking-legacy-history-brexit-a8929116.html.
19. https://www.pbs.org/wgbh/frontline/article/colin-powell-u-n-speech-was-a-great-intelligence-failure/.
20. https://en.wikipedia.org/wiki/Historical_rankings_of_presidents_of_the_United_States#Public_opinion_polls_on_recent_presidents.
21. Northouse, op. cit., p. 94.
22. https://futureofworking.com/directive-leadership-style-advantages-disadvantages-and-characteristics/.
23. Maxwell, John C. (2007), *The 21 Irrefutable Laws of Leadership*, Nashville, TN: Thomas Nelson, p. 163.
24. Greenleaf, Robert K. (1977), *Servant Leadership: A Journey into the Nature of Legitimate Power and Greatness*, New York: Paulist Press, p. 27.
25. Van Dierendonck, Dirk (2011), "Servant Leadership: A Review and Synthesis," *Journal of Management* 37 (July), pp. 1228–1261.
26. Conger, Jay A., and Rabindra N. Kanungo (1994), "Charismatic Leadership in Organizations: Perceived Behavioral Attributes and Their Measurement," *Journal of Organizational Behavior* 15, pp. 439–452.
27. Maxwell, op. cit., p. 171.
28. Von Clausewitz, Carl (1832/2018), *On War*, Digireads.com Publishing, pp. 127–128.

CHAPTER 2

1. Heather, Peter (2013), *The Restoration of Rome*, Oxford: Oxford University Press, p. 211; Anonymous (2017), *Clovis: History of the Founder of Frank Monarchy*, LM Publishers, p. 18.
2. Gregory of Tours (late sixth century/2014), *A History of the Franks*, First Rate Publishers, Book II.
3. Ibid., chapter 30.
4. Heather, op. cit. (2013), p. 212; Mitchell, Stephen (2007), *A History of the Late Roman Empire, A.D. 284–641*, Malden, MA: Blackwell, p. 212.
5. Wickham, Chris (2016), *Medieval Europe*, New Haven, CT: Yale University Press, pp. 31–32.
6. Gregory, op. cit., chapter 31.
7. Anonymous (2017), op. cit., p. 57.

8. Cantor, Norman F. (1994), *The Civilization of the Middle Ages*, New York: HarperPerennial, p. 113.

9. Gregory, op. cit., chapter 37.

10. Ibid., chapter 37.

11. Mitchell, op. cit., p. 213.

12. The only other major Germanic kingdom in the eighth century was the Lombard kingdom in Italy. This was a "latecomer" among Germanic kingdoms, being established in the late sixth century. It was annexed by the Frankish king Charlemagne in 774.

13. The German name for France (*Frankreich*) is even more revealing. It literally translates to "Empire of the Franks."

14. Clovis's Frankish name was Hlōdowig, which is the origin of Louis (French) and Ludwig (German).

15. Jackson, Julian (2018), *De Gaulle*, Cambridge, MA: Belknap, p. 25. When de Gaulle referred to Christianity, he meant Catholicism. Arianism had long disappeared.

16. Cantor, op. cit., p. 110.

17. Oman, Charles (1898/2017), *The Dark Ages 476–918 A.D.*, Augustine Books, chapter IV.

18. Ibid., chapter IV.

19. Siena College Research Institute, Presidential Expert Poll of 2010; https://en.wikipedia.org/wiki/Historical_rankings_of_presidents_of_the_United_States.

20. Anonymous, op. cit., pp. 76–77.

21. Steenkamp, Jan-Benedict (2017), *Global Brand Strategy: World-Wise Marketing in the Age of Branding*, New York: Palgrave MacMillan, chapter 8.

22. Barrage, Lint, et al. (2014), "Advertising as Insurance or Commitment? Evidence from the Oil Spill," NBER working paper 19838.

CHAPTER 3

1. Siemann, Wolfram (2017/2019), *Metternich: Statesman and Visionary*, translated by Daniel Steuer, Cambridge, MA: Belknap, chapter 8. At the time of the Congress of Vienna, he was foreign minister. He also became chancellor in 1821.

2. Kissinger, Henry A. (1994), *Diplomacy*, New York: Simon & Schuster, pp. 79, 82, 104.

3. Taylor, A.J.P. (1971), *The Struggle for the Mastery of Europe 1848–1918*, Oxford: Oxford University Press, p. 25.

4. Steinberg, Jonathan (2011), *Bismarck: A Life*, New York: Oxford University Press, pp. 111–113.

5. Apsler, Alfred (1972), *Iron Chancellor: Otto von Bismarck*, Folkestone: Bailey, pp. 49–50; Taylor (1971), p. 36, 41.

6. Taylor, op. cit., p. 27.

7. Ibid., pp. 14–15.

8. Apsler, op. cit., pp 30–31.

9. Steinberg, op. cit., pp. 70–76.

10. Ibid., pp. 93–94.

11. Apsler, op. cit., pp. 58, 65–66.

12. Steinberg, op. cit., p. 141 ff.

13. Apsler, op. cit., p. 76.

14. Definition taken from *Wikipedia.*

15. Apsler (1972), pp. 49–50; Taylor (1971), pp. 25–26.

16. Taylor, A.J.P. (1955), *Bismarck: The Man and the Statesman*, New York: Vintage Books, pp. 40–41.

17. Apsler, op. cit., p. 61. Steinberg, op. cit., pp. 121–123.

18. Kissinger, op. cit., pp. 123–127.

19. Steinberg, op. cit., p. 131.

20. Ibid., pp. 226–234.

21. Ibid., pp. 241–243.

22. Apsler, op. cit., p. 99.

23. Taylor (1955), op. cit., pp. 81–82.

24. Apsler, op. cit., pp. 112–113.

25. Steinberg, op. cit., chapter 8.

26. Taylor (1955), op. cit., chapters 11 and 12.

27. Kissinger, op. cit., p. 136.

28. Studemann, Frederick (2019), "Otto von Bismarck Is in the House as Brexit Goes a Bit Prussian," *Financial Times*, September 5.

29. Steenkamp, Jan-Benedict, with Laurens Sloot (2019), *Retail Disruptors: The Spectacular Rise and Impact of the Hard Discounters*, London: Kogan Page.

30. https://www.theguardian.com/business/2019/oct/05/tesco-dave-lewis-back-from-brink-it-could-have-gone-under.

CHAPTER 4

1. Pantsov, Alexander, with Steven Levine (2015), *Deng Xiaoping: A Revolutionary Life*, New York: Oxford University Press, p. 145.

2. Dikötter, Frank (2011), *Mao's Great Famine*, London: Bloomsbury.

3. Zhang, Weiwei (2012), *The China Wave: Rise of a Civilizational State*, Hackensack, NJ: World Century.

4. Kissinger, Henry (2012), *On China*, New York: Penguin, p. 396.

5. Pantsov with Levine, op. cit., p. 146.

6. Every five years, the CCP holds a National Congress, which comprises several thousands of party officials. The Central Committee consists of some 200 top leaders of the CCP. It convenes at least once a year at a plenary session ("plenum"). The Politburo is a group of around twenty-five people. The Standing Committee of the Politburo is the CCP's highest body. It is composed of five to nine members. The method by which membership in the Standing Committee/Politburo is determined has evolved over time. Mao himself selected and expelled Politburo members, while in the Deng era consultations among party elders determined membership. Source: Wikipedia.

7. Pantsov with Levine, op. cit., p. 185.

8. Ibid., p. 194.
9. Evans, Richard (1995), *Deng Xiaoping and the Making of Modern China*, London: Penguin, p. 164.
10. Pantsov with Levine, op. cit., p. 223.
11. Ibid., p. 267, 269.
12. Kissinger, op. cit., p. 323.
13. Ibid., p. 330.
14. Pantsov with Levine, op. cit., p. 328.
15. Vogel, Ezra (2011), *Deng Xiaoping and the Transformation of China*, Cambridge, MA: Belknap, p. 360.
16. Pantsov with Levine, op. cit., p. 370.
17. The fact that Bukharin, like Lenin, regarded NEP as a transitional period toward socialism was conveniently ignored.
18. Pantsov with Levine, op. cit., p. 366.
19. Ibid., p. 380.
20. https://www.nytimes.com/1997/09/17/world/a-great-tiptoe-forward-free-enterprise-in-china.html.
21. Lodish, Leonard, and Carl Mela (2007), "If Brands Are Built Over Years, Why Are They Managed Over Quarters?" *Harvard Business Review*, 85 (7/8), pp. 104–112.
22. Steenkamp, Jan-Benedict E. M., and Eric Fang (2011), "The Impact of Economic Contractions on the Effectiveness of R&D and Advertising," *Marketing Science*, 30 (4) pp. 628–645.
23. Vogel, op. cit., p. 382.
24. Kissinger, op. cit., pp. 400–401.
25. Steenkamp, Jan-Benedict (2017), *Global Brand Strategy: World-Wise Marketing in the Age of Branding*, New York: Palgrave MacMillan.

REFLECTIONS ON ADAPTIVE LEADERSHIP

1. Heifetz, Ronald A. et al. (2009), *The Practice of Adaptive Leadership*, Boston, MA: Harvard Business School Press.
2. Heifetz, Ronald A. and Donald L. Laurie (1997), "The Work of Leadership," *Harvard Business Review* 75 (1), pp. 124–134; quote taken from p. 124.
3. http://www.cnn.com/2004/ALLPOLITICS/09/30/kerry.comment/.

CHAPTER 5

1. The most important ancient source about the Persian Empire and the Greco-Persian Wars is the Greek historian Herodotus (c. 484–c. 425 B.C.), who wrote the seminal book *The Histories*. I use the translation by Aubrey de Sélincourt, revised by John Marincola and published in 2003 by Penguin Books, New York.
2. Holland, Tom (2005), *Persian Fire: The First World Empire and the Battle for the West*, New York: Anchor Books, pp. 235 and 237, and accompanying footnotes.
3. Plutarch was a Greco-Roman biographer who lived c. 47–c. 120 A.D. Plutarch's

best-known work is *Parallel Lives*, a series of biographies of famous Greeks and Romans, including Themistocles. I use the version edited by Arthur H. Clough, Oxford: Benediction Classics, published in 2015.

4. Holland, op. cit., p. 166.
5. Ibid., pp. 164–167.
6. Green, Peter (1996), *The Greco-Persian Wars*, Berkeley and Los Angeles, CA: University of California Press, p. 26.
7. Dando-Collins, Stephen (2013), *Rise of an Empire: How One Man United Greece to Defeat Xerxes's Persians,* New York: Wiley, p. 71.
8. Herodotus, op. cit., book 7, chapter 141; I excerpt the most relevant passage.
9. Ibid., book 8, chapter 49.
10. Green, op. cit., p. 164.
11. The chronology of the last week or two before Salamis is difficult to determine with complete certainty. Herodotus may have compressed the events on the various war councils into the twenty-four hours preceding the battle. See Green, op. cit., footnote on p. 174, for more information.
12. Fuller, J.F.C. (1954), *Military History of the Western World Volume I: From the Earliest Times to the Battle of Lepanto*, New York: Da Capo, pp. 39–41.
13. Plutarch, op. cit., p. 114.
14. Ibid., p. 114.
15. Gaddis, John L. (2018), *On Grand Strategy*, New York: Penguin Press, chapter 1.
16. Plutarch, op. cit., *Themistocles*, VI.2.
17. Holland, op cit., p. 303.
18. Plutarch, op. cit., *Themistocles*, V.2.
19. Holland, op. cit., p. 226.
20. Green, op. cit., p.171.
21. Dando-Collins, op. cit., p. 51.
22. Wright, Peter, and Barton Weitz (1977), "Time Horizon Effects on Product Evaluation Strategies," *Journal of Marketing Research* 14 (November), 429–443.
23. Steenkamp, Jan-Benedict E. M., Hans Baumgartner, and Elise Van der Wulp (1996), "Arousal Potential, Arousal, Stimulus Attractiveness, and the Moderating Role of Need for Stimulation," *International Journal of Research in Marketing* 13 (4), pp. 319–329.
24. Plutarch, op. cit., *Themistocles*, IV.2.
25. Herodotus, op. cit., 8.60.
26. Ibid., 8.80.

CHAPTER 6

1. Wilson, John (1973), *CB: A life of Sir Henry Campbell-Bannerman*, New York: St. Martin's Press, p. 300.
2. McCord, Norman (1991), *British History 1815–1906*, Oxford: Oxford University Press, pp. 390–394.
3. For the full text, see https://www.sahistory.org.za/archive/ peace-treaty-vereeniging-original-document.

4. In the period 1895–1905, Britain was governed by a coalition of the Conservative Party and the (far smaller) Liberal Unionist Party. The latter consisted of Liberals who broke away from the Liberal Party in 1886 in opposition to Irish Home Rule. Joseph Chamberlain was the leader of the Liberal Unionists.

5. Wilson, op. cit., p. 477.

6. In the nineteenth century, the two main parties in Britain were the Conservative Party and the Liberal Party. William E. Gladstone was the towering Liberal politician in the second half of the nineteenth century. He was prime minister four times between 1868 and 1894.

7. Hattersley, Roy (2006), *Campbell-Bannerman*, London: Haus Publishing, p. 21.

8. Wilson, op. cit., pp. 279–296.

9. Ibid., p. 327.

10. Hattersley, op. cit., p. 76.

11. Wilson, op. cit., p. 349.

12. Ibid., p. 350.

13. The conflict was instigated by Joseph Chamberlain, who championed a system of imperial preference. Thus, in his career, Chamberlain managed to wreck the two main political parties of his time and instigated the immensely costly and ethically questionable Boer War. His son Neville sold out Czechoslovakia in 1938 and nearly wrecked Britain. Quite a legacy for one family.

14. Pitt the Younger resigned as prime minister in 1801 over limited Catholic emancipation in Ireland, and Theresa May in 2019 over the Irish backstop, which Parliament refused to accept as part of the Brexit withdrawal agreement.

15. Taken from Hattersley, op. cit., p. 93.

16. Ibid.

17. Wilson, op. cit., pp. 477–478.

18. Steyn, Richard (2015), *Jan Smuts: Unafraid of Greatness*, Johannesburg: Jonathan Ball Publishers (Kindle version).

19. Ibid.

20. Wilson, op. cit., p. 484.

21. According to Lloyd George, before Campbell-Bannerman's speech only two Cabinet members (including Lloyd George) were with the prime minister, although this was disputed by Asquith. See Wilson, op. cit., pp. 482–483.

22. Ibid., pp. 489–490.

23. Steyn, op. cit.

24. Wilson, op. cit., p. 489.

25. Ibid., p. 492. German East (South-West) Africa is present-day Tanzania (Namibia). South Africa defeated the Germans in Namibia and played a significant role in defeating them in Tanzania.

26. Steyn, op. cit.

27. Craig, Gordon A. (1986), "The Political Leader as Strategist," in: *Makers of Modern Strategy*, Peter Paret (ed.), Princeton, NJ: Princeton University Press, pp. 481–509.

28. Wilson, op. cit., p. 492.

29. The first Punic War was fought from 264–241 B.C. Rome's peace conditions were so harsh that a war of revenge was unavoidable. In this second Punic War (218–201 B.C.), the Carthaginian general Hannibal inflicted crushing defeats upon Rome and nearly brought it to its knees.

30. Wilson, op cit., p. 487.

31. Hattersley, op. cit., p. 143.

32. Harris, Jose F., and Cameron Hazlehurst (1970), "Campbell-Bannerman as Prime Minister," *History* 55 (October), pp. 360–383.

33. Wilson, op. cit., p. 641. I added Angela Merkel.

34. Schuyler, Robert L. (1924), "Reviewed Work: The Life of the Right Hon. Sir Henry Campbell-Bannerman," *Political Science Quarterly* 39 (3), pp. 506–508.

35. Harris and Hazlehurst, op. cit.

36. Wilson, op. cit., p. 480.

37. Harris and Hazlehurst, op. cit.

38. Grey, E. (1925), *Twenty-Five Years*, London: Hodder & Stoughton, p. 65.

39. Massie, Robert K. (1991), *Dreadnought: Britain, Germany, and the Coming of the Great War*, New York: Ballantine Books, p. 551.

40. Wilson, op. cit., pp. 482–485.

41. Ibid., p. 466.

42. Hattersley, op. cit., p. 105.

43. Collins, Jim (2001), "Level 5 Leadership," *Harvard Business Review* 79 (1), pp. 66–76.

44. Schuyler, op cit., p. 507.

CHAPTER 7

1. Carl, Joachim (1957), *Das amerikanische Leih- und Pacht-Gesetz*, Berlin: Mittler & Sohn, p. 11.

2. Dallek, Robert (2017), *Franklin D. Roosevelt: A Political Life*, New York: Viking, pp. 281–282.

3. Ibid., p. 365.

4. www.thebalance.com/unemployment-rate-by-year-3305506 ; www.thebalance.com/us-gdp-by-year-3305543.

5. Dallek, op. cit., p. 396; Freidel, Frank (1990), *Franklin D. Roosevelt: A Rendezvous with Destiny*, Boston, MA: Little, Brown, p. 391.

6. Dallek, op. cit., p. 35.

7. Smith, Jean E. (2007), *FDR*, New York: Random House, p. 29.

8. Dallek, op. cit., p. 39.

9. Smith, op. cit., p. 182.

10. A recent medical diagnosis suggests that Roosevelt might have suffered from acute ascending polyneuritis rather than polio. Regardless, there was no effective treatment for either disease; see Smith, op. cit., p. 191.

11. Dallek, op. cit., pp. 104–105.

12. https://en.wikipedia.org/wiki/Party_divisions_of_United_States_Congresses.

13. For the transcript of this and other fireside chats, see https://www.presidency.ucsb.edu/documents/presidential-documents-archive-guidebook/fireside-chats-f-roosevelt.

14. Brands, H. W. (2008), *Traitor to His Class: The Privileged Life and Radical Presidency of Franklin Delano Roosevelt*, New York: Doubleday.

15. Smith, op. cit., chapters 17 and 18.

16. Dallek, op. cit., p. 354.

17. Smith, op. cit., p. 438.

18. Dallek, op. cit., p. 356.

19. Kimball, Warren F. (1969), *The Most Unsordid Act: Lend-Lease, 1939–1941*, Baltimore, MD: Johns Hopkins Press, pp. 111–119.

20. Ibid., p. 124.

21. http://docs.fdrlibrary.marist.edu/odllpc2.html.

22. Kimball, op. cit., p. 123.

23. Carl, op. cit., p. 22.

24. Freidel, op. cit., pp. 359–360.

25. Carl, op. cit., p. 23.

26. Kimball, op. cit., pp. 171–176.

27. Carl, op. cit., pp. 27, 29.

28. Freidel, op. cit., p. 393.

29. For an overview of nineteen different scholar survey results, see https://en.wikipedia.org/wiki/Historical_rankings_of_presidents_of_the_United_States.

30. https://www.presidency.ucsb.edu/documents/inaugural-address-8.

31. Bennis, Warren G. and Robert J. Thomas, (2002), "Crucibles of Leadership," *Harvard Business Review*, 80 (9), pp. 39–45.

32. Morgan, Ted (1985), *FDR*, New York: Simon & Schuster; Dallek, op. cit.

33. https://www.c-span.org/presidentsurvey2017/.

34. Dallek, op. cit., p. 399.

35. Freidel, op. cit., p. 370.

36. https://www.presidency.ucsb.edu/documents/fireside-chat-9.

37. Fireside chat on May 26, 1940.

38. Fireside chat on December 29, 1940.

39. For a cartoon in the Dutch newspaper *De Volkskrant*, see https://www.montesquieu-institute.eu/id/viwjgw8lf6sf/politiek_toerisme.

REFLECTIONS ON PERSUASIVE LEADERSHIP

1. Hewett, Kelly, et al. (2016), "Brand Buzz in the Echoverse," *Journal of Marketing* 80 (3), pp. 1–24.

2. Freidel, Frank (1990), *Franklin D. Roosevelt: A Rendezvous with Destiny*, Boston, MA: Little, Brown, pp. 354–355, 361.

3. https://www.presidency.ucsb.edu/documents/fireside-chat-12.

4. Wilson, John (1973), *CB: A life of Sir Henry Campbell-Bannerman*, New York: St. Martin's Press, p. 485.

5. Steyn, Richard (2015), *Jan Smuts: Unafraid of Greatness*, Johannesburg: Jonathan Ball Publishers.

CHAPTER 8

1. Kamen, Henry (2003), *Empire: How Spain Became a World Power 1492–1763*, New York: HarperCollins.
2. The name Aztecs was originally coined by the nineteenth-century German explorer Alexander von Humboldt. The Aztecs referred to themselves as Mexica.
3. Levy, Buddy (2009), *Conquistador: Hernán Cortés, King Montezuma, and the Last Stand of the Aztecs*, New York: Bantam Books, p. 2.
4. Cartwright, Mark (2018), "Aztec Sacrifice," Ancient History Encyclopedia.
5. Lopez de Gomara, Francisco (1552/1964), *Cortés: The Life of the Conqueror of Mexico by His Secretary*, Berkeley, CA: University of California Press, p. 8.
6. David A. Boruchoff (2008), "Hernán Cortés," *International Encyclopedia of the Social Sciences*, 2nd ed., vol. 2, pp. 146–49.
7. Hart, Michael H. (1978), "Hernando Cortés," in: *The 100 – A Ranking of the Most Influential Persons in History*, New York: Hart, pp. 349–354.
8. Levy, op. cit., pp. 45–46.
9. Ibid., p. 36.
10. Díaz del Castillo, Bernal (1568/2012), *The True History of the Conquest of New Spain*, translated, with an introduction and notes by Janet Burke and Ted Humphrey, Indianapolis, IN: Hackett, p. 106.
11. Wood, Michael (2001), *Conquistadors*, Berkeley, CA: University of California Press, p. 48.
12. Levy, op. cit., p. 75.
13. Díaz del Castillo, op. cit., p. 189.
14. Levy, op. cit., pp. 195–198.
15. Kamen, op. cit., pp. 103–104.
16. Landes, David (1999), *The Wealth and Poverty of Nations: Why Some Are So Rich and Some So Poor*, New York: Norton, especially chapters 7 and 20.
17. Kamen, op. cit., p. 104.
18. Díaz del Castillo, op. cit., p. 226.
19. Levy, op. cit., pp. 293–302.
20. Shin, Jihae, and Katherine L. Milkman (2016), "How Backup Plans Can Harm Goal Pursuit: The Unexpected Downside of Being Prepared for Failure," *Organizational Behavior and Human Decision Processes* 135 (July), pp. 1–9.
21. Levy, op. cit., pp. 220–221.
22. Lopez de Gomara, op. cit., p. 228.
23. Levy, op. cit., p. 204.
24. Lopez de Gomara, op. cit., pp. 229–230.
25. Levy, op. cit., pp. 191–192.
26. For Johnson, that applied primarily to his domestic policies (Medicare, civil rights legislation, etc.). His foreign policy mistakes (Vietnam) ultimately doomed his presidency.

27. More information on Stockholm syndrome can be found at https://en.wikipedia.org/wiki/Stockholm_syndrome.

CHAPTER 9

1. Broadberry, S. N., and Crafts, N.F.R. (2003), "UK Productivity Performance from 1950 to 1979: A Restatement of the Broadberry-Crafts View," *Economic History Review* 56, pp. 718–735.
2. Morgan, Kenneth O. (2010), "The Twentieth Century," in K. O. Morgan (ed.), *The Oxford History of Britain*, Oxford: Oxford University Press, p. 634.
3. www.nationalarchives.gov.uk/cabinetpapers/themes/sterling-devalued-imf-loan.htm.
4. Closed shop is a form of union security agreement under which the employer agrees to hire union members only, and employees must remain members of the union in order to remain employed.
5. Aitken, Jonathan (2013), *Margaret Thatcher: Power and Personality*, London: Bloomsbury.
6. Beckett, Claire (2006), *Thatcher*, London: Haus Publishing, p. 13.
7. www.bbc.co.uk/news/uk-politics-10377842.
8. Beckett, op. cit., p. 55.
9. Moore, Charles (2013), *Margaret Thatcher: From Grantham to the Falklands*, New York: Knopf, Chapter 13.
10. Ibid., pp. 388–392.
11. Aitken, op. cit., p. 456.
12. Ibid., p. 378.
13. Ibid., p. 442.
14. Moore, Charles (2016), *Margaret Thatcher: Volume Two: Everything She Wants,* Milton Keynes: Penguin, p. 150.
15. https://en.wikiquote.org/wiki/Arthur_Scargill.
16. Moore (2016), op. cit., p. 156.
17. Aitken, op. cit., p. 446.
18. https://en.wikipedia.org/wiki/UK_miners%27_strike.
19. Moore (2016), op. cit., p. 157.
20. Aitken, op. cit., p. 456.
21. http://news.bbc.co.uk/onthisday/hi/dates/stories/march/12/newsid_3503000/3503346.stm.
22. https://en.wikipedia.org/wiki/UK_miners%27_strike.
23. Morgan, op. cit., p. 635 ff.; Beckett, op. cit., pp. 48–53.
24. Thatcher, Margaret (2010), *Margaret Thatcher: The Autobiography*, New York: Harper, p. 329. This book was first published in two volumes, *The Downing Street Years* (1993) and *Path to Power* (1995).
25. Thatcher, op. cit., pp. 330–331.
26. Aitken, op. cit., pp. 249.
27. Ibid., pp. 183–184.

28. https://www.margaretthatcher.org/document/103485.

29. Aitken, op. cit., pp. 200–203.

30. Moore (2013), op. cit., pp. 641–642.

31. https://www.thrivetimeshow.com/business-podcasts/jack-welchs-public-hangings-introducing-merit- based-pay-and-how-to-gather-objective-reviews-ask-clay-anything/.

32. https://www.theverge.com/2019/12/9/21003787/away-luggage-steph-korey-ceo-new-lululemon-stuart-haselden-replacement-investigation.

REFLECTIONS ON DIRECTIVE LEADERSHIP

1. Beckett, Claire (2006), *Thatcher*, London: Haus Publishing, p. 58.

2. Levy, Buddy (2009), *Conquistador: Hernán Cortés, King Montezuma, and the Last Stand of the Aztecs*, New York: Bantam Books, p. 147.

3. Aitken, Jonathan (2013), *Margaret Thatcher: Power and Personality*, London: Bloomsbury, p. 561.

4. Levy, op. cit., pp. 37–43.

5. Mourinho was fired by Chelsea (2007, 2015), Real Madrid (2013), and Manchester United (2018).

CHAPTER 10

1. The Christian calendar (B.C/A.D.) was first worked out in the sixth century A.D. by Dionysius Exiguus. However, he placed the birth of Christ in the wrong year.

2. The word *apostle* comes from the Greek *apostolos*, which means "one who is sent off."

3. Acts, chapters 2–8.

4. Christ comes from the Greek *Christos*, the Greek equivalent to the Hebrew word *Messiah*, which means "the anointed one."

5. Paul was a disciple of Gamaliel (Acts 22:3), one of the greatest of Jewish scholars, and president of the Sanhedrin, according to the Talmud.

6. Acts, chapters 14 and 15.

7. Matthew 4:19. In this chapter, all Bible quotes are from the New International Version.

8. Matthew 16:17–19.

9. John 21:16.

10. Holzner, Josef (1937), *Paulus—Ein Heldenleben im Dienste Christi*, Freiburg im Breisgau: Herder. James the Just was either the half-brother or the cousin of Jesus.

11. For a compelling account of how papal authority became universally accepted in Europe by 1100–1200 A.D., see Heather, Peter (2013), *The Restoration of Rome*, especially pp. 207–414.

12. Acts, chapter 10.

13. Ibid., chapter 11.

14. De Jong, Johannes (1936), *Handboek der Kerkgeschiedenis Deel I*, Utrecht: Dekker & Van de Vegt, 3rd ed.

15. The section on the Council of Jerusalem draws heavily on Holzner, op. cit., chapter 19.

16. Acts 15:5.

17. Acts 15:10.

18. De Jong, op. cit., p. 46.

19. Holzner, op. cit., chapter 20.

20. Galatians 2:11–21; Holzner, op. cit., chapter 20.

21. Stark, Rodney (1997), *The Rise of Christianity*, New York: HarperOne, p. 58.

22. The "marketing" situation was actually even more favorable, as many Jews living outside of Palestine were thoroughly Hellenized and, according to Stark (1997, op. cit.), were a prime target market for Christianity, as it allowed them to continue to believe in the God of their forefathers (Christians accepted the Old Testament as God's Word), but without the social marginalization that came with the Law.

23. Stark, op. cit., Table 1.1. Estimates are approximate, given the absence of reliable census data.

24. Instructive is Acts 4:7–12.

25. Acts 4:13.

26. Walsh, William T. (1948/2005), *Peter the Apostle*, New York: Scepter. Of course, any assessment of Peter's qualities contains a fair amount of uncertainty.

27. John 13:37 and chapter 18.

28. Catholic doctrine disagrees with this observation and holds that Peter's positional power was the driving factor. The footnote to Acts 15:10–12 in which Peter announced his decision in the official Dutch Catholic Bible (Canisius translation, 7th edition, 1973), states (translated): "Thus, Peter, as head of the Church, makes the decisive and infallible ruling, to which all have to conform and be silent."

29. The latter is evident from the impact of his speech on Pentecost (Acts 2:14–41).

30. Walsh, op. cit., pp. 251–252.

31. Unilever was founded in 1930 by the merger of the Dutch margarine producer Margarine Unie and the British soapmaker Lever Brothers.

32. Walsh, op. cit., pp. 188, 207.

33. De Jong, op. cit., p. 47—translated from Dutch.

34. Definition provided by Dave Hofmann.

35. By 100 A.D., Christianity had become a religion for Gentiles. See Sim, David (2005), "How Many Jews Became Christians in the First Century? The Failure of the Christian Mission to the Jews," *HTS* 61 (1&2), pp. 417–440.

36. Collins, Jim (2001), "Level 5 Leadership," *Harvard Business Review* 79 (1), pp. 66–76.

CHAPTER 11

1. For this chapter, I am indebted to the seminal book by Robert K. Massie (1991), *Dreadnought: Britain, Germany, and the Coming of the Great War*, New York: Ballantine Books.

2. Kennedy, Paul (1987), *The Rise and Fall of the Great Powers*, New York: Random House, p. 149.

3. Davies, Norman (1996), *Europe: A History*, Oxford: Oxford University Press, p. 887.

4. Kennedy, op. cit., p. 149.

5. Massie, op. cit., p. xxv.

6. Four Sea Lords administered the Admiralty. The Fourth Sea Lord was responsible for supplying the fleet, the Third Sea Lord for the design and construction of ships, the Second Sea Lord for human resources, and the First Sea Lord for directing naval operations in war and peace. The First Lord (secretary of the navy) was a politician and member of the cabinet.

7. Massie , op. cit., p. 414.

8. Ibid., p. 399.

9. Mackay, Ruddock F. (1973), *Fisher of Kilverstone*, London: Oxford University Press.

10. Massie, op. cit., chapters 24 and 25.

11. Kennedy, Paul (1983), *The Rise and Fall of British Naval Mastery*, London: Macmillan, chapter 8.

12. Cuniberti, Vittorio (1903), "An Ideal Battleship for the British Fleet," *Jane's All the World's Fighting Ships*, pp. 407–409.

13. Sturton, Ian, ed. (2008), *Conway's Battleships: The Definitive Visual Reference to the World's All-Big-Gun Ships*, Annapolis, MD: Naval Institute Press.

14. Massie, op. cit., p. 487. His statement was somewhat exaggerated. In 1897, Britain had "only" 62 battleships versus 96 combined for Germany, France, Russia, Italy, U.S., and Japan. Kennedy (1983), op. cit.

15. Berghahn, Volker R. (1971), *Der Tirpitz-Plan: Genesis und Verfall einer innenpolitischen Krisenstrategie unter Wilhelm II*, Düsseldorf: Droste Verlag.

16. Profiles in Disruptive Leadership, https://quarterly.insigniam.com/leadership/profiles-in-disruptive- leadership/.

17. Hlavacek, James D. (2018), *Fat Cats Don't Hunt*, Asheville, NC: United Business Press, chapter 8.

18. Hlavacek, op. cit., p. 237.

19. Waters, Richard (2019), "FT Person of the Year: Satya Nadella," *Financial Times*, December 19, p. 9.

20. Hlavacek, op. cit., pp. 244–249.

21. Massie, op. cit. p. 418.

22. Isaacson, Walter (2011), *Steve Jobs*, New York: Simon & Schuster.

REFLECTIONS ON DISRUPTIVE LEADERSHIP

1. For disruption in grocery retailing, see Steenkamp, Jan-Benedict, with Laurens Sloot (2019), *Retail Disruptors: The Spectacular Rise and Impact of the Hard Discounters*, London: Kogan Page.

2. https://www.leapfrogging.com/wp-content/uploads/2017/03/Leadership-Competencies-for-Disruptive-Innovation.pdf.

3. Machiavelli, Nicolò (1513/2017), *The Prince*, Millennium Publications.

4. Massie, Robert K. (1991), *Dreadnought: Britain, Germany, and the Coming of the Great War*, New York: Ballantine Books, p. 489.

5. Barsh, J. et al. (2008), "Leadership and Innovation," *The McKinsey Quarterly*.
6. Kotter, John (2014), *Accelerate*, Cambridge, MA: Harvard Business Review Press.
7. Bass, Bernard M., and Bruce J. Avilo (1994), *Improving Organizational Effectiveness through Transformational Leadership*, Thousand Oaks, CA: Sage.
8. In chapter 11, I talked about the role of Fisher's superiors in helping him push through disruptive change. Here, I focus on his ability to build a following among others in the Royal Navy itself.
9. Acts 11:17, NIV.
10. Acts 2.

CHAPTER 12

1. See e.g., Tuchman, Barbara W. (1985), *The March of Folly*, New York: Random House, Part Four.
2. Chernov, Ron (2010), *Washington: A Life*, New York: Penguin, p. 428.
3. Ellis, Joseph J. (2005), *His Excellency George Washington*, New York: Vintage Books, pp. 270–271.
4. Ibid., p. 12.
5. Chernov, op. cit., chapters 3–5.
6. Ellis, op. cit., p. 62.
7. Ibid., pp. 68–69; Flexner, James (1974), *Washington: The Indispensable Man*, New York: New American Library, pp. 58–59.
8. https://www.historytoday.com/archive/death-george-washington.
9. Both quotes taken from Chernov, op. cit., p. 431.
10. Flexner, op. cit., p. 172.
11. Ibid., p. 173.
12. http://founders.archives.gov/documents/Hamilton/01-03-02-0155.
13. Flexner, op. cit., pp. 172–174.
14. http://founders.archives.gov/documents/Washington/99-01-02-10767.
15. Report on the Newburgh meeting is based on Flexner, op. cit., pp. 175–178.
16. Flexner, op. cit., p. 177.
17. For the full text of the Newburgh address, see www.mountvernon.org/education/primary-sources-2/article/newburgh-address-george-washington-to-officers-of-the-army-march-15-1783/.
18. Ellis, op. cit., p. 142.
19. Chernov, op. cit., pp. 435–436.
20. Ellis, op. cit., p. 146.
21. Ibid., p. 233.
22. Chernov, op. cit., pp. 674, 752.
23. Flexner, op. cit., p. 348.
24. Ibid., p. 361.
25. Chernov, op. cit., p. 757.
26. Ellis, op. cit., p. 74. Benedict Arnold was a U.S. general during the Revolutionary War

who defected to the British. He planned to surrender the fortifications at West Point to British forces for £20,000, but the plot was discovered in September 1780.

27. Ellis, op. cit., pp. 98–99.

28. Ibid., p. 74.

29. Taylor, A. (2018), "France to the Rescue!" *Wall Street Journal*, October 20, pp. C7–C8; Flexner, op. cit., p. 181.

30. Chernov, op. cit., p. 605.

31. Ibid., pp. 29–30.

32. Flexner, op. cit., p. 183.

33. Ellis, op. cit., p. 109; see also Walker, Sam (2018), "How to Lead Like Washington," *Wall Street Journal*, September 22, p. B5.

34. Chernov, op. cit., pp. 317–322.

35. Flexner, op. cit., p. 358.

36. Ellis, op. cit., pp. 222, 231.

37. Chernov, op. cit., p. 320.

38. *Financial Times* (2018), "Hubris Is an Ever-Present Risk for High-Flying Chief Executives," November 19.

39. https://www.conference-board.org/press/pressdetail.cfm?pressid=7551.

40. Hill, Andrew (2018), "Prepare to Tell Long-Serving Bosses Their Time Is Up," *Financial Times*, October 7; Gapper, John (2014), "The Perils of the Chief Who Stays Too Long at the Top," *Financial Times*, April 16.

CHAPTER 13

1. Wilson, John (1973), *CB: A life of Sir Henry Campbell-Bannerman*, New York: St. Martin's Press, p. 487.

2. For an overview of the Apartheid legislation, see https://en.wikipedia.org/wiki/Apartheid_legislation.

3. Carlin, John (2008), *Playing with the Enemy: Nelson Mandela and the Game That Made a Nation*, New York: Penguin, p. 41.

4. Mandela was keenly aware that, despite all the turmoil, the ANC was no match for the overwhelming might of the South African security apparatus. See, e.g., Mandela, Nelson (1994), *Long Walk to Freedom*, New York: Little, Brown, p. 525.

5. Mandela, op. cit., p. 368.

6. Sampson, Anthony (1999), *Mandela*, New York: Vintage Books, p. 192.

7. Ibid., p. 205.

8. Mandela, op. cit., p. 383.

9. Sampson, op. cit., p. 205.

10. Mandela, op. cit., p. 506.

11. Sampson, op. cit., p. 359.

12. Mandela, op. cit., pp. 566 and 589 ff.

13. Rossier, Nicholas (director, 2015), *The Other Man: F. W. de Klerk and the End of Apartheid*, documentary.

14. Sampson, op. cit., p. 293.

15. The remainder of this section is based on Carlin, op. cit.

16. Sampson, op. cit., p. 516.

17. Carlin, op. cit., p. 191. *Kaffir* is equivalent to the infamous "n-word."

18. Carlin, John (2007), "How Nelson Mandela Won the Rugby World Cup," *Daily Telegraph*, October 19; www.telegraph.co.uk/news/features/3634426/How-Nelson-Mandela-won-the-rugby-World-Cup.html.

19. Carlin, op. cit., p. 184.

20. Ibid., p. 223.

21. Ibid., p. 243.

22. Mandela, Nelson, and Mandla Langa (2017), *Dare Not Linger: The Presidential Years*, New York: Farrar, Straus, and Giroux, p. 210.

23. Sampson, op. cit., p. 516.

24. Carlin, op. cit., p. 244.

25. Ibid., p. 246.

26. Paragraph based on Rooke, David, and William R. Torbert (2005), "Seven Transformations of Leadership," *Harvard Business Review* 83 (4), pp. 66–76.

27. Paragraph based on Mandela, op. cit., p. ix.

28. Sampson, op. cit., p. 239.

29. Mandela and Langa, op. cit., pp. 214, 221.

30. Mandela, op. cit., p. 526.

31. Sampson, op. cit., p. 406.

32. Ibid., p. 406.

33. Ibid., p. 403.

34. Rooke and Torbert, op. cit., p. 72.

REFLECTIONS ON AUTHENTIC LEADERSHIP

1. Walumbwa, Fred O. et al. (2008), "Authentic Leadership: Development and Validation of a Theory-Based Measure," *Journal of Management* 34 (1), pp. 89–126.

2. www.forbes.com/sites/kevinkruse/2013/05/12/what-is-authentic-leadership/#238fda12def7.

3. George, Bill (2003), *Authentic Leadership*, San Francisco, CA: Jossey-Bass.

4. George, Bill (2015), *Discover Your True North*, Hoboken, NJ: Wiley.

5. Al Hussein, Zeid R. (2019), "A Principled Dissident Turns Despotic Premier," *Wall Street Journal*, December 10, p. A17.

6. Ellis, Joseph J. (2005), *His Excellency George Washington*, New York: Vintage Books, pp. 74–75.

7. Ibid., p. 37.

8. Walker, Sam (2018), "How to Lead Like Washington," *Wall Street Journal*, September 22, p. B5.

9. Quoted in Sampson, Anthony (1999), *Mandela*, New York: Vintage Books, p. 512.

10. Mandela, Nelson (1994), *Long Walk to Freedom*, New York: Little, Brown, p. 523.

CHAPTER 14

1. This applied especially to lay nurses. Religious nuns had (some) training and commanded more respect because of their life of self-sacrifice and their religious vows of chastity and obedience. They were primarily found in Catholic institutions.

2. Bostridge, Mark (2008), *Florence Nightingale: The Making of an Icon*, New York: Farrar, Straus and Giroux, p. 96.

3. Troubetzkoy, Alexis S. (2006), *A Brief History of the Crimean War*, London: Constable & Robinson, p. 208.

4. Description of conditions of the Barrack Hospital based on Hamilton, Lynn M. (2015), *Florence Nightingale: A Life Inspired*, Sudbury, MA: Wyatt North, pp. 40–42.

5. Bostridge, op. cit., p. 206.

6. Reef, Catherine (2017), *Florence Nightingale: The Courageous Life of a Legendary Nurse*, Boston, MA: Clarion Books, p. 16.

7. Bostridge, op. cit., pp. 35, 38, 71–72.

8. Hamilton, op. cit., pp. 9–13.

9. Reef, op. cit. p. 37.

10. Bostridge, op. cit., pp. 101–102; Reef, op. cit., p. 39.

11. Ibid., p. 115.

12. Ibid., pp. 147, 155.

13. Ibid., pp. 156–157.

14. Reef, op. cit., p. 66.

15. Bostridge, op. cit., pp. 190–191.

16. Ibid., p. 210.

17. Reef, op. cit., p. 90.

18. Ibid., pp. 110–111.

19. Bostridge, op. cit., pp. 283–284.

20. Ibid., pp. 284–285.

21. Ibid., pp. 287–292.

22. Hamilton, op. cit., pp. 92–99.

23. Reef, op. cit., p. 159.

24. Bostridge, op. cit., p. 291.

25. Hamilton, op. cit., p. 74.

26. Bostridge, op. cit., p. 341.

27. Greenleaf, Robert K. (1998), *The Power of Servant Leadership*, San Francisco, CA: Berrett-Koehler.

28. Barnabas was his nickname. His real name was Joseph; Acts 4:36.

29. Acts 15:36–41. The dangers facing the missionaries were indeed daunting as is evident from Paul's subsequent experiences. See 2 Corinthians 11:23–27.

30. Reef, op. cit., pp. 103–104.

31. Bostridge, op. cit., p. 226.

CHAPTER 15

1. "Jump Jim Crow" was a song-and-dance caricature of blacks performed by white actor Thomas Rice in blackface, which first surfaced in 1832. As a result of Rice's fame, "Jim Crow" became a pejorative expression meaning "Negro." When Southern legislatures passed laws of racial segregation directed against blacks at the end of the nineteenth century, these statutes became known as Jim Crow laws. Source: Wikipedia.
2. https://www.britannica.com/event/Plessy-v-Ferguson-1896.
3. Oates, Stephen B. (1994), *Let the Trumpet Sound*, New York: Harper Perennial, p. 179.
4. Ibid., p. 58.
5. Ibid., p. 57.
6. Ibid., p. 10.
7. Thoreau, Henry David (1849/2019), *On Civil Disobedience*.
8. Oates, op. cit., p. 21.
9. King, Martin Luther (1998), *The Autobiography of Martin Luther King Jr.*, New York: Grand Central Publishing, p. 17. This autobiography was published posthumously and edited by Clayborne Carson.
10. Ibid., p. 24.
11. King, Martin Luther (1958), *Toward Freedom: The Montgomery Story*, Boston, MA: Beacon Press, p. 8.
12. King (1998), op. cit., p. 44.
13. Ibid., p. 44.
14. Oates, op. cit., p. 51.
15. Ibid., pp. 65–69.
16. King (1998), op. cit., p. 68.
17. Oates, op. cit., p. 85.
18. King (1958), op. cit., p. 112.
19. Oates, op. cit., p. 86.
20. Ibid., p. 87.
21. King (1958), op. cit., p. 128.
22. Oates, op. cit., p. 92.
23. King (1998), op. cit., p. 87.
24. Oates, op. cit., Part Eight.
25. Branch, Taylor (2007), *At Canaan's Edge: America in the King Years, 1965–68*, New York: Simon & Schuster.
26. Oates, op. cit., p. 107.
27. For example, he received job offers with salaries up to $75,000, which is equal to $700,000 in 2019 dollars. Oates, op. cit., p. 115.
28. Oates, op. cit., p. 458.
29. Ibid., p. 218.
30. In the later years of the Johnson administration, the relationship between King and the president became increasingly tense as King became a vocal critic of the Vietnam War.
31. King (1998), op. cit., p. 330.
32. Ibid., pp. 330–331.

33. Ibid., p. 331.
34. Oates, op. cit., p. 335.
35. Ibid., pp. 194–195, 334–355.
36. Ibid., p. 289.

REFLECTIONS ON SERVANT LEADERSHIP

1. An article "Taking the Credit: Can Universities Tackle Academic Fraud?" that appeared in the *Financial Times* on September 7, 2019, details some abuses.
2. Northouse, Peter G. (2016), *Leadership: Theory and Practice*, Los Angeles, CA: Sage, p. 242.
3. Hlavacek, James D. (2018), *Fat Cats Don't Hunt*, Asheville, NC: United Business Press, pp. 183–185.
4. Liden, Robert C. et al. (2014), "Servant Leadership and Serving Culture: Influence on Individual and Unit Performance," *Academy of Management Journal* 57 (5), pp. 1434–1452.
5. Hlavacek, op. cit., p. 89. Drucker proposed twenty times more than the lowest-paid worker so my adapted benchmark is already considerably more lenient. But even then, the average S&P 500 company falls far short.
6. https://www.vox.com/policy-and-politics/2019/6/26/18744304/ceo-pay-ratio-disclosure-2018.
7. https://www.comparably.com/companies/wegmans/salaries; https://www.business.org/finance/accounting/hourly-wages-ceo-vs-employees/.
8. These principles are broadly based on Northouse, op. cit., chapter 10.
9. Ideal description based on Blanchard, Ken, and Renee Broadwell (2018), *Servant Leadership in Action*, Oakland, CA: Berrett-Koehler.
10. Anderson, Eugene W. and Mary W. Sullivan (1993), "The Antecedents and Consequences of Customer Satisfaction for Firms," *Marketing Science* 12 (2), pp. 125–143; Baumeister, Roy F. et al. (2001), "Bad Is Stronger Than Good," *Review of General Psychology* 5 (December), pp. 323–370.
11. Strachey, Lytton (1918/1948), *Eminent Victorians*, Harmondsworth: Penguin, pp. 111–161.
12. Bostridge, Mark (2008), *Florence Nightingale: The Making of an Icon*, New York: Farrar, Straus, and Giroux, chapter 21.
13. For some examples, see Oates, Stephen B. (1994), *Let the Trumpet Sound*, New York: Harper Perennial, pp. 314–316, 453–455.
14. https://standpointmag.co.uk/issues/june-2019/the-troubling-legacy-of-martin-luther-king/.
15. King told his followers about his weaknesses in a circumspect way. In his sermon "Unfullfilled Dreams," to the Ebenezer congregation on March 3, 1968, he said, "There are times that all of us know somehow that there is a Mr. Hyde and a Dr. Jekyll in us."
16. Northouse, op. cit., pp. 233–234.

17. French, John, and Bertram Raven (1959), "The Bases of Social Power," in *Studies in Social Power*, Ann Arbor: University of Michigan Press, pp. 150–67.

18. For full text of "Letter from a Birmingham Jail" see https://www.africa.upenn.edu/ Articles_Gen/Letter_Birmingham.html.

CHAPTER 16

1. Wilcken, Ulrich (1931/1967), *Alexander the Great*, transl. by G. C. Richards with introduction, notes, and bibliography by Eugene N. Borza, New York: Norton; chapter 1.

2. See Fuller, J.F.C. (1960), *The Generalship of Alexander the Great*, New York: Da Capo Press, chapter 2.

3. There are multiple accounts of Alexander's life from classical antiquity, including Arrian (c. 86–140 A.D.), *The Campaigns of Alexander*, transl. by Aubrey de Sélincourt, Harmondsworth: Penguin; and Plutarch (46–120 A.D.), *Parallel Lives*, edited by Arthur H. Clough, Oxford: Benediction Classics, pp. 624–663.

4. The actual size of Alexander's army is subject to some debate. I follow Wilcken, op. cit., p. 77.

5. Plutarch, op. cit., p. 639.

6. Wilcken, op. cit., pp. 111–112.

7. Ibid., pp. 111–112.

8. Fuller, J.F.C. (1954), *A Military History of the Western World, Vol. I*, New York: Da Capo Press, p. 97.

9. Fox, Robin L. (1975), *Alexander the Great*, London: Omega, p. 231.

10. Fuller (1960), op. cit., Figure 14 (p. 189) depicts Porus's dilemma with great clarity.

11. Green, Peter (1990), *Alexander to Actium: The Historical Evolution of the Hellenistic Age*, Berkeley, CA: University of California Press.

12. Rogers, Guy M. (2005), *Alexander: The Ambiguity of Greatness*, New York: Random House, pp. 290–293.

13. Ibid., p. 293.

14. Daniel 8:5–8; NIV. The goat stands for the Greeks/Macedonians and the prominent horn is Alexander. The two-horned ram is the Persian Empire, with the two horns referring to the Persians and the Medes. The four prominent horns are the four successor kingdoms. This interpretation is widely accepted by historians and Biblical scholars.

15. Naiden, F.S. (2019), *Soldier, Priest, and God: A Life of Alexander the Great*, Oxford: Oxford University Press, pp. 262–263.

16. Freeman, Philip (2008), *Julius Caesar*, New York: Simon & Schuster, p. 54.

17. Fuller (1954), op. cit., p. 88.

18. Renault, Mary (1975), *The Nature of Alexander*, New York: Pantheon, p. 107.

19. For the definitive account of Alexander's religious side, see Naiden, op. cit.

20. Ibid., chapter 9.

21. Wilcken, op. cit. p. 252.

22. Plutarch, op. cit., p. 633.

23. Description of the scene taken from Renault, op. cit., pp. 263–264.

24. Renault, op. cit., p. 95.

25. Plutarch, op. cit., p. 644.

26. Ibid., p. 645.

27. https://www.vox.com/policy-and-politics/2019/6/26/18744304/ ceo-pay-ratio-disclosure-2018.

28. Arrian, op. cit., pp. 360–365.

29. Fuller (1954), op. cit., p. 90.

30. Plutarch, op. cit., p. 635.

31. Ibid., pp. 639–640. Cyrus was the founder of the Persian Empire.

32. Arrian, op. cit., 7:29.

33. Renault, op. cit., p. 107.

34. Rogers, op. cit., pp. 175–180; Renault, op. cit., pp. 172–187. This tension was already described some 150 years earlier by Xerxes's uncle Artabanus when he told Themistocles, "[T]he laws of men are different, and one thing is honorable to one man, and to others another. It is the habit of the Greeks, we are told, to honor above all things, liberty and equality; but amongst our many excellent laws, we account this the most excellent, to honor the king, and to worship him, as the great preserver of the universe; if, then, you shall consent to our laws, and fall before the king and worship him, you may both see him and speak to him." Plutarch, op. cit., p. 118.

35. Steenkamp, Jan-Benedict (2017), *Global Brand Strategy: World-Wise Marketing in the Age of Branding*, New York: Palgrave MacMillan.

36. https://sso.agc.gov.sg/Act/PC1871?ProvIds=pr377A-#pr377A-.

37. Steenkamp, op. cit., p. 135.

38. https://www.rt.com/business/441849-cola-greeting-new-zealand/.

39. https://www.npr.org/sections/goatsandsoda/2018/12/01/671891818/ dolce-gabbana-ad-with-chopsticks- provokes-public-outrage-in-china.

40. https://www.theguardian.com/world/2017/oct/08/ dove-apologises-for-ad-showing-black-woman-turning-into-white-one.

41. Engels, Donald W. (1980), *Alexander the Great and the Logistics of the Macedonian Army*, Berkeley, CA: University of California Press, 1980.

CHAPTER 17

1. Fenby, Jonathan (2010), *The General: Charles de Gaulle and the France He Saved*, London: Simon & Schuster, p. 365.

2. Jackson, Julian (2018), *De Gaulle*, Cambridge, MA: Belknap, p. 596.

3. Fenby, op. cit., p. 132.

4. Jackson, op. cit., p. 44.

5. Ibid., p. 74.

6. The English translation of the speech can be found at https://www.bbc.com/ news/10339678.

7. First Republic: 1792–1804; Second Republic: 1848–1851; Third Republic: 1870–1940; Fourth Republic: 1946–1958; Fifth Republic: 1958–.

8. Williams, Charles (1995), *The Last Great Frenchman*, London: Abacus, p. 377.

9. Fenby, op. cit., pp. 412–414.

10. Davies, Norman (1996), *Europe: A History*, Oxford: Oxford University Press, p. 1073.

11. Fenby, op. cit., pp. 432–435.

12. Jackson, op. cit., p. 520.

13. Ibid., p. 522.

14. Ibid., p. 521.

15. Ibid., p. 530.

16. Ibid., p. 531.

17. Ibid., p. 531.

18. Ibid., p. 542.

19. Fenby, op. cit., p. 635.

20. *Financial Times* (2019), "Emmanuel Macron Has Issued a Wake-Up Call to Europe," November 9.

21. Jackson, op. cit., p. 529.

22. This paragraph is based on Fenby, op. cit., p. 132.

23. Jackson, op. cit., Chapter 22.

24. Fenby, op. cit., pp. 516–523.

25. Ibid., p. 5.

26. Fenby, op. cit., p. 406.

27. Chalaby, Jean K. (1998), "A Charismatic Leader's Use of the Media: De Gaulle and Television," *International Journal of Press/Politics* 3 (4), pp. 44–61.

28. Fenby, op. cit., p. 96.

29. An interesting resource is Stephen Joseph's (2011), *What Doesn't Kill Us: The New Psychology of Posttraumatic Growth*, Basic Books.

30. Fenby, op. cit., p. 636.

31. Ibid., p. 131.

32. Ibid., p. 315.

33. Ibid., p. 419.

34. Chalaby, op. cit., p. 55.

35. Fenby, op. cit., p. 419.

REFLECTIONS ON CHARISMATIC LEADERSHIP

1. Steenkamp, Jan-Benedict (2017), *Global Brand Strategy: World-Wise Marketing in the Age of Branding*, New York: Palgrave MacMillan, chapter 8.

2. Conger, Jay A., and Rabindra N. Kanungo (1994), "Charismatic Leadership in Organizations: Perceived Behavioral Attributes and Their Measurement," *Journal of Organizational Behavior* 15, pp. 439–452; Conger, Jay A., and Rabindra N. Kanungo (1987), "Toward a Behavioral Theory of Charismatic Leadership in Organizational Settings," *Academy of Management Review* 12 (4), pp. 637–647.

3. Weber, Max (1947), *The Theory of Social and Economic Organization*, New York: Oxford University Press.

4. Kotter, John (2012), *Leading Change*, Cambridge, MA: Harvard Business Review Press.

5. https://www.ikea.com/ms/sv_SE/pdf/reports-downloads/the-testament-of-a-furniture-dealer.pdf.

6. Naiden, F.S. (2019), *Soldier, Priest, and God: A Life of Alexander the Great*, Oxford: Oxford University Press provides a dozen examples, one at the end of each chapter.

7. Lussier, Robert N., and Christopher F. Achua (2015), *Leadership: Theory, Application & Skill Development*, Boston, MA: Cengage.

8. Conger and Kanungo (1987), op. cit., p. 644.

9. The story about Carlos Ghosn is based on Lewis, Leo et al. (2019), "The Downfall of Carlos Ghosn," *Financial Times*, November 7.

10. Howell, Jane M., and Bruce J. Avolio (1992), "The Ethics of Charismatic Leadership: Submission or Liberation?" *Academy of Management Executive* 6 (2), pp. 43–54.

CHAPTER 18

1. Siemann, Wolfram (2017/2019), *Metternich: Statesman and Visionary*, translated by Daniel Steuer, Cambridge, MA: Belknap, p. 90; see also chapter 4.

2. For example, leadership guru Ken Blanchard boldly claims: "The only way to get great results and great human satisfaction is with servant leadership." https://www.linkedin.com/learning/ken-blanchard-on-servant-leadership.

3. Aitken, Jonathan (2013), *Margaret Thatcher: Power and Personality*, London: Bloomsbury, p. 568.

4. Stott, Michael and Andres Schipani (2019), "Evo Morales's Legacy: A Polarised Bolivia," *Financial Times*, November 11.

5. Hill, Andrew (2018), "Prepare to Tell Long-Serving Bosses Their Time Is Up," *Financial Times*, October 7.

6. https://www.wsj.com/articles/under-armour-is-subject-of-federal-accounting-probe-11572819835.

APPENDICES

1. I developed the items based on Duckworth, Angela (2016), *Grit: The Power of Passion and Perseverance*, New York: Scribner; Sheard, Michael et al. (2009), "Progress Toward Construct Validation of the Sports Mental Toughness Questionnaire (SMTQ)," *European Journal of Psychological Assessment* 25 (3), pp. 186–193; Madrigal, Leilani et al. (2013), "Mind Over Matter: The Development of The Mental Toughness Scale (MTS)," *The Sport Psychologist*, 27, pp. 62–77. The interpretation of the scores is broadly based on Duckworth.

2. A number of items in this scale are adapted from Meynhardt et al. (2017), "Making Sense of a Most Popular Metaphor in Management: Towards a HedgeFox Scale for Cognitive Styles," *Administrative Sciences* 7 (3), p. 33; and https://www.forbes.com/

sites/jonyounger/2019/02/28/freelancers-are-you-more-fox-or-hedgehog-take-this-quiz-and-find-out/#1757887257a7.

3. SAILS draws upon the leadership literature, including: Conger, Jay A., and Rabindra N. Kanungo (1994), "Charismatic Leadership in Organizations: Perceived Behavioral Attributes and Their Measurement," *Journal of Organizational Behavior* 15, pp. 439–452; McClutcheon, Lynn (2000), "The Desirability of Control Scale: Still Reliable and Valid Twenty Years Later," *Current Research in Psychology* 5, pp. 1–9; Northouse, Peter G. (2016), *Leadership: Theory and Practice*, Los Angeles, CA: Sage; Parnell, John A., and William Crandall (2001), "Rethinking Participative Decision Making," *Personnel Review* 30 (5), pp. 523–535; Shearman, Sachiyo M., and Timothy R. Levine (2006), "Dogmatism Updated: A Scale Revision and Validation," *Communication Quarterly* 54 (3), pp. 275–291; Svedholm-Häkkinen, Annika M., and Marjaana Lindeman (2018), "Actively Open-Minded Thinking: Development of a Shortened Scale and Disentangling Attitudes towards Knowledge and People," *Thinking & Reasoning* 24 (1), pp. 21–40; van Dierendonck, Dirk, and Inge Nuijten (2011), "The Servant Leadership Survey: Development and Validation of a Multidimensional Measure," *Journal of Business and Psychology* 26 (3), pp. 249–267; Walumbwa, Fred O. et al. (2008), "Authentic Leadership: Development and Validation of a Theory-Based Measure," *Journal of Management* 34 (1), pp. 89–12.

4. *The Economist* (2018), "History Lessons," August 25, p. 55.

5. Maj. Dan Finkenstadt (USAF) proposed the use of SAILS as part of a 360-degree exercise. He also developed an initial version of Figure A.1.

INDEX

Figures and tables are indicated by an italicized *f* or *t* following a page number. Endnotes are indicated by an italicized *n* following a page number, and followed by a chapter number and an endnote number.

A

Achilles, xxiii
action orientation, 156
Acts of the Apostles, 162–63, 246
Adams, John, 198
adaptive leadership, 20–67
 examples of, 18
  Bismarck, Otto von, 31–45
  Clovis, 20–30
  Deng Xiaoping, 46–62
 four-step procedure for, 28–29
 leader vs. follower influence, 10, 11*f*
 overview, 11
 persuasive leadership vs., 12
 questions to ask, 67
 reflections on, 63–67
  displaying mental flexibility, 64–66
  identifying adaptive challenges, 63–64
  maintaining credibility, 66–67
  recognizing that locus for change is in the leader, 64
Adeimantus, 76
Adenauer, Konrad, 299
Aegina, 81, 123
Aesopian classifications. *See* animal metaphors; *names of specific metaphors*
Afghanistan, 280–81
African National Congress (ANC), 210–16, 220, 223–24; 361*n*13:4

Afrika Korps, 112
Afrikaners, 209–10, 215–20, 222–24, 228, 230. *See also* Boers
Aiken, Jonathan, 324
AiMark, 82–83
Aitken, Jonathan, 149
Alamanni, 21*f*, 22, 23*f*, 24
Alaric II, 26
alchemists, 221
Aldi, 43
Alexander the Great, xxii–xxiii, 18, 78, 274–91
 biography, 276
 empire of, 277*f*
 Greco-Persian Wars, 276–79
 Hellenistic period, 282
 historical context, 274–75
 lessons learned from, 283–90
  combining vision with flexibility, 284–85
  creation and communication of vision, 312–13
  deep emotional bond with followers, 315
  desire to change status quo, 312
  exemplary acts of great personal risk and sacrifice, 314
  letting followers share in successes, 286–87
  limited time span, 315–16
  limits of charisma, 289
  loyalty to and faith in followers, 285–86
  moral outlook, 287–88

planning, 289–90
    reciprocal relationship with followers, 285–87
    sharing followers' hardships, 286
rejection of Persian offer, 279–80
successor kingdoms, 281–82, 282f
Algerian War of Independence, 293–94, 315–16
All Blacks rugby team, 217–18
Alvarado, Pedro de, 133
Amazon, 182
AMD, 121–22
America First Committee, 109
Ananias, 163
Anastasius, 27
ANC (African National Congress), 210–16, 220,
    223–24; 361n13:4
Andrew, 162
Angola, 211, 228
animal metaphors (Aesopian classifications), 4–10.
    See also names of specific metaphors
    eagles, 7f, 8
    foxes, 5–7, 7f
    Hedgefox Scale, 10
    hedgehogs, 4–5, 7f
    identifying yours, 321–23
    ostriches, 7f, 9
Antioch, 161–63, 165–68
apartheid, 210–12, 214, 216, 219–20, 223
Apple, 182, 184, 187
Archilochus, 4
Argentina, 145, 202, 222
Arianism, 24, 28, 64–66
Aristotle, 276
Arnold, Benedict, 206; 361n12:26
Arrian, 288
Artabanus, 79; 367n16:34
Articles of Confederation, 195
Asia Minor, 275–76, 278, 284
Asquith, H. H., 89, 91–92, 96–97, 184; 352n6:21
Athens, 275. See also Themistocles
Atlantic Charter, 112
Attlee, Clement, 140
Augustine, 271
Augustus, 8
Aung San Suu Kyi, 227
Austen, Jane, 236
Australia, 217
Austria, 31–39, 42–43, 64, 101
authentic leadership, 194–231
    examples of, 18
        Mandela, Nelson, 209–25
        Washington, George, 194–208
    moral standards, 10, 11f, 13–14
    overview, 13–14

questions to ask, 230–31
reflections on, 226–30
    consistent integrity, 227–28
    meaningful relationships with followers, 230
    self-discipline, 229
    strong values, 226–27
    willingness to pay the price, 229
autocratic leadership, 12–13
Away, 150
Aztecs, 127–36, 127f, 355n8:2

B

Babylon, 279, 284
Baghdadi, Abu Bakr al-, 317
Baker, Jim, 267
Balfour, Arthur, 91–92, 177, 183, 184
Ballmer, Steve, 182
Bannerman, Henry, 88
Barnabas, 161–62, 165, 166, 246, 262; 364n14:28
Barrack Hospital, 235, 238–41, 323
Bass, Bernard, 191
Bechuanaland, 86, 86f
Bell, Tim, 142
Ben & Jerry's, 311
Bennis, Warren, 113, 168
Beresford, Charles, 184–85, 190
Berlin, Isaiah, 4, 6–7, 28
Berlin Wall, 211
bin Laden, Osama, 317
Bismarck, Otto von, 18, 31–45; 348n3:1
    biography, 34–36
    historical context, 31–34
    lessons learned from, 40–44, 63–66
        consistency, 42
        credibility through personal background,
            42–43
        devising appropriate strategy for attaining
            goals, 42
        flexibility, 42, 64–65
        focus, 320
        identifying adaptive challenges, 63
        maintaining credibility, 66
        recognizing that locus for change is in the
            leader, 63
    unification of Germany, 36–40, 38f
Bismarck (Steinberg), 320
BlackBerry, 187
Blanchard, Ken, 265; 369n18:2
Blockbuster, 187
Boers, 86–89, 86f, 91–95, 123. See also Afrikaners
Boer War, 87, 89–90, 123, 215; 352n6:13

Bolivia, 325
Bollinger, Kate, 65
Borders, 187
Boston Tea Party, 197
Boston University, 252
Bostridge, Mark, 237, 323
Botha, Louis, 93–94
Botha, P. W., 223
BP, 29
Bracebridges, 237
Braddock, Edward, 195
Brand Breakout (Steenkamp), xxi
Branson, Richard, 307–8
Brexit, 6, 9, 91, 121; 352*n*6:14
Brezhnev, Leonid, 207
Britain, Battle of, 102
British Steel Corporation, 143
Browder v. Gayle, 257
Brown, Jani (Engelbrecht), 219, 223
Buddha, xxii
Bukharin, Nikolai, 53; 350*n*4:17
Burgess, Steve, 228
Burma, 227
Bush, George H. W., 5
Bush, George W., 9, 28
Butler, Gerard, 73

C

Caesar, Julius, 200–202, 283
Callaghan, James, 141–42, 144
Cambodia, 201
Cambyses, 284
Cameron, David, 6
Campbell-Bannerman (Hattersley), 323
Campbell-Bannerman, Henry, 18, 85–99, 90*f*, 184,
    209, 323; 352*n*6:21
  biography, 88–91
  historical context, 85–88
  lessons learned from, 95–98
    appealing to self-interest, 123
    communication skills, 120
    giving credit to others, 97
    keeping enemies close, 96
    lack of ambition, 98
    listening, 96
    maintaining credibility, 119
    making oneself indispensable, 97
    managing gap in vision with followers, 118
    persuading proximate followers through distal
        followers, 121
  reconciliation with Boers, 92–95

Cantor, Norman, 27
Cape Colony, 93
Cape of Good Hope, 94
Cape Province, 85–86
Carter, Jimmy, 110–11
cash-and-carry policy, 107, 114
Catholicism, 64
  administrative role after fall of Rome, 25
  Arianism vs., 24
  celibacy, 187
  Clovis' conversion and utilization of, 23–29
  de Gaulle and, 348*n*2:15
  nuns as nurses, 363*n*14:1
  Peter's positional power, 358*n*10:28
Catholic People's Party, 43, 65
CB (Wilson), 323
CCP (Chinese Communist Party), 47, 49–51, 53,
    56, 59; 349*n*4:6
Ceylon, 173
Chaeronea, Battle of, 275–76
Challe, Maurice, 300–301
Chamberlain, Joseph, 87, 89; 352*n*6:4, 352*n*6:13
change
  coping with, 2–3
  desire to change status quo, 312
  maintaining credibility when changing position,
    67
  making followers aware of change in position, 29
  recognizing that locus for change is in the leader,
    64
charismatic leadership, 274–318
  examples of, 18
    Alexander the Great, 274–91
    de Gaulle, Charles, 292–310
    King, Martin Luther, Jr., 259
  messianic quality, 10, 11*f*
  overview, 15
  questions to ask, 318
  reflections on, 311–17
    creation and communication of vision, 312–13
    deep emotional bond with followers, 315
    desire to change status quo, 312
    evil side of charismatic leadership, 316–17
    exemplary acts of great personal risk and
        sacrifice, 314
    limited time span, 315–16
Charlemagne, 348*n*2:12
Charles I, 129
Charles V, 129, 134
Chernov, Ron, 206–7
Chiang Kai-shek, 47
China, 43, 157, 201, 290. *See also* Deng Xiaoping
Chinese Academy of Social Sciences, 54

Chinese Communist Party (CCP), 47, 49–51, 53, 56, 59; 349n4:6
Cholula, 131, 134
Christian Democratic Party (the Netherlands), 65, 80, 82, 116, 121
Churchill, Winston, 296f
  Boer War and reconciliation, 87, 92–94, 97, 209
  de Gaulle and, 296–97, 303
  Roosevelt and, 107, 111–12
  Royal Navy, 179
  Stalin and, 212
  voted out, 78
  warnings ignored, 81
Civil Rights Act, 258
Civil War, 250
Clarke, Mary, 236
Clark, Jim, 261–62
Clausewitz, Carl von, 16
Cleitus, 288
Clinton, Bill, 6, 28, 57, 322
closed shops, 140; 356n9:4
Clotilda, 22, 24
Clovis, 18, 20–30; 348n2:14
  biography, 22
  conquest over Germanic kingdoms, 23–27, 23f
  conversion to Catholicism, 23–26
  historical context, 20–22
  lessons learned from, 27–30, 64, 66–67
    assessing competitors, 29
    benefiting from aura, 29
    flexibility, 28, 64–65
    identifying obstacles and barriers, 28
    maintaining credibility, 66–67
    making followers aware of change in position, 29
    moral standards, 28–29
    recognizing that locus for change is in the leader, 63
Coca-Cola, 290
coercive power, 270
Coetsee, Kobie, 219
Collins, Jim, 97–98
Columbia University, 103
common goals, leadership and, 2
communication. See also persuasive leadership
  communication skills, 119–20, 262
  of vision, 312–13
Confucius, xxii
Conger, Jay, 311
Congress of Vienna, 32–33, 33f, 36; 348n3:1
Conquistador (Levy), 321
Conservative Party (Britain), 352n6:6
  Cameron and, 6
  Campbell-Bannerman and, 90; 352n6:4
  Fisher and, 184

Johnson and, 121
May and, 9
Nightingale and, 237
Thatcher and, 140–42, 144–45, 149, 151–52, 157
consistency, 42, 227–29
Constitutional Convention, 204, 205
Continental Army, 197–98, 200–202
Continental Congress, 197–98, 201
control
  need for control, 154–55
  over emotions, 206–7
Cook, Tim, 182
Corbyn, Jeremy, 148
Corinth, 72, 75–76, 80, 275
Cornelius, 164–65, 191
Corn Laws, 91
Cornwallis, Charles, 198
Cortés, Hernán, 18, 126–38
  advance to Tenochtitlán, 130–32, 131f
  biography, 128–29
  fall of Tenochtitlán, 133–34
  historical context, 126–28
  lessons learned from, 134–37
    action orientation, 156
    determination, 135
    leading by example, 136
    leading from the front, 155
    learning from the past, 136–37
    motivation to succeed, 321
    need for control, 154
    not overstaying your welcome, 157
    resilience, 136
    stiffening resolve of wobbly followers, 155–56
    time to go, 324–25
    scuttling his fleet, 129–30
    withdrawal and retreat, 131f, 133
Costco, 264–65
Coty, René, 294, 298
Council of Jerusalem, 165–67
courage, 149–50, 189–90. See also disruptive leadership
Cox, James, 103
"creative destruction," 175, 182–83
credibility
  leveraging, 115
  maintaining, 66–67, 119
  through personal background, 42–43
Crimean War, 235, 237–38, 242
Cromwell, Oliver, xxiii, 200
Crozer Theological Seminary, 252
crucibles, 113, 168
Cuba, 128–30
Cultural Revolution, 47–48, 50, 53, 55
Cyrus, 71
Czechoslovakia, 101, 106; 352n6:13

D

Daley, Richard, 258
Damon, Matt, 220
Daniel, 283; 366*n*16:14
Darius I, 71–72, 81
Darius III, 278–81, 283, 286, 288
Das Kapital (Marx), 53
Day of the Jackal, The (Forsyth), 307
Deepwater Horizon oil spill, 29
de Gaulle, Charles, 18, 27, 40, 292–310, 296*f*, 348*n*2:15
  biography, 294–99
  historical context, 292–94
  lessons learned from, 303–9
    creation and communication of vision, 312–13
    deep emotional bond with followers, 315
    desire to change status quo, 312
    emotional power, 307–8
    exemplary acts of great personal risk and sacrifice, 314
    inner strength, 306
    limited time span, 315–16
    myth making, 307–8
    public restraint, 306–7
    self-confidence, 320–21
    time to go, 324–26
  return to office, 298–99
  self-imposed postwar exile, 297–98
  severing ties with Algeria, 299–303
  World War II, 295–97
de Gaulle, Henri, 294
De Gaulle (Jackson), 321
de Klerk, F. W., 211, 213–15, 218, 228
Delft University of Technology, 55
Delouvrier, Paul, 300
Democratic Party, 89, 103–4, 104*t*, 106, 121
Democratic-Republicans, 198–99, 206, 230
Deng Xiaoping, xxiii, xxv, 18, 46–62, 51*f*, 322–23; 349*n*4:6
  biography, 48–51
  historical context, 46–48
  lessons learned from, 57–61, 63–67
    buy-in from followers, 59–60
    decentralized decision making, 60
    displaying mental flexibility, 64–65
    focus on big picture, 58
    identifying adaptive challenges, 63–64
    long-term focus, 58–59
    maintaining credibility, 66–67
    recognizing that locus for change is in the leader, 63
    setting short-term policies in light of long-term goals, 58–59

    trying to lead while your predecessor is still around, 61
  Reform and Opening Up program, 51–57
    modernization of agriculture, 53
    modernization of industry, 53–54
    modernization of science and technology, 55
    results of, 55–57, 56*t*
Deng Xiaoping (Pantsov and Levine), 323
Denmark, 37
Deutscher Bund (German Confederation), 33–34, 36, 38–39, 42
Dexter Avenue Baptist Church, 253
Diamond, Jared, xxii
Díaz del Castillo, Bernal, 126
Dionysius Exiguus, 357*n*10:1
Diplomacy (Kissinger), 41, 320
directive leadership, 126–58
  examples of, 18
    Cortés, Hernán, 126–38
    Thatcher, Margaret, 139–53
  leader vs. follower influence, 10, 11*f*
  limited shelf life of, 151–52, 157
  overview, 12–13
  questions to ask, 158
  reflections on, 154–57
    action orientation, 156
    leading from the front, 155
    need for control, 154–55
    not overstaying your welcome, 157
    stiffening resolve of wobbly followers, 155–56
disruptive leadership, 160–92
  examples of, 18
    Fisher, Jacky, 171–86
    Peter, 160–70
  leader vs. follower influence, 10, 11*f*
  overview, 13
  questions to ask, 192
  reflections on, 187–92
    conviction of righteousness of cause, 190
    courage, 189–90
    guiding coalitions, 191–92
    nurturing disruptive mindset, 188–89
distal followers, 245–47
  defined, 120
  emotional power, 308
  persuading proximate followers through, 121
diversification strategy, 43–44
Dolce & Gabbana, 290
Dove, 290
Dreadnought, 176–83, 177*f*, 178*f*, 190
"Dropping the Pilot" (cartoon), 40, 41*f*
Drucker, Peter, xxiv–xxv, 265
Duckworth, Angela, 321
du Plessis, Morné, 217–18

E

eagle-like qualities and leaders
  Alexander the Great, 284
  aspiring to be, 321–22
  Augustus, 8
  Bismarck, Otto von, 41
  Campbell-Bannerman, Henry, 95
  Clovis, 28
  Cortés, Hernán, 135
  de Gaulle, Charles, 304
  Deng Xiaoping, 57
  Fisher, Jacky, 179
  King, Martin Luther, Jr., 260
  Lincoln, Abraham, 8
  Mandela, Nelson, 220, 322
  overview, 7f, 8
  Peter, 167
  Roosevelt, Franklin D., 112
  Stalin, Joseph, 8
  Thatcher, Margaret, 151
  Themistocles, 79
  tower perspective, 322
  Washington, George, 205
Ebenezer Baptist Church, 251, 259
Economist, The, xxv
Edge of the Sword, The (*Le fil de l'épée*) (de Gaulle),
  305–6
Edward VII, 87, 123, 183
Egypt, 112, 173, 202, 207, 228, 279, 284
Eisenhower, Dwight D., 95, 257, 260
el-Alamein, Battle of, 112
Ellis, Joseph, 195, 229
Eminent Victorians (Strachey), 267
emotional intelligence, 3, 335, 338
Employment Act, 146
enemies and competitors
  assessing, 29
  keeping close, 96
  knowing, 222–23
  speaking language of, 222
Erdogan, Recep, 137, 157
EU (European Union), 152, 293, 299
European Central Bank, 304
European Commission, 304
European Council, 304
European Economic Community, 293
European Marketing Academy, 155
European Union (EU), 152, 293, 299
Eurybiades, 76, 80, 82
Evian Accords, 302, 308
example, leading by, 13, 136
expectation-disconfirmation theory, 267–68, 268f
expertise, defined, 66
expert power, 270

F

Facebook, xxiv
Falklands War, 145
family contract system, 50, 53, 60
Fashoda, 294
FBI, 260, 268
FDR (Morgan), 321
Federal Diet, 34–36, 64
Federalist Papers, 201
Federalists, 198–99, 230
Fenby, Jonathan, 303, 307–8
FIFA World Cup, 216
Financial Times, 207
Finkenstadt, Dan, xix
fireside chats, 104–5, 115–16, 120
Firth, Colin, 120
Fisher, Jacky, 9, 18, 171–86, 175f
  biography, 173–75
  historical context, 171–73
  HMS *Dreadnought*, 176–79, 177f, 178f
  lessons learned from, 179–85
    continuously challenging, analyzing, and
     learning, 180–81
    conviction of righteousness of cause, 190
    courage, 190
    ensuring top-level support, 183
    guiding coalitions, 191–92
    having thick skin, 184–85
    nurturing disruptive mindset, 189
    prioritizing long-term goals, 181–83
    unrelenting focus, 184
flattery, 8, 79, 82
flexibility. *See also* adaptive leadership
  aligning means and ends, 28, 205
  combining vision with, 284–85
  mental, 64–66
  in tactics vs. in strategy, 42
Flexner, James, 202–6
FLN (*Front de Libération Nationale*), 293, 300
Florence Nightingale (Bostridge), 323
focus
  on big picture, 58
  grit and, 320
  long-term, 58–59
  tower perspective, 322
  unrelenting, 184
focus strategy, 43–44
Forbes, 226
Ford, Henry, 137
Ford, Henry, II, 61
Forsyth, Frederick, 307
Fortune (magazine), xxiv
fox-like qualities and leaders, 5–7
  aspiring to be eagle-like, 322

examples of, 6, 322–23
overview, 5–6, 7*f*
France. *See also* de Gaulle, Charles
    Bismarck and, 39–40, 42–43, 65
    after Congress of Vienna, 32–34
    Crimean War, 235
    Deng Xiaoping in, 48
    German name for, 348*n*2:13
    Revolutionary War, 206
    Trafalgar, 172
    World War II, 100–102, 112, 114
Franks, 20–22, 21*f*, 24–29. *See also* Clovis
Freeman, Morgan, 220
French and Indian War, 195
French Revolution, 9, 31, 194–95, 199, 200, 235
Friedrich Wilhelm IV, 34–35
Front de Libération Nationale (FLN), 293, 300
Fuller, J.F.C., 274, 280, 287

G

Gaddafi, Muammar, 228
Gaddis, John Lewis, 5–6, 78
Gamaliel, 357*n*10:5
Gandhi, xxiii, 252
Gang of Four, 50–51, 65
Garrow, David, 268
Gaugamela, Battle of, xxii, 280, 284, 289
Gaul, 22, 26, 28
Gaullists, 300–301, 303
General Electric (GE), xxiv, 150, 325
George, Bill, 226, 230
George III, 5, 194, 204
George VI, 120
Gerlach, Leopold von, 35, 37
German Confederation (*Deutscher Bund*), 33–34, 36,
    38–39, 42
Germanic kingdoms, 20–29, 21*f*, 22*f*, 63, 167;
    348*n*2:12
German Reich, 34, 40
Germany, 57, 207. *See also* Bismarck, Otto von
    Anglo-German naval arms race, 172–73, 174,
        178–80
    Franco-German alliance, 299
    Hitler and Nazism, 5, 81, 100–101, 106–7, 109,
        112, 120, 312
    Nightingale in, 237
    postwar economy, 140
    South African support against, 93–94; 352*n*6:25
    World War II, 100–101, 106–7, 109, 112–13,
        120, 122–23, 292–93, 295, 297
Gerwarth, Robert, 31
Ghosn, Carlos, xxiv, 316–17
Ginsburg, Ruth Bader, 243

Gladstone, William E., 88–89; 352*n*6:6
Global Brand Strategy (Steenkamp), xxi
Gorbachev, Mikhail, 223
Gorgias, 275
Gormley, Joe, 145
Graham, Billy, 267
Great Britain, 43, 57, 200. *See also* Campbell-
    Bannerman, Henry; Mandela, Nelson;
    Nightingale, Florence; Thatcher, Margaret;
    United Kingdom
    American Revolution, 195–96
    China and, 46–47
    Congress of Vienna, 31–32
    Crimean War, 235
    World War II, 100–102, 106–12, 111*t*, 114, 123,
        292
Great Chinese Famine, 47
Great Depression, 101–2, 113, 116, 119
Great Leap Forward, 47, 49–50
Greece, 226. *See also* Alexander the Great;
    Themistocles
Greenleaf, Robert, 14, 246
Green New Deal, 258
Green, Peter, 80
Gregory of Tours, 22, 24–26, 29
Grey, Edward, 89, 91, 96–97
grit, 320–21, 326
    components of, 320–21
        focus, 320
        motivation to succeed, 321
        resilience, 321
        self-confidence, 320–21
    defined, 320
    as trait of great leaders, 3–4
Grit (Duckworth), 321
Grit Scale, 4, 18, 320, 329–31
    calculating and interpreting score, 331
    instructions for, 329
    questionnaire, 330
Groton school, 103
guiding coalitions, 191–92
Guns, Germs, and Steel (Diamond), xxii
Guomindang (Kuomintang) party, 47, 49

H

Habsburg Dynasty, 33
Haldane, Richard, 89, 91, 96–97
Hall, John, 242, 245
Hamilton, Alexander, 198, 201–2, 206
Hannibal, 281; 353*n*6:29
Harding, Warren, 103
Harry, Duke of Sussex, 227
Harvard Business Review, xxiv

Harvard University, 103
Hastings, Reed, 187
Hattersley, Roy, 95, 323
Heath, Edward, 140, 144
Hedgefox Scale, 18, 321, 332–33
    calculating and interpreting score, 333
    instructions for, 332
    questionnaire, 332–33
Hedgehog and the Fox, The (Berlin), 4
hedgehog-like qualities and leaders, 4–5, 65, 326
    aspiring to be eagle-like, 321–22
    de Gaulle, Charles, 303–4
    Deng Xiaoping, 57
    George III, 5
    Hitler, Adolf, 5, 112–13
    Mandela, Nelson, 220
    Mao Zedong, 57
    Nightingale, Florence, 244, 323
    overview, 4–5, 7f
    Reagan, Ronald, 5
    Scargill, Arthur, 151
    Thatcher, Margaret, 151
    Theodoric, 28
    Xerxes, 78–79
Heifetz, Ronald, 63–64
Henley, William Ernest, 221–22
Herbert, Elizabeth, 237
Herbert, Sidney, 235, 237, 238–39, 245
Herod Agrippa, 163
Herodotus, 79, 120; 350n5:1; 351n5:11
Hippocrates, 288
Hispaniola, 126
History of the Franks (Gregory of Tours), 22
Hitler, Adolf, 5, 12, 42, 100–101, 106, 112, 122, 290, 295, 317
HMS Dreadnought, 176–83, 177f, 178f, 190
Hobhouse, Emily, 89
Holt, Cameron G., xvii–xx
Holt Street Church, 255
Hong Kong, 54, 58
Hoover, Herbert, 104
Hoover, J. Edgar, 260
Hoskyns, John, 150
Howe, Geoffrey, 152, 326
Hua Guofeng, 51
Humbert, Agnes, 305–6
Humboldt, Alexander von, 355n8:2
humility, 3, 97–98, 168–69
Hungary, 39
Hunt, Maria, 241–42
Hussein, Saddam, 317
Hu Yaobang, 58

I

Iacocca, Lee, 61
idealized influence, 191–92
"I Have a Dream" (King), 258, 269
IJRM (International Journal of Marketing), 155
IKEA, 289, 313
Illustrated London News, 240
Il Principe (The Prince) (Machiavelli), xxiii, 13, 189–90, 267, 326
IMF (International Monetary Fund), 140, 304
Immelt, Jeff, 325
immigration, 149–50
India, 174, 243, 281, 284–85
indispensability, 97, 205, 207, 228, 315, 324, 326
individualized consideration, 191
Indochina, 293, 300
Industrial Revolution, 172
influence
    leadership and, 2
    leader vs. follower influence, 10, 11f
Inkerman Café, 241
inspirational motivation, 191
institutional power, 270
integrity, 95, 168. See also authentic leadership;
        servant leadership
    consistent, 227–29
    as trait of great leaders, 3
Intel, 121–22
intellectual stimulation, 191
intelligence
    emotional intelligence, 3, 335, 338
    as trait of great leaders, 3
International Committee of the Red Cross, 244
International Journal of Marketing (IJRM), 155
International Monetary Fund (IMF), 140, 304
International Nurses Day, 244
intuition, 113–15, 150
Invictus (film), 220
"Invictus" (Henley), 221–22
Ionia, 71, 77–78
Ionian Revolt, 71
Iran, 280
Iraq war, 9, 66, 181
Irish Home Rule, 91; 352n6:4, 352n6:6
Isaacson, Walter, 183
Isocrates, 275
Issus, Battle of, 278, 278f, 284, 287–88
Italy, 32, 39, 43, 290

J

Jackson, Julian, 321
James the Just, 163, 165
Jane's Fighting Ships, 176

Japan, 176
China and, 47
World War II, 112–13, 122–23
Jay, John, 198, 204
Jefferson, Thomas, 198, 206
Jesus Christ, xxii, 24, 160–63, 167–68; 357*n*10:4
Jewish Law (Mosaic Law), 162, 163–66
Jiang Qing, 50
Jiang Zemin, 57
Jim Crow laws, 250, 253–54, 256–57; 364*n*15:1
Jobs, Steve, 137, 169, 184, 187
John, 165
Johnson, Boris, 121
Johnson, Lyndon, 137, 258, 260; 356*n*8:26;
        365*n*15:30
Jones, Felicity, 243
Jones, Jim, 317
Jong, Johannes de, 168
Joseph, Keith, 144
Judaism, 162–67, 169
Judas Iscariot, 163
Junkers, 34
Jutland, 179

K

Kamprad, Ingvar, 313
Kanungo, Rabindra, 311
Kenan-Flagler Business School, xix, 2, 219
Kennedy, John F., 116, 260
Kennedy, Paul, xxii
Kerry, John, 66
Khan, Adil, 289
Kim Il-sung, 317
King, Coretta Scott, 252–54
King, Martin Luther, Jr., xxiii, 18, 221, 249–63, 253*f*
    assassination, 258–59
    biography, 251–54
    historical context, 249–51
    lessons learned from, 259–62; 365*n*15:27,
        365*n*15:30
        communication skills, 262
        creating value for the community, 269
        deprioritizing institutional power for expert
            power, 271
        emotional healing, 269
        ethical behavior, 268
        molder of consensus, 261
        putting followers' interests above self-interest,
            260, 265
    MIA bus boycott, 254–57
King, Martin Luther, Sr., 251–52
King's Speech, The (film), 120
Kipling, Rudyard, 92

Kips liver sausage, 122
Kissinger, Henry, 40–41, 320
Kodak, 187
Kohl, Helmut, 207
Koran, 283
Korey, Steph, 150–51
Kotter, John, 191, 312
Kreuzzeitung, 35
Kruger, Paul, 87, 89
Kruisinga, Roelof, 82
Kruse, Kevin, 226
Ku Klux Klan, 251
Kuomintang (Guomindang) party, 47, 49

L

labor unions. *See* Thatcher, Margaret
Labour Party (Britain), 140–42, 148–49, 151
Landale, Karen, xix
Landes, David, xxii
Landtag (Prussian Chamber of Deputies), 35–36
language, of opponents, 222
La Noche Triste, 133, 136
Lawson, Nigel, 152, 326
leadership. *See also names of specific leadership styles
        and leaders*
    animal metaphors, 4–10
    books about, xvii
    complex human society and, 1–2
    components of, 2–3
    courses and programs, 2
    defined, 2–3
    importance of, xvii
    as journey rather than destination, xviii–xix
    learning from historical leaders, xxii–xxv, 16–18
        basis for choice of case studies in book, 16–17
        format of book, 17–18
    personal nature of, xvii–xviii
    styles of, xxi
        dimensional comparison, 10, 11*f*
        identifying your dominant style, 323–24
        overview, 10–15
        SAILS, 15–16
    traits of great leaders, 3–4
leader vs. follower influence, 11*f*
Leclerc, Philippe, 297
Lee, Henry, 199
Le fil de l'épée (*The Edge of the Sword*) (de Gaulle),
        305–6
legitimate power, 270
Le Monde, 307
Lend-Lease program, 107–12, 111*t*, 114–15
Lenin, Vladimir, 49, 53–54
Leonidas, 73

"Letter from a Birmingham Jail" (King), 270–71
"Level 5 leaders," 97–98, 169
Levy, Buddy, 321
Lewis, Anthony, 229
Leyen, Ursula von der, 322
Liberal Imperialists, 89–92, 96–97
Liberal Party (Britain), 88–89, 90, 184; 352n6:4
Liberal Unionist Party (Britain), 352n6:4
Libya, 228
Lidl, 43
limited time span, 324–26
    charismatic leadership, 315–16
    directive leadership, 151–52, 157
    examples of leaders who stayed too long, 324–25
    warning signs indicating you should consider
        stepping down, 325–26
Lincoln, Abraham, 8, 169
listening, 60, 135, 168–69, 316
    individualized consideration, 191
    with open mind, 96
Lloyd George, David, 89, 91, 94, 97; 352n6:21
Lombards, 348n2:12
London Morning Chronicle, The, 199
London Times, 235, 238
Long March, 49
Long Walk to Freedom (Mandela), 221, 223, 322
Louis-Napoleon (Napoleon III), 32, 36, 39–40,
        41–42, 65, 320
Louis XIV, 301
Louis XVI, 9
Lyttelton Constitution, 88, 92, 97

M

Macao, 54
Macdonald, John, 240–41
Macedon. *See* Alexander the Great
Machiavellian leadership, 11
Machiavelli, Niccolò, xxiii, 13, 189–91, 267, 270, 326
Macmillan, Harold, 142
Macron, Emmanuel, 303
Madison, James, 198, 206
Mandela, Nelson, 18, 95, 209–25, 214f, 322;
        361n13:4
    biography, 211–15
    historical context, 209–11
    lessons learned from, 220–24
        action logic, 221
        communicating commitment, 223
        consistent integrity, 227–29
        knowing your enemy, 222–23
        leading flock without losing it, 223–24

    meaningful relationships with followers, 230
    speaking language of your opponent, 222
    strong values, 227
    time to go, 326
    willingness to pay the price, 229
    rugby and national reconciliation, 216–20
Manson, Charles, 317
Mao Zedong, xxiii, 46–52, 55, 57, 61, 317; 349n4:6
Marathon, 71–72, 74, 79
Mark, 246
marketing
    expectation-disconfirmation, 267, 268f
    five bases of power, 270
    goals of, xxi
    principles of persuasion, 81
    pull strategies, 121
    purpose branding, 311
    research and supply-line control, 290
    social judgment theory, 114
market segmentation, 244
Marshall, John, 200
Marshall Plan, 139, 293
Martin (saint), 26–27, 29
Marxism, 48, 53–54, 57, 65, 145
Marx, Karl, 53
Massie, Robert, 173
Massu, Jacques, 294, 301
Maya, 127
May, Theresa, 9; 352n6:14
McGovern, George, 43
McKinsey, 119
McNeil, William, xxii
Medicare, 111
Meghan, Duchess of Sussex, 227
Mendes France, Pierre, 293
Merkel, Angela, 6, 95, 322
Mesopotamia, 279, 281, 287
messianic quality, 11f
Metternich, Klemens von, 32, 322
Mexico, 43, 127–29, 134
Mexico City, 134
MIA (Montgomery Improvement Association) bus
        boycott, 254–57, 270
Microsoft, 182
Miletus, 288
Milner, Alfred, 87–88, 92
Mitterrand, François, 293
Molotov-Ribbentrop Pact, 101
Monroe Doctrine, 107
Monroe, James, 198
Montezuma II, 127, 129–33, 135, 137
Montgomery Improvement Association (MIA) bus
        boycott, 254–57, 270

Morales, Evo, 325
moralistic leadership, 14
moral standards, 10, 11*f*, 13–14, 28–29, 266–68, 287–88. *See also* authentic leadership; integrity; servant leadership
Morehouse College, 251
Morgan, Ted, 321
Morgenthau, Henry, 110
Mosaic Law (Jewish Law), 162, 163–66
Mount Vernon, 195, 227–28
Mourinho, José, 157
Mozambique, 211
Mubarak, Hosni, 207, 228
Mugabe, Robert, 207, 228
Muhammad, xxii
Museveni, Yoweri, 228
Musk, Elon, 169
myth making, 307–8

N

NAACP (National Association for the Advancement of Colored People), 254–55
Nadella, Satya, 182
Namibia, 352*n*6:25
Napoleon I, 31, 40, 200, 235, 280, 290
Napoleonic Wars, 31, 235
Napoleon III (Louis-Napoleon), 32, 36, 39–40, 41–42, 65, 320
Narváez, Pánfilo de, 133, 156
Nasionale Party (National Party), 210
Natal, 86, 86*f*, 93
National Association for the Advancement of Colored People (NAACP), 254–55
National Coal Board, 144–45
National Party (Nasionale Party), 210
National Union of Mineworkers (NUM), 140, 142–48, 156
Nation, The, 262
Nazism, 81, 100–101, 106–7, 109, 112, 120, 312
Nelson, Horatio, 172–73
Neocles, 73
NEP (New Economic Policy), 48–49, 53–54; 350*n*4:17
Nero, 163
Netflix, 187
Netherlands, 43, 80, 216, 222, 258
Neutrality Acts, 106
Neutrality Law, 107
Newburgh conspiracy, 202–3
New Deal, 104–5

New Economic Policy (NEP), 48–49, 53–54; 350*n*4:17
New York Times, The, 57, 229, 244
New Zealand, 217
Niebuhr, Reinhold, 271
Nietzsche, Friedrich, 306
Nigeria, 260
Nightingale, Fanny, 236
Nightingale, Florence, 18, 234–48, 238*f*, 262, 323
    Barrack Hospital, 238–41
    biography, 236–38
    Crimean military hospitals, 242
    historical context, 234–36; 363*n*14:1
    "Lady with the Lamp," 240–41, 245, 270
    lessons learned from, 244–47
        creating value for the community, 269
        deprioritizing institutional power for expert power, 271
        emotional healing, 269
        ethical behavior, 267–68
        putting followers' interests above self-interest, 265
        self-effacement, 245
        serving needs of both distal and immediate followers, 245–47
    Nightingale School of Nursing, 243
    writing and statistics, 243–44
Nightingale, Parthenope, 236
Nightingale, William, 236
Nixon, Richard, 43
Nobel Peace Prize, 215, 219, 227, 258, 259
Nokia, 187
Normandy, 297
North Korea, 201
Notes on Hospitals (Nightingale), 244
Notes on Nursing (Nightingale), 244
NUM (National Union of Mineworkers), 140, 142–48, 156
Núñez de Balboa, Vasco, 127

O

Oates, Stephen B., 254, 262
Obama, Barack, 104, 116, 220
Ocasio-Cortez, Alexandria, 258
Ocean, Billy, 3–4
Odoacer, 20–21
Odysseus, 200
Oman, Charles, 28
Omni Hotels & Resorts, 180
On Civil Disobedience (Thoreau), 251, 256
On the Basis of Sex (film), 243

On War (Clausewitz), 16
Opis mutiny, 287, 289, 316
opium wars, 47
Oracle of Delphi, 74–75
Orange Free State (Orange River Colony), 86, 86*f*, 88, 93
ostrich-like qualities and leaders
    Bush, George W., 9
    Louis XVI, 9
    May, Theresa, 9
    Montezuma II, 135
    Napoleon III, 41
    overview, 7*f*, 9
    Tojo, Hideki, 113
Ostrogoths, 21*f*, 22, 23*f*, 26–28, 65
Ottoman Empire, 235
Otumba, Battle of, 133, 136
Oxford Dictionary, 187
Oxford University, 141

P

Pakistan, 202
Panhellenic League, 275–76, 284, 288
Panoramic Alphabet of Peace, 234
Parallel Lives (Plutarch), xxiii
Parks, Rosa, 254
Parmenio, 279, 286, 288
Pasteur, Louis, 239
Paul, 161–62, 165, 168, 246, 262; 357*n*10:5; 364*n*14:29
PayPal, 289
Peace of Paris, 198, 205
Peace of Vereeniging, 87–88, 95
Pearl Harbor, 112, 122
People's Liberation Army, 49
Persia, 71–79, 71*f*, 72*f*, 81, 121, 274–76, 278–82, 284–88; 350*n*5:1. *See also* Alexander the Great; Themistocles; Xerxes
persuasive leadership, 70–124
    adaptive leadership vs., 12
    examples of, 18
        Campbell-Bannerman, Henry, 85–99
        Roosevelt, Franklin D., 100–117
        Themistocles, 70–84
    leader vs. follower influence, 10, 11*f*
    overview, 12
    questions to ask, 124
    reflections on, 118–23
        appealing to self-interest, 123
        communication skills, 119–20
        hiding ulterior intentions, 122–23
        maintaining credibility, 119
        managing gap in vision with followers, 118–19
        persuading proximate followers through distal followers, 120–22
Pétain, Philippe, 292, 295–97
Peter, 18, 160–70, 164*f*; 358*n*10:28
    biography, 162–63
    Council of Jerusalem, 163–67
    historical context, 161–62
    lessons learned from, 167–69
        conviction of righteousness of cause, 190
        courage, 190
        firmness, 168–69
        guiding coalitions, 191–92
        humility, 168–69
        integrity, 168
        listening, 168–69
        nurturing disruptive mindset, 189
    "marketing" of Christianity, 161, 166; 358*n*10:22
Philip, 285–86
Philip II, 275–76, 279
Piech, Ferdinand, 61
pieds-noirs, 293, 299–303
Pienaar, François, 217–18, 220
Pischetsrieder, Bernd, 61
Pitt, William, the Younger, 352*n*6:14
Planck, Kevin, 325
Plataea, 77
Plessy v. Ferguson, 250
Pliny the Elder, 9
Plutarch, 73, 78, 80, 286; 351*n*5:3
Poland, 101
Pol Pot, 317
Pompidou, Georges, 303
"post-war consensus," 147–48
Powell, Colin, 9
Prince, The (*Il Principe*) (Machiavelli), xxiii, 13, 189–90, 267, 326
Princeton, Battle of, 205
Prior, Jim, 148–49
Pritchett, Laurie, 260–61
Private Label Strategy (Steenkamp), xxi
process, leadership as, 2
proximate followers, 245–46
    defined, 120
    emotional power, 308
    persuading, 120–21
Prussia, 31–43, 65
Prussian-Austrian war, 39, 42
Prussian Chamber of Deputies (*Landtag*), 35–36
Prussian Diet, 35
pull strategies, 121–22
Punch magazine, 40

Punic Wars, 353n6:29
Putin, Vladimir, 137, 157

R

Ray, James, 258
Reagan, Ronald, 5, 110–11, 122
Realpolitik, 36, 41, 260
Red Army, 49
Reece, Gordon, 142
referent power, 270
Reform and Opening Up program (China), 51–60
    modernization of agriculture, 53
    modernization of industry, 53–54
    modernization of science and technology, 55
    results of, 55–57, 56t
relational nature of leadership, 2
relationship building, 80
    deep emotional bond with followers, 315
    limited skill in, 150
    meaningful relationships with followers, 230
    reciprocal relationship with followers, 285–87
Remigius, 24–25
Renault, Mary, 288
Renault-Nissan-Mitsubishi Alliance, xxiv, 316
Republican Party, 6, 104t, 106
Retail Disruptors (Steenkamp), xxi
Revolutionary War, 194–98, 201, 227, 229;
    361n12:26
reward power, 270
Reynaud, Paul, 295–97
Rhineland, 101
Rhodesia, 86, 86f
Rice, Thomas, 364n15:1
Richards, Frederick, 178, 181–82
Ripuarian Franks, 21–22, 23f
Rise and Fall of the Great Powers, The (Kennedy), xxii
Rise of the West, The (McNeil), xxii
Rivonia Trial, 212–13
Rivonia trial, 223
Robben Island prison, 212–13
Robespierre, Maximilien de, 201
Rochambeau, Comte de, 198
Rockefeller, John D., 137
Rohingya Muslims, 227
Roman Empire, 8, 20, 22, 24–27, 161, 163, 166,
    200–201, 280, 282; 353n6:29. *See also*
    Clovis; Peter
Rommel, Erwin, 112
Rooke, David, 221
Roon, Albrecht von, 36
Roosevelt, Franklin D., xxii, 18, 100–117, 105f, 204

    biography, 102–6
    de Gaulle and, 297, 303
    helping Great Britain, 106–12
        Lend-Lease program, 107–12, 111t
        overcoming isolationism, 106–8
    historical context, 100–102
    lessons learned from, 112–16
        appealing to self-interest, 123
        communication skills, 120
        credibility, 115
        hiding ulterior intentions, 122–23
        intimacy with audience, 116
        maintaining credibility, 119
        managing gap in vision with followers, 118
        metaphors, 116
        persuading proximate followers through distal
            followers, 121
        political intuition, 113–15
        resilience, 321
        self-confidence, 113
        time to go, 324–25
    polio, 113, 321; 354n7:10
Roosevelt, Theodore, 103
Rosebery, Earl of, 89
Roxane, 281
Royal Dutch Shell, 42, 317
Royal Navy, 9, 106–7, 171–74, 176–80, 183–85, 190,
    199; 359n11:6
Royal Statistical Society, 242
Rugby World Cup, 216–20
Russia, 31–33, 35, 201, 235, 290
Rutte, Mark, 322

S

Saatchi & Saatchi, 142, 289
Sabotage Act, 212
SAILS. *See* Steenkamp Assessment Instrument for
    Leadership Styles
Saint-Cyr military academy, 294
Salamis, Battle of, 75–78, 76f, 122; 351n5:11
Salan, Raoul, 300
Salian Franks, 21–22
Sampson, Anthony, 212–13
Santora, Tom, 180
Santos, José Eduardo dos, 228
Sapphira, 163
Sardinia, 235
satyagraha, 252, 255, 260
Saudi Arabia, 289
Scargill, Arthur, 144–45, 151
Schleswig-Holstein, 37–38

Schumpeter, Joseph, 175
SCLC (Southern Christian Leadership
        Conference), 257, 262
Sea Lords, 359n11:6
Second Naval Law, 173
Selborne, Lord, 183
self-confidence, 113, 168, 174, 308
    as component of grit, 320–21
    as trait of great leaders, 3
self-discipline, 229. *See also* authentic leadership
self-interest
    appealing to, 123
    putting followers' interests above, 260, 265
Selma (film), 258
servant leadership, 234–71
    compensation of CEO vs. median employee,
        264–65, 287
    examples of, 18
        King, Martin Luther, Jr., 249–63
        Nightingale, Florence, 234–48
        Peter, 167
    expectation-disconfirmation theory, 267–68, 268f
    moral standards, 10, 11f
    overview, 14–15
    questions to ask, 271
    reflections on, 264–71
        creating value for the community, 269
        deprioritizing institutional power for expert
            power, 270–71
        emotional healing, 269
        ethical behavior, 266–68
        putting followers' interests above self-interest,
            265–66
    skepticism about, 264
    in theory vs. practice, 266t
Services Marketing (Zeithaml), xxi
SEZ (Special Economic Zones), 54
Sharpeville Massacre, 210, 212
Simon, Hermann, xxiv
Simon-Kucher & Partners, xxiv
Singapore, 289
Sisi, Abdel Fattah el-, 202
Slack, 151
Smith, Adam, 265
Smuts, Jan, 85, 92–94, 96, 123
sociability, 3
social judgment theory, 114–15, 115f
social responsibility, 14, 29
Socrate, 271
SOEs (state-owned enterprises), 58–59
source credibility, 66–67
South Africa. *See* Mandela, Nelson
South African Communist Party, 211–13

Southern Christian Leadership Conference
        (SCLC), 257, 262
Southwest Airlines, 264–65
Soviet Union, 8, 207, 223
    central planning, 52
    Deng Xiaoping in, 48–49
    détente with, 149
    World War II, 101, 112, 292
Spain, 172. *See also* Cortés, Hernán
Sparta, 70, 72–73, 76, 78, 80, 275
Special Economic Zones (SEZ), 54
Spender, J. A., 95–96
Springboks rugby team, 216–20, 223, 224
Squadron Command, xvii–xviii
Stalin, Joseph, 8, 12, 212, 306, 317
Stanley, Mary, 239–40, 270
Stark, Rodney, 166
state-owned enterprises (SOEs), 58–59
Steenkamp Assessment Instrument for Leadership
        Styles (SAILS), 15–16, 18, 323–24, 334–45
    actual leadership profile questionnaire, 335–37
    aspirational leadership profile questionnaire,
        338–40
    calculating and interpreting score, 340–45
    developing leaders, 324, 334, 342–43
    instructions for, 334–35, 338
    seasoned leaders, 324, 334, 341–42
    starting leaders, 324, 334, 342
    360 leaders, 324, 334, 343–45, 344f
Steenkamp, Jan-Benedict, xviii–xx
Steenkamp, Paulus, 42, 55, 169
Steenkamp, Piet (author's father), xxvi, 43, 65, 82,
        98, 100, 116, 120–21
Steenkamp, Thomas, 80, 82
Steinberg, Jonathan, 320
Stewart, Martha, 137
Stockholm syndrome, 137
St. Peter's Basilica, 163
Strachey, Lytton, 267
Sudan, 294
Sudetenland, 101
Swaggart, Jimmy, 267
Syagrius, 22, 23f
Syria, 278–79

T

Taiwan, 47, 54, 58
Tambo, Oliver, 211, 224
Tanzania, 352n6:25
Taylor, A.J.P., 32
Tebbit, Norman, 143, 149

Tenochtitlán, 127, 130–31, 132*f,* 133–34, 135
Tesco, 43–44
Thatcher, Denis, 141, 324
Thatcher, Margaret, 18, 58, 139–53, 143*f*
   aftermath of victory over unions, 147–48
   biography, 141–42
   historical context, 139–41
   lessons learned from, 148–52
      action orientation, 156
      behaving with caution, 149
      courage, 149–50
      determination to succeed, 148–49
      insecurity and vulnerability, 149
      intuition, 150
      leading from the front, 155
      need for control, 154–55
      not overstaying your welcome, 157
      relationship building, 150
      self-confidence, 149
      stiffening resolve of wobbly followers, 155–56
      time to go, 324–26
   National Union of Mineworkers (NUM), 144–48
   trade-union legislation, 143, 146, 148
Thebes, 275–76, 288
Themistocles, 18, 70–84
   Battle at Salamis, 75–78, 76*f*
   biography, 73–75
   historical context, 70–73
   lessons learned from, 78–83
      appealing to self-interest, 123
      communication skills, 119–20
      hiding ulterior intentions, 122
      invoking threats, 81
      maintaining credibility, 119
      managing gap in vision with followers, 118
      not making it about yourself, 80–81
      persuading proximate followers through distal
         followers, 121
      playing tough, 82–83
      relationship building, 80
      time to go, 324, 326
      using flattery, 82
Theodoric the Great, 27–28, 65
Theodosius I, 167
Thermopylae, 73
Third Force, 214
Thoreau, Henry David, 251, 256
300 (film), 73
Thucydides Trap, xxii, 56–57
Tlaxcalans, 129–31, 133
Tojo, Hideki, 113
Torbert, William, 221

Towards a Professional Army (*Vers l'Armée de Métier*)
   (de Gaulle), 295
tower perspective, 322
Trafalgar, 172–73
Transvaal, 86–88, 86*f,* 93–94, 97
TRC (Truth and Reconciliation Commission), 215
Trevelyan, George M., 94
triremes, 74–75, 77
Truman, Harry S., xxiii, 95
Trump, Donald, 116, 267
trustworthiness, 3, 66, 119, 124
Truth and Reconciliation Commission (TRC), 215
Turkey, 161, 238, 242
Turnbull, Andrew, 146
Tutu, Desmond, 215, 219
Tyre, 279

U

Uganda, 228
U.K. Independence Party (UKIP), 6
ulterior intentions, hiding, 80, 122–23
UNC (University of North Carolina), xix, 2
Under Armour, 325
U.N. High Commissioner for Human Rights, 227
Unilever, 168; 358*n*10:31
Unionist government (Britain), 88–90, 92–93, 97
United Kingdom, 6, 43, 243. *See also* Great Britain
United States, 9, 172, 176, 228, 287, 292, 304. *See
   also* King, Martin Luther, Jr.; Roosevelt,
   Franklin D.; Washington, George
University of Cambridge, 88
University of Fort Hare, 211
University of Glasgow, 88
University of North Carolina (UNC), xix, 2
University of Salamanca, 128
University of Witwatersrand, 211
U.N. Security Council, 292
U.S. Air Force, xvii–xix
U.S. Army, xxii
U.S. Constitution, 195, 198, 204, 250
U.S. Declaration of Independence, 195, 205, 249
U.S. special ops, xxii
U.S. Supreme Court, 105–6, 121, 250, 257
utopian leadership, 14

V

Valley of Mexico, 132, 132*f*
values. *See also* authentic leadership
   clash of, 289
   strong, 226–27

Vandals, 21, 21*f*
Velázquez de Cuéllar, Diego, 128–30, 133–34, 154, 156
Verdun, Battle of, 294
Versailles Peace Conference, 94
Versailles, Treaty of, 100
Vers l'Armée de Métier (Towards a Professional Army) (de Gaulle), 295
Verwoerd, Betsy, 223
Verwoerd, Hendrik, 223
Victoria, 85, 171, 242
Videla, Jorge Rafael, 222
Vienna system, 32–34, 36–40, 63–64
Vietnam War, 89; 365*n*15:30
Virgin Group, 307–8
Virginia, 195, 198
Visigoths, 21–22, 21*f*, 23*f*, 26–27, 64
vision. *See also* charismatic leadership; eagle-like qualities and leaders; hedgehog-like qualities and leaders
    combining with flexibility, 284–85
    creation and communication of, 312–13
    managing gap in vision with followers, 118
Voting Rights Act, 258, 262

W
Wall Street Crash, 101
Washington, George, xxiii, 16–17, 18, 107, 194–208, 197*f*, 199*f*
    biography, 196–200
    historical context, 194–96
    lessons learned from, 205–7
        control over emotions, 206–7
        flexibility, 205
        integrity, 205–6, 227–28
        learning from experience, 206
        meaningful relationships with followers, 230
        not shirking from danger, 205–6
        self-discipline, 229
        strong values, 227
        time to go, 326
        willingness to pay the price, 229
    resigning as commander in chief, 198, 200–203
    resigning as president, 199, 203–4
Washington, Martha Custis, 195
Watts, Philip, 176
Wealth and Poverty of Nations, The (Landes), xxii
Wealth of Nations, The (Smith), 265
Weber, Max, 312
Wegmans, 264–65
Welch, Jack, xxiv, 150
West Point, 57, 180, 181; 361*n*12:26
Wilcken, Ulrich, 279–80
Wilhelm I, 35–36, 40, 66

Wilhelm II, 172
Willem Alexander, 222
Wilson, Harold, 142
Wilson, John, 323
Wilson, Woodrow, 103
Winfrey, Oprah, 315
Woodruff, Todd, 181
World War I
    Anglo-German naval arms race, 179
    de Gaulle, Charles, 294
    effect of on participation in WWII, 101
    South African support for Britain, 93
    Versailles Peace Conference, 94
World War II, 120, 179, 212, 292–93. *See also* Roosevelt, Franklin D.
    de Gaulle, Charles, 295–97
    Roosevelt, Franklin D., 100–102, 106–14, 111*t*, 122–23

X
Xenophon, xxiii
Xerxes, 4, 72, 77–79, 122, 276; 367*n*16:34
Xi Jinping, 56, 58

Y
Yorktown, 206
Yutar, Percy, 223

Z
Zhao Ziyang, 58
Zhou Enlai, 48–50
Zimbabwe, 207, 228
Zorreguieta, Máxima, 222
Zuckerberg, Mark, xxiv

ABOUT THE AUTHOR

JAN-BENEDICT STEENKAMP (doctor honoris causa; PhD, MSc, BSc [all summa cum laude]) is the C. Knox Massey Distinguished Professor of Marketing at the University of North Carolina's Kenan-Flagler Business School. He is an honorary professor at the European Institute for Advanced Studies in Management, fellow of the European Marketing Academy, and chairman of the International Board of Experts at the Institute for Nation(al) Branding. He was a member of the selection committee of the Spinoza Prize, nicknamed the Dutch Nobel Prize. He is co-founder and executive director of the Institute AiMark.

Since his days as an undergraduate student at Wageningen University, the Netherlands (1977–1981), he has held a variety of leadership positions at four universities in three countries, at professional organizations, nonprofits, research councils, and a political party. Most recently, he was chairman of the Marketing Area at the Kenan-Flagler Business School from 2006 to 2018, during which time the department's global ranking improved from #24 to #7.

A prolific writer, he is the author of four previous business books. Translations of his books have appeared in Chinese, Dutch, Portuguese, Russian, Spanish, and Turkish. *Brand Breakout* was selected as "Best Business Book 2013: Globalization" by *Strategy+Business*, the magazine of global consultancy Strategy& (formerly Booz & Company). *Global Brand Strategy* was runner-up for the Len Berry Award recognizing books that have had a significant impact in marketing. *Retail Disruptors* was selected as one of the "Best Business Books for 2019" by Yahoo! Finance.

He has also written over one hundred articles for leading marketing and management journals as well as leading practitioner outlets such as *Harvard Business Review, Management and Business Review, Business Strategy Review, Long Range Planning,* and *Financial Times.* He has published a dozen business case studies, including multiple cases on the role of inspired leadership in company success, all of which are available through the Case Center. His work has received more than 50,000 citations and he has a Hirsch index of 81.

He has taught, consulted, and given executive seminars on all continents and to a multitude of organizations including the U.S. Military Academy at West Point. His work has been featured in *Bloomberg Businessweek, The Economist, Financial Times, The New York Times, The Wall Street Journal,* newspapers in China, Europe, India, and South Korea, and he has been interviewed on television in the United States, Europe, China, South Africa, and India.

A naturalized Dutch-American, he has taught at universities in Austria, Belgium, China, India, the Netherlands, South Africa, Spain, the United Kingdom, and the United States. He has been recognized as a "Teaching All-Star" by UNC's MBA program. In 2005, the Royal Netherlands Academy of Sciences awarded him the Muller lifetime prize for "exceptional achievements in the area of the behavioral and social sciences." His award was the first time the prize had been granted to an academic in any area of business administration. He also has received an honorary doctorate from Aarhus University (Denmark) and lifetime achievement honors from the American Marketing Association (twice) and the European Marketing Academy.